D0850530

Checklist of Writings on American Music 1640–1992

Guy A. Marco

The Scarecrow Press, Inc.
Lanham, Md., and London
1996

SCARECROW PRESS, INC.

Published in the United States of America
by Scarecrow Press, Inc.
4720 Boston Way
Lanham, Maryland 20706

4 Pleydell Gardens, Folkestone
Kent CT20 2DN, England

The third volume in this series, *Literature of American Music III, 1983–1992* by Guy A. Marco, covers the years 1983-1992. The series itself was begun in 1977 by David Horn with the book *Literature of American Music in Books and Folk Music Collections: A Fully Annotated Bibliography.*

The second volume, published in 1988 by David Horn, with Richard Jackson, was called *The Literature of American Music in Books and Folk Music Collections: A Fully Annotated Bibliography, Supplement I.*

British Cataloguing-in-Publication Information Available

Library of Congress Cataloging-in-Publication Data

Marco, Guy A.
Checklist of writings on American Music, 1640–1992. / by Guy A. Marco.
p.   cm.
1. Horn, David 1942-   Literature of American music in books and folk music collections—Indexes.   2. Marco, Guy A.   Literature of American music in books and folk music collections, 1983-1993—Indexes.   3. Music—United States—History and criticism—Indexes.   I. Title.
ML120.U5M137   1996   016.78'0973—dc 20   95-26773   CIP

ISBN 0-8108-3133-3 (cloth : alk. paper)

CONTENTS

INTRODUCTION

This cumulative author index covers all three volumes in the LOAM series (*Literature of American Music III, 1983–1992* by Guy A. Marco, published in 1996; *The Literature of American Music in Books and Folk Music Collections: A Fully Annotated Bibliography, Supplement I,* by David Horn with Richard Jackson in 1988; and *Literature of American Music in Books and Folk Music Collections: A Fully Annotated Bibliography,* by David Horn in 1977). The index gives publisher and date along with author and title. It has been named *Checklist of Books on American Music, 1640–1992* to emphasize that it does have the intention of bringing together — for the first time in print — the titles of the significant monographic writings on music and musical life in the nation.

CUMULATIVE INDEX
VOLS. I, II, AND III

1

Adams, Charles B. Our Moravian hymn heritage / Charles B. Adams. — Bethlehem, Pa. : Moravian Church in America, 1984. — II, A-27.

Adams, Edie. Sing a pretty song / Edie Adams. — New York : Morrow, 1990. — III, 679.

Adams, Frank. Wurlitzer jukeboxes and other nice things, 1934–1974 / Frank Adams. — Seattle : AMR Publishing, 1983. — SA 63.

Adams, Juliette Graves. Chapters from a musical life / Juliette Graves Adams. — Chicago : Crosby Adams, 1903. — II, 150.

Adams, Russell L. Great negroes past and present / Russell L. Adams. — Chicago : Afro-Am Pub. Co., 1963. — I, 702.

Adler, B. Tougher than leather : the authorized biography of Run-DMC / B. Adler. — New York : New American Library, 1987. — III, 936.

Adler, Bill. Bill Adler's love letters to Elvis / Bill Adler. — New York : Grosset & Dunlap, 1978. — II, 1293.

Adler, David. Elvis, my dad : the unauthorized biography of Lisa Marie Presley / David Adler and Ernest Andrews. — New York : St. Martin's, 1990. — III, 815.

Adler, Irene. I remember Jimmy : the life and times of Jimmy Durante / Irene Adler. — Westport, Conn. : Arlington House, 1980. — II, 994.

Adler, Larry. It ain't necessarily so / Larry Adler. — New York : Grove, 1984. — III, 595.

Adler, Richard. You gotta have heart : an autobiography / Richard Adler; with Lee Davis. — New York : D. I. Fine, 1990. — III, 448.

Agostinelli, Anthony J. The Newport jazz festival, Rhode Island, 1954–1971 : a bibliography, discography and filmography / Anthony J. Agostinelli. — Providence, R.I. : Author, 1977. — II, 672.

Agostinelli, Anthony J. The Newport jazz festival, Rhode Island, 1954–1971 : a significant era in the development of jazz / Anthony J. Agostinelli. — Providence, R.I. : Author, 1978. — II, 673.

Ahrens, Pat J. Union Grove : the first fifty years / Pat J. Ahrens. — Columbia, S.C. : Author, 1974. — II, 322.

Aikin, J. B. The Christian minstrel / J. B. Aikin. — Philadelphia : T. K. Collins, 1846. — I, 532.

Ainsworth, Henry. The book of psalmes / Henry Ainsworth. — Amsterdam : Giles Thorp, 1612. — I, 186.

Albert, George. Cash Box black contemporary singles charts, 1960–1984 / George Albert and Frank Hoffmann; with Lee Ann Hoffmann. — Metuchen, N.J. : Scarecrow, 1986. — III, 249.

Albertson, Chris. Bessie / Chris Albertson. — New York : Stein & Day, 1972. — I, 851.

Albertson, Chris. Bessie Smith : empress of the blues / ed. Chris Albertson. — New York : Walter Kane, 1975. — II, 550.

Albertson, Chris. Jelly Roll Morton. — Alexandria, Va. : Time-Life Records, 1979. — III, 564.

Albertson, Chris. Louis Armstrong. — Alexandria, Va. : Time-Life Records, 1978. — III, 597.

Alda, Frances. Men, women, and tenors / Frances Alda. — Boston : Houghton Mifflin, 1937. — II, 127.

Aldrich, Richard. Concert life in New York, 1902–1923 / Richard Aldrich. — New York : Putnam, 1941. — I, 105.

Alessandrini, Marjorie. Le rock au feminin / Marjorie Alessandrini. — Paris : Albin Michel, 1980. — II, 1179.

Alexander, J. Heywood. It must be heard : a survey of the musical life of Cleveland, 1836–1918 / J. Heywood Alexander. — Cleveland : Western Reserve Historical Society, 1982. — II, A-30.

Alexander, Michael J. The evolving keyboard style of Charles Ives / Michael J. Alexander. — New York : Garland, 1989. — III, 489.

Allan, Francis D. Allan's lone star ballads / Francis D. Allan. — Galveston, Tex. : Sawyer, 1874. — I, A-231.

Allan, Johnnie. Memories : a pictorial history of South Louisiana music, 1920–1980s / Johnnie Allan. — Lafayette, La. : Jadfel, 1988. — III, 384.

Allen, Bob. George Jones : the saga of an American singer / Bob Allen. — Garden City, N.Y. : Doubleday, 1984. — II, A-253.

Allen, Bob. Waylon and Willie : the full story in words and pictures of Waylon Jennings & Willie Nelson / Bob Allen. — New York : Quick Fox, 1979. — II, 404.

Allen, Daniel. Bibliography of discographies : volume 2 : jazz / Daniel Allen. — New York : Bowker, 1981. — II, A-363.

Allen, Jules Verne. Cowboy lore / Jules Verne Allen. — San Antonio, Tex. : Naylor, 1933. — I, 558.

Allen, Ray. Singing in the spirit : African-American sacred quartets in New York City / Ray Allen. — Philadelphia : University of Pennsylvania Press, 1991. — III, 1037.

Allen, Richard. A collection of hymns and spiritual songs / Richard Allen. — Philadelphia : John Ormrod, 1801. — I, 729.

Allen, Walter C. Hendersonia : the music of Fletcher Henderson and his musicians / Walter C. Allen. — Highland Park, N.J. : Author, 1973. — I, 1117.

Allen, Walter C. King Joe Oliver / Walter C. Allen and Brian Rust. — Belleville, N.J. : Allen, 1955. — I, 1130.

Allen, William Francis. Slave songs of the United States / William Francis Allen [et al]. — New York : Simpson, 1867. — I, 768.

Altman, Richard. The making of a musical : Fiddler on the roof / Richard Altman and Mervyn Kaufman. — New York : Crown, 1971. — II, 923.

Altman, Rick. Genre : the musical : a reader / ed. Rick Altman. — London : Routledge & Kegan Paul, 1987. — III, 1279.

Altman, Rick. Genre : the musical : a reader / ed. Rick Altman. — London : Routledge & Kegan Paul, 1981. — II, A-581.

Alverson, Margaret Blake. Sixty years of California song / Margaret Blake Alverson. — Oakland, Calif. : Author, 1913. — II, 117.

Alvey, R. Gerald. Dulcimer maker : the craft of Homer Ledford / R. Gerald Alvey. — Lexington : University Press of Kentucky, 1984. — II, A-204.

Amburn, Ellis. Dark star : the Roy Orbison story / Ellis Amburn. — New York : Knightsbridge, 1991. — III, 807.

Amburn, Ellis. Pearl : the obsessions and passions of Janis Joplin : a biography / Ellis Amburn. — New York : Warner Books, 1992. — III, 753.

American folk music occasional, No. 1. — Berkeley, Calif. : American Folk Music Occasional, 1964. — I, 754.

American folklore films and videotapes : an index. — Memphis, Tenn. : Center for Southern Folklore, 1976. — II, 269.

American Music Center. Catalog of the American Music Center library. — New York : The Center, 1975–1978. — II, 163.

American Music Center. Compositions, libretti, and translations. — New York : The Center, 1978. — II, 226.

American Music Center. The National Endowment for the Arts composer : librettist program collection at the American Music Center. — New York : The Center, 1979. — II, 227.

American musical directory 1861. — New York : Thomas Hutchinson, 1861. — II, 151.

American Society of Composers, Authors and Publishers. 30 years of motion picture music. — New York : ASCAP, 1960. — II, 800.

American Society of Composers, Authors and Publishers. 40 years of show business tunes. — New York : ASCAP, 1958. — II, 799.

American Society of Composers, Authors and Publishers. ASCAP biographical dicitonary / comp. for the American Society of Composers, Authors and Publishers by Jaques Cattell Press. — 4th ed. — New York : Bowker, 1980. — III, 86.

American Society of Composers, Authors and Publishers. ASCAP hit songs. — New York : ASCAP, 1977. — II, 797.

American Society of Composers, Authors and Publishers. ASCAP index of performed compositions. — New York : ASCAP, 1952–1978. — II, 798.

American Society of Composers, Authors and Publishers. Country and western music : ASCAP music on records. — New York : ASCAP, 196-?. — II, 465.

American war songs. — Philadelphia : Colonial Dames of America, 1925. — II, 867.

Ames, Russell. The story of American folk song / Russell Ames. — New York : Grosset & Dunlap, 1960. — I, 436.

Ammer, Christine. Unsung : a history of women in American music / Christine Ammer. — Westport, Conn. : Greenwood, 1980. — II, 20.

Amram, David. Vibrations : the adventures and musical times of David Amram / David Amram. — New York : Viking, 1971. — I, 299.

Ancelet, Barry J. Makers of Cajun music / Barry J. Ancelet. — Austin : University of Texas Press, 1984. — III, 1206.

Andersen, Christopher P. Madonna, unauthorized / Christopher P. Andersen. — New York : Simon & Schuster, 1991. — III, 768.

Anderson, Bill. Whisperin' Bill : an autobiography : a life of music, love, tragedy & triumph / Bill Anderson. — Atlanta : Longstreet Press, 1989. — III, 680.

Anderson, Dennis. The hollow horn : Bob Dylan's reception in the United States and Germany / Dennis Anderson. — Munich : Hobo Press, 1981. — II, A-780.

Anderson, Donna K. Charles T. Griffes : an annotated bibliography-discography / Donna K. Anderson. — Detroit : Information Coordinators, 1977. — II, 185.

Anderson, Donna K. The works of Charles Tomlinson Griffes : a descriptive catalogue / Donna K. Anderson. — Ann Arbor, Mich. : UMI Press, 1983. — II, A-124.

Anderson, E. Ruth. Contemporary American composers / E. Ruth Anderson. — 2nd ed. — Boston : G. K. Hall, 1982. — II, 164.

Anderson, Gillian B. Freedom's voice in poetry and song / Gillian B. Anderson. — Wilmington, Del. : Scholarly Resources, 1977. — II, 868.

Anderson, Gillian B. Music for silent films, 1894–1929 / Gillian B. Anderson. — Washington : Library of Congress, 1988. — III, 1024.

Anderson, Gillian B. Music in New York during the American revolution / Gillian B. Anderson. — Boston : Music Library Association, 1987. — III, 392.

Anderson, Ian. Rock record collectors guide / Ian Anderson. — London : MRP Books, 1977. — II, 1117.

Anderson, Jervis. Harlem : the great black way, 1900–1950 / Jervis Anderson. — London : Orbis, 1982. — II, A-279.

Anderson, Jervis. This was Harlem / Jervis Anderson. — New York : Farrar, Straus & Giroux, 1982. — II, A-279.

Anderson, John Murray. Out without my rubbers / John Murray Anderson; as told to Hugh Abercrombie Anderson. — New York : Library Publishers, 1954. — II, 918.

Anderson, Marian. My Lord, what a morning : an autobiography / Marian Anderson. — New York : Viking, 1956. — I, 706.

Anderson, Robert. Gospel music encyclopedia / Robert Anderson and Gail North. — New York : Sterling, 1979. — II, 38.

Anderton, Barrie. Sonny boy! : the world of Al Jolson / Barrie Anderton. — London : Jupiter Books, 1975. — II, 1003.

Andresen, Uwe. Keith Jarrett : sein Leben, seine Musik, seine Schallplatten / Uwe Andresen. — Gauting-Buchendorf, Germany : Oreos, 1985. — III, 551.

Andrews, Edward D. The gift to be simple : songs, dances and rituals of the American Shakers / Edward D. Andrews. — New York : Augustin, 1940. — I, 552.

Andrus, Helen Josephine. A century of music in Poughkeepsie, 1802–1911 / Helen Josephine Andrus. — Poughkeepsie, N.Y. : F. B. Howard, 1912. — I, A-25.

Annals of the Metropolitan Opera : the complete chronicle of performances and artists : chronology 1883–1985 / ed. Gerald Fitzgerald. — New York : Metropolitan Opera Guild; Boston : G. K. Hall, 1989. — III, 1018.

Annual review of jazz studies / ed. Edward Berger, David Cayer, Dan Morgenstern, and Lewis Porter. — Metuchen, N.J. : Scarecrow, 1982- . — III, 1074.

Antheil, George. Bad boy of music / George Antheil. — Garden City, N.Y. : Doubleday, 1945. — I, 300.

Appel, Richard G. The music of the Bay Psalm Book, 9th edition (1698) / Richard G. Appel. — Brooklyn : Institute for Studies in American Music, 1975. — I, 189.

Appelbaum, Stanley. Stars of the American musical theater in historic photographs / Stanley Appelbaum and James Camner. — New York : Dover, 1981. — II, A-568.

Appleton, Jon H. The development and practice of electronic music / Jon H. Appleton and Ronald C. Perera. — Englewood Cliffs, N.J. : Prentice-Hall, 1975. — II, 154.

Apthorp, William Foster. By the way : being a collection of short essays on music and art in general / William Foster Apthorp. — Boston : Copeland & Day, 1898. — I, A-26.

Aquila, Richard. That old time rock & roll : a chronicle of an era, 1954–1963 / Richard Aquila. — New York : Schirmer, 1989. — III, 1168.

Aranza, Jacob. Backward masking unmasked : backward satanic messages of rock and roll exposed / Jacob Aranza. — Shreveport, La. : Huntington House, 1983. — II, A-710.

Archer, Robyn. A star is torn / Robyn Archer and Diana Simmonds. — London : Virago, 1986; New York : Dutton, 1987. — III, 435.

Archive of American Folk Song. Check-list of recorded songs in the English language in the Library of Congress Archive of American Folk Song to July 1940. — Washington : Library of Congress, 1942. — I, 433.

Ardoin, John. Callas at Juilliard : the master classes / John Ardoin. — New York : Knopf, 1987. — III, 1267.

Ardoin, John. The Callas legacy / John Ardoin; foreword by Terrence McNally. — Rev. "compact disc edition." — New York : Scribner's, 1991. — III, 690.

Ardoin, John. The stages of Menotti / John Ardoin. — Garden City, N.Y. : Doubleday, 1985. — II, A-131.

Arganian, Lillian. Stan Kenton : the man and his music / Lillian Arganian. — East Lansing, Mich. : Artistry, 1989. — III, 957.

Arian, Edward. Bach, Beethoven, and bureaucracy : the case of the Philadelphia Orchestra / Edward Arian. — University : University of Alabama Press, 1971. — II, 55.

Armistead, Samuel G. Judeo-Spanish ballads from New York collected by Mair Jose Benardete / ed. Samuel G. Armistead and Joseph H. Silverman. — Berkeley : University of California Press, 1981. — III, 1276.

Armitage, Andrew D. Annual index to popular music record reviews / Andrew D. Armitage and Dean Tudor. — Metuchen, N.J. : Scarecrow, 1973. — I, 1145.

Armitage, Merle. Accent on life / Merle Armitage. — Ames : Iowa State University Press, 1965. — S. 919.

Armitage, Merle. George Gershwin / Merle Armitage. — London : Longmans, Green, 1938. — I, 1276.

Armitage, Merle. George Gershwin : man and legend / Merle Armitage. — New York : Duell, Sloan & Pearce, 1958. — I, 1277.

Armsby, Leonora. We shall have music / Leonora Armsby. — San Francisco : Pisani, 1960. — I, A-27.

Armstrong, Doug. Wild Bill Davison : a celebration : an illustrated tribute / Doug Armstrong. — Ottawa : Leith Music, 1991. — III, 631.

Armstrong, Louis. Louis Armstrong : a self-portrait / Louis Armstrong; the interview by Richard Meryman. — New York : Eakins Press, 1971. — I, 1081.

Armstrong, Louis. Satchmo : my life in New Orleans / Louis Armstrong. — New York : Prentice-Hall, 1954. — I, 1082.

Armstrong, Louis. Swing that music / Louis Armstrong. — London : Longmans, Green, 1937. — I, 1083.

Armstrong, Mrs. M. F. Hampton and its students, by two of its teachers / Mrs. M. F. Armstrong and Helen W. Ludlow. — New York : Putnam, 1874. — I, 769.

Armstrong, Orland Kay. Old massa's people : the old slaves tell their story / Orland Kay Armstrong. — Indianapolis : Bobbs-Merrill, 1931. — II, 593.

Armstrong, W. G. A record of opera in Philadelphia / W. G. Armstrong. — Philadelphia : Porter & Coates, 1884. — I, 158.

Armstrong, William H. Organs for America : the life and work of David Tannenberg / William H. Armstrong. — Philadelphia : University of Pennsylvania Press, 1967. — II, 80.

Arnaudon, Jean-Claude. Dictionnaire du blues / Jean-Claude Arnaudon. — Paris : Filipacchi, 1977. — II, 537.

Arnaz, Desi. A book / Desi Arnaz. — New York : Morrow, 1976. — II, 1063.

Arnold, Byron. Folksongs of Alabama / Byron Arnold. — University : University of Alabama Press, 1950. — I, 491.

Arnold, Eddy. It's a long way from Chester County / Eddy Arnold. — Old Tappan, N.J. : Hewitt House, 1969. — II, 466.

Arnold, Elliott. Deep in my heart : a story based on the life of Sigmund Romberg / Elliott Arnold. — New York : Duell, Sloan & Pearce, 1949. — I, 1300.

Aronson, Rudolph. Theatrical and musical memoirs / Rudolph Aronson. — New York : McBride, Nast, 1913. — II, 128.

Aros, Andrew A. Elvis : his films and recordings / Andrew A. Aros. — Diamond Bar, Calif. : Applause Productions, 1980. — II, 1309.

Arpin, P. Life of Louis Moreau Gottschalk / P. Arpin. — New York, 1853. — I, 226.

Artis, Bob. Bluegrass / Bob Artis. — New York : Hawthorn Books, 1975. — I, 623.

Arvey, Verna. In one lifetime / Verna Arvey. — Fayetteville : University of Arkansas Press, 1984. — II, A-139.

Arvey, Verna. William Grant Still / Verna Arvey. — New York : Fischer, 1939. — I, 347.

Asbury, Samuel E. Old-time white camp-meeting spirituals / Samuel E. Asbury and Henry E. Meyer. — Austin : Texas Folk-Lore Society, 1932. — I, 537.

ASCAP biographical dictionary of composers, authors and publishers. — New York : ASCAP, 1966. — I, 1146.

ASCAP. 30 years of motion picture music. — New York : ASCAP, 1958. — I, A-247.

ASCAP. 40 years of hit tunes. — New York : ASCAP, 1956. — I, A-232.

ASCAP. ASCAP hit tunes. — New York : ASCAP, 1967. — I, A-232.

Ashby, Clifford. Trouping through Texas : Harley Sadler and his tent show / Clifford Ashby. — Bowling Green, Ohio : Bowling Green State University Popular Press, 1982. — II, A-562.

Asher, Don. Notes from a battered grand : a memoir / Don Asher. — New York : Harcourt Brace Jovanovich, 1992. — III, 536.

Asriel, Andre. Jazz : Analysen und Aspekte / Andre Asriel. — 2nd ed. — Berlin : Lied der Zeit, 1977. — II, 687.

Association of Recorded Sound Collections. A preliminary directory of sound recordings collections in the United States and Canada / Association of Recorded Sound Collections, Program Committee. — New York : New York Public Library, 1967. — I, 175.

Astaire, Fred. Steps in time / Fred Astaire. — New York : Harper, 1959. — I, 1316.

Astrup, Arne. Gerry Mulligan discography / Arne Astrup. — Soeburg, Denmark : Bidstrup, 1989. — III, 345.

Astrup, Arne. The John Haley Sims (Zoot Sims) discography / Arne Astrup. — Lyngby, Denmark : Danish Discographical Publishing Co., 1980. — II, 653.
Astrup, Arne. The Stan Getz discography / Arne Astrup. — Hellerup, Denmark : Author, 1978. — II, 649.
Atherton, Lewis. Main street on the middle border / Lewis Atherton. — Bloomington : Indiana University Press, 1954. — I, 88.
Atkins, Chet. Country gentleman / Chet Atkins. — Chicago : Regnery, 1974. — II, 392.
Atkins, Irene Kahn. Source music in the dramatic motion picture / Irene Kahn Atkins. — Rutherford, N.J. : Fairleigh Dickinson University Press, 1983. — II, A-593.
Atkins, John. The Carter family / John Atkins [et al.]. — London : Old Time Music, 1973. — I, 634.
Atkinson, Bob. Songs of the open road : the poetry of folk rock and the journey of the hero / Bob Atkinson. — New York : New American Library, 1974. — II, 463.
Attali, Jacques. Noise : the political economy of music / Jacques Attali. — Minneapolis : University of Minnesota Press, 1985. — II, A-528.
Austin, Bill Joe. The beat goes on and on and on / Bill Joe Austin. — Erwin, N.C. : Carolina Arts and Publishing House, 1978. — II, 1066.
Austin, Mary. The American rhythm : studies and reexpressions of Amerindian songs / Mary Austin. — 2nd ed. — Boston : Houghton Mifflin, 1930. — I, 387.
Austin, William W. Music in the 20th century, from Debussy through Stravinsky / William W. Austin. — New York : Norton, 1966. — I, 264.
Austin, William W. "Susanna," "Jeanie," and "The old folks at home" : the songs of Stephen C. Foster from his time to ours / William W. Austin. — New York : Macmillan, 1975. — II, 877.
Autry, Gene. Back in the saddle again / Gene Autry. — Garden City, N.Y. : Doubleday, 1978. — II, 393.
Avakian, George. Jazz from Columbia : a complete jazz catalog / George Avakian. — New York : Columbia Records, 1956. — I, 933.
Avshalomov, Jacob. The concerts reviewed : 65 years of the Portland Youth Philharmonic / Jacob Avshalomov. — Portland, Ore. : Amadeus, 1991. — III, 1000.
Ayars, Christine Merrick. Contributions to the art of music in America by the music industries of Boston, 1640 to 1936 / Christine Merrick Ayars. — New York : Wilson, 1937. — I, 164.
Aylesworth, Thomas G. A history of movie musicals / Thomas G. Aylesworth. — Greenwich, Conn. : Bison Books, 1984. — II, A-582.
Babington, Bruce. Blue skies and silver linings : aspects of the Hollywood musical / Bruce Babington and Peter William Evans. — Manchester : Manchester University Press, 1985. — II, A-583.
Backus, Rob. Fire music : a political history of jazz / Rob Backus. — Chicago : Vanguard, 1976. — II, 777.
Bacon, Ernst. Notes on the piano / Ernst Bacon. — Syracuse, N.Y. : Syracuse University Press, 1963. — I, 357.
Baez, Joan. And a voice to sing with : a memoir / Joan Baez. — New York : Summit Books, 1987. — III, 681.

Baez, Joan. Daybreak / Joan Baez. — New York : Dial, 1968. — I, 601.

Baggelaar, Kristin. Folk music : more than a song / Kristin Baggelaar and Donald Milton. — New York : Crowell, 1976. — II, 270.

Baggelaar, Kristin. The folk music encyclopeadia / Kristin Baggelaar and Donald Milton. — London : Omnibus, 1977. — II, 270.

Bahr, Donald M. Piman Shamanism and staging sickness / Donald M. Bahr [et al]. — Tuscon : University of Arizona Press, 1974. — II, 245.

Bailey, Pearl. Between you and me : a heartfelt memoir on learning, loving, and living / Pearl Bailey. — New York : Doubleday, 1989. — III, 682.

Bailey, Pearl. Talking to myself / Pearl Bailey. — New York : Harcourt, Brace, Jovanovich, 1971. — I, A-269.

Bailey, Pearl. The raw pearl / Pearl Bailey. — New York : Harcourt, Brace & World, 1968. — II, 985.

Baker, Barbara. Black gospel music styles, 1942–1975 / Barbara Baker. — Dissertation, University of Maryland, 1978. — II, 623.

Baker, David. Arranging and composing for the small ensemble / David Baker. — Chicago : Maher, 1970. — I, 979.

Baker, David. Charlie Parker, alto saxophone / David Baker. — New York : Hansen House, 1978. — II, 765.

Baker, David. J. J. Johnson, trombone / David Baker. — New York : Hansen House, 1979. — II, 755.

Baker, David. Jazz improvisation / David Baker. — Chicago : Maher, 1969. — I, 980.

Baker, David. Jazz pedagogy / David N. Baker. — Chicago : Maher, 1979. — II, 685.

Baker, David. The black composer speaks / ed. David Baker [et al]. — Metuchen, N.J. : Scarecrow, 1978. — II, 505.

Baker, Glenn A. Monkeemania : the true story of the Monkees / Glenn A. Baker. — New York : St. Martin's, 1986. — III, 924.

Baker, Glenn A. The new music / Glenn A. Baker and Stuart Coupe. — London : Ring, 1980. — II, A-697.

Baker, Houston A. Blues, ideology, and Afro-American literature / Houston A. Baker. — Chicago : University of Chicago Press, 1984. — II, A-327.

Baker, Josephine. Joséphine / Josephine Baker and Jo Bouillon. — Paris : Laffont, 1976. — II, 1067.

Baker, Paul. Contemporary Christian music / Paul Baker. — Rev. ed. — Westchester, Ill. : Crossway Books, 1985. — II, A-711.

Baker, Robb. Bette Midler / Robb Baker. — 2nd ed. — New York : Fawcett, 1979. — II, 1291.

Baker, Theodore. Über die Musik der nordamerikanischen Wilden / Theodore Baker. — Leipzig : Breitkopf und Härtel, 1882. — I, 388.

Bakker, Dick. Billie and Teddy on microgroove, 1932–1944 / Dick Bakker. — Alphen aan den Rijn, Netherlands : Micrography, 1975. — I, 938.

Bakker, Dick. Clarence Williams on microgroove / Dick Bakker. — Alphen aan den Rijn, Netherlands : Micrography, 1976. — II, 655.

Bakker, Dick. Duke Ellington on microgroove, 1923–1942 / Dick Bakker. — Alphen aan den Rijn, Netherlands : Micrography, 1974. — I, 939.

Balkind, Frankfort Gips. Listen up : the lives of Quincy Jones / Frankfort Gips

Balkind, Nelson George, and Courtney Sale Ross. — New York : Warner Books, 1990. — III, 493.

Ballanta, Nicholas George Julius. Saint Helena Island spirituals / Nicholas George Julius Ballanta. — New York : Schirmer, 1925. — I, 770.

Ballantine, Christopher. Music and its social meanings / Christopher Ballantine. — New York : Gordon and Breach, 1984. — II, A-126.

Balliett, Whitney. American musicians : fifty-six portraits in jazz / Whitney Balliet. — New York : Oxford, 1986. — III, 426.

Balliett, Whitney. American singers : twenty-seven portraits in song / Whitney Balliett. — 2nd ed. — New York : Oxford, 1988. — III, 436.

Balliett, Whitney. Barney, Bradley, and Max : sixteen portraits in jazz / Whitney Balliett. — New York : Oxford, 1989. — III, 400.

Balliett, Whitney. Dinosaurs in the morning : 41 pieces on jazz / Whitney Balliett. — Philadelphia : Lippincott, 1962. — I, 1011.

Balliett, Whitney. Ecstasy at the Onion : thirty-one pieces on jazz / Whitney Balliett. — Indianapolis : Bobbs-Merrill, 1971. — I, 1013.

Balliett, Whitney. Goodbyes and other messages : a journal of jazz, 1981–1990 / Whitney Balliett. — New York : Oxford, 1991. — III, 1130.

Balliett, Whitney. Improvising : sixteen jazz musicians and their art / Whitney Balliett. — New York : Oxford University Press, 1977. — II, 698.

Balliett, Whitney. Jelly Roll, Jabbo, and Fats / Whitney Balliett. — New York : Oxford University Press, 1983. — II, A-423.

Balliett, Whitney. New York notes : a journal of jazz, 1972–1975 / Whitney Balliett. — Boston : Houghton Mifflin, 1976. — II, 699.

Balliett, Whitney. Night creature : a journal of jazz / Whitney Balliett. — New York : Oxford University Press, 1981. — II, A-424.

Balliett, Whitney. Such sweet thunder / Whitney Balliett. Indianapolis : Bobbs-Merrill, 1966. — I, 1012.

Balliett, Whitney. Super drummer : a profile of Buddy Rich / Whitney Balliett. — Indianapolis : Bobbs-Merrill, 1968. — I, 1137.

Balliett, Whitney. The sound of surprise : 46 pieces on jazz / Whitney Balliett. — New York : Dutton, 1959. — I, 1010.

Balmir, Guy-Claude. Du chant au poème / Guy-Claude Balmir. — Paris : Payot, 1982. — II, A-292.

Balys, Jonas. Lietuviu dainos Amerikoj / ed. Jonas Balys. — Boston : Lietiviu Enciklopedijos Leidykla, 1958. — II, 442.

Bandel, Betty. Sing the Lord's song in a strange land : the life of Justin Morgan / Betty Bandel. — Rutherford, N.J. : Fairleigh Dickinson University Press, 1981. — II, A-71.

Bane, Michael. The outlaws : revolution in country music / Michael Bane. — New York : Country Music Magazine Press, 1978. — II, 374.

Bane, Michael. White boy singing the blues / Michael Bane. — New York : Penguin, 1982. — II, A-712.

Bane, Michael. Who's who in rock / Michael Bane. — New York : Everest House, 1981. — II, A-649.

Bane, Michael. Willie : an unauthorized biography of Willie Nelson / Michael Bane. — New York : Dell, 1984. — II, A-259.

Bangs, Lester. Blondie / Lester Bangs. — New York : Simon & Schuster, 1980. — II, 1189.

Bangs, Lester. Psychotic reactions and carburetor dung / Lester Bangs; ed. with introduction by Greil Marcus. — New York : Knopf, 1987. — III, 1169.

Banney, Howard F. Return to sender : the first complete discography of Elvis tribute and novelty records, 1956–1986 / Howard F. Banney; photographs by Charles Weitz. — Ann Arbor, Mich. : Pierian, 1987. — III, 250.

Baraka, Amiri. The autobiography of Leroi Jones/Amiri Baraka / Amiri Baraka. — New York : Freundlich Books, 1984. — II, A-280.

Baraka, Imamu Amiri. The music : reflections on jazz and blues / Imamu Amiri Baraka and Amina Baraka. — New York : Morrow, 1987. — III, 1215.

Baral, Robert. Revue : the great Broadway period / Robert Baral. — New York : Fleet Press, 1962. — I, 1245.

Barbour, James Murray. Church music of William Billings / James Murray Barbour. — East Lansing : Michigan State University Press, 1960. — I, 201.

Barker, Danny. A life in jazz / Danny Barker; ed. Alyn Shipton. — New York : Oxford; London : Macmillan, 1986. — III, 577.

Barlow, William. "Looking up at down" : the emergence of blues culture / William Barlow. — Philadelphia : Temple University Press, 1989. — III, 1146.

Barnes, Edwin N. C. American music : from Plymouth Rock to Tin Pan Alley / Edwin N. C. Barnes. — Washington : Music Education Publications, 1936. — I, A-1.

Barnes, Edwin N. C. American women in creative music / Edwin N. C. Barnes. — Washington : Music Education Publications, 1936. — I, 44.

Barnes, Ken. Sinatra and the great song stylists / Ken Barnes. — London : Ian Allan, 1972. — I, 1322.

Barnes, Ken. The Beach Boys / Ken Barnes. — New York : Sire Books, 1976. — II, 1184.

Barnes, Ken. The Crosby years / Ken Barnes. — London : Elm Tree Books, 1980. — II, 988.

Barnes, William Harrison. The contemporary American organ / William Harrison Barnes. — 8th ed. — Glen Rock, N.J. : J. Fischer, 1964. — II, 81.

Barnes, William Harrison. Two centuries of American organ building / William Harrison Barnes and Edward B. Gammons. — Glen Rock, N.J. : J. Fischer, 1970. — II, 82.

Barnet, Charlie. Those swinging years : the autobiography of Charlie Barnet / Charlie Barnet; with Stanley Dance. — Baton Rouge : Louisiana State University Press, 1984. — II, A-456.

Barr, Steven C. The (almost) complete 78 rpm record dating guide / Steven C. Barr. — Toronto : Author, 1979. — II, 1022.

Barr, Steven C. The almost complete 78 rpm record dating guide (II) / Steven C. Barr. — Rev. ed. — Huntington Beach, Calif. : Yesterday Once Again, 1992. — III, 194.

Barron, Lee. Odyssey of the mid-nite flyer : a history of Midwest bands / Lee Barron. — Omaha, Nebr. : Author, 1987. — III, 1134.

Barry, Phillips. British ballads from Maine / Phillips Barry [et al]. — New Haven, Conn. : Yale University Press, 1929. — I, 477.

Barry, Phillips. Folk music in America / Phillips Barry. — New York : National Service Bureau, 1939. — I, 437.

Barry, Phillips. Maine woods songster / Phillips Barry. — Cambridge, Mass. : Powell, 1939. — I, 478.

Barry, Ron. All American Elvis : the Elvis Presley American discography / Ron Barry. — Phillipsburg, N.J. : Spectator Service, 1976. — II, 1310.

Barsamian, Jacques. L'age d'or de la pop music / Jacques Barsamian. — Paris : Ramsay, 1982. — II, A-698.

Barsamian, Jacques. L'age d'or du rock 'n' roll / Jacques Barsamian and François Jouffa. — Paris : Ramsay, 1980. — II, 1277.

Bart, Teddy. Inside music city, U.S.A. / Teddy Bart. — Nashville : Aurora, 1970. — I, 630.

Barth, Jack. Roadside Elvis : the complete state-by-state travel guide for Elvis Presley fans / Jack Barth. — Chicago : Contemporary Books, 1991. — III, 816.

Barthel, Norma. Ernest Tubb, the original E. T. / Norma Barthel. — Roland, Okla. : Country Roads Publications, 1984. — II, A-268.

Bartlette, Reginald J. Off the record : Motown by master number, 1959–1989 : volume 1, singles / Reginald J. Bartlette. — Ann Arbor, Mich. : Popular Culture, Ink., 1991. — III, 213.

Barton, William E. Old plantation hymns / William E. Barton. — Boston : Lamson, Wolffe, 1899. — I, 771.

Bartsch, Ernst. Neger, Jazz und tiefer Süden / Ernst Bartsch. — Leipzig : Brockhaus, 1956. — I, A-191.

Barzun, Jacques. Music in American life / Jacques Barzun. — Garden City, N.Y. : Doubleday, 1956. — I, 358.

Bas-Rabérin, Philippe. Le blues moderne, 1945–1973 / Philippe Bas-Rabérin. — 2nd ed. — Paris : Albin Michel, 1979. — II, 541.

Basart, Ann Phillips. Serial music : a classified bibliography of writings on twelve-tone and electronic music / Ann Phillips Basart. — Berkeley : University of California Press, 1961. — I, 250.

Bashe, Philip. Teenage idol, travelin' man : the complete biography of Rick Nelson / Philip Bashe. — New York : Hyperion, 1992. — III, 800.

Basie, Count. Good morning blues : the autobiography of Count Basie / Count Basie; as told to Albert Murray. — New York : Random House, 1985. — II, A-457.

Baskerville, David. Music business handbook and career guide / David Baskerville; foreword by Stan Cornyn. — 5th ed. — Los Angeles : Sherwood Co., 1990. — III, 1255.

Baskerville, Stephen W. Nothing else to fear : new perspectives on America in the thirties / Stephen W. Baskerville and Ralph Willett. — Manchester : Manchester University Press, 1985. — II, A-314.

Bassett, John. The Bing Crosby LP-ography / John Bassett and Bert Bishop. — Cwmbran, Wales : International Crosby Circle, 1973. — I, 1326.

Bassett, John. The Bing Crosby mini-discography, 1926–1974 / John Bassett. — 2nd ed. — Cwmbran, Wales : International Crosby Circle, 1974. — I, 1326.

Bastin, Bruce. Crying for the Carolines / Bruce Bastin. — London : Studio Vista, 1971. — I, 820.

Bastin, Bruce. Never sell a copyright : Joe Davis and his role in the New York music scene, 1916–1978 / Bruce Bastin. — Chigwell, Essex, England : Storyville, 1990. — III, 393.

Bastin, Bruce. Red River blues : the blues tradition in the southeast / Bruce Bastin. — Urbana : University of Illinois Press, 1986. — III, 1147.

Battcock, Gregory. Breaking the sound barrier : a critical anthology of the new music / ed. Gregory Battcock. — New York : Dutton, 1981. — II, A-88.

Bauer, Barbara. Bing Crosby / Barbara Bauer. — New York : Pyramid, 1977. — II, 1073.

Bauldie, John. Bob Dylan and "Desire" / John Bauldie. — Bury, Lancs., England : Wanted Man, 1984. — II, A-781.

Bauldie, John. Wanted man : in search of Bob Dylan / ed. John Bauldie. — New York : Citadel, 1990. — III, 717.

Bauman, Richard. "And other neighborly names" : social process and cultural image in Texas folklore / Richard Bauman and Roger D. Abrahams. — Austin : University of Texas Press, 1981. — II, A-199.

Baumbach, Robert W. Look for the dog : an illustrated guide to Victor talking machines, 1901–1929 / Robert W. Baumbach. — Woodland Hills, Calif. : Stationery X-Press, 1981. — III, 1252.

Baumol, William J. Performing arts : the economic dilemma / William J. Baumol and William G. Bowen. — New York : Twentieth Century Fund, 1966. — I, 359.

Baxter, Brian. The films of Judy Garland / Brian Baxter. — Bembridge, England : BCW, 1977. — II, 1078.

Baxter, J. R. Gospel song writers biography / J. R. Baxter and Videt Polk. — Dallas : Stamps-Baxter, 1971. — I, 70.

Bay psalm book. [Whole book of psalmes; Psalms hymns and spiritual songs.] I, 188.

Bayard, Samuel Preston. Dance to the fiddle, march to the fife : instrumental folk tunes in Pennsylvania / Samuel Preston Bayard. — University Park : Pennsylvania State University Press, 1982. — III, 20.

Bayard, Samuel Preston. Hill country tunes : instrumental folk music of Southwestern Pennsylvania / Samuel Preston Bayard. — Philadelphia : American Folklore Society, 1944. — I, 517.

Bazelon, Irwin. Knowing the score : notes on film music / Irwin Bazelon. — New York : Van Nostrand Reinhold, 1975. — II, 935.

Bechet, Sidney. Treat it gentle : an autobiography / Sidney Bechet. — New York : Hill & Wang, 1960. — II, 737.

Beck, Earl Clifton. Lore of the lumber camps / Earl Clifton Beck. — Ann Arbor : University of Michigan Press, 1948. — I, 566.

Beck, Earl Clifton. Songs of the Michigan lumberjacks / Earl Clifton Beck. — Ann Arbor : University of Michigan Press, 1941. — I, 566.

Beck, Earl Clifton. They all knew Paul Bunyan / Earl Clifton Beck. — Ann Arbor : University of Michigan Press, 1956. — I, 567.

Beck, Horace P. Folklore in action / Horace P. Beck. — Philadelphia : American Folklore Society, 1962. — II, 277.

Becker, Howard S. Art worlds / Howard S. Becker. — Berkeley : University of California Press, 1982. — II, A-143.

Becker, Howard S. Outsiders : studies in the sociology of deviance / Howard S. Becker. — New York : Free Press, 1963. — II, 667.

Bego, Mark. Aretha Franklin, the queen of soul / Mark Bego. — New York : St. Martin's, 1989. — III, 723.

Bego, Mark. Bette Midler, outrageously divine : an unauthorized biography / Mark Bego. — New York : New American Library, 1987. — III, 787.

Bego, Mark. Cher! / Mark Bego. — New York : Pocket Books, 1986. — III, 700.

Bego, Mark. Doobie Brothers / Mark Bego. — New York : Fawcett, 1980. — III, 903.

Bego, Mark. Ice, ice, ice : the extraordinary Vanilla Ice story / Mark Bego. — New York : Dell, 1991. — III, 881a.

Bego, Mark. Linda Ronstadt : it's so easy! / Mark Bego. — Austin, Tex. : Diamond Books, 1990. — III, 852.

Bego, Mark. Madonna : blonde ambition / Mark Bego. — New York : Harmony Books, 1992. — III, 769.

Bego, Mark. Michael! / Mark Bego. — New York : Pinnacle Books, 1984. — III, 743.

Bego, Mark. On the road with Michael : the Michael Jackson story, part 2 / Mark Bego. — London : Zomba, 1984. — III, 744.

Bego, Mark. Whitney! / Mark Bego. — Toronto : PaperJacks, 1986. — III, 738.

Behague, Gerard. Performance practice : ethnomusicological perspectives / ed. Gerard Behague. — Westport, Conn. : Greenwood, 1984. — II, A-205.

Behrman, S. N. People in a diary : a memoir / S. N. Behrman. — Boston : Little, Brown, 1972. — I, 1278.

Belden, H. M. Ballads and songs collected by the Missouri Folk-Lore Society / H. M. Belden. — 2nd ed. — Columbia : University of Missouri Press, 1955. — I, 498.

Belfy, Jeanne. The Louisville Orchestra new music project / Jeanne Belfy. — Louisville : University of Louisville, 1983. — II, A-31.

Bell, Malcolm F. Theme songs of the dance band era / Malcolm F. Bell. — Memphis, Tenn. : KWD, 1981. — II, A-369.

Bellocq, E. J. Storyville portraits : photographs from the New Orleans red light district, circa 1912 / E. J. Bellocq. — New York : Museum of Modern Art, 1970. — I, A-192.

Belsito, Peter. Hardcore California : a history of punk and new wave / Peter Belsito and Bob Davis. — Berkeley, Calif. : Last Gasp of San Francisco, 1983. — II, A-704.

Belsito, Peter. Streetart : the punk poster in San Francisco / Peter Belsito [et al]. — Berkeley, Calif. : Last Gasp of San Francisco, 1981. — II, A-705.

Belz, Carl. The story of rock / Carl Belz. — 2nd ed. — New York : Oxford University Press, 1972. — I, 1348.

Benedict, Brad. Phonographics : contemporary album cover art and design / Brad Benedict and Linda Barton. — New York : Collier, 1977. — II, 1272.

Benjaminson, Peter. The story of Motown / Peter Benjaminson. — New York : Grove, 1979. — II, 565.

Bennett, Bill. Capitol record listing, 101 thru 3031 / Bill Bennett. — Zephyrhills, Fla. : Joyce Record Club, 1987. — III, 200.

Bennett, H. Stith. On becoming a rock musician / H. Stith Bennett. — Amherst : University of Massachusetts Press, 1980. — II, 1148.

Bennett, Lerone. Before the Mayflower : a history of the negro in America / Lerone Bennett. — 3rd ed. — Chicago : Johnson, 1969. — I, 659.

Bennett, Robert Russell. Instrumentally speaking / Robert Russell Bennett. — Melville, N.Y. : Belwin-Mills, 1975. — II, 912.

Bennett, Roy C. The songwriter's guide to writing and selling hit songs / Roy C. Bennett. — Englewood Cliffs, N.J. : Prentice-Hall, 1983. — II, A-737.

Benson, Dennis C. The rock generation / Dennis C. Benson. — Nashville : Abingdon, 1976. — II, 1131.

Benson, Louis F. The English hymn : its development and use in worship / Louis F. Benson. — London : Hodder and Stoughton, 1915. — I, 65.

Benston, Kimberly W. Baraka : the renegade and the mask / Kimberly W. Benston. — New Haven, Conn. : Yale University Press, 1976. — II, 488.

Berendt, Joachim Ernst. Blues / Joachim Ernst Berendt. — Munich : Nymphenburger, 1957. — I, 867.

Berendt, Joachim Ernst. Der Jazz / Joachim Ernst Berendt. — Stuttgart : Deutsche Verlags-Anstalt, 1950. — I, A-193.

Berendt, Joachim Ernst. Das Jazzbuch / Joachim Ernst Berendt. — Rev. ed. — Frankfurt : Fischer, 1973. — I, 960.

Berendt, Joachim Ernst. Die Story des jazz / Joachim Ernst Berendt. — Stuttgart : Deutsche Verlagsanstalt, 1975. — II, 691.

Berendt, Joachim Ernst. Ein Fenster aus Jazz / Joachim Ernst Berendt. — Rev. ed. — Frankfurt : Fischer, 1978. — II, 700.

Berendt, Joachim Ernst. Jazz : a photo history / Joachim Ernst Berendt. — London : Deutsch, 1979. — II, 679.

Berendt, Joachim Ernst. Jazz optisch / Ernst Joachim Berendt. — Munich : Nymphenburger, 1954. — I, A-194.

Berendt, Joachim Ernst. Photo-Story des Jazz / Joachim Ernst Berendt. — Frankfurt : Kruger, 1978. — II, 679.

Berendt, Joachim Ernst. Spirituals : geistliche Lieder der Neger Amerikas / Joachim Ernst Berendt and Paridam von dem Knesebeck. — Munich : Nymphenburger, 1955. — I, A-170.

Berendt, Joachim Ernst. The jazz book : from New Orleans to rock and free jazz / Joachim Ernst Berendt. — New York : Hill, 1975. — I, 960.

Berendt, Joachim Ernst. The jazz book : from ragtime to fusion and beyond / Joachim Ernst Berendt and Gunther Huesmann. — Brooklyn : Lawrence Hill Books, 1992. — III, 1075.

Berendt, Joachim Ernst. The story of jazz : from New Orleans to rock / Joachim Ernst Berendt. — Englewood Cliffs, N.J. : Prentice- Hall, 1978. — II, 691.

Berendt, Joachim Ernst. Variationen über Jazz / Joachim Ernst Berendt. — Munich : Nymphenburger, 1956. — I, A-195.

Berg, Charles Merrell. An investigation of the motives for and realization of music to accompany the American silent films 1896–1927 / Charles Merrell Berg. — New York : Arno, 1976. — II, 936.

Bergan, Ronald. Glamorous musicals : fifty years of Hollywood's ultimate fantasy / Ronald Bergan. — London : Octopus, 1984. — II, A-584.

Bergendorff, Conrad. One hundred years of oratorio at Augustana : a history of the Handel Oratorio Society, 1881–1980 / Conrad Bergendorff. — Rock Island, Ill. : Augustana Historical Society, 1981. — II, A-33.

Berger, Arthur. Aaron Copland / Arthur Berger. — New York : Oxford University Press, 1953. — I, 316.

Berger, Kenneth. Band encyclopedia / Kenneth Berger. — Evansville, Ind. : Band Associates, 1960. — I, 1192.

Berger, Kenneth. The March King and his band : the story of John Philip Sousa / Kenneth Berger. — New York : Exposition Press, 1957. — I, 1203.

Berger, Melvin. The story of folk music / Melvin Berger. — New York : S. G. Phillips, 1976. — II, 426.

Berger, Morroe. Benny Carter / Morroe Berger; notes on the music by Edward Berger. — Alexandria, Va. : Time-Life Records, 1980. — III, 615.

Berger, Morroe. Benny Carter : a life in American music / Morroe Berger [et al]. — Metuchen, N.J. : Scarecrow, 1982. — II, A-463.

Bergman, Billy. Hot sauces : Latin and Caribbean pop / Billy Bergman, — New York : Morrow, 1985. — II, A-181.

Bergman, Billy. Reggae and Latin pop : hot sauces / Billy Bergman. — Poole, Dorset, England : Blandford, 1985. — II, A-181.

Bergman, Marian. Russian-American song and dance book / Marian Bergman. — New York : Barnes, 1947. — II, 443.

Bergmann, Leola Nelson. Music master of the middle west : the story of F. Melius Christiansen and the St. Olaf Choir / Leola Nelson Bergmann. — Minneapolis : University of Minnesota Press, 1944. — II, 118.

Bergreen, Laurence. As thousands cheer : the life of Irving Berlin / Laurence Bergreen. — New York : Viking, 1990. — III, 415.

Berlin, Edward A. Ragtime : a musical and cultural history / Edward A. Berlin. — Berkeley : University of California Press, 1980. — II, 531.

Berman, Connie. Diana Ross, supreme lady / Connie Berman. — New York : Popular Library, 1978. — II, 620.

Berman, Connie. Linda Ronstadt : an illustrated biography / Connie Berman. — Carson City, Nev. : Proteus, 1979. — II, 1239.

Berman, Connie. The official Dolly Parton scrapbook / Connie Berman. — New York : Grosset & Dunlap, 1978. — II, 467.

Berman, Leslie. Grass roots international folk directory / Leslie Berman and Heather Wood. — New York : Grass Roots, 1985. — II, A-165.

Bernard, Kenneth A. Lincoln and the music of the Civil War / Kenneth A. Bernard. — Caldwell, Idaho : Caxton Printers, 1966. — I, 1193.

Bernhardt, Clyde E. B. I remember : eighty years of black entertainment, big bands and the blues : an autobiography by jazz trombonist and blues singer Clyde E. B. Bernhardt / Clyde E. B. Bernhardt; with Sheldon Harris; foreword by John F. Szwed. — Philadelphia : University of Pennsylvania Press, 1986. — III, 608.

Bernlef, J. Charles Ives / J. Bernlef and Reinbert de Leeuw. — Amsterdam : De Bezige Bij, 1969. — I, 326.

Bernstein, Leonard. Findings / Leonard Bernstein. — New York : Simon & Schuster, 1982. — II, A-110.

Bernstein, Leonard. The joy of music / Leonard Bernstein. — New York : Simon & Schuster, 1959. — I, 1250.

Bernstein, Leonard. The unanswered question : six talks at Harvard / Leonard Bernstein. — Cambridge, Mass. : Harvard University Press, 1976. — II, 174.

Berry, Chuck. Chuck Berry : the autobiography / Chuck Berry; foreword by Bruce Springsteen. — New York : Harmony Books, 1987. — III, 683.

Berry, Jason. Up from the cradle of jazz : New Orleans music since World War II / Jason Berry, Jonathan Foose, and Tad Jones. — Athens : University of Georgia Press, 1986. — III, 1148.

Berry, Lemuel. Biographical dictionary of black musicians and music educators / Lemuel Berry. — Guthrie, Okla. : Educational Book Publishers, 1978. — II, 501.

Berry, Peter E. And the hits just keep on comin' / Peter E Berry. — Syracuse, N.Y. : Syracuse University Press, 1977. — II, 1107.

Berton, Ralph. Remembering Bix : a memoir of the jazz age / Ralph Berton. — New York : Harper & Row, 1974. — I, 1089.

Bethell, Tom. George Lewis : a jazzman from New Orleans / Tom Bethell. — Berkeley : University of California Press, 1977. — II, 758.

Bethke, Robert D. Adirondack voices : woodsmen and wood lore / Robert D. Bethke. — Urbana : University of Illinois Press, 1980. — III, 8.

Betrock Alan. Girl groups : the story of a sound / Alan Betrock. — New York : Delilah, 1982. — II, A-763.

Beyer, Jimmy. Baton Rouge blues / Jimmy Beyer. — Baton Rouge, La. : Arts and Humanities Council of Greater Baton Rouge, 1980. — II, 543.

Biagioni, Egino. Herb Flemming : a jazz pioneer around the world / Egino Biagioni. — Alphen aan de Rijn, Netherlands : Micrography, 1977. — II, 747.

Bianco, David. Heat wave : the Motown fact book / David Bianco. — Ann Arbor, Mich. : Pierian, 1988. — III, 214.

Bianco, David. Who's new wave in music / David Bianco. — Ann Arbor, Mich. : Pierian Press, 1985. — II, A-650.

Bidwell, Ron. Columbia 78 rpm record listing 37000 thru 41963 : working draft / Ron Bidwell. — Zephyrhills, Fla. : Joyce Record Club, 1989. — III, 202.

Bierhorst, John. A cry from the earth : music of the North American Indians / John Bierhorst. — New York : Four Winds, 1979. — II, 236.

Bierhorst, John. The sacred path : spells, prayers and power songs of the American Indians / John Bierhorst. — New York : Morrow, 1983. — II, A-155.

Bierley, Paul E. Hallelujah trombone / Paul E. Bierley. — Columbus, Ohio : Integrity Press, 1982. — II, A-550.

Bierley, Paul E. John Philip Sousa : a descriptive catalog of his works / Paul E. Bierley. — Urbana : University of Illinois Press, 1973. — I, 1205.

Bierley, Paul E. John Philip Sousa : American phenomenon / Paul E. Bierley. — New York : Appleton-Century-Crofts, 1973. — I, 1204.

Bierley, Paul E. John Philip Sousa, American phenomenon / Paul E. Bierley; foreword by Arthur Fiedler. — 2nd ed. — Columbus, Ohio : Integrity, 1986. — III, 521.

Bierley, Paul E. The music of Henry Fillmore and Will Huff / Paul E. Bierley. — Columbus, Ohio : Integrity, 1982. — III, 162.

Bierley, Paul E. The works of John Philip Sousa / Paul E. Bierley. — Columbus, Ohio : Integrity, 1984. — III, 181.

Big Mama. Them gospel songs : lore of the black church experience / Big Mama. — Aurora, Colo. : National Writers Press, 1990. — III, 1038.

Bigard, Barney. With Louis and the Duke : the autobiography of a jazz clarinetist / Barney Bigard; with Barry Martin. — London : Macmillan, 1985. — III, 609.

Bigsby, C. W. E. Approaches to popular culture / ed. C. W. E. Bigsby. — London : Arnold, 1976. — II, 551.

Bigsby, C. W. E. Superculture : American popular culture and Europe / C. W. E. Bigsby. — London : Paul Elek, 1975. — II, 1132.

Bijl, Leen. Monk on records / Leen Bijl and Fred Canté. — 2nd ed. — Amsterdam : Golden Age Records, 1985. — III, 344.

Billard, François. Lennie Tristano / François Billard. — Montpellier, France : Limon, 1988. — III, 573.

Billings, William. The complete works of William Billings / ed. Karl Kroeger; Richard Crawford, editorial consultant — Boston : Colonial Society of Massachusetts, and American Musicological Society; distributed by University Press of Virginia, 1977–1990. — III, 16.

Bindas, Kenneth J. America's musical pulse : popular music in twentieth-century society / Kenneth J. Bindas. — New York : Greenwood, 1992. — III, 1054.

Binder, Abraham. The Jewish music movement in America / Abraham W. Binder. — New ed. — New York : Jewish Music Council of the National Jewish Welfare Board, 1975. — II, 205.

Binzler, Alan. Bob Dylan : the illustrated record / Alan Binzler, — New York : Harmony, 1978. — II, 1201.

Bird, Christiane. Jazz and blues lover's guide to the United States : with more than 900 hot clubs, cool joints, landmarks and legends, from boogie-woogie to bop and beyond / Christiane Bird. — New York : Addison Wesley, 1991. — III, 1109.

Birge, Edward Bailey. History of public school music in the United States / Edward Bailey Birge. — 2nd ed. — Philadelphia : Ditson, 1937. — I, 170.

Birosik, Patti Jean. The new age music guide : profiles and recordings of 500 top new age musicians / Patti Jean Birosik. — New York : Collier Books, 1989. — III, 251.

Bishop, A. S. The A-Z of Bing Crosby / A. S. Bishop and J. D. Bassett. — Cwmbran, Wales : International Crosby Circle, 1971. — I, 1326.

Bishop, Cardell. The San Carlo Opera Company, 1919–1955 / Cardell Bishop. — Cudahy, Calif. : Author, 1978. — II, 68.

Bishop, Ian Courtney. The Gibson guitar from 1950 / Ian Courtney Bishop. — London : Musical New Services, 1977–1979. — II, 91.

Bissonnette, Big Bill [William E.]. The jazz crusade : the inside story of the great New Orleans jazz revival of the 1960s / Big Bill Bissonnette. — Bridgeport, Conn. : Special Request Music Service, 1992. — III, 390.

Black, Douglas C. Matrix numbers : their meaning and history / Douglas C. Black. — Melbourne : Australia Jazz Quarterly, 1946. — I, 952.

Blackburn, Richard. Rockabilly : a comprehensive discography of reissues / Richard Blackburn. — [n.p.] : Author, 1976. — II, 1108.

Blacking, John. Venda children's songs / John Blacking. — Johannesburg : Witwatersrand University Press, 1967. — I, 718.

Blackley, Becky. The autoharp book / Becky Blackley. — Brisbane, Calif. : i.a.d. Publications, 1983. — III, 994.

Blackstone, Orin. Index to jazz / Orin Blackstone. — 2nd ed. — New Orleans : Author, [1949]. — I, 925.

Blackwell, Lois S. The wings of the dove : the story of gospel music in America / Lois S. Blackwell. — Norfolk, Va. : Donning, 1978. — II, 39.

Blair, John. The illustrated discography of hot rod music, 1961–1965 / John Blair and Stephen J. McParland. — Ann Arbor, Mich. : Popular Culture, Ink., 1990. — III, 252.

Blair, John. The illustrated discography of surf music 1959–1965 / John Blair. — Riverside, Calif. : J. Bee, 1978. — II, 1109.

Blair, John. The illustrated discography of surf music 1961–1965 / John Blair. — 2nd ed. — Ann Arbor, Mich. : Pierian Press, 1985. — II, 1109.

Blake, Benjamin. The Kingston Trio on record / Benjamin Blake, Jack Rubeck, and Allan Shaw. — Naperville, Ill. : Kingston Korner, 1986. — III, 921a.

Blancq, Charles. Sonny Rollins : the journey of a jazzman / Charles Blancq. — Boston : Twayne, 1983. — II, A-499.

Blandford, Edmund L. Artie Shaw : a bio-discography / Edmund L. Blandford. — Hastings, England : Castle Books, 1973. — I, 1139.

Blassingame, John W. Black New Orleans, 1860–1880 / John W. Blassingame. — Chicago : University of Chicago Press, 1973. — II, 489.

Blegen, Theodore C. Norwegian emigrant songs and ballads / ed. Theodore C. Blegen and Martin B. Ruud. — London : Oxford University Press, 1936. — II, 444.

Blesh, Rudi. Combo : USA : eight lives in jazz / Rudi Blesh. — Philadelphia : Chilton, 1971. — I, 1075.

Blesh, Rudi. Shining trumpets : a history of jazz / Rudi Blesh. — 2nd ed. — New York : Knopf, 1958. — I, 1025.

Blesh, Rudi. They all played ragtime / Rudi Blesh and Harriet Janis. — 4th ed. — New York : Oak, 1971. — I, 799.

Blesh, Rudi. This is jazz / Rudi Blesh. — San Francisco : Author, 1943. — I, 1026.

Bloch, Peter. Le-le-lo-lai : Puerto Rican music and its performers / Peter Bloch. — New York : Plus Ultra, 1973. — II, 431.

Block, Adrienne Fried. Women in American music : a bibliography of music and literature / Adrienne Fried Block and Carol Neuls-Bates. — Westport, Conn. : Greenwood, 1979. — II, 21.

Block, Geoffrey H. Charles Ives : a bio-bibliography / Geoffrey H. Block; foreword by J. Peter Burkholder — New York : Greenwood, 1988. — III, 169.

Bloom, Ken. American song : the complete musical theatre companion, 1900–1984 / Ken Bloom. — New York : Facts on File, 1985. — III, 131.

Bloomfield, Arthur J. 50 years of the San Francisco opera / Arthur J. Bloomfield. — San Francisco : San Francisco Book Co., 1972. — I, A-49.

Bloomfield, Arthur J. The San Francisco Opera / Arthur J. Bloomfield. — Sausalito, Calif. : Comstock, 1978. — II, 79.

Bluestein, Gene. The voice of the folk : folklore and American literary theory / Gene Bluestein. — Amherst : University of Massachusetts Press, 1972. — I, 438.

Blum, Daniel. A pictorial treasury of opera in America / Daniel Blum. — New York : Greenberg, 1954. — I, A-50.

Blum, David. The art of quartet playing : the Guarneri Quartet in conversation with David Blum / David Blum. — New York : Knopf, 1986. — III, 1266.

Blume, August G. The 1987/88 music business directory / August G. Blume. — San Anselmo, Calif. : Music Industry Resources, 1987. — III, 37.

Blume, August G. The 1987/88 music radio directory / August G. Blume. — San Anselmo, Calif. : Music Industry Resources, 1987. — III, 38.

Blumenfeld, Aaron. The art of blues and barrelhouse improvisation / Aaron Blumenfeld. — Berkeley, Calif. : Author, 1979. — II, 615.

Blumenthal, George. My 60 years in show business / George Blumenthal. — New York : Osberg, 1936. — II, 880.

Board of Music Trade of the United States of America. Complete catalogue of sheet music and musical works published by the Board of Music Trade. — New York, 1870. — I, 165.

Boardman, Herbert R. Henry Hadley, ambassador of harmony / Herbert R. Boardman. — Atlanta : Emory University, 1932. — I, A-75.

Boas, Franz. The social organization and the secret societies of the Kwakiutl Indians / Franz Boas. — Washington : Government Printing Office, 1897. — I, 401.

Boatright, Mody C. A good tale and a bonnie tune / ed. Mody C. Boatright [et al]. — Dallas : Southern Methodist University Press, 1964. — I, 420.

Boatwright, Mody C. Gib Morgan, minstrel of the oil fields / Mody C. Boatwright. — Austin : Texas Folk-Lore Society, 1945. — I, A-95.

Bockris, Victor. Uptight : the Velvet Underground story / Victor Bockris and Gerald Malanga. — London : Omnibus, 1983. — II, A-850.

Boddie, David L. We've come a long way together : the story of a drum corps / David L. Boddie. — New Rochelle, N.Y. : C. W. Dickerson, 1981. — II, A-552.

Boeckmann, Charles. And the beat goes on : a survey of pop music in America / Charles Boeckmann. — Washington : Luce, 1972. — II, 1258.

Boer, Wim de. Breathless : the Jerry Lee Lewis long play album guide / Wim de Boer. — Best, Netherlands : DeWitte, 1983. — II, A-807.

Boeringer, James. Morning star : the life and works of Francis Florentine Hagen (1815–1907), Moravian evangelist and composer / James Boeringer. — Winston-Salem, N.C. : Moravian Music Foundation Press, 1986. — III, 483.

Boette, Marie. Sing hipsy doodle and other folk songs of West Virginia / ed. Marie Boette. — Parsons, W.Va. : McClain Printing, 1971. — II, 318.

Bogaert, Karel. Blues lexicon : blues, cajun, boogie woogie, gospel / Karel Bogaert. — Antwerp, Belgium : Standaard, 1972. — I, 805.

Boggs, Beverly B. An index of selected folk recordings / Beverly B. Boggs. — Chapel Hill : University of North Carolina, 1984. — II, A-169.

Boggs, Vernon W. Salsiology : Afro-Cuban music and the evolution of salsa in New York City / Vernon W. Boggs. — New York : Greenwood, 1992. — III, 1051.

Bogle, Donald. Brown sugar : eighty years of America's black female superstars / Donald Bogle. — New York : Harmony, 1980. — II, 502.

Bogue, Merwyn. Ish Kabibble : the autobiography of Merwyn Bogue / Merwyn Bogue; with Gladys Bogue Reilly. — Baton Rouge : Louisiana State University Press, 1989. — III, 611.

Bond, Carrie Jacobs. The roads to melody / Carrie Jacobs Bond. — New York : Appleton, 1927. — II, 879.

Bond, Johnny. Mimmie Rodgers : an annotated discography / Johnny Bond. — Los Angeles : John Edwards Memorial Foundation, 1978. — II, 416.

Bond, Johnny. Reflections : the autobiography of Johnny Bond / Johnny Bond. — Los Angeles : John Edwards Memorial Foundation, 1976. — II, 394.

Bond, Johnny. The Tex Ritter story / Johnny Bond. — New York : Chappell Music Co., 1976. — II, 415.

Bond, Sherry. The songwriter's and musician's guide to Nashville / Sherry Bond. — Cincinnati, Ohio : Writer's Digest Books, 1991. — III, 1249.

Bonighton, Ian. Ives and Varèse / Ian Bonighton and Richard Middleton / Milton Keynes, England : Open University Press, 1979. — II, 191.

Bonnerjea, Biren. Index to Bulletins 1–100 of the Bureau of American Ethnology / Biren Bonnerjea. — Washington : Smithsonian Institution, 1963. — I, 384.

Bono, Sonny. And the beat goes on / Sonny Bono. — New York : Pocket Books, 1991. — III, 684.

Bontemps, Arna. Anyplace but here / Arna Bontemps. — New York : Hill & Wang, 1966. — I, 660.

Bontemps, Arna. They seek a city / Arna Bontemps and Jack Conroy. — Garden City, N.Y. : Doubleday, 1945. — I, 660.

Bookbinder, Robert. The films of Bing Crosby / Robert Bookbinder. — Secaucus, N.J. : Citadel, 1977. — II, 989.

Bookspan, Martin. André Previn : a biography / Martin Bookspan and Rosa Yockey. — Garden City, N.Y. : Doubleday, 1981. — II, A-144.

Boone, Pat. A new song / Pat Boone. — Carol Stream, Ill. : Creation House, 1970. — II, 1071.

Boone, Pat. A new song / Pat Boone. — Nashville : Impact Books, 1981. — II, A-245.

Boone, Pat. A new song / Pat Boone. — Rev. ed. — Altamonte Springs, Fla. : Creation House, 1988. — III, 685.

Boone, Pat. Together : 25 years with the Boone family / Pat Boone. — Nashville : Nelson, 1979. — II, 1072.

Booth, Mark W. American popular music : a reference guide / Mark. W. Booth. — Westport, Conn. : Greenwood, 1983. — II, A-505.

Booth, Mark W. The experience of songs / Mark W. Booth. — New Haven, Conn. : Yale University Press, 1981. — II, A-529.

Booth, Stanley. Rythm [sic] oil : a journey through the music of the American south / Stanley Booth. — New York : Pantheon, 1991. — III, 1149.

Bordman, Gerald. American musical comedy : from *Adonis* to *Dreamgirls* / Gerald Bordman. — New York : Oxford, 1981. — III, 1009.

Bordman, Gerald. American musical revue : from *The Passing Show* to *Sugar Babies* / Gerald Bordman. — New York : Oxford University Press, 1985. — II, A-563.

Bordman, Gerald. American musical theatre : a chronicle / Gerald Bordman. — New York : Oxford University Press, 1978. — II, 906.

Bordman, Gerald. American musical theatre : a chronicle / Gerald Bordman. — 2nd ed. — New York : Oxford, 1992. — III, 1010.

Bordman, Gerald. American operetta : from *HMS Pinafore* to *Sweeney Todd* / Gerald Bordman. — New York : Oxford University Press, 1981. — II, A-573.

Bordman, Gerald. Days to be happy, years to be sad : the life and music of Vincent Youmans / Gerald Bordman. — New York : Oxford University Press, 1982. — II, A-610.

Bordman, Gerald. Jerome Kern : his life and music / Gerald Bordman. — New York : Oxford University Press, 1980. — II, 955.

Boretz, Benjamin. Perspectives on American composers / Benjamin Boretz and Edward T. Cone. — New York : Norton, 1971. — I, 292.

Bornemann, Ernest. A critic looks at jazz / Ernest Bornemann. — London : Jazz Music Books, 1946. — I, 987.

Borroff, Edith. American operas : a checklist / Edith Borroff and J. Bunker Clark. — Warren, Mich. : Harmonie Park, 1992. — III, 137.

Borroff, Edith. Music in Europe and the United States : a history / Edith Borroff. — Englewood Cliffs, N.J. : Prentice-Hall, 1971. — I, 32.

Borroff, Edith. Three American composers / Edith Borroff. — Lanham, Md. : University Press of America, 1986. — III, 408.

Bortin, Virginia. Elinor Remick Warren : her life and her music / Virginia Bortin. — Metuchen, N.J. : Scarecrow, 1987. — III, 532.

Botkin, B. A. American play-party song / B. A. Botkin. — Lincoln : University of Nebraska Press, 1937. — I, 448.

Botkin, B. A. Lay my burden down : a folk history of slavery / B. A. Botkin. — Chicago : University of Chicago Press, 1945. — I, 730.

Botkin, B. A. Sidewalks of America / B. A. Botkin. — Indianapolis : Bobbs-Merrill, 1954. — I, 449.

Botkin, B. A. Treasury of American folklore / B. A. Botkin. — New York : Crown, 1944. — I, 450.

Botts, Rick. A complete identification guide to the Wurlitzer jukebox / Rick Botts. — Des Moines, Iowa : Jukebox Collector Newsletter, 1984. — II, A-64.

Boucourechliev, Andre. Stravinsky / Andre Boucourechliev; trans. from the French by Martin Cooper. — New York : Holmes & Meier, 1987. — III, 524.

Boulard, Garry. Just a gigolo : the life and times of Louis Prima / Garry Boulard. — Lafayette : Center for Louisiana Studies, University of Southwestern Louisiana, 1989. — III, 660.

Bowden, Betsy. Performed literature : words and music by Bob Dylan / Betsy Bowden. — Bloomington : Indiana University Press, 1982. — II, A-782.

Bowdich, Thomas Edward. Mission from Cape Coast Castle to Ashantee / Thomas Edward Bowdich. — London : Murray, 1819. — I, 712.

Bowers, Q. David. Put another nickel in : a history of coin-operated pianos and orchestrions / Q. David Bowers. — New York : Vestal, 1966. — I, 160.

Bowles, Garrett H. Ernst Krenek : a bio-bibliography / Garrett H. Bowles. — Westport, Conn. : Greenwood, 1989. — III, 170.

Bowling, Lance. Joseph Wagner : a retrospective of a composer-conductor / Lance Bowling. — Lomita, Calif. : Charade Record Co., 1976. — II, 204.

Bowman, Kent A. Voices of combat : a century of liberty and war songs, 1765–1865 / Kent A. Bowman. — New York : Greenwood, 1987. — III, 1209.

Boyd, Brian G. Willard Robison and his piano : a discography / Brian G. Boyd. — Toronto : Author, 1990. — III, 351.

Boyd, Herb. Detroit jazz who's who / Herb Boyd. — Detroit : Jazz Research Institute, 1983. — II, A-442.

Boyd, Jenny. Musicians in tune / Jenny Boyd; with Holly George-Warren. — New York : Fireside, 1992. — III, 1259.

Boyd, Maurice. Kiowa voices : ceremonial dance, ritual and song / Maurice Boyd. — Fort Worth, Tex. : Texas Christian University Press, 1981. — II, A-156.

Boyer, Horace C. An analysis of black church music / Horace C. Boyer. — Dissertation, Eastman School of Music, 1973. — II, 624.

Boyer, Walter E. Songs along the Mahantongo : Pennsylvania Dutch folksongs / ed. Walter E. Boyer [et al]. — Lancaster, Pa. : Pennsylvania Dutch Folklore Center, 1951. — II, 297.

Bradford, Perry. Born with the blues / Perry Bradford. — New York : Oak, 1965. — I, 834.

Bradley, Carol June. Music collections in American libraries : a chronology / Carol June Bradley. — Detroit : Information Coordinators, 1981. — II, A-10.

Bradley, Carol June. Richard S. Hill : tributes from friends / ed. Carol June Bradley and James B. Coover. — Detroit : Information Coordinators, 1987. — III, 53.

Bradley, Van Allen. Music for the millions : the Kimball piano and organ story / Van Allen Bradley. — Chicago : Regnery, 1957. — II, 87.

Bradshaw, Jon. Dreams that money can buy : the tragic life of Libby Holman. New York : Morrow, 1985. — II, A-618.

Brady, Frank. Barbra Streisand : an illustrated biography / Frank Brady. — New York : Grosset & Dunlap, 1979. — II, 1014.

Brahms, Caryl. Song by song : the lives and work of 14 great lyric writers / Caryl Brahms and Ned Sherrin. — Bolton, Lancs., England : Anderson, 1984. — II, A-574.

Brand, Oscar. Ballad mongers : the rise of modern folk song / Oscar Brand. — New York : Funk & Wagnalls, 1962. — I, 579.

Brand, Oscar. Songs of '76 : a folksinger's history of the Revolution / Oscar Brand. — New York : Evans, 1972. — II, 869.

Brandel, Rose. The music of Central Africa / Rose Brandel. — The Hague : Nijhoff, 1961. — I, 719.

Brandelius, Jerilyn Lee. Grateful Dead family album / Jerilyn Lee Brandelius. — New York : Warner Books, 1989. — III, 908.

Branen, Jeff. How to stage a minstrel show / Jeff Branen and Frederick G. Johnson. — Chicago : Denison, 1921. — I, A-248.

Brask, Ole. Jazz people / Ole Brask. — New York : Abrams, 1976. — II, 680.

Braun, D. Duane. Toward a theory of popular culture / Duane D. Braun. — Ann Arbor, Mich. : Ann Arbor Publishers, 1969. — I, 1163.

Brawley, Benjamin. The negro genius : a new appraisal of the achievement of the American negro in literature and the fine arts / Benjamin Brawley. — New York : Dodd, Mead, 1937. — I, 661.

Bredel, Marc. Edgard Varèse / Marc Bredel. — Paris : Mazarine, 1984. — II, A-142.

Breland, Roger. In search of a lovely moment / Roger Breland. — Nashville : T. Nelson, 1990. — III, 943.

Breman, Paul. Blues, en andere wereldlijke volksmuziek van de Noordamerikaanse neger / Paul Breman. — The Hague : Servire, 1961. — I, A-171.

Breman, Paul. Spirituals : Nooramerikaanse geestelijke volksliederen / Paul Breman. — The Hague : Servire, 1959. — I, A-172.

Bremer, Frederika. The homes of the New World : impressions of America / Frederika Bremer. — New York : Harper, 1853. — I, 731.

Brewer, J. Mason. American negro folklore / J. Mason Brewer. — Chicago : Quadrangle Books, 1968. — II, 518; II, 596.

Brewer, J. Mason. The word on the Brazos / J. Mason Brewer. — Austin : University of Texas Press, 1953. — II, 597.

Brewer-Giorgio, Gail. The Elvis files : was his death faked? / Gail Brewer-Giorgio : foreword by Raymond A. Moody, Jr., and Monte W. Nicholson. — New York : Shapolsky; Toronto : McGraw-Hill Ryerson; Lancaster, England : Impala Books, 1990. — III, 817.

Brewster, Paul G. Ballads and songs of Indiana / Paul G. Brewster. — Bloomington : Indiana University Press, 1940. — I, 487.

Bricktop. Bricktop / Bricktop; with James Haskins. — New York : Atheneum, 1983. — III, 686.

Bridges, Glenn. Pioneers in brass / Glenn Bridges. Detroit : Sherwood, 1965. — I, 1194; II, 875.

Briegleb, Ann. Directory of ethnomusicological sound recording collections in the U.S. and Canada / Ann Briegleb. — Ann Arbor, Mich. : Society for Ethnomusicology, 1971. — II, 271.

Briggs, John. Leonard Bernstein : the man, his work and his world / John Briggs. — Cleveland : World, 1961. — I, 303.

Briggs, John. Requiem for a yellow brick brewery : a history of the Metropolitan Opera / John Briggs. — Boston : Little, Brown, 1969. — I, 146.

Brignano, Russell C. Black Americans in autobiography / Russell C. Brignano. — Durham, N.C. : Duke University Press, 1974. — I, 650.

Brindle, Reginald Smith. The new music : the avant-garde since 1945 / Reginald Smith Brindle. — London : Oxford University Press, 1975. — II, 155.

Brink, Carol. Harps in the wind : the story of the singing Hutchinsons / Carol Brink. — New York : Macmillan, 1947. — I, 1219.

Brinkmann, Reinhold. Avantgarde, Jazz, Pop / Reinhold Brinkmann. — Mainz, Germany : Schott, 1978. — II, 156.

Brinkmann, Reinhold. Die neue Musik und die Tradition / Reinhold Brinkmann. — Mainz, Germany : Schott, 1978. — II, 689.

Brinkmann, Reinhold. Improvisation und neue Musik : acht Kongressreferate / Reinhold Brinkmann. — Mainz, Germany : Schott, 1979. — II, 688.

Britt, Judith S. Nothing more agreeable : music in George Washington's family / Judith S. Britt. — Mount Vernon, Va. : Mount Vernon Ladies' Association of the Union, 1984. — II, A-72.

Britt, Stan. Dexter Gordon : a musical biography / Stan Britt; discography by Don Tarrant. — New York : Da Capo, 1989. — III, 639.

Britt, Stan. The jazz guitarists / Stan Britt. — Poole, Dorset, England : Blandford Press, 1984. — II, A-447.

Britton, Allen Perdue. American sacred music imprints, 1698–1810 : a bibliography / Allen Perdue Britton and Irving Lowens; completed by Richard Crawford. — Worcester, Mass. : American Antiquarian Society, 1990. — III, 124.

Broadcast Music, Inc. All time pin up tunes 1940–1962. — New York : BMI, 1963. — II, 801.

Broadcast Music, Inc. BMI performindex. — New York : BMI, 194-? — II, 802.

Broadcast Music, Inc. The explosion of American music, 1940–1990 : BMI 50th anniversary. — Nashville : Country Music Foundation, 1990. — III, 43.

Broder, Nathan. Samuel Barber / Nathan Broder. — New York : Schirmer, 1954. — I, 302.

Bronson, Bertrand Harris. The ballad as song / Bertrand Harris Bronson. — Berkeley : University of California Press, 1969. — II, 282.

Bronson, Bertrand Harris. The singing tradition of Child's popular ballads / Bertrand Harris Bronson. — Princeton, N.J. : Princeton University Press, 1976. — II, 283.

Bronson, Bertrand Harris. Traditional tunes of the Child ballads / Bertrand Harris Bronson. — Princeton, N.J. : Princeton University Press, 1959–1971. — I, 464.

Bronson, Fred. *Billboard's* hottest hot 100 hits / Fred Bronson. — New York : Billboard Books, 1991. — III, 253.

Bronson, Fred. The *Billboard* book of number one hits / Fred Bronson. — New York : Billboard, 1985. — II, A-670.

Brookhart, Edward. Music in American higher education : an annotated bibliography / Edward Brookhart. — Warren, Mich. : Harmonie Park, 1988; published for the College Music Society. — III, 97.

Brooks, Edward. The Bessie Smith companion / Edward Brooks. — Cavendish, N.Y. : Da Capo, 1983. — II, A-324.

Brooks, Elston. I've heard those songs before, volume II : the weekly top ten hits of the last six decades / Elston Brooks. — Fort Worth, Tex. : Summit Group, 1991. — III, 148.

Brooks, Henry M. Olden-time music : a compilation from newspapers and books / Henry M. Brooks. — Boston : Ticknor, 1888. — I, 180.

Brooks, Tilford. America's black musical heritage / Tilford Brooks. — Englewood Cliffs, N.J. : Prentice-Hall, 1984. — II, A-293.

Broonzy, William. Big Bill blues / William Broonzy and Yannick Bruynoghe. — London : Cassell, 1955. — I, 835.

Brosi, George. Appalachian literature and music : a comprehensive catalogue / George Brosi. — Berea, Ky. : Appalachian Book & Record Store, 1981. — II, A-186.

Brosnac, Donald. The electric guitar : its history and construction / Donald Brosnac. — Los Angeles : Panjandrum Press, 1975. — II, 92.

Brosnac, Donald. The steel string guitar : its construction, origin and design / Donald Brosnac. — 2nd ed. — Los Angeles : Panjandrum Press, 1975. — II, 93.

Broughton, Viv. Black gospel : an illustrated history of the gospel sound / Viv Broughton. — Poole, Dorset, England : Blandford Press, 1985. — II, A-357.

Broven, John. South to Louisiana : the music of the Cajun bayous / John Broven. — II, A-274.

Broven, John. Walking to New Orleans / John Broven. — Bexhill-on-Sea : Blues Unlimited, 1974. — I, 883.

Brown, Charles T. Proceedings of NAJE research / ed. Charles T. Brown. — Manhattan, Kans. : National Association of Jazz Educators, 1981. — II, A-425.

Brown, Charles T. The art of rock 'n' roll / Charles T. Brown. — Englewood Cliffs, N.J. : Prentice-Hall, 1983. — II, A-691.

Brown, Denis. Sarah Vaughan : a discography / Denis Brown. — Westport, Conn. : Greenwood, 1991. — III, 363.

Brown, Geoff. Diana Ross / Geoff Brown. — London : Sidgwick & Jackson, 1981. — II, A-355.

Brown, Geoff. Michael Jackson : body and soul : an illustrated biography / Geoff Brown. — London : Virgin Books, 1984. — II, A-804.

Brown, James. James Brown : the godfather of soul / James Brown; with Bruce Tucker. — New York : Macmillan, 1986. — II, 688.

Brown, Malcolm H. Papers of the Yugoslav-American seminar on music / Malcolm H. Brown. — Bloomington : Indiana University School of Music, 1970. — II, 206.

Brown, Marion. Recollections : essays, drawings, miscellanea / Marion Brown. — Frankfurt am Main, Germany : J. A. Schmitt, 1984. — III, 613.

Brown, Rae Linda. Music, printed and manuscript, in the James Weldon Johnson collection of negro arts and letters : an annotated catalog / Rae Linda Brown. — New York : Garland, 1982. — II, A-285.

Brown, Rodger Lyle. Party out of bounds : the B-52's, REM, and the kids who rock Athens, Georgia / Rodger Lyle Brown. — New York : Penguin, 1991. — III, 1170.

Brown, Scott E. James P. Johnson : a case of mistaken identity / Scott E. Brown; discography by Robert Hilbert; foreword by Dan Morgenstern. — Metuchen, N.J. : Scarecrow Press and Institute of Jazz Studies, 1986. — III, 553.

Brown, Sterling A. The negro caravan : writings by American negroes / ed. Sterling A. Brown [et al]. — New York : Dryden Press, 1941. — I, 672.

Brown, T. Allston. A history of the New York stage from the first performance in 1732 to 1901 / T. Allston Brown. — New York : Dodd, Mead, 1903. — I, A-60.

Brown, T. Allston. History of the American stage / T. Allston Brown. — New York : Dick & Fitzgerald, 1870. — I, A-59.

Brown, Virginia Pounds. Toting the lead row : Ruby Pickens Tartt, Alabama folklorist / Virginia Pounds Brown and Laurella Owens. — University : University of Alabama Press, 1981. — II, A-185.

Brown, William Wells. Anti-slavery harp / William Wells Brown. — Boston : Bela Marsh, 1848. — I, 732.

Brown, William Wells. Narrative of William Wells Brown, a fugitive slave, written by himself / William Wells Brown. — Boston : Anti-Slavery Office, 1847. — I, 733.

Browne, Ray B. Challenges in American culture / Ray B. Browne [et al]. Bowling Green, Ohio : Bowling Green State University Popular Press, 1970. — II, 207.

Browne, Ray B. Heroes of popular culture / Ray B. Browne, [et al]. — Bowling

Green, Ohio : Bowling Green State University Popular Press, 1972. — II, 354.

Browne, Ray B. New voices in American studies / ed. Ray B. Browne [et al]. — West Lafayette, Ind. : Purdue University Press, 1966. — II, 284.

Browne, Ray B. Rituals and ceremonies in popular culture / Ray B. Browne. — Bowling Green, Ohio : Bowling Green State University Popular Press, 1980. — II, 887.

Browne, Ray B. The Alabama folk lyric / Ray B. Browne. — Bowling Green, Ohio : Bowling Green State University Popular Press, 1979. — II, 304.

Browning, Norma Lee. Joe Maddy of Interlochen : profile of a legend / Norma Lee Browning. — Chicago : Contemporary Books, 1992. — III, 969.

Broyles, Michael. "Music of the highest class" : elitism and populism in antebellum Boston / Michael Broyles. — New Haven, Conn. : Yale University Press, 1992. — III, 388.

Brubaker, Robert L. Making music Chicago style / Robert L. Brubaker. — Chicago : Chicago Historical Society, 1985. — II, A-33.

Bruce, Dickson D. And they all sang hallelujah / Dickson D. Bruce. — Knoxville : University of Tennessee Press, 1974. — II, 319.

Bruce, Graham. Bernard Herrmann : film music and narrative / Graham Bruce. — Ann Arbor, Mich. : UMI Research Press, 1985. — II, A-601.

Bruchac, Joseph. The poetry of pop / Joseph Bruchac. — Paradise, Calif. : Dustbooks, 1973. — II, 1265.

Brunn. H. O. The story of the Original Dixieland Jazz Band / H. O. Brunn. — Baton Rouge : Louisiana State Univerity Press, 1960. — I, 1132.

Brunnings, Florence E. Folk song index / Florence E. Brunnings. — New York : Garland, 1981. — II, A-166.

Brunvand, Jan Harold. The study of American folklore / Jan Harold Brunvand. — 2nd ed. — New York : Norton, 1978. — II, 278.

Bruyninckx, Walter. 50 years of recorded jazz, 1917–1967 / Walter Bruyninckx. — Mechelen : Author, 1968. — 932.

Bruyninckx, Walter. 60 years of recorded jazz, 1917–1977 / Walter Bruyninckx. — Mechelen, Belgium : Author, 1980? — III, 230.

Bruyninckx, Walter. Discography : traditional jazz, 1897–1985 / Walter Bruyninckx. — Mechelen, Belgium : Copy Express, 1988? — III, 228.

Bruyninckx, Walter. Jazz discography / Walter Bruyninckx. — 2nd ed. — Mechelen, Belgium : Author, 1984- . — II, A-367.

Bruyninckx, Walter. Jazz : modern jazz, be-bop, hard bop, West Coast / Walter Bruyninckx. — Mechelen, Belgium : 60 Years of Recorded Jazz Team, 1985. — III, 234.

Bruyninckx, Walter. Jazz : swing, 1920–1988 : swing, dance bands & combos / Walter Bruyninckx. — Mechelen, Belgium : Copy Express, 1988? — III, 231.

Bruyninckx, Walter. Jazz : the vocalists, 1917–1986 : singers and crooners / Walter Bruyninckx. — Mechelen, Belgium : Copy Express, 1988. — III, 229.

Bruyninckx, Walter. Modern jazz : modern big band / Walter Bruyninckx. — Mechelen, Belgium : 60 Years of Recorded Jazz Team, 1986. — III, 232.

Bruyninckx, Walter. Progressive jazz : free—third stream fusion / Walter Bruyninckx. — Mechelen, Belgium : 60 Years of Recorded Jazz Team, 1984–1987. — III, 233.

Bryan, George B. Ethel Merman : a bio-bibliography / George B. Bryan. —
New York : Greenwood, 1992. — III, 188.
Bryant, Carolyn. And the band played on, 1776–1976 / Carolyn Bryant. —
Washington : Smithsonian Institution, 1975. — II, 1032.
Buchanan, Annabel Morris. Folk hymns of America : Annabel Morris
Buchanan. — New York : Fischer, 1938. — I, 538.
Büchmann-Moller, Frank. You got to be original, man! : the music of Lester
Young / Frank Büchmann-Moller; foreword by Lewis Porter. — New York :
Greenwood, 1990. — III, 364.
Büchmann-Moller, Frank. You just fight for your life : the story of Lester Young /
Frank Büchmann-Moller; foreword by Lewis Porter. — New York : Praeger,
1990. — III, 676.
Buckley, Gail Lumet. The Hornes : an American family / Gail Lumet Buckley. —
New York : Knopf, 1986. — III, 736.
Buckner, Reginald T. Jazz in mind : essays on the history and meanings of jazz /
ed. Reginald T. Buckner and Steven Weiland. — Detroit : Wayne State Uni-
versity Press, 1992. — III, 1097.
Budds, Michael J. Jazz in the sixties : the expansion of musical resources and
techniques / Michael J. Budds. — 2nd ed. — Iowa City : University of Iowa
Press, 1990. — III, 1076.
Budds, Michael J. Jazz in the sixties / Michael J. Budds. — Iowa City : Univer-
sity of Iowa Press, 1978. — II, 716.
Buerkle, Jack V. Bourbon Street black : the New Orleans black jazzman / Jack
V. Buerkle and Danny Barker. — New York : Oxford University Press,
1973. — I, 1062.
Buffington, Albert F. Dutchified German spirituals / Albert F. Buffington. —
Lancaster, Pa. : Franklin and Marshall College, 1965. — I, 539.
Buholzer, Meinrad. Auf der Suche nach Cecil Taylor / Meinrad Buholzer, Abi
S. Rosenthal, and Valerie Wilmer. — Hofheim, Germany : Wolke Verlag,
1990. — III, 572.
Bull, Storm. Index to biographies of contemporary composers / Storm Bull. —
Metuchen, N.J. : Scarecrow, 1964, 1974. — I, 251.
Bumgardner, Thomas A. Norman Dello Joio / Thomas A. Bumgardner. —
Boston : Twayne, 1986. — III, 465.
Burbank, Richard. Twentieth century music / Richard Burbank. — New York :
Facts on File, 1984. — II, A-86.
Burchill, Jaulie. The boy looked at Johnny : the obituary of rock and roll / Julie
Burchill and Tony Parsons. — London : Pluto Press, 1978. — II, 1125.
Burford, Cary Clive. We're loyal to you, Illinois / Cary Clive Burford. —
Danville, Ill. : Interstate, 1952. — II, 1033.
Burk, Bill E. Elvis : a 30-year chronicle / Bill E. Burk. — Tempe, Ariz. : Os-
borne Enterprises, 1985. — II, A-822.
Burk, Cassie. America's musical heritage / Cassie Burk [et al]. — Chicago :
Laidlaw, 1942. — I, A-2.
Burkhardt, Werner. Lester Young : ein Porträt / Werner Burkhardt and Joachim
Gerth. — Wetzlar, Germany : Pegasus, 1959. — II, 789.
Burkholder, J. Peter. Charles Ives : the ideas behind the music / J. Peter Burk-
holder. — New Haven, Conn. : Yale University Press, 1985. — II, A-127.

Burleigh, Harry T. Negro spirituals / Harry T. Burleigh. — New York : Ricordi, 1917–1928. — I, A-173.

Burman, Linda C. The technique of variation in an American fiddle tune / Linda C. Burman. — Los Angeles : John Edwards Memorial Foundation, 1968. — I, 518.

Burman-Hall, Linda C. Southern American folk fiddle styles / Linda C. Burman-Hall. — Los Angeles : John Edwards Memorial Foundation, 1976. — II, 323.

Burnim, Mellonee V. The black gospel music tradition : symbol of ethnicity / Mellonee V. Burnim. — Dissertation, Indiana University, 1980. — II, 625.

Burrows, Abe. Honest, Abe : is there really no business like show business? / Abe Burrows. — Boston : Little, Brown, 1980. — II, 945.

Burt, Jesse. The history of gospel music / Jesse Burt and Duane Allen. — Nashville : K & S Press, 1971. — I, 71.

Burt, Olive Woolley. American murder ballads and their stories / Olive Wooley Burt. — New York : Oxford University Press, 1958. — II, 285.

Burt, Rob. 25 years of teen-screen idols / Rob Burt. — Poole, Dorset, England : Blandford, 1983. — II, A-748.

Burt, Rob. West Coast story / Rob Burt and Patsy North. — London : Hamlyn, 1977. — II, 1262.

Burton, Frederick. American primitive music, with especial attention to the songs of the Ojibways / Frederick Burton. — New York : Moffat, Yard, 1909. — I, 402.

Burton, Jack. The blue book of Broadway musicals / Jack Burton. — Watkins Glen, N.Y. : Century House, 1952. — I, 1251.

Burton, Jack. The blue book of Hollywood musicals / Jack Burton. — Watkins Glen, N.Y. : Century House, 1953. — I, 1263.

Burton, Jack. The blue book of Tin Pan Alley / Jack Burton. — Rev. ed. — Watkins Glen, N.Y. : Century House, 1962. — I, 1147.

Burton, Jack. The index of American popular music / Jack Burton. — Watkins Glen, N.Y. : Century House, 1957. — I, 1148.

Burton, Thomas G. Some ballad folks / Thomas G. Burton. — Boone, N.C. : Appalachian Consortium Press, 1981. — II, A-175.

Burton, Thomas G. The East Tennessee State University collection of folklore / ed. Thomas G. Burton and Ambrose N. Manning. — Johnson City : East Tennessee State University, 1967–1969. — II, 317.

Burton, Thomas G. Tom Ashley, Sam McGee, Bukka White : Tennessee traditional singers / Thomas G. Burton. — Knoxville : University of Tennessee Press, 1981. — II, A-233.

Bushell, Garvin. Jazz from the beginning / Garvin Bushell; as told to Mark Tucker; introduction by Lawrence Gushee. — Ann Arbor : University of Michigan Press, 1988. — III, 614.

Busnar, Gene. Superstars of country music / Gene Busnar. — New York : Messner, 1984. — II, A-238.

Busnar, Gene. The superstars of rock / Gene Busnar. — New York : Messner, 1980–1984. — II, 1169; II, 1278.

Butcher, Geoffrey. Next to a letter from home : Glenn Miller's wartime band / Geoffrey Butcher. — Edinburgh, Scotland : Mainstream, 1986. — III, 959.

Butcher, Margaret Just. The negro in American culture : based on materials left by Alain Locke / Margaret Just Butcher. — 2nd ed. — New York : Knopf, 1972. — I, 662.

Butterfield, Arthur. Encyclopedia of country music / Arthur Butterfield. — London : Multimedia Publications, 1985. — II, A-217.

Butterworth, Hezekiah. The story of the hymns and tunes / Hezekiah Butterworth and Theron Brown. — New York : American Tract Society, 1906. — II, 28.

Butterworth, Neil. A dictionary of American composers / Neil Butterworth. — New York : Garland, 1983. — II, A-7.

Butterworth, Neil. The music of Aaron Copland / Neil Butterworth. — London : Toccata, 1985. — II, A-117.

Byworth, Tony. Giants of country music / Tony Byworth. — London : Hamlyn, 1984. — II, A-239.

Cabaj, Janice. The Elvis image ; Janice Cabaj. — Smithtown, N.Y. : Exposition, 1982. — II, A-823.

Cable, Paul. Bob Dylan : his unreleased recordings / Paul Cable. — London : Scorpion, 1978. — II, 1194.

Cage, John. A year from Monday / John Cage. — Middletown, Conn. : Wesleyan University Press, 1967. — I, 308.

Cage, John. Empty words : writings '73-'78 / John Cage. — Middletown, Conn. : Wesleyan University Press, 1979. — II, 177.

Cage, John. For the birds / John Cage. — Boston : Marion Boyars, 1981. — II, 178.

Cage, John. M : writings '67-'72 / John Cage. — Middletown, Conn. : Wesleyan University Press, 1973. — I, 305.

Cage, John. Notations / John Cage. — New York : Something Else Press, 1969. — I, 306.

Cage, John. Pour les oiseaux / John Cage. — Paris : Belfon, 1976. — II, 178.

Cage, John. Silence : lectures and writings / John Cage. — Middletown, Conn. : Wesleyan University Press, 1968. — I, 307.

Cahill, Marie. Madonna / Marie Cahill. — New York : Smithmark, 1991. — III, 770.

Cahn, Sammy. I should care : the Sammy Cahn story / Sammy Cahn. — New York : Arbor House, 1974. — I, 1272.

Cahn, Sammy. The songwriter's rhyming dictionary / Sammy Cahn. — New York : Facts on File, 1983. — II, A-548.

Cahn, William. Good night, Mrs. Calabash : the secret of Jimmy Durante / William Cahn. — New York : Duell, Sloan & Pearce, 1963. — II, 995.

Cain, Robert. Whole lotta shakin' goin' on : Jerry Lee Lewis / Robert Cain. — New York : Dial, 1981. — II, A-808.

California State College, San Diego. Library. Afro-American bibliography. San Diego : California State College, 1970. — I, A-145.

Callahan, Charles. The American classic organ : a history in letters / Charles Callahan. — Richmond, Va. : Organ Historical Society, 1990. — III, 989a.

Callas, Jackie. Sisters : a revealing portrait of the world's most famous diva / Jackie Callas. — London : Macmillan, 1989. — III, 691.

Callender, Red. Unfinished dream / Red Callender. — London : Quartet, 1985. — II, A-462.

Calloway, Cab. Of Minnie the moocher and me / Cab Calloway and Bryant Rollins. — New York : Crowell, 1976. — II, 741.

Calman, Charles Jeffrey. The Mormon Tabernacle Choir / Charles Jeffrey Calman. — New York : Harper & Row, 1979. — II, 64.

Calt, Stephen. King of the Delta blues : the life and music of Charlie Patton / Stephen Calt and Gayle Wardlow. — Newton, N.J. : Rock Chapel, 1988. — III, 812.

Cambiare, Celestin Pierre. East Tennessee and Western Virginia mountain ballads / Celestin Pierre Cambiare. — London : Mitre Press, 1934. — I, A-96.

Campa, Arthur L. Hispanic folklore studies of Arthur L. Campa / Arthur L. Campa. — New York : Arno, 1976. — II, 291.

Campa, Arthur L. Spanish-American folksongs from the collection of Leonora Curtin / Arthur Leon Campa. — [n.p.] : Independent Music, 1946. — II, 432.

Campbell, Jane. Old Philadelphia music / Jane Campbell. — Philadelphia : City Historical Society, 1926. — I, A-29.

Campbell, John C. The Southern highlander and his homeland / John C. Campbell. — New York : Russell Sage Foundation, 1921. — I, 90.

Campbell, Olive Dame. English folk songs from the Southern Appalachians / Olive Dame Campbell and Cecil J. Sharp. — New York : Putnam, 1917. — I, 469.

Campbell, Patricia J. Passing the hat : street performers in America / Patricia J. Campbell. — New York : Delacorte, 1981. — II, A-519.

Camus, Raoul F. Military music of the American Revolution / Raoul F. Camus. — Chapel Hill : University of North Carolina Press, 1976. — II, 870.

Canada, Lena. To Elvis with love / Lena Canada. — New York : Everest House, 1978. — II, 1294.

Cane, Giampiero. Canto nero : il free jazz degli anni sessanta / Giampiero Cane. — Bologna : Cooperativa Libreria, 1982. — II, A-438.

Canot, Theodore. Captain Canot, or twenty years as an African slaver / Theodore Canot. — London : Routledge, 1854. — I, 713.

Cantor, Eddie. My life is in your hands / Eddie Cantor. — Rev. ed. — New York : Blue Ribbon Books, 1932. — I, A-270.

Cantor, Eddie. Ziegfeld, the great glorifier / Eddie Cantor and David Freedman. — New York : A. H. King, 1934. — I, A-249.

Cantwell, Robert. Bluegrass breakdown : the making of the old southern sound / Robert Cantwell. — Urbana : University of Illinois Press, 1984. — II, A-229.

Caraeff, Ed. Dolly : close up, up close / Ed Caraeff and Richard Amdur. — New York : Delilah, 1983. — II, A-261.

Carawan, Guy. Ain't you got a right to the tree of life? / Guy Carawan and Candie Carawan. — New York : Simon & Schuster, 1966. — I, 742.

Carawan, Guy. Freedom is a constant struggle / Guy Carawan and Candie Carawan. — New York : Oak, 1968. — I, 743.

Carawan, Guy. We shall overcome : songs of the Southern freedom movement / Guy Carawan and Candie Carawan. — New York : Oak, 1963. — I, 744.

Card, Caroline. Discourse in ethnomusicology : essays in honor of George List /. ed. Caroline Card [et al]. — Bloomington : Ethnomusicology Publications Group, Indiana University, 1978. — II, 279.

Card, Caroline. Discourse in ethnomusicology 2 : a tribute to Alan P. Merriam / ed. Caroline Card. — Bloomington : Indiana University, 1981. — II, A-358.

Carden, Joy. Music in Lexington before 1840 / Joy Carden. — Lexington, Mass. : Lexington-Fayette County Historical Commission, 1980. — II, 56.

Cardew, Cornelius. Stockhausen serves imperialism, and other articles / Cornelius Cardew. — London : Latimer, 1974. — I, 309.

Caress, Jay. Hank Williams : country music's tragic king / Jay Caress. — New York : Stein & Day, 1979. — II, 419.

Carey, David A. Directory of recorded jazz and swing music / David A. Carey and Albert J. McCarthy. — London : Cassell [varies] : 1949–1957. — I, 926.

Carey, Gary. Judy Holiday : an intimate life story / Gary Carey. — New York : Seaview Books, 1982. — II, A-616.

Carey, Gary. Lenny, Janis & Jimi / Gary Carey. — New York : Pocket Books, 1975. — II, 1279.

Carey, George G. Maryland folk legends and folk songs / ed. George G. Carey. — Cambridge, Md. : Tidewater Publishers, 1971. — II, 313.

Carey, Joseph Kuhn. Big noise from Notre Dame : a history of the collegiate jazz festival / Joseph Kuhn Carey. — Notre Dame, Ind. : University of Notre Dame Press, 1986. — III, 48.

Carles, Philippe. Free jazz : black power / Philippe Carles and Jean-Louis Comolli. — Paris : Éditions du Champ Libre, 1971. — II, 717.

Carlisle, Dolly. Ragged but right : the life and times of George Jones / Dolly Carlisle. — Chicago : Contemporary Books, 1984. — II, A-254.

Carlson, Effie B. A bio-bibliographical dictionary of twelve-tone and serial composers / Effie B. Carlson. — Metuchen, N.J. : Scarecrow, 1970. — I, 252.

Carman, Judith. Art-song in the United States, 1801–1976 : an annotated bibliography / Judith Carman [et al]. — New York : NATS, 1976. — II, 25.

Carmer, Carl. Songs of the rivers of America / Carl Carmer. — New York : Farrar & Rinehart, 1942. — I, 451.

Carmer, Carl. Stars fell on Alabama / Carl Carmer. — New York : Literary Guild, 1934. — II, 305.

Carmichael, Hoagy. Sometimes I wonder : the story of Hoagy Carmichael / Hoagy Carmichael; with Stephen Longstreet. — New York : Farrar, Straus & Giroux, 1965. — I, 1094.

Carmichael, Hoagy. The stardust road / Hoagy Carmichael. — New York : Rinehart, 1946. — I, 1093.

Carner, Gary. Jazz performers : an annotated bibliography of biographical materials / comp. Gary Carner; foreword by John Chilton. — New York : Greenwood, 1990. — III, 111.

Carney, George O. Oklahoma's folk music traditions : a resource guide / George O. Carney. — Stillwater : Oklahoma State University, 1979. — II, 452.

Carney, George O. The sounds of people and places : readings in the geography of American folk and popular music / ed. George O. Carney. — Rev. ed. — Lanham, Md. : University Press of America, 1987. — III, 1214.

Carney, George O. The sounds of people and places : readings in the geography of music / George O. Carney. — Washington : University Press of America, 1979. — II, 833.

Carnovale, Norbert. Gunther Schuller : a bio-bibliography / Norbert Carnovale. — New York : Greenwood, 1987. — III, 180.

Carpenter, Paul S. Music : an art and a business / Paul S. Carpenter. — Norman : University of Oklahoma Press, 1950. — I, 360.

Carr, Ian. Jazz : the essential companion / Ian Carr, Digby Fairweather, and Brian Priestley. — London : Grafton Books, 1987; Englewood Cliffs, N.J. : Prentice-Hall, 1988. — III, 69.

Carr, Ian. Keith Jarrett : the man and his music / Ian Carr. — London : Grafton, 1991. — III, 552.

Carr, Ian. Miles Davis : a critical biography / Ian Carr. — London : Quartet, 1982. — II, A-469.

Carr, Patrick. The illustrated history of country music / Patrick Carr. — Garden City, N.Y. : Doubleday, 1979. — II, 367.

Carr, Roy. Elvis : the complete illustrated record / Roy Carr and Mick Farren. — London : Eel Pie, 1982 — II, A-824.

Carr, Roy. The hip : hipsters, jazz and the beat generation / Roy Carr, Brian Case, and Fred Dellar. — London : Faber & Faber, 1986. — III, 1273.

Carrick, Peter. A tribute to Fred Astaire / Peter Carrick. — London : Hale, 1984. — II, A-612.

Carrington, John F. Talking drums of Africa / John F. Carrington. — London : Kingsgate, 1949. — I, A-158.

Carroll, Brendan G. Erich Wolfgang Korngold, 1897–1957 / Brendan G. Carroll. — Paisley, Scotland : Wilfion Books, 1984. — II, A-604.

Carruth, Hayden. Sitting in : selected writings on jazz, blues, and related topics / Hayden Carruth. — Iowa City : University of Iowa Press, 1986. — III, 1216.

Carson, Gerald. The roguish world of Doctor Brinkley / Gerald Carson. — New York : Rinehart, 1960. — I, 611.

Carter, Elliott. The writings of Elliott Carter / Elliott Carter. — Bloomington : Indiana University Press, 1977. — II, 182.

Carter, Janette. Living with memories / Janette Carter. — Hilton, Va. : Carter Family Memorial Center, 1983. — II, A-246.

Carter, Lawrence T. Eubie Blake : keys to memory / Lawrence T. Carter. — Detroit : Balamp, 1979. — II, 534.

Carter, Morris. Isabella Stewart Gardner and Fenway Court / Morris Carter. — Boston : Houghton Mifflin, 1925. — II, 119.

Carter, Randolph. The world of Flo Ziegfeld / Randolph Carter. — New York : Praeger, 1974. — I, 1246.

Carter, William. Preservation Hall : music from the heart / William Carter. — New York : Norton, 1991. — III, 932.

Case, Brian. Harmony encyclopedia of jazz / Brian Case and Stan Britt; rev. Chrissie Murray. — 3rd ed. — New York : Harmony Books, 1987. — III, 69a.

Case, Brian. The illustrated encyclopedia of jazz / Brian Case and Stan Britt. — New York : Harmony Books, 1978. — II, 629.

Caserta, Peggy. Going down with Janis / Peggy Caserta. — Secaucus, N.J. : Lyle Stuart, 1975. — II, 1290.

Casey, Betty. Dance across Texas / Betty Casey. — Austin : University of Texas Press, 1985. — II, A-200.

Cash, Johnny. Man in black / Johnny Cash. — Grand Rapids, Mich. : Zondervan, 1975. — II, 396.

Cash, June Carter. Among my klediments / June Carter Cash. — Grand Rapids, Mich. : Zondervan, 1979. — II, 397.
Cash, June Carter. From the heart / June Carter Cash. — Englewood Cliffs, N.J. : Prentice-Hall, 1987. — III, 699.
Casper, Joseph Andrew. Vincente Minnelli and the film musical / Joseph Andrew Casper. — South Brunswick, N.J. : Barnes, 1977. — II, 926.
Cassidy, Bruce. Dinah! : a biography / Bruce Cassidy. — New York : Watts, 1979. — II, 1086.
Cassidy, Claudia. Lyric Opera of Chicago / Claudia Cassidy. — Chicago : Lyric Opera of Chicago, 1979. — II, 76.
Castell, David. The films of Barbra Streisand / David Castell. — Bembridge, England : BCW, 1977. — II, 1091.
Castelli, Vittorio. The Bix bands : a Bix Beiderbecke discobiography / Vittorio Castelli [et al]. — Milan : Raretone, 1972. — II, 642.
Castle, Irene. Castles in the air / Irene Castle; as told to Bob and Wanda Duncan. — Garden City, N.Y. : Doubleday, 1958. — II, 986.
Catlin, George. Letters and notes on the manners, customs and condition of the North American Indians / George Catlin. — New York : Wiley & Putnam, 1841. — I, A-88.
Catrambone, Gene. The golden touch : Frankie Carle / Gene Catrambone. — Roslyn Heights, N.Y. : Libra, 1981. — III, 538.
Cazden, Norman. Folk songs of the Catskills / Norman Cazden. — Albany : State University of New York Press, 1982. — II, A-194.
Cazden, Norman. Notes and sources for folk songs of the Catskills / Norman Cazden. — Albany : State University of New York Press, 1981. — II, A-195.
Cazden, Norman. The Abelard folk song book / ed. Norman Cazden. — New York : Abelard Schuman, 1958. — II, 341.
Cazort, Jean E. Born to play : the life and career of Hazel Harrison / Jean E. Cazort and Constance Tibbs Hobson. — Westport, Conn. : Greenwood, 1983. — III, 543.
Cebe, Gilles. Fred Astaire / Gilles Cebe. — Paris : Veyrier, 1981. — II, A-613.
Celentano, John. A catalogue of contemporary American chamber music / John Celentano and C. Reynolds. — Lawrenceville, N.J. : American String Teachers Association, 1975. — II, 228.
Cerchiari, Luca. Il jazz degli anni settanta / Luca Cerchiari [et al]. — Milan : Gammalibri, 1980. — II, 778.
Cerulli, Dom. The jazz word / ed. Dom Cerulli [et al]. — New York : Ballantine, 1960. — I, 1014.
Cerutti, Gustave. Discographie Archie Shepp 1960–1980 / Gustave Cerutti and Guido Maertens. — Sierre, Switzerland : Jazz 360 Degree, 1981. — II, A-385.
Chadwick, George W. Horatio Parker / George W. Chadwick. — New Haven, Conn. : Yale University Press, 1921. — I, 242.
Chalker, Bryan. Country music / Bryan Chalker. — London : Phoebus, 1976. — II, 384.
Chambers, H. A. Treasury of negro spirituals / H. A. Chambers. — New York : Emerson Books, 1963. — I, 772.
Chambers, Iain. Urban rhythms : pop music and popular culture / Iain Chambers. — London : Macmillan, 1985. — II, A-692.

Chambers, Jack. The music and times of Miles Davis / Jack Chambers. — Toronto : University of Toronto Press, 1983–1985. — II, A-470.

Chambers, John Richard. Milestones 1 : the music and times of Miles Davis to 1960 / John Richard Chambers. — Toronto : University of Toronto Press, 1983. — III, 626.

Chambers, John Richard. Milestones 2 : the music and times of Miles Davis since 1960 / John Richard Chambers. — New York : Beech Tree Books, 1985. — III, 627.

Chametzky, Jules. Black and white in American culture : an anthology from "The Massachusetts Review" / Jules Chametzky and Sidney Kaplan. — Amherst : University of Massachusetts Press, 1969. — I, 673.

Champe, Flavia Waters. The Matachines dance of the upper Rio Grande : history, music, and choreography / Flavia Waters Champe. — Lincoln : University of Nebraska Press, 1983. — III, 12.

Chandler, Edna White. The night the camel sang / Edna White Chandler. — St. Johnsbury, Vt. : New Amberola Graphic, 1990. — III, 672.

Chapin, Schuyler, Leonard Bernstein : notes from a friend / Schuyler Chapin; foreword by Peter Ustinov. — New York : Walker, 1992. — III, 453.

Chapin, Schuyler. Musical chairs : a life in music / Schuyler Chapin. — New York : Putnam, 1977. — II, 208.

Chappell, Louis W. Folk-songs of Roanoke and the Albemarle / Louis W. Chappell. — Morgantown, W.Va. : Ballad Press, 1939. — I, A-97.

Chappell, Louis W. John Henry : a folk-lore study / Louis W. Chappell. — Jena : Frommann, 1933. — I, 755.

Chapple, Steve. Rock 'n' roll is here to pay / Steve Chapple and Reebee Garofalo. — Chicago : Nelson-Hall, 1977. — II, 1153.

Charbonnier, Georges. Entretiens avec Edgard Varèse / Georges Charbonnier. — Paris : Belfond, 1970. — I, 351.

Charles, Daniel. Gloses sur John Cage / Daniel Charles. — Paris : Union Générale d'Éditions, 1978. — II, 179.

Charles, Ray. Brother Ray : Ray Charles' own story / Ray Charles and David Ritz. — New York : Dial, 1978. — II, 570.

Charnin, Martin. Annie : a theatre memoir / Martin Charnin. — New York : Dutton, 1977. — II, 924.

Charters, Ann. Nobody : the story of Bert Williams / Ann Charters. — New York : Macmillan, 1970. — I, 1229.

Charters, Ann. Ragtime songbook / Ann Charters. — New York : Oak, 1965. — I, A-174.

Charters, Samuel B. Jazz : a history of the New York scene / Samuel B. Charters and Leonard Kunstadt. — New York : Doubleday, 1962. — I, 1072.

Charters, Samuel B. Jazz : New Orleans / Samuel B. Charters. — Rev. ed. — New York : Oak, 1963. — I, 1063.

Charters, Samuel B. Jelly Roll Morton's last night at the Jungle Inn : an imaginary memoir / Samuel B. Charters. — London : Boyars, 1984. — II, A-490.

Charters, Samuel B. Poetry of the blues / Samuel B. Charters. — New York : Oak, 1963. — I, 858.

Charters, Samuel B. Robert Johnson / Samuel B. Charters. — New York : Oak, 1973. — I, 842.

Charters Samuel B. Sweet as the showers of rain : the bluesmen / Samuel B. Charters. — New York : Oak, 1977. — II, 545.

Charters, Samuel B. The bluesmen : the story and the music of the men who made the blues / Samuel B. Charters. — New York : Oak, 1967. — I, 827.

Charters, Samuel B. The country blues / Samuel B. Charters. — New York : Rinehart, 1959. — I, 828.

Charters, Samuel B. The legacy of the blues / Samuel B. Charters. — London : Calder & Boyars, 1975. — I, 829.

Charters, Samuel. The roots of the blues / Samuel Charters. — London : Boyars, 1981. — II, A-315.

Chase, Gilbert. American composer speaks : a historical anthology, 1770–1965 / Gilbert Chase. — Baton Rouge : Louisiana State University Press, 1966. — I, 33.

Chase, Gilbert. America's music : from the pilgrims to the present / Gilbert Chase; foreword by Richard Crawford; discographical essay by William Brooks. — 3rd ed. — New York : McGraw-Hill, 1987. — III, 367.

Chase, Gilbert. America's music from the pilgrims to the present / Gilbert Chase. — Rev. ed. — New York : McGraw-Hill, 1966. — I, 25.

Chase, Richard. American folk tales and songs and other examples of English-American tradition / ed. Richard Chase. — New York : New American Library, 1956. — II, 286.

Chasins, Abram. Leopold Stokowski / Abram Chasins. — New York : Hawthorn, 1979. — II, 229.

Chasins, Abram. Music at the crossroads / Abram Chasins. — New York : Macmillan, 1972. — I, 361.

Chauncey, Nathaniel. Regular singing defended and proved to be the only true way of singing the songs of the Lord / Nathaniel Chauncey. — New London, Conn. : T. Green, 1728. — I, 200.

Cheney, Simeon Pease. The American singing book / Simeon Pease Cheney. — Boston : White, Smith, 1879. — I, 11.

Cheney, Thomas E. Mormon songs from the Rocky Mountains / Thomas E. Cheney. — Austin : University of Texas Press, 1968. — I, 557.

Cherrington, George. Jazz catalogue : a discography of all British jazz releases / George Cherrington and Brian Knight. — London : Jazz Journal, 1960–1971. — I, 929.

Chevalier, Dominique. Viva! Zappa / Dominique Chevalier. — London : Omnibus, 1986. — III, 893.

Chevigny, Paul. Gigs : jazz and the cabaret laws in New York City / Paul Chevigny. — New York : Routledge, 1991. — III, 1289.

Chew, V. K. Talking machines, 1887–1914 : some aspects of the early history of the gramophone / V. K. Chew. — London : H.M.S.O., 1967. — I, 176.

Child, Francis James. English and Scottish popular ballads / Francis James Child. — Boston : Houghton Mifflin, 1882–1898. — I, 465.

Chilton, John. A jazz nursery : the story of the Jenkins' Orphanage bands / John Chilton. — London : Bloomsbury Book Shop, 1980. — II, 709.

Chilton, John. Billie's blues : a survey of Billie Holiday's career, 1933–1959 / John Chilton. — London : Quartet, 1975. — I, 1119.

Chilton, John. Bunny Berigan / John Chilton. — Alexandria, Va. : Time-Life Records, 1982. — III, 606.

Chilton, John. Jazz / John Chilton. — New York : McKay, 1979. — II, 692.

Chilton, John. Let the good times roll : the story of Louis Jordan and his music / John Chilton. — London : Quartet, 1992. — III, 650.

Chilton, John. McKinney's music : a bio-discography of McKinney's Cotton Pickers / John Chilton. — London : Bloomsbury Book Shop, 1978. — II, 761.

Chilton, John. Sidney Bechet : the wizard of jazz / John Chilton. — New York : Oxford, 1987. — III, 602.

Chilton, John. Stomp off, let's go! : the story of Bob Crosby's Bob Cats and big band / John Chilton. — London : Jazz Book Service, 1983. — II, A-467.

Chilton, John. The song of the hawk : the life and recordings of Coleman Hawkins / John Chilton. — New York : Quartet; Ann Arbor : University of Michigan Press, 1990. — III, 641.

Chilton, John. Who's who of jazz / John Chilton. — London : Bloomsbury Book Shop, 1970. — I, 901.

Chinn, Jennie A. Folk roots : an exploration of the folk arts and cultural traditions of Kansas / Jennie A. Chinn. — Manhattan, Kans. : University for Man, 1982. — II, A-190.

Chipman, Bruce L. Hardening rock : an organic anthology of the adolescence of rock 'n' roll / ed. Bruce L. Chipman. — Boston : Little, Brown, 1972. — II, 1137.

Chipman, John H. Index to top-hit tunes (1900–1950) / John H. Chipman. — Boston : Humphries, 1962. — I, 1149.

Christeson, R. P. The old-time fiddler's repertory : 245 traditional tunes / R. P. Christeson. — Columbia : University of Missouri Press, 1973. — I, A-98.

Christeson, R. P. The old-time fiddler's repertory / ed. R. P. Christeson. — Columbia : University of Missouri Press, 1973–1984. — II, 324.

Christgau, Robert. Any old way you choose it / Robert Christgau. — Baltimore : Penguin, 1973. — I, 1362.

Christgau, Robert. Christgau's record guide : rock albums of the seventies / Robert Christgau. — New Haven, Conn. : Ticknor & Fields, 1981. — II, A-682.

Church music and musical life in Pennsylvania in the eighteenth century / Committee on Historical Research, National Society of the Colonial Dames of America. — Philadelphia : The Society, 1926–1947. — I, 120.

Churchill, Allen. The great white way : a recreation of Broadway's golden era of theatrical entertainment / Allen Churchill. — New York : Dutton, 1962. — II, 881.

Cimino, Al. Great record labels / Al Cimino. — Secaucus, N.J. : Chartwell, 1992. — III, 1236.

Cipolla, Wilma Reid. A catalog of the works of Arthur Foote, 1853–1937 / Wilma Reid Cipolla. — Detroit : Information Coordinators, 1980. — II, 144.

Claghorn, Charles Eugene. Biographical dictionary of American music / Charles Eugene Claghorn. — West Nyack, N.Y. : Parker, 1973. — I, 12.

Claghorn, Charles Eugene. Biographical dictionary of jazz / Charles Eugene Claghorn. — Englewood Cliffs, N.J. : Prentice-Hall, 1982. — III, 409.

Claghorn, Charles Eugene. The mocking bird : the life and diary of its author, Septimus Winner / Charles Eugene Claghorn. — Philadelphia : Magee Press, 1937. — I, A-234.

Claghorn, Gene. Women composers and hymnists : a concise biographical dictionary / Gene Claghorn. — Metuchen, N.J. : Scarecrow, 1984. — II, A-16.

Claire, Vivian. Judy Collins / Vivian Claire. — New York : Flash Books, 1977. — II, 357.

Claire, Vivian. Linda Ronstadt / Vivian Claire. — New York : Flash Books, 1978. — II, 1240.

Clapton, Diana. Lou Reed and the Velvet Underground / Diana Clapton. — London : Proteus, 1982. — II, A-837.

Clark, Dick. Rock, roll & remember / Dick Clark and Richard Robinson. — New York : Crowell, 1976. — II, 1154.

Clark, J. Bunker. Music at KU : a history of the University of Kansas Music Department / J. Bunker Clark. — Lawrence : University of Kansas, Dept. of Music and Dance, 1986. — III, 1264.

Clark, J. Bunker. The dawning of American keyboard music / J. Bunker Clark. — Westport, Conn. : Greenwood, 1988. — III, 992.

Clark, Kenneth S. Music in industry / Kenneth S. Clark. — New York : National Bureau for the Advancement of Music, 1929. — I, 362.

Clark, Laverne Harrell. They sang for horses : the impact of the horse on Navajo and Apache folklore / Laverne Harrell Clark. — Tucson : University of Arizona Press, 1966. — II, 246.

Clark, Ronald W. Edison : the man who made the future / Ronald V. Clark. — New York : Putnam, 1977. — II, 104.

Clarke, Garry E. Essays on American music / Garry E. Clarke. — Westport, Conn. : Greenwood, 1977. — II, 13.

Clarke, John Henrik. Harlem, U.S.A. / John Henrik Clarke. — Rev. ed. — New York : Collier, 1971. — I, 972.

Claypool, Bob. Saturday night at Gilley's / Bob Claypool. — New York : Grove, 1980. — II, 382.

Clayson, Alan. Only the lonely : Roy Orbison's life and legacy / Alan Clayson. — New York : St. Martin's, 1990. — III, 808.

Clayton, Buck. Buck Clayton's jazz world / Buck Clayton; assisted by Nancy Miller Elliott; discography compiled by Bob Weir. — London : Macmillan, 1986. — III, 617.

Clayton, Peter. Jazz A-Z / Peter Clayton and Peter Gammond. — London : Guinness Superlatives, 1986. — III, 70.

Clee, Ken. The directory of American 45 rpm records / Ken Clee. — Philadelphia : Author, 1981–1985. — II, A-514.

Clements, William M. Native American folklore, 1879–1979 : an annotated bibliography / William M. Clements. — Athens, Ohio : Swallow Press, 1984. — II, A-157.

Cleveland Public Library. Catalog of folklore and folk songs / Cleveland Public Library, John G. White Department. — Boston : G. K. Hall, 1964. — I, 428.

Cleveland Public Library. Index to negro spirituals. — Cleveland : The Library, 1937. — I, 785.

Clifford, Mike. Harmony encyclopedia of rock / Mike Clifford. — 6th ed. — New York : Harmony Books, 1988. — III, 79a.

Clifford, Mike. The illustrated encyclopedia of black music / Mike Clifford [et al]. — London : Salamander, 1982. — II, A-286.

Clifford, Mike. The illustrated rock handbook / Mike Clifford [et al]. — London : Salamander, 1983. — II, A-651.

Cline, Beverly Fink. The Lombardo story / Beverly Fink Cline. — Don Mills, Ontario : Musson, 1979. — II, 760.

Cline, Dallas. Cornstalk fiddle and other homemade instruments / Dallas Cline. — New York : Oak, 1976. — II, 456.

Clinkscale, Edward H. A musical offering : essays in honor of Martin Bernstein / ed. Edward H. Clinkscale and Claire Brook. — New York : Pendragon, 1977. — II, 188.

Clooney, Rosemary. This for remembrance : the autobiography of Rosemary Clooney / Rosemary Clooney; with Raymond Strait. — New York : Playboy Press, 1977. — II, 987.

Clurman, Harold. The fervent years : the story of the group theatre and the thirties / Harold Clurman. — New York : Knopf, 1945. — II, 1040.

Coakley, Mary Lewis. Mister music maker : Lawrence Welk / Mary Lewis Coakley. — Garden City, N.Y. : Doubleday, 1958. — II, 1094.

Cobb, Buell E. The sacred harp : a tradition and its music / Buell E. Cobb. — Athens, Ga. : University of Georgia Press, 1978. — II, 320.

Cochran, Robert. For love and for money : the writings of Vance Randolph / Robert Cochran and Michael Luster. — Batesville : Arkansas College Folklore Archive, 1979. — II, 453.

Cochran, Robert. Vance Randolph : an Ozark life / Robert Cochran. — Urbana : University of Illinois Press, 1985. — II, A-196.

Cocke, Marian J. I called him babe : Elvis Presley's nurse remembers / Marian J. Cocke. — Memphis : Memphis University Press, 1979. — II, 1295.

Coeuroy, André. Le jazz / André Coeuroy and André Schaeffner. — Paris : C. Aveline, 1926. — I, A-197.

Coffin, Levi. Reminiscences of Levi Coffin, the reputed president of the underground railroad / Levi Coffin. — Cincinnati : Western Tract Society, 1876. — I, 734.

Coffin, Tristram P. American folklore / Tristram P. Coffin. — Washington : Voice of America, 1968. — I, 439.

Coffin, Tristram P. British traditional ballad in North America / Tristram P. Coffin. — 2nd ed. — Philadelphia : American Folklore Society, 1963. — I, 466.

Coffin, Tristram P. Folklore in America / Tristram P. Coffin and Hennig Cohen. — New York : Doubleday, 1970. — I, 452.

Coffin, Tristram P. Our living traditions : an introduction to American folklore / Tristram P. Coffin. — New York : Basic Books, 1968. — I, 439.

Cohen, Aaron I. International discography of women composers / Aaron I. Cohen. — Westport, Conn. : Greenwood, 1984. — II, A-17.

Cohen, Anne B. Poor Pearl, poor girl : the murdered-girl stereotype in ballad and newspaper / Anne B. Cohen. — Austin : University of Texas Press, 1973. — II, 287.

Cohen, Lily Young. Lost spirituals / Lily Young Cohen. — New York : Walter Neale, 1928. — II, 523.

Cohen, Mitchell S. Carole King : a biography in words and pictures / Mitchell S. Cohen. — New York : Sire Books, 1976. — II, 1213.

Cohen, Mitchell S. Simon & Garfunkel / Mitchell S. Cohen. — New York : Sire Books, 1977. — II, 1315.

Cohen, Norm. Long steel rail : the railroad in American folksong / Norm Cohen. — Urbana : University of Illinois Press, 1981. — II, A-213.

Cohen, Norm. Robert W. Gordon and the second wreck of the "Old 97" / Norm Cohen. — Los Angeles : John Edwards Memorial Foundation, 1974. — I, 612.

Cohen, Norman. Railroad folksongs on record : survey / Norman Cohen. — Los Angeles : John Edwards Memorial Foundation, 1970. — I, 571.

Cohen-Stratyner, Barbara Naomi. Popular music, 1900–1919 : an annotated guide to American popular songs / Barbara Naomi Cohen-Stratyner. — Detroit : Gale Research, 1988. — III, 104.

Cohn, Arthur. The collector's twentieth-century music in the Western hemisphere / Arthur Cohn. — Philadelphia : Lippincott, 1961. — I, 253.

Cohn, Nik. Awopbopaloobop alopbamboom ; pop from the beginning / Nik Cohn. — London : Paladin, 1970. — I, 1349.

Cohn, Nik. Pop from the beginning / Nik Cohn. — London : Weidenfeld & Nicolson, 1969. — I, 1349.

Cohn, Nik. Rock from the beginning / Nik Cohn. — New York : Stein & Day, 1969. — I, 1349.

Coker, Jerry. Improvising jazz / Jerry Coker. — Englewood Cliffs, N.J. : Prentice-Hall, 1964. — I, 981.

Coker, Jerry. Listening to jazz / Jerry Coker. — Englewood Cliffs, N.J. : Prentice-Hall, 1978. — II, 663.

Coker, Jerry. The jazz idiom / Jerry Coker. — Englewood Cliffs, N.J. : Prentice-Hall, 1975. — II, 662.

Colbeck, Julian. Zappa : a biography / Julian Colbeck. — London : Virgin, 1987. — III, 895.

Colbert, Warren E. Who wrote that song? / Warren E. Colbert. — New York : Revisionist Press, 1975. — II, 821.

Colcord, Joanna C. Roil and go : songs of American sailormen / Joanna C. Colcord. — Indianapolis : Bobbs-Merrill, 1924. — I, 573.

Colcord, Joanna C. Songs of American sailormen / Joanna C. Colcord. — Rev. ed. — New York : Norton, 1938. — I, 573.

Cole, Bill. John Coltrane / Bill Cole. — New York : Schirmer, 1976. — II, 742.

Cole, Bill. Miles Davis : a musical biography / Bill Cole. — New York : Morrow, 1974. — I, 1099.

Cole, Maria. Nat King Cole : an intimate biography / Maria Cole. — New York : Morrow, 1971. — I, 1324.

Coleman, Bill. Trumpet story / Bill Coleman. — London : Macmillan, 1988. — III, 618.

Coleman, Emily R. Complete Judy Garland : the ultimate guide to her career in films, records, concerts, radio, and television, 1935–1969 / Emily R. Coleman. — New York : Harper & Row, 1990. — III, 724.

Coleman, Janet. Mingus/Mingus : two memoirs / Janet Coleman and Al Young. — Berkeley, Calif. : Creative Arts, 1989. — III, 588.

Colin, Sid. Ella : the life and times of Ella Fitzgerald / Sid Colin. — London : Elm Tree, 1986. — III, 720.

Collaer, Paul. Music of the Americas : an illustrated music ethnology of the Eskimo and American Indian peoples / Paul Collaer. — New York : Praeger, 1973. — I, 389.

Collectable 45s. — London : Vintage Record Centre, 1981. — II, A-684.

Collectable EPs. — London : Vintage Record Centre, 1982–1985. — II, A-683.

Collection jazz (series). — III, 1111.

Collectors classics. Bexhill-on-Sea, England : Blues Unlimited, 1964–1966. — II, 616.

Collier, Graham. Inside jazz / Graham Collier. — London : Quartet, 1973. — I, 961.

Collier, Graham. Jazz : a student's and teacher's guide / Graham Collier. — Cambridge, England : Cambridge University Press, 1975. — I, 962.

Collier, James Lincoln. Benny Goodman and the swing era / James Lincoln Collier. — New York : Oxford, 1989. — III, 952.

Collier, James Lincoln. Duke Ellington / James Lincoln Collier. — New York : Oxford, 1987. — III, 467.

Collier, James Lincoln. Louis Armstrong / James Lincoln Collier. — New York : Oxford University Press, 1983. — II, A-455.

Collier, James Lincoln. The great jazz artists / James Lincoln Collier. — New York : Four Winds Press, 1977. — II, 701.

Collier, James Lincoln. The making of jazz : a comprehensive history / James Lincoln Collier. — Boston : Houghton Mifflin, 1978. — II, 693.

Collier, James Lincoln. The reception of jazz in America : a new view / James Lincoln Collier. — Brooklyn : Institute for Studies in American Music, 1988. — III, 110.

Collings, Henrietta. Georgia's heritage of song / ed. Henrietta Collings. — Athens : University of Georgia Press, 1955. — II, 306.

Collins, Ace. Bette Midler / Ace Collins. — New York : St. Martin's, 1989. — III, 788.

Collins, Judy. Trust your heart : an autobiography / Judy Collins. — Boston : Houghton Mifflin, 1987. — III, 704.

Collins, Lee. Oh, didn't he ramble / Lee Collins, as told to Mary Collins. — Urbana : University of Illinois Press, 1974. — I, 1095.

Collinson, John. The jazz legacy of Don Ewell / John Collinson and Eugene Kramer; with seventeen piano transcriptions by Ray Smith; and additional contributions by William Russell . . . [et al]. — Chigwell, Essex, England : Storyville, 1991. — III, 540.

Collis, John. The rock primer / John Collis. — Harmondsworth, England : Penguin, 1980. — II, 1118.

Colman, Stuart. They kept on rockin' / Stuart Colman. — Poole, Dorset, England : Blandford, 1982. — II, A-756.

Colyer, Ken. New Orleans and back / Ken Colyer. — Delph, Yorkshire, England : Brooks & Pratt, 1968. — I, 1064.

Combs, Josiah H. Folk-songs from the Kentucky highlands / Josiah H. Combs. — New York : Schirmer, 1939. — I, A-99.

Combs, Josiah H. Folk-songs of the Southern United States / Josiah H. Combs. — Austin : University of Texas Press, 1967. — I, 488.

Complete catalogue of royalty and non-royalty productions and grand and comic operas, musical comedies and other musical productions. — New York : Tams-Witmark, 1922- . II, 1023.

Condon, Eddie. Eddie Condon's treasury of jazz / Eddie Condon and Richard Gehmann. — New York : Dial, 1956. — I, 1015.

Condon, Eddie. The Eddie Condon scrapbook of jazz / Eddie Condon and Hank O'Neal. — New York : St. Martin's, 1973. — I, 1097.

Condon, Eddie. We called it music : a generation of jazz / Eddie Condon. — New York : Holt, 1947. — I, 1098.

Cone, James H. The spirituals and the blues : an interpretation / James H. Cone. — New York : Seabury, 1972. — I, 786.

Cone, John Frederick. Oscar Hammerstein's Manhattan Opera Company / John Frederick Cone. — Norman : University of Oklahoma Press, 1966. — I, 156.

Confronting Stravinsky : man, musician, and modernist / ed. Jann Pasler. — Berkeley : University of California Press, 1986. — III, 525.

Conn, Charles Paul. The Barbara Mandrell story / Charles Paul Conn. — New York : Putnam, 1988. — III, 778.

Conn, Charles. The new Johnny Cash / Charles Conn. — Old Tappan, N.J. : Revell, 1973. — II, 468.

Connelly, Will. The musician's guide to independent record production / Will Connelly. — Chicago : Contemporary Books, 1981. — II, A-738.

Connor, D. Russell. B. G. — on the record / D. Russell Connor and Warren W. Hicks. — New Rochelle, N.Y. : Arlington House, 1969. — I, 1115.

Connor, D. Russell. Benny Goodman : listen to his legacy / D. Russell Connor. — Metuchen, N.J. : Scarecrow Press and The Institute of Jazz Studies, 1988. — III, 313.

Connor, Donald Russell. The record of a legend : Benny Goodman. — Donald Russell Connor. — New York : Let's Dance, 1984. — II, A-480.

Conrad, Earl. Billy Rose, Manhattan primitive / Earl Conrad. — Cleveland : World, 1968. — II, 1041.

Conrad, Glenn R. The Cajuns : essays on their history and culture / ed. Glenn R. Conrad. — 2nd ed. — Lafayette : Center for Louisiana Studies, University of Southwestern Louisiana, 1978. — II, 424.

Considine, J. D. Van Halen! / J. D. Considine. — New York : Quill, 1985. — III, 944.

Considine, Shaun. Barbra Streisand : the woman, the myth, the music / Shaun Considine. — New York : Delacorte, 1985. — II, A-641.

Convention of Local Phonograph Companies of the United States, 1890. Proceedings. — Nashville : Country Music Foundation Press, 1974. — I, 177.

Conversations with jazz musicians. — Detroit : Gale, 1977. — II, 730.

Cook, Bruce. Listen to the blues / Bruce Cook. — New York : Scribner's, 1973. — I, 859.

Cook, Harold E. Shaker music : a manifestation of American culture / Harold E. Cook. — Lewisburg, Pa. : Bucknell University Press, 1973. — I, 553.

Cooke, George Willis. John Sullivan Dwight, Brook-farmer, editor, and critic of music : a biography / George Willis Cooke. — New ed. — Hartford, Conn. : Transcendental Books, 1973. — I, 212.

Coon, O. Wayne. Some problems with musical public-domain materials under United States copyright law / Wayne O. Coon. — Los Angeles : John Edwards Memorial Foundation, 1973. — I, 602.

Cooper, Alice. Me, Alice : the autobiography of Alice Cooper / Alice Cooper; with Steven Gaines. — New York : Putnam, 1976. — II, 1190.

Cooper, B. Lee. A resource guide to themes in contemporary American song

Corenthal, Michael G. Iconography of recorded sound, 1886–1986 / Michael G. Corenthal. — Milwaukee, Wisc. : Yesterday's Memories, 1986. — III, 1237.
Corenthal, Michael G. The illustrated history of Wisconsin music / Michael G. Corenthal. — Milwaukee, Wisc. : Yesterday's Memories, 1991. — III, 385.
Cornfeld, Robert. Just country : country people, stories, music / Robert Cornfeld. — New York : McGraw-Hill, 1976. — II, 363.
Cortez, Diego. Private Elvis / Diego Cortez. — Stuttgart : Fey, 1978. — II, 1222.
Coryell, Julie. Jazz-rock fusion : the people, the music / Julie Coryell and Laura Friedman. — New York : Dell, 1978. — II, 718.
Coryton, Demitri. Hits of the '60s : the million sellers / Demitri Coryton and Joseph Murrells. — London : Batsford, 1990. — III, 256.
Coslow, Sam. Cocktails for two : the many lives of giant songwriter Sam Coslow / Sam Coslow. — New Rochelle, N.Y. : Arlington House, 1977. — II, 946.
Costello, Mark. Signifying rappers / Mark Costello and David Foster Wallace. — New York : Ecco, 1990. — III, 1167.
Cott, Jonathan. Bob Dylan / Jonathan Cott. — New York : Rolling Stone Press, 1984. — II, A-783.
Cotten, Lee. All shook up : Elvis day-by-day, 1954–1977 / Lee Cotten. — Ann Arbor, Mich. : Pierian, 1985. — II, A-825.
Cotten, Lee. Jailhouse rock : the bootleg records of Elvis Presley, 1970–1983 / Lee Cotten and Howard A. DeWitt. — Ann Arbor, Mich. : Pierian, 1983. — II, A-817.
Cotten, Lee. Shake, rattle & roll : the golden age of American rock 'n' roll. Volume 1, 1952–1955 / Lee Cotten. — Ann Arbor, Mich. : Pierian, 1989. — III, 1171.
Cotten, Lee. The Elvis catalog : memorabilia, icons and collectibles celebrating the king of rock 'n' roll / Lee Cotten. — Garden City, N.Y. : Doubleday, 1987. — III, 818.
Cotton, John. Singing of psalms, a gospel ordinance / John Cotton. — London: Hannah Allan, 1647. — I, 192.
Country music who's who / ed. Thurston Moore. — Cincinnati : Cardinal Enterprises, 1960. — I, 604.
Country : the music and the musicians / foreword by Paul Kingsbury. — Nashville : Country Music Foundation Press; New York : Abbeville, 1988. — III, 1158.
Coupe, Stuart. The new rock 'n' roll / Stuart Coupe and Glenn A. Baker. — London : Omnibus, 1983. — II, A-652.
Courlander, Harold. A treasury of Afro-American folklore / ed. Harold Courlander. — New York : Crown, 1976. — II, 598.
Courlander, Harold. Haiti singing / Harold Courlander. — Chapel Hill : University of North Carolina Press, 1939. — I, 681.
Courlander, Harold. Negro folk music, U.S.A. / Harold Courlander. — New York : Columbia University Press, 1963. — I, 756.
Courlander, Harold. Negro songs from Alabama / Harold Courlander. — New York : Wenner-Gren Foundation, 1960. — I, 745.
Cowell, Henry. American composers on American music : a symposium / Henry Cowell. — New York : Ungar, 1962. — I, 293.

Cowell, Henry. Charles Ives and his music / Henry Cowell and Sidney Cowell. — Rev. ed. — London : Oxford University Press, 1969. — I, 327.

Cowell, Henry. New musical resources / Henry Cowell. — New York : Knopf, 1930. — I, 319.

Cox, John Harrington. Folk songs mainly from West Virginia / ed. John Harrington Cox. — New York : National Service Bureau, 1939. — II, 320.

Cox, John Harrington. Folk songs of the South / John Harrington Cox. — Cambridge, Mass. : Harvard University Press, 1925. — I, 507.

Cox, John Harrington. Traditional ballads and folk-songs mainly from West Virginia / ed. John Harrington Cox. — Philadelphia : American Folklore Society, 1964. — II, 320.

Cox, John Harrington. Traditional ballads from West Virginia / ed. John Harrington Cox. — New York : National Service Bureau, 1939. — II, 320.

Cox, John Harrington. Traditional ballads, mainly from West Virginia / John Harrington Cox. — New York : National Service Bureau, 1939. — I, A-101.

Craft, Robert. Stravinsky : glimpses of a life / Robert Craft. — New York : St. Martin's, 1992. — III, 526.

Craig, Warren. Sweet and lowdown : America's popular songwriters / Warren Craig. — Metuchen, N.J. : Scarecrow, 1978. — II, 803.

Craig, Warren. The great songwriters of Hollywood / Warren Craig. — San Diego : Barnes, 1980. — II, 927.

Cranor, Rosalind. Elvis collectibles / Rosalind Cranor. — 2nd ed. — Johnson City, Tenn. : Overmountain, 1987. — III, 819.

Cranor, Rosalind. Elvis collectibles / Rosalind Cranor. — Paducah, Ky. : Collection Books, 1983. — II, A-818.

Craven, Robert R. Symphony orchestras of the United States : selected profiles / Robert R. Craven. — Westport, Conn. : Greenwood, 1986. — III, 999.

Crawford, Ralston. Music in the street : photographs of New Orleans / Ralston Crawford. — New Orleans : William Ransom Hogan Archive, 1983. — II, A-443.

Crawford, Richard. A celebration of American music : words and music in honor of H. Wiley Hitchcock / ed. Richard Crawford, R. Allen Lott, and Carol J. Oja. — Ann Arbor : University of Michigan Press, 1989. — III, 366.

Crawford, Richard. A historian's introduction to early American music / Richard A. Crawford. — Worcester, Mass. : American Antiquarian Society, 1979. — II, 139.

Crawford, Richard. American studies and American musicology : a point of view and a case in point / Richard A. Crawford. — Brooklyn : Institute for Studies in American Music, 1975. — I, 34.

Crawford, Richard. Andrew Law, American psalmodist / Richard A. Crawford. — Evanston, Ill. : Northwestern University Press, 1968. — I, 207.

Crawford, Richard. Jazz standards on record, 1900–1942 : a core repertory / Richard Crawford and Jeffrey Magee. — Chicago : Center for Black Music Research, Columbia College, 1992. — III, 236.

Crawford, Richard. Studying American music / Richard Crawford. — Brooklyn : Institute for the Study of American Music, 1985. — II, A-14.

Crawford, Richard. The Civil War songbook / ed. Richard Crawford. — New York : Dover, 1946. — II, 1028.

Crawford, Richard. The core repertory of early American psalmody / ed. Richard Crawford. — Madison, Wisc. : A-R Editions, 1984. — III, 15.
Cray, Ed. The erotic muse : American bawdy songs / Ed Cray. — 2nd ed. — Urbana : University of Illinois Press, 1992. — III, 25.
Cripe, Helen. Thomas Jefferson and music / Helen Cripe. — Charlottesville : University of Virginia Press, 1974. — I, 208.
Crite, Allan Rohan. Three spirituals from heaven to earth / Allan Rohan Crite. — Cambridge, Mass. : Harvard University Press, 1948. — II, 599.
Crite, Allan Rohan. Were you there when they crucified my Lord? / Allan Rohan Crite. — Cambridge, Mass. : Harvard University Press, 1944. — II, 600.
Croce, Arlene. The Fred Astaire and Ginger Rogers book / Arlene Croce. — New York : Outerbridge and Lazard, 1972. — II, 971.
Crosby, Bing. Call me lucky / Bing Crosby. — New York : Simon & Schuster, 1953. — I, 1325.
Crosby, David. Long time gone : the autobiography of David Crosby / David Crosby; with Carl Gottlieb. — New York : Doubleday, 1988. — III, 706.
Crosby, Gary. Goin my way / Gary Crosby and Ross Firestone. — Garden City, N.Y. : Doubleday, 1985. — II, A-623.
Crosby, Kathryn. My life with Bing / Kathryn Crosby. — Wheeling, Ill. : Collage, 1983. — II, A-624.
Crosby, Ted. Bing / Ted Crosby and Larry Crosby. — Los Angeles : Bolton Printing Co., 1937. — I, 1327.
Crosby, Ted. The story of Bing Crosby / Ted Crosby. — Cleveland : World, 1946. — I, 1327.
Cross, Charles R. Backstreets : Springsteen : the man and his music / Charles R. Cross [et al]. — London : Sidgwick & Jackson, 1989. — III, 863.
Cross, Lowell M. A bibliography of electronic music / Lowell M. Cross. — Toronto : University of Toronto Press, 1967. — I, 279.
Cross, Wilbur. The Conway Twitty story : an authorized biography / Wilbur Cross and Michael Kosser. — Garden City, N.Y. : Doubleday, 1986. — III, 880.
Crow, Bill. From Birdland to Broadway : scenes from a jazz life / Bill Crow. — New York : Oxford, 1992. — III, 1077.
Crow, Bill. Jazz anecdotes / Bill Crow. — New York : Oxford 1992. — III, 1078.
Crowther, Bruce. Benny Goodman / Bruce Crowther. London : Apollo, 1988. — III, 953.
Crowther, Bruce. Gene Krupa : his life and times / Bruce Crowther. — New York : Universe, 1987. — III, 652
Crowther, Bruce. The big band years / Bruce Crowther and Mike Pinfold; Franklin S. Driggs, picture editor. — New York : Facts on File, 1988. — III, 1135
Crowther, Bruce. The jazz singers : from ragtime to the new wave / Bruce Crowther and Mike Pinfold. — Poole, Dorset, England; New York : Blandford, 1986. — III, 438
Crumbaker, Marge. Up and down with Elvis Presley / Marge Crumbaker and Gabe Tucker. — New York : Putnam, 1981. — II, A-826.

Crump, George D. Write it down : a history of country music in Hampton Roads / George D. Crump. — Norfolk, Va. : Donning, 1985. — II, A-236.

Cugat, Xavier. Rumba is my life / Xavier Cugat. — New York : Didier, 1948. — II, 1075.

Culbertson, Evelyn Davis. He heard America singing : Arthur Farwell, composer and crusading music educator / Evelyn Davis Culbertson. — Metuchen, N.J. : Scarecrow, 1992. — III, 472

Cummings, Tony. The sound of Philadelphia / Tony Cummings. — London : Methuen, 1975. — II, 566.

Cummins, Marjorie W. The Tache-Yokuts : Indians of the San Joaquin Valley / Marjorie W. Cummins. — Fresno, Calif. : Pioneer Publishing, 1979. — II, 259.

Cummins, Paul F. Dachau song / Paul F. Cummins. — New York : P. Lang, 1992. — III, 965

Cumnock, Frances. Catalog of the Salem congregation music / Frances Cumnock. — Chapel Hill : University of North Carolina Press, 1980. — II, 43.

Cunard, Nancy. Negro anthology / ed. Nancy Cunard. — New York : Ungar, 1970. — I, 674.

Cuney-Hare, Maud. Negro musicians and their music / Maud Cuney-Hare. — Washington : Associated Publishers, 1936. — I, 682.

Cunningham, Lyn Driggs. Sweet, hot and blue : St. Louis' musical heritage / Lyn Driggs Cunningham and Jimmy Jones. — Jefferson, N.C. : McFarland, 1989. — III, 417

Curtis, Edward S. The North American Indian : being a series of volumes picturing and describing the Indians of the United States, the Dominion of Canada and Alaska / Edward S. Curtis. — Cambridge, Mass. : Harvard University Press, 1907–1930. — I, 390.

Curtis, George William. Early letters to John S. Dwight / George William Curtis. — New York : Harper, 1898. — II, 142.

Curtis, Jim. Rock eras : interpretations of music and society, 1954–1984 / Jim Curtis. — Bowling Green, Ohio : Bowling Green State University Popular Press, 1987. — III, 1172.

Curtis, Natalie. The Hampton series of negro folk songs / Natalie Curtis. — New York : Schirmer, 1918–1919. — I, A-175.

Curtis, Natalie. The Indians' book : an offering by the American Indians of Indian lore, musical and narrative / Natalie Curtis. — New York : Harper, 1923. — I, 391.

Cuscuna, Michael. The Blue Note label / Michael Cuscuna and Michel Ruppli. — New York : Greenwood, 1988. — III, 199.

Cusic, Don. Randy Travis : king of the new country traditionalists / Don Cusic. — New York : St. Martin's, 1990. — III, 876.

Cusic, Don. Reba : country music's queen / Don Cusic. — New York : St. Martin's, 1991. — III, 781.

Cusic, Don. Sandi Patti : the voice of gospel / Don Cusic. — New York : Doubleday, 1988. — III, 811.

Cusic, Don. The sound of light : a history of gospel music / Don Cusic. — Bowling Green, Ohio : Bowling Green State University Popular Press, 1990. — III, 1039.

Cuthbert, John A. West Virginia folk music / John A. Cuthbert. — Morgantown : West Virgina University Press, 1982. — II, A-203.

Cyporyn, Dennis. The bluegrass songbook / Dennis Cyporyn. — New York : Macmillan, 1972. — I, A-127.

D'Alessio, Gregory. Old troubadour : Carl Sandburg with his guitar friends / Gregory D'Alessio. — New York : Walker, 1987. — III, 854.

Dachs, David. Anything goes : the world of popular music / David Dachs. — Indianapolis : Bobbs-Merrill, 1964. — II, 825.

Dachs, David. Encyclopedia of pop/rock / David Dachs. — New York : Scholastic Book Service, 1972. — II, 1247.

Dachs, David. John Denver / David Dachs. — New York : Pyramid, 1976. — II, 1192; II, 1208.

Dahl, David. Young Judy / David Dahl and Barry Kehoe. — New York : Mason Charter, 1975. — II, 997.

Dahl, Linda. Stormy weather : the music and lives of a century of jazz women / Linda Dahl. — New York : Pantheon, 1984. — II, A-452.

Daigle, Pierre V. Tears, love and laughter : the story of the Acadians / Pierre V. Daigle. — Church Point, La. : Acadian Publishing, 1972. — I, 647.

Dale, Rodney. The world of jazz / Rodney Dale. — Oxford : Phaidon, 1980. — II, 681.

Dallas, Karl. Singers of an empty day / Karl Dallas. — London : Kahn & Averill, 1971. — II, 1170.

Dalton, David. Janis / David Dalton. — New York : Simon & Schuster, 1971. — II, 1211.

Dalton, David. "Mr. Mojo risin" : Jim Morrison, the last holy fool / David Dalton. — New York : St. Martin's, 1991. — III, 791a.

Dalton, David. Piece of my heart : the life, times and legend of Janis Joplin / David Dalton. — New York : St. Martin's, 1986. — III, 754.

Dalton, David. Rock 100 / David Dalton and Lenny Kaye. — New York : Grosset & Dunlap, 1977. — II, 1096.

Daly, John Jay. A song in his heart / John Jay Daly. — Philadelphia : Winston, 1951. — I, 1236.

Damon, S. Foster. Series of old American songs / S. Foster Damon. — Providence, R.I. : Brown University Library, 1936. — I, A-236.

Damrosch, Walter. My musical life / Walter Damrosch. — New York : Scribner, 1930. — I, 363.

Damsker, Matt. Rock voices : the best lyrics of an era / ed. Matt Damsker. — New York : St. Martin's, 1980. — II, 1138.

Danca, Vince. Bunny : a bio-discography of jazz trumpeter Bunny Berigan / Vince Danca. — Rockford, Ill. : Author, 1978. — II, 643.

Dance, Helen Oakley. Stormy Monday : the T-Bone Walker story / Helen Oakley Dance; foreword by B. B. King. — Baton Rouge : Louisiana State University Press, 1987. — III, 594.

Dance, Stanley. Duke Ellington / Stanley Dance. — Alexandria, Va. : Time-Life Records, 1978. — III, 468.

Dance, Stanley. Earl Hines / Stanley Dance. — Alexandria, Va. : Time-Life Records, 1980. — III, 544.

Dance, Stanley. Jazz era : the forties / Stanley Dance [et al]. — London : MacGibbon & Kee, 1961. — I, 902.

Dance, Stanley. Johnny Hodges / Stanley Dance; notes on the music by Gary Giddens. — Alexandria, Va. : Time-Life Records, 1981. — III, 646.

Dance, Stanley. The world of Count Basie / Stanley Dance. — New York : Scribner's, 1980. — II, 736.

Dance, Stanley. The world of Duke Ellington / Stanley Dance. — New York : Scribner's, 1970. — I, 1106.

Dance, Stanley. The world of Earl Hines / Stanley Dance. — New York : Scribner's, 1977. — II, 753.

Dance, Stanley. The world of swing / Stanley Dance. — New York : Scribner's, 1974. — I, 1040.

Dandridge, Dorothy. Everything and nothing : the Dorothy Dandridge tragedy / Dorothy Dandridge and Earl Conrad. — New York : Abelard-Schuman, 1970. — II, 975.

Daniel, Oliver. Stokowski : a counterpoint of view / Oliver Daniel. — New York : Dodd, Mead, 1982. — II, A-146.

Daniel, Wayne W. Pickin' on Peachtree : a history of country music in Atlanta, Georgia / Wayne W. Daniel. — Urbana : University of Illinois Press, 1990. — III, 1159.

Daniels, William F. The American 45 and 78 rpm record dating guide / William F. Daniels. — Westport, Conn. : Greenwood, 1983. — II, A-515.

Danker, Frederick E. The repertory and style of a country singer : Johnny Cash / Frederick E. Danker. — Los Angeles : John Edwards Memorial Foundation, 1973. — I, 636.

Dankworth, Avril. Jazz : an introduction to its musical basis / Avril Dankworth. — London : Oxford University Press, 1968. — I, 963.

Dannen, Fredric. Hit men : power brokers and fat money inside the music business / Fredric Dannen. — New York : Times Books, 1990. — III, 1238.

Danzi, Michael. American musician in Germany, 1924–1939; memoirs of the jazz, entertainment, and movie world in Berlin during the Weimar republic and the Nazi era—and in the United States / Michael Danzi; as told to Rainer E. Lotz. — Schmitten, Germany : Norbert Ruecker; distributed by Legacy Books, Hatboro, Pa., 1986. — III, 578.

DaPonte, Lorenzo. Memoirs / Lorenzo DaPonte [various editors, publishers, dates]. — I, 147.

Darby, William. American film music : major composers, techniques, trends, 1915–1990 / William Darby and Jack DuBois. — Jefferson, N.C. : McFarland, 1990. — III, 1025.

Darensbourg, Joe. Telling it like it is / Joe Darensbourg; ed. Peter Vacher; supplementary material compiled by Peter Vacher. — Basingstoke, England : Macmillan, 1987. — III, 624.

Darling, Charles W. The new American songster / Charles W. Darling. — Lanham, Md. : University Press of America, 1983. — II, A-176.

Darlington, Marwood. Irish Orpheus : the life of Patrick S. Gilmore, bandmaster extraordinary / Marwood Darlington. — Philadelphia : Olivier-Nancy-Klein, 1950. — I, 1195.

DaSilva, Fabio. The sociology of music / Fabio DaSilva. — Notre Dame, Ind. : Notre Dame University Press, 1984. — II, A-520.

DaSilva, Owen. Mission music of California / Owen DaSilva. — Los Angeles : Lewis, 1941. — I, A-102.

Dauer, Alfons. Blues aus 100 Jahren /Alfons Michael Dauer. — Frankfurt : Fischer, 1983. — II, A-328.

Dauer, Alfons. Jazz, die magische Musik / Alfons Dauer. — Bremen : Schünemann, 1961. — I, A-198.

Dauer, Alfons. Tradition afrikansicher Blasorchester und Entstehung des Jazz / Alfons Michael Dauer. — Graz, Austria : Akademisce Druck- und Verlagsanstalt, 1985. — II, A-435.

David, Andrew. Country music stars : people at the top of the charts / Andrew David. — New York : Domas Books, 1980. — II, 385.

David, Hans T. Musical life in the Pennsylvania settlements of the Unitas Fratrum / Hans T. David. — Winston-Salem, N.C. : Moravian Music Foundation, 1959. — I, 78.

Davies, Hugh. International electronic music catalog / Hugh Davies. — New York : Independent Electronic Music Center, 1968. — I, 280.

Davies, John R. T. Morton's music / John R. T. Davies and Laurie Wright. — London : Storyville, 1968. — I, 941.

Davies, John R. T. Music of Thomas "Fats" Waller with complete discography / John R. T. Davies. — Rev. ed. — London : Friends of Fats, 1953. — I, 942.

Davies, Samuel. Letters from the Rev. Samuel Davies &c. shewing the state of religion in Virginia, particularly among the negroes / Samuel Davies. — London : R. Pardon, 1757. — I, A-163.

Davis, Arthur Kyle. Folk-songs of Virginia / Arthur Kyle Davis. — Durham, N.C. : Duke University Press, 1949. — I, 503.

Davis, Arthur Kyle. Traditional ballads of Virginia / Arthur Kyle Davis. — Cambridge, Mass. : Harvard University Press, 1929. — I, 504.

Davis, Brian. John Coltrane discography / Brian Davis. — Hockley, Essex, England : Author, 1977. — II, 645.

Davis, Charlie. That band from Indiana / Charlie Davis. — Oswego, N.Y. : Mathom, 1983. — II, A-468.

Davis, Clive. Clive : inside the record business / Clive Davis; with James Willwerth. — New York : Morrow, 1975. — II, 1155.

Davis, Elizabeth A. Index to the New World Recorded Anthology of American Music : a user's guide to the initial one hundred records / Elizabeth A. Davis. — New York : Norton, 1981. — II, A-1.

Davis, Francis. In the moment : jazz in the 1980s / Francis Davis. — New York : Oxford, 1986. — III, 1112.

Davis, Francis. Outcats : jazz composers, instrumentalists, and singers / Francis Davis. — New York : Oxford, 1990. — III, 401.

Davis, Gary. Rev. Gary Davis : the holy blues / Gary Davis; ed. Stefan Grossman. — New York : Robbins, 1970. — I, 837.

Davis, Gerald L. I got the word in me and I can sing it, you know / Gerald L. Davis. — Philadelphia : University of Pennsylvania Press, 1985. — II, A-359.

Davis, Jerome. Talking Heads / Jerome Davis. — New York : Vintage, 1986. — III, 939.

Davis, John P. American negro reference book / John P. Davis. — Englewood Cliffs, N.J. : Prentice-Hall, 1966. — I, 675.

Davis, Lenwood G. A Paul Robeson research guide / Lenwood G. Davis. — Westport, Conn. : Greenwood, 1982. — II, A-306.

Davis, Lorrie. Letting down my hair : two years with the love rock tribe / Lorrie Davis. — New York : Arthur Fields, 1973. — II, 1266.

Davis, Miles. Miles : the autobiography / Miles Davis; with Quincy Troupe. — New York : Simon & Schuster, 1989. — III, 635.

Davis, Nathan. WRitings in jazz / Nathan Davis. — Dubuque, Iowa : Gorsuch Scarisbrick, 1978. — II, 694.

Davis, Paul. New life in country music / Paul Davis. — Worthing, Sussex, England : Henry Walter, 1976. — II, 386.

Davis, Ronald L. A history of music in American life / Ronald L. Davis. — Malabar, Fla. : Robert Krieger, 1980–1982. — II, 10.

Davis, Ronald L. History of opera in the American West / Ronald L. Davis. — Englewood Cliffs, N.J. : Prentice-Hall, 1965. — I, 159.

Davis, Ronald L. Opera in Chicago / Ronald L. Davis. — New York : Appleton-Century, 1966. — II, 77.

Davis, Sammy. Yes I can : the story of Sammy Davis, Jr. / Sammy Davis. — London : Cassell, 1965. — I, 1328.

Davis, Sharon. I heard it through the grapevine : Marvin Gaye : a biography / Sharon Davis. — Edinburgh, Scotland : Mainstream, 1991. — III, 725.

Davis, Sharon. Motown : the history / Sharon Davis. — Enfield, England : Guinness, 1988. — III, 1239.

Davis, Sheila. The craft of lyric writing / Sheila Davis. — Cincinnati : Writer's Digest, 1985. — II, A-549.

Davison, Archibald T. Protestant church music in America / Archibald T. Davison. — Boston : Schirmer, 1933. — I, 56.

Davisson, Ananias. Kentucky harmony / Ananias Davisson. — 4th ed. — Harrisburg, Va. : Author, 1821. — I, 525.

Day, Aidan. Jokerman : reading the lyrics of Bob Dylan / Aidan Day. — Oxford, England : Blackwell, 1988. — III, 1301.

Day, Charles H. Fun in black / Charles H. Day. — New York : DeWitt, 1874. — I, A-250.

Day, Doris. Doris Day : her own story / Doris Day; with A. E. Hotchner. — New York : Morrow, 1976. — II, 993.

Deakins, Betty. Bluegrass directory : 1985–86 / Betty Deakins. — Murphys, ·Calif. : BD Products, 1986. — III, 1145.

Dean, Roger T. New structures in jazz and improvised music since 1960 / Roger T. Dean. — Philadelphia : Open University, 1991. — III, 1079.

Dean, Talmage W. A survey of twentieth century Protestant church music in America / Talmage W. Dean. — Nashville : Broadman, 1988. — III, 1032.

DeAngulo, Jaime. The music of the Indians of Northern California / Jaime DeAngulo; ed. Peter Garland. — Santa Fe, N.M. : Soundings, 1988. — III, 1230.

Deans, Mickey. Weep no more, my lady / Mickey Deans and Ann Pinchot. — New York : Hawthorne, 1972. — I, 1319.

Dearing, James W. Making money making music (no matter where you live) /

James W. Dearing. — 2nd ed. — Cincinnati, Ohio : Writer's Digest Books, 1990. — III, 1256.

Dearling, Robert. The Guinness book of recorded sound / Robert Dearling and Celia Dearling; with Brian Rust. — Enfield, Middlesex, England : Guinness Books, 1984. — II, A-69.

DeBarbin, Lucy. Are you lonesome tonight? : the untold story of Elvis Presley's one true love and the child he never knew / Lucy DeBarbin and Dary Matera. — New York : Villard, 1987. — III, 820.

Deboer, Kee. Daniel Pinkham : a bio-bibliography / Kee Deboer and John B. Ahouse. — New York : Greenwood, 1988. — III, 176.

DeCraen, Hugo. Marion Brown : discography / Hugo DeCraen and Eddy Janssens. — Brussels : New Think, 1985. — III, 290.

DeCurtis, Anthony. Present tense : rock & roll and culture / Anthony DeCurtis. — Durham, N.C. : Duke University Press, 1992. — III, 1188.

Deffaa, Chip. Swing legacy / Chip Deffaa; foreword by George T. Simon. — Metuchen, N.J. : Scarecrow Press and the Institute of Jazz Studies, Rutgers University, 1989. — III, 1080.

Deffaa, Chip. Voices of the jazz age : profiles of eight vintage jazzmen / Chip Deffaa. — Urbana : University of Illinois Press, 1990. — III, 427.

DeKoven, Mrs. Reginald. A musician and his wife / Mrs. Reginald DeKoven. — New York : Harper, 1926. — I, 1273.

Delamater, Jerome. Dance in the Hollywood musical / Jerome Delamater. — Ann Arbor, Mich. : UMI Research Press, 1981. — II, A-585.

Delaplaine, Edward S. John Philip Sousa and the national anthem / Edward S. Delaplaine. — Frederick, Md. : Great Southern Press, 1983. — II, A-553.

Delaunay, Charles. Hot discographie, 1943 / Charles Delaunay. — Paris : Collection du Hot Club de France, 1944. — I, 924.

Delaunay, Charles. Hot discographie encyclopédique / Charles Delaunay and Kurt Mohr. — Paris : Jazz Disques, 1951–1952. — I, 924.

Delaunay, Charles. Hot discography / Charles Delaunay. — 3rd ed. — New York : Commodore Music Shop, 1940. — I, 924.

Delaunay, Charles. New hot discography / Charles Delaunay. — New York : Criterion Music, 1948. — I, 924.

Delbanco, Nicholas. The Beaux Arts Trio / Nicholas Delbanco. — London : Gollancz, 1985. — III, 900.

DeLerma, Dominique-René. Bibliography of black music / Dominique-René DeLerma. — Westport, Conn. : Greenwood, 1981–1984. — II, A-287.

DeLerma, Dominique-René. Black concert and recital music : a provisional repertoire list / Dominique-René DeLerma. — Bloomington, Ind. : Afro-American Music Opportunities Association, 1975. — II, 506.

DeLerma, Domimique-René. Black music and musicians in *The New Grove Dictionary of American Music* and *The New Harvard Dictionary of Music* / Dominique-René DeLerma and Marsha J. Reisser. — Chicago : Center for Black Music Research, Columbia College, 1989. — III, 112a.

DeLerma, Dominique-René. Black music in our culture / Dominique-René DeLerma. — Kent, Ohio : Kent State University Press, 1970. — I, 663.

DeLerma, Dominique-René. Charles Edward Ives, 1874–1954 : a bibliography of his music / Dominique-René DeLerma. — Kent, Ohio : Kent State University Press, 1970. — I, 328.

DeLerma, Dominique-René. Concert music and spirituals : a selective bibliography / Dominique-René DeLerma. — Nashville : Institute for Research in Black American Music, Fisk University, 1981. — II, A-299.

DeLerma, Dominique-René. Discography of concert music by black composers / Dominique-René DeLerma. — Minneapolis : AAMOA Press, 1973. — I, 684.

DeLerma, Dominique-René. Reflections on Afro-American music / ed. Dominique-René DeLerma. — Kent, Ohio : Kent State University Press, 1973. — I, 685.

DeLerma, Dominique-René. The black American musical heritage : a preliminary bibliography / Dominique-René DeLerma. — Kent, Ohio : School of Library Science, Kent State University, 1969. — I, A-147.

DeLio, Thomas. Circumscribing the open universe / Thomas DeLio. — Lanham, Md. : University Press of America, 1984. — II, A-89.

DeLio, Thomas. Continuous lines : issues and ideas in music of the 60s and 70s / Thomas DeLio. — Lanham, Md. : University Press of America, 1985. — II, A-100.

Dellar, Fred. NME Guide to rock cinema / Fred Dellar. — London : Hamlyn, 1981. — II, A-653.

Dellar, Fred. The illustrated encyclopedia of country music / Fred Dellar and Roy Thompson. — New York : Harmony, 1977. — II, 358.

Dellar, Fred. The Omnibus rock discography / Fred Dellar and Barry Lazell. — London : Omnibus, 1982. — II, A-671.

Delmore, Alton. Truth is stranger than publicity / Alton Delmore. — Nashville : Country Music Foundation Press, 1977. — II, 399.

DeLong, Thomas A. Pops : Paul Whiteman, king of jazz / Thomas A. DeLong. — Piscataway, N.J. : New Century, 1983. — II, A-502.

DeLong, Thomas A. The mighty music box : the golden age of musical radio / Thomas A. DeLong. — Los Angeles : Amber Crest Books, 1980. — II, 827.

Demeusy, Bertrand. Hot Lips Page / Bertrand Demeusy [et al]. — Basel : Jazz Publications, 1961. — I, 943.

DeMicheal, Don. Red Norvo / Don DeMicheal. — Alexandria, Va. : Time-Life Records, 1980. — III, 656.

DeMille, Agnes. And promenade home / Agnes DeMille. — Boston : Little, Brown, 1956. — II, 920.

Demorest, Steve. Alice Cooper / Steve Demorest. — New York : Popular Library, 1974. — II, 1287.

Denisoff, R. Serge. American protest songs of war and peace : a selected bibliography and discography / R. Serge Denisoff. — Los Angeles : California State College, Center for the Study of Armament and Disarmament, 1970. — I, 580.

Denisoff, R. Serge. Great day coming : folk music and the American left / R. Serge Denisoff. — Urbana : University of Illinois Press, 1971. — I, 581.

Denisoff, R. Serge. Risky business : rock in film / R. Serge Denisoff and William D. Romanowski. — New Brunswick, N.J. : Transaction, 1991. — III, 1280.

Denisoff, R. Serge. Sing a song of social significance / R. Serge Denisoff. — 2nd ed. — Bowling Green, Ohio : Bowling Green State University Popular Press, 1983. — III, 1055.

Denisoff, R. Serge. Sing a song of social significance / R. Serge Denisoff. — Bowling Green, Ohio : Bowling Green State University Popular Press, 1972. — I, 582.

Denisoff, R. Serge. Solid gold : the popular record industry / R. Serge Denisoff. — New Brunswick, N.J. : Transaction Books, 1975. — II, 1156.

Denisoff, R. Serge. Songs of protest, war and peace : a bibliography and discography / R. Serge Denisoff. — Santa Barbara, Calif. : ABC-Clio, 1973. — I, 580.

Denisoff, R. Serge. Sounds of social change : studies in popular culture / R. Serge Denisoff and Richard A. Peterson. — Chicago : Rand McNally, 1972. — I, 583.

Denisoff, R. Serge. Tarnished gold : the record industry revisited / R. Serge Denisoff. — New Brunswick, N.J. : Transaction Books, 1985. — II, A-739.

Denisoff, R. Serge. Waylon : a biography / R. Serge Denisoff; discography by John L. Smith. — Knoxville : University of Tennessee Press, 1983. — III, 749.

Dennison, Sam. Scandalize my name : black imagery in American popular song / Sam Dennison. — New York : Garland, 1982. — II, A-539.

Dennison, Tim. The American negro and his amazing music / Tim Dennison. — New York : Vantage, 1963. — II, 498.

Denselow, Robin. When the music's over : the story of political pop / Robin Denselow. — London : Faber & Faber, 1989. — III, 1046.

Densmore, Frances. Cheyenne and Arapaho music / Frances Densmore. — Los Angeles : Southwest Museum, 1936. — I, A-89.

Densmore, Frances. Chippewa music / Frances Densmore. — Washington : Government Printing Office, 1910–1913. — I, 403.

Densmore, Frances. Choctaw music / Frances Densmore. — Washington : Government Printing Office, 1943. — I, 403.

Densmore, Frances. Mandan and Hidatsa music / Frances Densmore. — Washington : Government Printing Office, 1923. — I, 403.

Densmore, Frances. Menominee music / Frances Densmore. — Washington : Government Printing Office, 1932. — I, 403.

Densmore, Frances. Music of Santo Domingo Pueblo, New Mexico / Frances Densmore. — Los Angeles : Southwest Museum, 1938. — I, A-90.

Densmore, Frances. Music of the Acoma, Isleta, Cochiti, and Zuni pueblos / Frances Densmore. — Washington : Government Printing Office, 1957. — I, 403.

Densmore, Frances. Music of the Indians of British Columbia / Frances Densmore. — Washington : Government Printing Office, 1943. — I, A-91.

Densmore, Frances. Music of the Maidu Indians of California / Frances Densmore. — Los Angeles : Southwest Museum, 1958. — II, 247.

Densmore, Frances. Nootka and Quileute music / Frances Densmore. — Washington, : Government Printing Office, 1939. — I, 403.

Densmore, Frances. Northern Ute music / Frances Densmore. — Washington : Government Printing Office, 1922. — I, 403.

Densmore, Frances. Papago music / Frances Densmore. — Washington : Government Printing Office, 1929. — I, 403.

Densmore, Frances. Pawnee music / Frances Densmore. — Washington : Government Printing Office, 1929. — I, 403.

Densmore, Frances. Seminole music / Frances Densmore. — Washington : Government Printing Office, 1956. — I, 403.

Densmore, Frances. Teton Sioux music / Frances Densmore. — Washington : Government Printing Office, 1918. — I, 403.

Densmore, Frances. The American Indians and their music / Frances Densmore. — New York : Woman's Press, 1926. — I, 392.

Densmore, Frances. The study of Indian music / Frances Densmore. — Seattle : Shorey Book Store, 1966. — I, 393.

Densmore, Frances. Yuman and Yaqui music / Frances Densmore. — Washington : Government Printing Office, 1932. — I, 403.

Densmore, John. Riders on the storm : my life with Jim Morrison and the Doors / John Densmore. — New York : Dell, 1991. — III, 904.

Dent, Roberta Yancy. Paul Robeson : tributes and selected writings / ed. Roberta Yancy Dent. — New York : Paul Robeson Archives, 1976. — II, 512.

DeSantis, Florence Stevenson. Gershwin / Florence Stevenson DeSantis. — New York : Treves, 1987. — III, 475.

DesBarres, Pamela. I'm with the band : confessions of a groupie / Pamela DesBarres. — New York : Morrow, 1987. — III, 976.

DesBarres, Pamela. Take another little piece of my heart : a groupie grows up / Pamela DesBarres. — New York : Morrow, 1992. — III, 975.

DesCordobes, Dominique. Ratt / Dominique DesCordobes. — New York : Ballantine, 1986. — III, 935.

Despard, Mabel H. The music of the United States / Mabel H. Despard. — New York : Muirhead, 1936. — I, A-4.

Dethlefson, Ronald. Edison blue amberol recordings, 1912–1914 / Ronald Dethlefson. — Brooklyn : APM Press, 1980. — II, 1024.

Detroit Public Library. Catalog of the E. Azalia Hackley Memorial Collection of Negro Music, Dance, and Drama. — Boston : G. K. Hall, 1979. — II, 496.

Dett, R. Nathaniel. Religious folk-songs of the negro, as sung at Hampton Institute / Nathaniel R. Dett. — Hampton, Va. : Hampton Institute Press, 1927. — I, 773.

DeTurk, David A. The American folk scene : dimensions of the folksong revival / David A. DeTurk and A. Poulin. — New York : Dell, 1967. — I, 603.

DeVeaux, Alexis. Don't explain : a song of Billie Holiday / Alexis DeVeaux. — [n.p.] : Writers and Readers Publishing, 1988. — III, 730.

DeVeaux, Scott Knowles. The music of James Scott / Scott Knowles DeVeaux. — Washington : Smithsonian Institution Press, 1992. — III, 18.

DeVenney, David P. American masses and requiems : a descriptive guide / David P. DeVenney. — Berkeley, Calif. : Fallen Leaf, 1991. — III, 121.

DeVenney, David P. Early American choral music : an annotated guide / David P. DeVenney. — Berkeley, Calif. : Fallen Leaf, 1988. — III, 155.

DeVenney, David P. Nineteenth-century American choral music : an annotated guide / David P. DeVenney. — Berkeley, Calif. : Fallen Leaf, 1987. — III, 122.

Dew, Joan. Singers & sweethearts : the women of country music / Joan Dew. — Garden City, N.Y. : Doubleday, 1977. — II, 387.

Dexter, Dave. Jazz cavalcade : the inside story of jazz / Dave Dexter. — New York : Criterion, 1946. — I, A-191.

Dexter, Dave. Playback / Dave Dexter. — New York : Billboard Publications, 1976. — II, 668.

Diamond, Stanley. Theory and practice / Stanley Diamond. — The Hague : Mouton, 1980. — II, 260.

Dichter, Harry. Early American sheet music / Harry Dichter and Elliott Shapiro. — New York : Bowker, 1941. — I, 1150.

Dickens, H. The films of Ginger Rogers / H. Dickens. — Secaucus, N.J. : Citadel, 1975. — II, 1084.

Dickerson, P. J. Collectable 45s of the swinging sixties / P. J. Dickerson and M. A. Gordon. — London : Vintage Centre, 1984–1985. — II, A-685.

Dickey, Dan William. The Kennedy corridos : a study of the ballads of an American hero / Dan William Dickey. — Austin : Center for Mexican American Studies, University of Texas, 1978. — II, 292.

Dickson, Harry Ellis. Arthur Fiedler and the Boston Pops : an irreverent memoir / Harry Ellis Dickson. — Boston : Houghton Mifflin, 1981. — II, A-34.

Dickson, Harry Ellis. Gentlemen, more dolce please! : an irreverent memoir of thirty years in the Boston Symphony Orchestra / Harry Ellis Dickson. — Boston : Beacon, 1969. — II, 48.

Dickstein, Morris. Gates of Eden : American culture in the sixties / Morris Dickstein. — New York : Basic Books, 1977. — II, 1195.

Didimus, Henry. Biography of Louis Moreau Gottschalk / Henry Didimus. — Philadelphia : Deacon & Peterson, 1853. — I, A-70.

Dietz, Betty Warner. Musical instruments of Africa / Betty Warner Dietz and Michael Babatunde Olatunji. — New York : Day, 1965. — I, A-159.

Dietz, Howard. Dancing in the dark / Howard Dietz. — New York : Quadrangle, 1974. — II, 947.

DiMedio, Annette Maria. Frances McCollin : her life and music / Annette Maria DiMedio; foreword by Sam Dennison. — Metuchen, N.J. : Scarecrow, 1990. — III, 500.

DiMeglio, John E. Vaudeville U.S.A. / John DiMeglio. — Bowling Green, Ohio : Bowling Green State University Popular Press, 1973. — II, 889.

DiMucci, Dion. The wanderer : Dion's story / Dion DiMucci; with Davin Seay. — New York : Beech Tree Books, 1988. — III, 710.

DiOrio, Al. Borrowed time : the 37 years of Bobby Darin / Al DiOrio. — Philadelphia : Running Press, 1981. — II, A-776.

DiOrio, Al. Little girl lost / Al DiOrio. — New York : Arlington House, 1973. — II, 998.

Directory of music collections in the midwestern United States / comp. Publications Committee, Music Library Association, Midwest Chapter. — Oberlin, Ohio : The Chapter, 1990. — III, 93.

Directory of music faculties in colleges and universities, U.S. and Canada / comp. and ed. Craig R. Short. — 13th ed. — Missoula, Mont. : CMS Publications, 1990. — III, 27.

Directory of music libraries and collections in New England, 1985 / comp. Publications Committee, Music Library Association, New England Chapter. — 7th ed. — Hanover, N.H. : The Chapter, 1985. — III, 94.

Directory of music research libraries / Rita Benton, general editor. — V.1., 2nd ed. — Canada / Marian Kahn and Helmut Kallmann; United States / Charles Lindahl. — Kassel, Germany : Bärenreiter, 1983. — III, 92.

Dister, Alain. Frank Zappa et les Mothers of Invention / Alain Dister and Urban Gwerder. — Paris : Albin Michel, 1975. — II, 1246.

Diton, Carl. Thirty-six South Carolina spirituals / ed. Carl Diton. — New York : Schirmer, 1930. — II, 601.

Dixon, Christa. Wesen und Wandel geistlicher Volkslieder : negro spirituals / Christa Dixon. — Wuppertal, Germany : Jugenddienst Verlag, 1967. — I, 787.

Dixon, Joan DeVee. George Rochberg : a bibliographic guide to his life and works / Joan DeVee Dixon. — Stuyvesant, N.Y. : Pendragon, 1992. — III, 178.

Dixon, Robert M. W. Blues and gospel records, 1902–1942 / R. M. W. Dixon and John Godrich. — Kenton, England : Steve Lane, 1964. — I, 806.

Dixon, Robert M. W. Blues and gospel records, 1902–1943 / Robert M. W. Dixon and John Godrich. — 3rd ed. — London : Storyville, 1982. — III, 220.

Dixon, Robert M. W. Recording the blues / Robert M. W. Dixon and John Godrich. — London : Studio Vista, 1970. — I, 813.

Djedje, Jacqueline Cogdell. American black spiritual and gospel songs from southeast Georgia / Jacqueline Cogdell Djedje. — Los Angeles : Center for Afro-American Studies, University of California, 1978. — II, 529.

Dobrin, Arnold. Aaron Copland : his life and times / Arnold Dobrin. — New York : Crowell, 1967. — I, 317.

Dobrin, Arnold. Voices of joy, voices of freedom / Arnold Dobrin. — New York : Coward, McCann & Geoghegan, 1972. — I, A-152.

Docks, L. R. 1915–1965 American premium record guide / L. R. Docks. — Florence, Ala. : Books Americana, 1980. — II, 810.

Doctor, Gary L. The Sinatra scrapbook / Gary L. Doctor. — New York : Citadel, 1991. — III, 859.

Dodds, Warren. The Baby Dodds story / Warren Dodds; as told to Larry Gara. — Los Angeles : Contemporary Press, 1959. — I, 1102.

Dodge, Charles. Computer music : synthesis, composition, and performance / Charles Dodge and Thomas A. Jerse. — New York : Schirmer, 1985. — II, A-92.

Dodge, Consuelo. The Everly brothers : ladies love outlaws / Consuelo Dodge. — Starke, Fla. : CIN-DAV, 1991. — III, 906.

Doe, Andrew. The Doors in the their own words / Andrew Doe and John Tobler. — London : Omnibus, 1988. — III, 905.

Doerflinger, William Main. Shantymen and shantyboys : songs of the sailor and lumberman / William Main Doerflinger. — New York : Macmillan, 1951. — I, 574.

Dolph, Edward Arthur. "Sound off!" : soldier songs from the Revolution to World War II / Edward Arthur Dolph. — New York : Farrar & Rinehart, 1942. — I, A-237.

Dolph, Edward Arthur. "Sound off!" : soldier songs from Yankee Doodle to Parley Voo / Edward Arthur Dolph. — New York : Cosmopolitan Book Corp., 1929. — I, A-237.

Donnan, Elizabeth. Documents illustrative of the slave trade to America / Elizabeth Donnan. — Washington : Carnegie Institution, 1930–1935. — I, 714.

Doran, James M. Erroll Garner : the most happy piano / James M. Doran. — Metuchen, N.J. : Scarecrow, 1985. — II, A-478.

Dorman, James E. Recorded Dylan : a critical review and discography / James E. Dorman. — Pinedale, Calif. : Soma Press, 1982. — II, A-784.

Dorough, Prince. Popular music culture in America / Prince Dorough. — New York : Ardsley House, 1992. — III, 1056.

Dorson, Richard M. American folklore / Richard M. Dorson. — Chicago : University of Chicago Press, 1959. — I, 440.

Dorson, Richard M. Buying the wind : regional folklore in the United States / Richard M. Dorson. — Chicago : University of Chicago Press, 1964. — I, 453.

Douglas-Home, Robin. Sinatra / Robin Douglas-Home. — London : Joseph, 1962. — I, A-274.

Douglass, Frederick. Life and times of Frederick Douglass, written by himself / Frederick Douglass. — Rev. ed. — Boston : DeWolfe, Fiske, 1892. — I, 735.

Dowdey, Landon Gerald. Journey to freedom : a casebook with music / Landon Gerald Dowdey. — Chicago : Swallow, 1969. — I, 584.

Dower, Catherine. Puerto Rican music following the Spanish-American War / Catherine Dower. — Lanham, Md. : University Press of America, 1983. — III, 399.

Dowley, Tim. Bob Dylan : from a hard rain to a slow train / Tim Dowley and Barry Dunnage. — Tunbridge Wells, England : Midas Books, 1983. — II, A-785.

Downes, Olin. Olin Downes on music / Olin Downes. — New York : Simon & Schuster, 1957. — I, 106.

Downes, Olin. Treasury of American song / Olin Downes and Elie Siegmeister. — 2nd ed. — New York : Knopf, 1943. — I, 454.

Downey, Pat. The golden age of top 40 music (1955–1973) on compact disc / Pat Downey. — Boulder, Colo. : P. Downey Enterprises, 1992. — III, 257.

Downing, David. Future rock / David Downing. — St. Albans, England : Panther, 1976. — II, 1133.

Dox, Thurston J. American oratorios and cantatas : a catalog of works written in the United States from colonial times to 1985 / Thurston J. Dox. — Metuchen, N.J. : Scarecrow, 1986. — III, 96.

Doyle, David Noel. American and Ireland, 1776–1976 : the American identity and the Irish question / David Noel Doyle and Owen Dudley Edwards. — Westport, Conn. : Greenwood, 1980. — II, 445.

Doyle, John G. Louis Moreau Gottschalk, 1829–1869 : a bibliographical study and catalog of works / John G. Doyle. — Detroit : Information Coordinators, 1983. — II, A-80.

Dragonwagon, Crescent. Stevie Wonder / Crescent Dragonwagon. — New York : Flash Books, 1977. — II, 573.

Drake, James A. Richard Tucker : a biography / James A. Drake; discography by Patricia Ann Kiser. — New York : Dutton, 1984. — III, 877.

Draper, Robert. Huey Lewis and the News / Robert Draper. — New York : Ballantine, 1986. — III, 764.

Draper, Robert. ZZ Top / Robert Draper. — New York : Ballantine, 1984. — III, 946.

Drew, David. Über Kurt Weill / David Drew. — Frankfurt : Suhrkamp, 1975. — I, 1305.

Driggs, Franklin. Black beauty, white heat : a pictorial history of classic jazz, 1920–1950 / Franklin Driggs and Harris Lewine. — New York : Morrow, 1982. — II, A-395.

Drinkrow, John. The vintage musical comedy book / John Drinkrow. — Reading, England : Osprey, 1974. — II, 898.

Driver, Harold E. Indians of North America / Harold E. Driver. — 2nd ed. — Chciago : University of Chicago Press, 1969. — I, 394.

Drone, Jeanette Marie. Index to opera, operetta and musical comedy synopses in collections and periodicals / Jeanette Marie Drone. — Metuchen, N.J. : Scarecrow, 1978. — II, 899.

Drummond, Andrew H. American opera librettos / Andrew H. Drummond. — Metuchen, N.J. : Scarecrow, 1973. — I, 52.

Drummond, Robert Rutherford. Early German music in Philadelphia / Robert Rutherford Drummond. — New York : Appleton, 1910. — I, 116.

Druxman, Michael B. The musical : from Broadway to Hollywood / Michael B. Druxman. — South Brunswick, N.J. : Barnes, 1980. — II, 928.

Dubal, David. Evenings with Horowitz : a personal portrait / David Dubal. — New York : Birch Lane, 1991. — III, 548.

Duberman, Martin Bauml. Paul Robeson / Martin Bauml Duberman. — New York : Knopf, 1988. — III, 6.

DuBois, W. E. Burghardt. Sound of black folk : essays and sketches / W. E. Burghardt DuBois. — Chicago : McClurg, 1903. — I, 788.

Duchossoir, Andre. Gibson / Andre Duchossoir. — Winona, Minn. : Leonard, 1981. — II, A-57.

Dufayet, Jean-Jacques. Stevie Wonder / Jean-Jacques Dufayet. — Paris : Plasma, 1982. — II, A-356.

Duff, Arlie. Y'all come : country music / Arlie Duff. — Austin, Tex. : Eakin Press, 1983. — II, A-234.

Dufrechou, Carole. Neil Young / Carole Dufrechou. — New York : Quick Fox, 1978. — II, 1245.

Duke University Library. The Frank C. Brown Collection of North Carolina Folklore / Duke University Library. — Durham, N.C. : Duke University Press, 1952–1964. — I, 501.

Duke, Vernon. Passport to Paris / Vernon Duke. — Boston : Little, Brown, 1955. — I, 1274.

Dunaway, David King. How can I keep from singing? : Pete Seeger / David King Dunaway. — New York : McGraw-Hill, 1981. — II, A-215.

Dunbar, Tom. From Bob Will to Ray Benson : a history of Western swing music, vol. 1 / Tom Dunbar. — Austin, Tex. : Term Publications, 1988. — III, 1205.

Duncan, Robert. Only the good die young : the rock 'n' roll book of the dead / Robert Duncan. — New York : Harmony Books, 1986. — III, 439.

Duncan, Robert. The noise : notes from a rock 'n' roll era / Robert Duncan. — New York : Ticknor & Fields, 1984. — II, A-713.

Dundes, Alan. Mother wit from the laughing barrel : readings in the interpretation of Afro-American folklore / ed. Alan Dundes. — New printing, with addendum. — New York : Garland, 1981. — II, 520.

Dundy, Elaine. Elvis and Gladys : the genesis of a king / Elaine Dundy. — New York : Macmillan, 1985. — II, A-827.

Dunham, Henry M. The life of a musician / Henry M. Dunham. — New York : Richmond Borough Publishing and Printing, 1931. — II, 146.

Dunham, Katherine. A touch of innocence / Katherine Dunham. — New York : Harcourt, Brace & World, 1959. — II, 1043.

Dunham, Katherine. Journey to Accompong / Katherine Dunham. — New York : Holt, 1946. — II, 1042.

Dunkleberger, A. C. King of country music : the life story of Roy Acuff / A. C. Dunkleberger. — Nashville : Williams, 1971. — I, 633.

Dunlap, William. A history of the American theatre / William Dunlap. — New York : Harper, 1832. — I, A-61.

Dunn, Don. The making of "No, No, Nanette" / Don Dunn. — Secaucus, N.J. : Citadel, 1972. — I, 1252.

Dunning, John. Tune in yesterday : the ultimate encyclopedia of old-time radio, 1925–1976 / John Dunning. — Englewood Cliffs, N.J. : Prentice-Hall, 1976. — II, 828.

Dunson, Josh. Anthology of American folk music / Josh Dunson and Ethel Raim. — New York : Oak, 1973. — I, A-103.

Dunson, Josh. Freedom in the air : song movements of the sixties / Josh Dunson. — New York : International Publishers, 1965. — I, 585.

Dupuis, Robert. Bunny Berigan : elusive legend of jazz / Robert Dupuis. — Baton Rouge : Louisiana State University Press, 1991. — III, 607.

Duran, Gustavo. 14 traditional Spanish songs from Texas / ed. Gustavo Duran. — Washington : Pan American Union, 1942. — II, 433.

Durant, Alan. Conditions of music / Alan Durant. — London : Macmillan, 1984. — II, A-728.

Durant, J. B. A student's guide to American jazz and popular music / J. B. Durant. — Scottsdale, Ariz. : Author, 1984. — II, A-399.

Durante, Jimmy. Night clubs / Jimmy Durante and Jack Kofoed. — New York : Knopf, 1931. — II, 1026.

Durham, Frank. DuBose Heyward : the man who wrote "Porgy" / Frank Durham. — Columbia : University of South Carolina Press, 1954. — I, 1279.

Durham, Lowell. Abravanel! / Lowell Durham. — Salt Lake City : University of Utah Press, 1989. — III, 949.

Durrett, Warren. Warren Durrett : his piano and his orchestra / Warren Durrett. — Shawnee Mission, Kans. : Author, 1987. — III, 1126.

Duxbury, Janell R. Rockin' the classics and classicizin' the rock : a selectively annotated discography / Janell R. Duxbury. — Westport, Conn. : Greenwood, 1985. — III, 278.

Dwight, Billy. Motley Crue / Billy Dwight. — New York : Ballantine, 1986. — III, 927.

Dwyer, Richard A. Songs of the gold rush / Richard A. Dwyer and Richard E. Lingenfelter. — Berkeley : University of California Press, 1964. — I, 513.

Dylan, Bob. Approximately complete works / Bob Dylan. — Amsterdam : De Bezige Bij, Thomas Rap, 1970. — I, A-286.

Dylan, Bob. Bob Dylan in his own words / Bob Dylan; compiled by Miles. — London : Omnibus, 1978. — II, 1196.

Dylan, Bob. Tarantula / Bob Dylan. — New York : Macmillan, 1971. — I, A-287.

Dylan, Bob. Writings and drawings / Bob Dylan. — New York : Knopf, 1973. — I, 1373.

Eagon, Angelo. Catalog of published concert music by American composers / Angelo Eagon. — 2nd ed. — Metuchen, N.J. : Scarecrow, 1960. — First suppl., 1971; second suppl., 1974. — I, 3.

Eaklor, Vicki Lynn. American antislavery songs : a collection and analysis / Vicki Lynn Eaklor. — Westport, Conn. : Greenwood, 1988. — III, 1208.

Eames, Wilberforce. A list of editons of the "Bay Psalm Book" / Wilberforce Eames. — New York, 1885. — I, A-65.

Easton, Carol. Straight ahead : the story of Stan Kenton / Carol Easton. — New York : Morrow, 1973. — II, 756.

Eatherly, Pat Travis. In search of my father / Pat Travis Eatherly. — Nashville : Broadman, 1987. — III, 875.

Eaton, Quaintance. Musical U.S.A. / ed. Quaintance Eaton. — New York : Allen, Towne & Heath, 1949. — I, 91.

Eaton, Quaintance. Opera caravan : adventures of the Metropolitan on tour, 1883–1956 / Quaintance Eaton. — New York : Farrar, Strauss and Cudahy, 1957. — I, 148.

Eaton, Quaintance. The miracle of the Met / Quaintance Eaton. — New York : Meredith Press, 1968. — I, A-52.

Eberly, Philip K. Music in the air : changing tastes in popular music, 1920–80 / Philip K. Eberly. — New York : Hastings House, 1982. — II, A-522.

Ebony (periodical). The negro handbook. — Chicago : Johnson, 1974. — I, 676.

Eckland, K. O. Jazz West 1945–1985 : the A-Z guide to West Coast jazz music / K.O. Eckland; photographs by Ed Lawless. — Carmel-by-the-Sea, Calif. : Cypress, 1986. — III, 71.

Eckstorm, Fannie Hardy. Minstrelsy of Maine / Fannie Hardy Eckstorm. — Boston : Houghton Mifflin, 1927. — I, A-104.

Eddy, Chuck. Stairway to hell : the 500 best heavy metal albums in the universe / Chuck Eddy. — New York : Harmony Books, 1991. — III, 279.

Eddy, Mary O. Ballads and songs from Ohio / Mary O. Eddy. — New York : Augustin, 1939. — I, 486.

Eden, Myrna G. Energy and individuality in the art of Anna Huntington, sculptor, and Amy Beach, composer / Myrna G. Eden. — Metuchen, N.J. : Scarecrow, 1987. — III, 1270.

Edison, musicians, and the phonograph / ed. and with an introduction by John Harvith and Susan Edwards Harvith. — Westport, Conn. : Greenwood, 1987. — III, 418.

Edmunds, John. Some twentieth century American composers : a selective bibliography / John Edmunds and Gordon Boelzner. — New York : New York Public Library, 1959, 1960. — I, 284.

Edwards, Allen. Flawed words and stubborn sounds : a conversation with Elliott Carter / Allen Edwards. — New York : Norton, 1971. — I, 312.

Edwards, Anne. Judy Garland : a biography / Anne Edwards. — New York : Simon & Schuster, 1975. — II, 999.

Edwards, Anne. Judy Garland : a biography / Anne Edwards. — London : Constable, 1975. — I, A-275.

Edwards, Arthur C. Music in the United States / Arthur C. Edwards and W. Thomas Marrocco. — Dubuque, Iowa : Brown, 1968. — I, 29.

Edwards, Ernie. Big bands discography / Ernie Edwards. — Whittier, Calif. : Jazz Discographies Unlimited, 1965–1968. — I, A-192.

Edwards, George Thornton. Music and musicians of Maine / George Thornton Edwards. — Portland, Me. : Southworth, 1928. — I, 102.

Edwards, John. The published works of the late John Edwards. Kingswinford, England : Society for the Preservation and Promotion of Traditional Country Music, 1973. — I, 613.

Edwards, John W. Rock 'n' roll through 1969 : discographies of all performers who hit the charts beginning in 1955 / John W. Edwards. — Jefferson, N.C. : McFarland, 1992. — III, 280.

Eells, George. The life that late he led : a biography of Cole Porter. — George Eells. — New York : Putnam, 1967. — I, 1292.

Egan, Robert F. Music and the arts in the community : the community music school in America / Robert F. Egan. — Metuchen, N.J. : Scarecrow, 1989. — III, 1261.

Ehrenstein, David. Rock on film / David Ehrenstein and Bill Reed. — New York : Delilah, 1982. — II, A-749.

Ehrlich, Cyril. The piano : a history / Cyril Ehrlich. — London : Dent, 1976. — II, 88.

Eisen, Jonathan. The age of rock 1 / Jonathan Eisen. — New York : Random House, 1969. — I, 1363.

Eisen, Jonathan. The age of rock 2 / Jonathan Eisen. — New York : Random House, 1970. — I, 1364.

Eisen, Jonathan. Twenty-minute fandangos and forever changes : a rock bazaar / Jonathan Eisen. — New York : Random House, 1971. — II, 1134.

Eisler, Hanns. A rebel in music : selected writings / Hanns Eisler. — New York : International Publishers, 1978. — II, 209.

Eisler, Hanns. Composing for the films / Hanns Eisler. — New York : Oxford University Press, 1947. — I, 1306.

Eisler, Paul E. The Metropolitan Opera : the first twenty-five years, 1883–1908 / Paul E. Eisler. — Croton-on-Hudson, N.Y. : North River Press, 1984. — II, A-42.

Eliason, Robert E. Early American brass makers / Robert E. Eliason. — Nashville : Brass Press, 1979. — II, 97.

Eliason, Robert E. Keyed bugles in the United States / Robert E. Eliason. — Washington : Smithsonian Institution Press, 1972. — II, 98.

Eliot, Marc. Death of a rebel / Marc Eliot. — Garden City, N.Y. : Anchor, 1979. — II, 1220.

Eliot, Marc. Death of a rebel : a biography of Phil Ochs / Marc Eliot. — Rev. ed. — New York : Watts, 1989. — III, 805.

Eliot, Marc. Down thunder road : the making of Bruce Springsteen / Marc Eliot; with Mike Appel. — New York : Simon & Schuster, 1992. — III, 864.

Eliot, Marc. Rockonomics : the money behind the music / Marc Eliot. — New York : Watts, 1989. — III, 1173.

Elkus, Jonathan. Charles Ives and the American band tradition : a centennial tribute / Jonathan Elkus. — Exeter, England : University of Exeter, 1974. — I, 329.

Elliker, Calvin. Stephen Collins Foster : a guide to research / Calvin Elliker. — New York : Garland, 1988. — III, 164.

Ellington, Duke. Piano method for the blues / Duke Ellington. — New York : Robbins, 1943. — I, 868.

Ellington, Edward Kennedy. Music is my mistress / Edward Kennedy Ellington. — Garden City, N.Y. : Doubleday, 1973. — I, 1105.

Ellington, Mercer. Duke Ellington in person : an intimate memoir / Mercer Ellington; with Stanley Dance. — Boston : Houghton Mifflin, 1978. — II, 745.

Ellinwood, Leonard. Bibliography of American hymnals / Leonard Ellinwood and Elizabeth Lockwood. — New York : University Music Editions for the Hymn Society of America, 1983. — III, 125.

Ellinwood, Leonard. Dictionary of American hymnology : first line index / Leonard Ellinwood. — New York : University Music Editions, 1984. — III, 126.

Ellinwood, Leonard. History of American church music / Leonard Ellinwood. — New York : Morehouse-Gorham, 1953. — I, 57.

Elliott, Brad. Surf's up : the Beach Boys on record 1961–1981 / Brad Elliott. — Ann Arbor, Mich. : Pierian, 1982. — II, A-768.

Ellis, Jack C. The film book bibliography, 1940–1975 / Jack C. Ellis. — Metuchen, N.J. : Scarecrow, 1979. — II, 1053.

Ellis, Robert. The pictorial album of rock / Robert Ellis. — London : Salamander, 1981. — II, A-750.

Ellison, Mary. Extensions of the blues / Mary Ellison. — London : Calder, 1989. — III, 1150.

Ellison, Mary. Lyrical protest : black music's struggle against discrimination / Mary Ellison. — New York : Praeger, 1989. — III, 1217.

Ellison, Ralph. Shadow and act / Ralph Ellison. — New York : Random House, 1964. — I, 1016.

Elrod, Bruce C. A history of American popular music / Bruce C. Elrod. — 2nd ed. — Columbia, S.C. : Colonial Printing Co., 1982. — II, 1250.

Elrod, Bruce C. Your hit parade : April 20, 1935 to June 7, 1958 : American top 10 hits, 1958–1984 / Bruce C. Elrod. — 3rd ed. — White Rock, S.C. : Author, 1985. — III, 1056a.

Elsner, Constanze. Stevie Wonder / Constanze Elsner. — London : Everest Books, 1977. — II, 574.

Elson, Louis C. The history of American music / Louis C. Elson. — Rev. ed. — New York : Macmillan, 1925. — I, 21.

Elson, Louis C. The national music of America and its sources / Louis C. Elson. — Rev. ed. — Boston : Page, 1924. — I, 1183.

Elsworth, John Van Varick. The Johnson organs : the story of one of our famous American organbuilders / John Van Varick Elsworth. — Harrisville, N.H. : Boston Organ Club, 1984. — II, A-52.

Embree, Edwin R. 13 against the odds / Edwin R. Embree. — New York : Viking, 1944. — I, A-153.

Emery, Lynne Fauley. Black dance in the United States from 1619 to 1970 /

Lynne Fauley Emery. — Palo Alto, Calif. : National Press Books, 1972. — I, 686.

Emurian, Ernest K. Stories of Civil War songs / Ernest K. Emurian. — Natick, Mass. : W. A. Wilde, 1960. — II, 872.

Emurian, Ernest K. The sweetheart of the Civil War : the true story of the song "Lorena" / Ernest K. Emurian. — Natick, Mass. : W. A. Wilde, 1962. — II, 873.

Encyclopedia of black America. — New York : McGraw-Hill, 1981. — II, A-276.

Encyclopedia of recorded sound in the United States / ed. Guy A. Marco; contributing ed. Frank Andrews. — New York : Garland, 1993. — III, 83.

Encyclopedia of rock / ed. Phil Hardy and Dave Laing; additional material by Stephen Barnard and Don Perretta. — [Rev. ed.] — New York : Schirmer, 1988. — III, 79.

Endres, Clifford. Austin city limits / Clifford Endres. — Austin : University of Texas Press, 1987. — III, 1160.

Eng, Steve. A satisfied mind : the country music life of Porter Wagoner / Steve Eng. — Nashville : Rutledge Hill, 1992. — III, 882.

Engel, Lehman. Planning and producing the musical show / Lehman Engel. — Rev. ed. — New York : Crown, 1966. — I, A-252.

Engel, Lehman. The American musical theater : a consideration / Lehman Engel. — Rev. ed. — New York : Macmillan, 1975. — I, 1253.

Engel, Lehman. The critics / Lehman Engel. — New York : Macmillan, 1976. — II, 913.

Engel, Lehman. The making of a musical / Lehman Engel. — New York : Macmillan, 1977. — II, 914.

Engel, Lehman. Their words are music : the great theatre lyricists and their lyrics / Lehman Engel. — New York : Crown, 1975. — II, 915.

Engel, Lehman. This bright day : an autobiography / Lehman Engel. — New York : Macmillan, 1974. — I, 1254.

Engel, Lehman. Words with music / Lehman Engel. — New York : Macmillan, 1972. — II, 916.

Enstice, Wayne. Jazz spoken here : conversations with twenty-two musicians / Wayne Enstice and Paul Rubin. — Baton Rouge : Louisiana State University Press, 1992. — III, 1095.

Epstein, Dena J. Music publishing in Chicago before 1871 : the firm of Root and Cady, 1858–1871 / Dena J. Epstein. — Detroit : Information Coordinators, 1969. — I, 166.

Epstein, Dena J. Sinful tunes and spirituals : black folk music to the Civil War / Dena J. Epstein. — Urbana : University of Illinois Press, 1977. — II, 521.

Epstein, Dena J. The folk banjo : a documentary history / Dena J. Epstein. — Los Angeles : John Edwards Memorial Foundation, 1976. — II, 325.

Equiano, Olaudah. The interesting narrative of the life of Olaudah Equiano / Olaudah Equiano. — London : Author, 1789. — I, 715.

Eremo, Judie. Country musicians / Judie Eremo. — Cupertino, Calif. : Grove, 1987. — III, 402.

Eremo, Judie. New age musicians / Judie Eremo. — Cupertino, Calif. : GPI Publications, 1989. — III, 405.

Erenberg, Lewis. Steppin' out : New York nightlife and the transformation of American culture, 1890–1930 / Lewis A. Erenberg. — Westport, Conn. : Greenwood, 1981. — II, A-527.

Erlewine, Michael. All music guide : the best CDs, albums & tapes : the experts' guide to the best releases from thousands of artists in all types of music / Michael Erlewine, Stephen Thomas Erlewine, and Scott Bultman. San Francisco : Miller Freeman, 1992. — III, 258.

Erlich, Lillian. What jazz is all about / Lillian Erlich. — Rev. ed. — New York : Messner, 1975. — I, 964.

Errigo, Angie. The illustrated history of rock album covers / Angie Errigo and Steve Leaning. — London : Octopus, 1969 — II, 1166.

Erskine, John. The Philharmonic-Symphony Society of New York : its first hundred years / John Erskine. — New York : Macmillan, 1943. — I, 112.

Erwin, Pee Wee. This horn for hire / Pee Wee Erwin; as told to Warren W. Vaché, Sr.; foreword by William M. Weinberg. — Metuchen, N.J. : Scarecrow Press and The Institute of Jazz Studies, 1987. — III, 633.

Escott, Colin. Catalyst : the Sun Records story / Colin Escott and Martin Hawkins. — London : Aquarius Books, 1975. — I, 1342.

Escott, Colin. Elvis Presley : the illustrated discography / Colin Escott and Martin Hawkins. — London : Omnibus, 1981. — II, 1223.

Escott, Colin. Good rockin' tonight : Sun Records and the birth of rock 'n' roll / Colin Escott; with Martin Hawkins. — New York : St. Martin's, 1991. — III, 1250.

Escott, Colin. The Conway Twitty rock 'n' roll years / Colin Escott and Richard Weize. — Bremen, Germany : Bear Family Records, 1985. — II, A-849.

Escott, Colin. The Elvis session file : 20 years of Elvis / Colin Escott and Martin Hawkins. — Bexhill-on-Sea, Sussex, England : Swift Record Distributors, 1974. — II, 1223.

Escott, Colin. The killer / Colin Escott; discography by Richard Weize. — Bremen, Germany : Bear Family Records, 1986. — III, 765.

Escott, Colin. The Sun session file / Colin Escott and Martin Hawkins. — Ashford, Kent, England : Authors, 1973–1974. — I, 1343.

Esquire's jazz book / ed. Paul Eduard Miller. — New York : Smith & Durrell, 1944. — I, 1017.

Ethnic recordings in America : a neglected heritage. — Washington : American Folklife Center, 1982. — II, A-179.

Ettema, James S. Individuals in mass media organizations : creativity and constraint / ed. James S. Ettema and D. Charles Whitney. — Beverly Hills, Calif. : : Sage Publications, 1982. — II, A-227.

Evans, David. Tommy Johnson / David Evans. — London : Studio Vista, 1971. — I, 843.

Evans, Frederick William. Shaker music / Frederick William Evans. — Albany, N.Y. : Weed, Parsons, 1875. — I, 554.

Evans, Mark. Scott Joplin and the ragtime years / Mark Evans. — New York : Dodd, Mead, 1976. — II, 617.

Evans, Mark. Soundtrack : the music of the movies / Mark Evans. — New York : Hopkinson and Blake, 1975. — II, 937.

Evans, Mary Garrettson. Music and Edgar Allan Poe : a bibliographical study / Mary Garrettson Evans. — Baltimore : Johns Hopkins Press, 1939. — II, 26.

Evans, Tom. Guitars : from the renaissance to rock / Tom Evans and Mary Anne Evans. — New York : Panjandrum, 1977. — II, 94.

Evensmo, Jan. Jazz solography series, v.1–14 / Jan Evensmo. — Hosle, Norway : Author, 1975–1983. — II, 640.

Evensmo, Jan. Tenor saxophonists of the period 1930–1942 / Jan Evensmo. — Oslo : Author, 1969. — I, 934.

Ewen, David. All the years of American popular music / David Ewen. — Englewood Cliffs, N.J. : Prentice-Hall, 1977. — II, 834.

Ewen, David. American composers : a biographical dictionary / David Ewen. — New York : Putnam, 1982. — II, A-8.

Ewen, David. American composers today : a biographical and critical guide / David Ewen. — New York : Wilson, 1949. — I, 285.

Ewen, David. American popular songs from the Revolutionary War to the present / David Ewen. — New York : Random House, 1966. — I, 1151.

Ewen, David. American songwriters / David Ewen. — New York : H. W. Wilson, 1987. — III, 410.

Ewen, David. Complete book of the American musical theater / David Ewen. — Rev. ed. — New York : Holt, 1959. — I, 1222.

Ewen, David. Composers of tomorrow's music : a non-technical introduction to the musical avant-garde movement / David Ewen. — New York : Dodd, Mead, 1971. — I, 254; II, 157.

Ewen, David. Composers since 1900 : a biographical and critical guide : first supplement / David Ewen. — New York : Wilson, 1981. — II, A-87.

Ewen, David. David Ewen introduces modern music / David Ewen. — Rev. ed. — New York : Chilton, 1969. — I, 271.

Ewen, David. Great men of American popular song / David Ewen. — Rev. ed. — Englewood Cliffs, N.J. : Prentice-Hall, 1972. — I, 1152.

Ewen, David. History of popular music / David Ewen. — New York : Barnes & Noble, 1961. — I, A-238.

Ewen, David. Journey to greatness : the life and music of George Gershwin / David Ewen. — New York : Holt, 1956. — I, 1280.

Ewen, David. Leonard Bernstein : a biography for young people / David Ewen. — Rev. ed. — Philadelphia : Chilton, 1967. — I, A-76.

Ewen, David. Men of popular music / David Ewen. — Chicago : Ziff-Davis, 1944. — I, 1153.

Ewen, David. New complete book of the American musical theater / David Ewen. — New York : Holt, Rinehart & Winston, 1970. — I, 1222.

Ewen, David. Panorama of American popular music / David Ewen. — Englewood Cliffs, N.J. : Prentice-Hall, 1957. — I, 1167.

Ewen, David. Popular American composers from revolutionary times to the present / David Ewen. — New York : Wilson, 1962. — I, 1154.

Ewen, David. Richard Rodgers / David Ewen. — New York : Holt, 1957. — I, 1296.

Ewen, David. The story of America's musical theater / David Ewen. — Rev. ed. — New York : Chilton, 1968. — I, 1223.

Ewen, David. The world of 20th century music / David Ewen. — Englewood Cliffs, N.J. : Prentice-Hall, 1968. — I, 255.

Ewen, David. The world of Jerome Kern : a biography / David Ewen. — New York : Holt, 1960. — I, 1290.

Ewing, George W. The well-tempered lyre : songs and verse of the temperance movement / ed. George W. Ewing. — Dallas : Southern Methodist University Press, 1977. — II, 1029.

Faber, Charles F. The country music almanac / Charles F. Faber. — Lexington, Ky. : Author, 1978–1979. — II, 359.

Fagan, Ted. The encyclopedic discography of Victor recordings / Ted Fagan and William R. Moran. — Westport, Conn. : Greenwood, 1983. — II, A-516.

Fahey, John. Charley Patton / John Fahey. — London : Studio Vista, 1970. — I, 850.

Fairbairn, Ann. Call him George / Ann Fairbairn. — Rev. ed. — New York : Crown, 1969. — I, 1122.

Fancourt, Leslie. John Lee Hooker : a discography / Leslie Fancourt. — Faversham, Kent, England : Author, 197-?. — II, 548.

Farah, Cynthia. Country music : a look at the men who made it / Cynthia Farah. — El Paso, Tex. : C. M. Pub., 1981. — II, A 240.

Farber, Donald C. The amazing story of *The Fantasticks* : America's longest-running play / Donald C. Farber and Robert Viagas. — New York : Citadel, 1991. — III, 511.

Fark, Reinhard. Die missachtet Botschaft / Reinhard Fark. — Berlin : Volker Spiess, 1971. — II, 779.

Farkas, Andrew. Lawrence Tibbett, singing actor / Andrew Farkas; introduction and discography by William Moran. — Portland, Ore. : Amadeus, 1989. — III, 871.

Farnsworth, Marjorie. The Ziegfeld Follies / Marjorie Farnsworth. — New York : Putnam, 1956. — I, 1247.

Farragher, Scott. Music city Babylon / Scott Farragher. — New York : Birch Lane, 1992. — III, 1161.

Farrell, Susan Caust. Directory of contemporary American musical instrument makers / Susan Caust Farrell. — Columbia : University of Missouri Press, 1981. — III, 34.

Farren, Mick. Rock 'n' roll circus : the illustrated rock concert / Mich Farren and George Snow. — London : Pierrot, 1978. — II, 1142.

Farwell, Arthur. Music in America / Arthur Farwell and Dermot W. Darby. — New York : National Society of Music, 1915. — I, 23.

Farwell, Brice. A guide to the music of Arthur Farwell and to the microfilm collection of his work / Brice Farwell. — Briarcliff Manor, N.Y. : Author, 1972. — I, 320.

Faulkner, Robert R. Hollywood studio musicians / Robert R. Faulkner. — Chicago : Aldine Atherton, 1971. — I, 1307.

Fawcett, Anthony. California rock, California sound / Anthony Fawcett. — Los Angeles : Reed Books, 1978. — II, 1129.

Fay, Amy. More letters of Amy Fay : the American years, 1879–1916 / Amy Fay; ed. Margaret William McCarthy. — Detroit : Information Coordinators, 1986. — III, 541.

Feather, Leonard. Encyclopedia of jazz / Leonard Feather. — New York : Horizon, 1955. — I, 903.

Feather, Leonard. Encyclopedia of jazz in the sixties / Leonard Feather. — New York : Horizon, 1966. — I, 904.

Feather, Leonard. From Satchmo to Miles / Leonard Feather. — New York : Stein & Day, 1972. — I, 1076.

Feather, Leonard. Inside be-bop / Leonard Feather. — New York : Robbins, 1949. — II, 719.

Feather, Leonard. Inside jazz / Leonard Feather. — New York : Da Capo, 1977. — II, 719.

Feather, Leonard. New edition of the *Encyclopedia of jazz* / Leonard Feather. — New York : Horizon, 1960. — I, 903.

Feather, Leonard. The book of jazz from then until now / Leonard Feather. — Rev. ed. — New York : Horizon, 1965. — I, 965.

Feather, Leonard. The encyclopedia of jazz in the seventies / Leonard Feather and Ira Gitler. — New York : Horizon, 1976. — II, 630.

Feather, Leonard. The jazz years : earwitness to an era / Leonard Feather. — New York : Quartet, 1986. — III, 966.

Feather, Leonard. The passion for jazz / Leonard Feather. — New York : Horizon, 1980. — II, 702.

Feather, Leonard. The pleasures of jazz / Leonard Feather. — New York : Horizon, 1976. — II, 703.

Feder, Stuart. Charles Ives "My father's song" : a psychoanalytic biography / Stuart Feder. — New Haven, Conn. : Yale University Press, 1992. — III, 490.

Fedor, Ferenz. The birth of Yankee Doodle / Ferenz Fedor. — New York : Vantage, 1976. — II, 864.

Fehl, Fred. On Broadway / Fred Fehl [et al]. — Austin : University of Texas Press, 1978. — II, 907.

Fein, Art. The L.A. musical history tour : a guide to the rock and roll landmarks of Los Angeles / Art Fein. — Boston : Faber & Faber, 1990. — III, 1201.

Feinstein, Elaine. Bessie Smith / Elaine Feinstein. — New York : Viking, 1985. — II, A-325.

Feintuch, Burt. Kentucky folkmusic : an annotated bibliography / Burt Feintuch. — Lexington : University Press of Kentucky, 1985. — II, A-191.

Feist, Leonard. An introduction to popular music publishing in America / Leonard Feist. — New York : National Music Publishers' Association, 1980. — II, 829.

Feldman, Jim. Prince / Jim Feldman. — New York : Ballantine, 1984. — III, 847.

Feldman, Morton. Essays / Morton Feldman. — Kerpen, Germany : Beginner Press, 1985. — II, A-122.

Fellers, Frederick P. Discographies of commercial recordings of the Cleveland Orchestra (1924–1977) and the Cincinnati Orchestra (1917–1977) / Frederick P. Fellers and Betty Meyers. — Westport, Conn. : Greenwood, 1978. — II, 57.

Fellers, Frederick P. The Metropolitan Opera on record : a discography of the commercial recordings / Frederick P. Fellers. — Westport, Conn. : Greenwood, 1984. — III, 247.

Felton, Harold W. Cowboy jamboree : western songs & lore / Harold W. Felton. — New York : Knopf, 1951. — II, 337.

Fennell, Frederick. Time and the winds : a short history of the use of wind instruments in the orchestra, band, and the wind ensemble / Frederick Fennell. — Kenosha, Wisc. : Leblanc, 1954. — II, 45.

Fenner, Thomas P. Cabin and plantation songs as sung by Hampton students / Thomas P. Fenner and Frederic G. Rathbun. — New York : Putnam, 1891. — I, 774.

Fenner, Thomas P. Religious folk songs of the Negro as sung on the plantations / Thomas P. Fenner. — Hampton, Va. : Hampton Institute Press, 1909. — I, 774.

Fenton, William N. Symposium on Cherokee and Iroquois culture / William N. Fenton and John Gulick. — Washington : Smithsonian Institution, 1961. — I, 404.

Ferber, Edna. A peculiar treasure / Edna Ferber. — New York : Doubleday, Doran, 1939. — II, 922.

Ferencz, George Joseph. Robert Russell Bennett : a bio-bibliography / George Joseph Ferencz. — New York : Greenwood, 1990. — III, 158.

Ferguson, [C.]. Mainstream jazz reference and price guide, 1949–1965 / [Charles] Ferguson & [Michael] Johnson. — Phoenix, Ariz. : O'Sullivan Woodside, 1984. — III, 237.

Ferguson, John Allen. Walter Holtkamp, American organ builder / John Allen Ferguson. — Kent, Ohio : Kent State University Press, 1979. — II, 130.

Ferguson, Otis. The Otis Ferguson reader / Otis Ferguson. — Highland Park, Ill. : December Press, 1982. — II, A-426.

Fergusson, Erna. Dancing gods : Indian ceremonials of New Mexico and Arizona / Erna Fergusson. — New York : Knopf, 1931. — I, 405.

Ferlingere, Robert D. A discography of rhythm and blues and rock 'n' roll vocal groups, 1945 to 1965 / Robert D. Ferlingere. — Pittsburg, Calif. : Author, 1976. — II, 556.

Fernett, Gene. Swing out : great negro dance bands / Gene Fernett. — Midland, Mich. : Pendell, 1970. — I, 1041.

Fernett, Gene. Thousand golden horns : the exciting age of America's greatest dance bands / Gene Fernett. — Midland, Mich. : Pendell, 1966. — I, A-194.

Ferris, William. Blues from the Delta / William Ferris. — Garden City, N.Y. : Anchor, 1979. — II, 544.

Ferris, William. Blues from the Delta / William R. Ferris. — London : Studio Vista, 1970. — I, 821.

Ferris, William. Folk music and modern sound / William Ferris and Mary L. Hart. — University : University of Mississippi Center for the Study of Southern Culture, 1982. — II, A-173.

Ferris, William. Mississippi black folklore : a research bibliography / William R. Ferris. — Hattiesburg : University Press of Mississippi, 1971. — I, 807.

Fesperman, John T. Flentrop in America : an account of the work and influence of the Dutch organ builder D. A. Flentrop in the United States, 1939–1977 / John T. Fesperman. — Raleigh, N.C. : Sunbury, 1981. — II, A-53.

Feuer, Jane. The Hollywood musical / Jane Feuer. — Bloomington : Indiana University Press, 1982. — II, A-586.

Ffrench, Florence. Music and musicians in Chicago / Florence Ffrench. — Chicago : Author, 1899. — I, 125.

Fichter, George S. American Indian music and musical instruments / George S. Fichter. — New York : McKay, 1978. — II, 237.

Field, Shelly. Career opportunities in the music industry / Shelly Field. — 2nd ed. — New York : Facts on File, 1990. — III, 1257.

Fife, Austin. Cowboy and Western songs : a comprehensive anthology / Austin E. Fife and Alta S. Fife. — New York : Potter, 1969. — I, 508.

Fife, Austin. Heaven on horseback : revivalist songs and verse in the cowboy idiom / Austin Fife and Alta Fife. — Logan : Utah State University Press, 1970. — I, 559.

Figueroa, Rafael. Salsa and related genres : a bibliographical guide / Rafael Figueroa. — Westport, Conn. : Greenwood, 1992. — III, 147.

Filby, P. W. Star-spangled books / P. W. Filby and Edward G. Howard. — Baltimore : Maryland Historical Society, 1972. — I, 1184.

Film music I / ed. Clifford McCarty. — New York : Garland, 1989. — III, 1026.

Filtgen, Gerd. John Coltrane : sein Leben, seine Musik, seine Schallplatten / Gerd Filtgen and Michael Ausserbauer. — Gauting-Buchendorf, Germany : Oreos, 1983. — III, 622.

Finch, Christopher. Rainbow : the stormy life of Judy Garland / Christopher Finch. — New York : Grosset & Dunlap, 1975.—II, 1000.

Finck, Henry T. My adventures in the golden age of music / Henry T. Finck. — New York : Funk & Wagnalls, 1926. — I, A-71.

Finell, Judith Greenberg. The contemporary music performance directory / Judith Greenberg Finell. — New York : American Music Center, 1975. — S. 210.

Finger, Charles J. Frontier ballads / Charles J. Finger. — London : Heinemann, 1927. — I, 509.

Finger, Charles J. Sailor chanties and cowboy songs / Charles J. Finger. — Girard, Kans. : Haldeman-Julius, 1923. — I, A-105.

Fink, Michael. Inside the music business : music in contemporary life / Michael Fink. — New York : Schirmer, 1989. — III, 1240.

Finkelstein, Sidney. Composer and nation : the folk heritage of music / Sidney Finkelstein. — New York : International Publishers, 1960. — I, 421.

Finkelstein, Sidney. Jazz : a people's music / Sidney Finkelstein. — New York : Citadel, 1948. — I, 991.

Finn, Julio. The bluesman : the musical heritage of black men and women in the Americas / Julio Finn; illustrations by Willa Woolston. — London : Quartet, 1987. — III, 1151.

Finney, Ross Lee. Profile of a lifetime : a musical autobiography / Ross Lee Finney. — New York : C. F. Peters, 1992. — III, 473.

Finney, Ross Lee. Thinking about music : the collected writings of Ross Lee Finney / Ross Lee Finney; ed. with a preface by Frederic Goossen. — Tuscaloosa : University of Alabama Press, 1990. — III, 55.

Firestone, Ross. Swing, swing, swing : the life & times of Benny Goodman / Ross Firestone. — New York : Norton, 1992. — III, 954.

Fisher, John. Call them irreplaceable / John Fisher. — London : Elm Tree Books, 1976. — II, 822.

Fisher, Miles Mark. Negro slave songs in the United States / Miles Mark Fisher. — Ithaca, N.Y. : Cornell University Press, 1963. — I, 789.

Fisher, William Arms. Music festivals in the United States : an historical sketch / William Arms Fisher. — Boston : American Choral and Festival Alliance, 1934. — I, 92.

Fisher, William Arms. One hundred and fifty years of music publishing in the United States / William Arms Fisher. — Boston : Ditson, 1933. — I, 167.

Fisher, William Arms. Seventy negro spirituals / ed. William Arms Fisher. — Boston : Ditson, 1926. — II, 602.

Fisher, William Arms. Ye olde New England psalm tunes / William Arms Fisher. — Boston : Ditson, 1930. — I, A-66.

Fithian, Philip Vickers. Journal and letters, 1767–1774 / Philip Vickers Fithian. — Princeton, N.J. : Princeton University Library, 1900–1934. — I, A-164.

Fitterling, Thomas. Thelonious Monk : sein Leben, seine Musik, seine Schallplatten / Thomas Fitterling. — Waakirchen, Germany : Oreos, 1987. — III, 563.

Fitzgerald, F-stop. Weird angle / F-stop Fitzgerald. — Berkeley, Calif. : Last Gasp of San Francisco, 1982. — II, A-751.

Flanagan, Bill. Written in my soul : rock's great songwriters talk about creating their music / Bill Flanagan. — Chicago : Contemporary Books, 1986. — III, 411.

Flanagan, Cathleen C. American folklore : a bibliography, 1950–1974 / Cathleen Flanagan and John T. Flanagan. — Metuchen, N.J. : Scarecrow, 1977. — II, 272.

Flanders, Helen Hartness. Ancient ballads, traditionally sung in New England / Helen Hartness Flanders; critical anaylses by Tristram P. Coffin; music annotations by Bruno Nettl. — Philadelphia : University of Pennsylvania Press, 1960–1965. — I, 475.

Flanders, Helen Hartness. Ballads migrant in New England / Helen Hartness Flanders and Marguerite Olney. — New York : Farrar, Straus & Young, 1953. — I, 476.

Flanders, Helen Hartness. Country songs of Vermont / Helen Hartness Flanders. — New York : Schirmer, 1937. — I, 479.

Flanders, Helen Hartness. Green Mountain songs / Helen Hartness Flanders. — Boston : Worley, 1934. — I, 479.

Flanders, Helen Hartness. New Green Mountain songster / Helen Hartness Flanders [et al]. — New Haven, Conn. : Yale University Press, 1939. — I, 480.

Flanders, Helen Hartness. Vermont folk-songs and ballads / Helen Hartness Flanders. — Brattleboro, Vt. : Stephen Daye Press, 1931. — I, 481.

Fleischer, Leonore. Dolly : here I come again / Leonore Fleischer. — Toronto : PaperJacks, 1987. — III, 810.

Fleischer, Leonore. John Denver / Leonore Fleischer. — New York : Flass Books, 1976. — II, 1193.

Fleischer, Leonore. Joni Mitchell / Leonore Fleischer. — New York : Flash Books, 1976. — II, 1218.

Fleming, Richard. John Cage at seventy-five / ed. Richard Fleming and William Duckworth. — Lewisburg, Pa. : Bucknell University; distributed by Associated University Presses, 1989. — III, 459.

Fletcher, Alice C. A study of Omaha Indian music / Alice C. Fletcher. — Cambridge, Mass. : Peabody Museum, 1893. — I, 406.

Fletcher, Alice C. Indian games and dances with native songs / Alice C. Fletcher. — Boston : Birchard, 1915. — I, 395.

Fletcher, Alice C. Indian story and song from North America / Alice C. Fletcher. — Boston : Small, Maynard, 1900. — I, 396.

Fletcher, Alice Cunningham. The Hako : a Pawnee ceremony / Alice Cunningham Fletcher. — Washington : Government Printing Office, 1904. — I, A-92.

Fletcher, Peter. Roll over rock / Peter Fletcher. — London : Stainer & Bell, 1981. — II, A-729.

Fletcher, Tom. The Tom Fletcher story : 100 years of the negro in show business / Tom Fletcher. — New York : Burdge, 1954. — I, 1230.

Fletcher, Tony. Remarks : the story of R.E.M. / Tony Fletcher. — New York : Bantam, 1990. — III, 933.

Flinn, Caryl. Strains of utopia : gender, nostalgia, and Hollywood film music / Caryl Flinn. — Princeton, N.J. : Princeton University Press, 1992. — III, 1027.

Flippo, Chet. Everybody was kung-fu dancing : chronicles of the lionized and notorious / Chet Flippo. — New York : St. Martin's, 1991. — III, 1174.

Flippo, Chet. Your cheatin' heart : a biography of Hank Williams / Chet Flippo. — New York : Simon & Schuster, 1981. — II, A-270.

Flower, John. Moonlight serenade : a bio-discography of the Glenn Miller civilian band / John Flower. — New Rochelle, N.Y. : Arlington House, 1972. — I, 1125.

Floyd, Samuel A. Black music in the United States : an annotated bibliography of selected references and research materials / Samuel A. Floyd and Marsha J. Reissner. — Milwood, N.Y. : Kraus, 1983. — II, A-288.

Floyd, Samuel A., Jr. Black music biography : an annotated bibliography / Samuel A. Floyd, Jr. and Marsha J. Reisser. — White Plains, N.Y. : Kraus International, 1987. — III, 112.

Floyd, Samuel A., Jr. Black music in the Harlem renaissance : a collection of essays / ed. Samuel A. Floyd, Jr. — Westport, Conn. : Greenwood, 1990. — III, 1229.

Foner, Philip S. American labor songs of the 19th century / Philip S. Foner. — Urbana : University of Illinois Press, 1975. — I, 577.

Foner, Philip S. The case of Joe Hill / Philip S. Foner. — New York : International Publishers, 1965. — I, 592.

Fong-Torres, Ben. Hickory wind : the life and times of Gram Parsons / Ben Fong-Torres. — New York : Pocket Books, 1991. — III, 809.

Fong-Torres, Ben. The Rolling Stone rock 'n' roll reader / Ben Fong-Torres. — New York : Bantam, 1974. — I, 1365.

Fong-Torres, Ben. What's that sound? / ed. Ben Fong-Torres. — Garden City, N.Y. : Anchor, 1976. — II, 1171.

Foote, Arthur. Arthur Foote, 1853–1937 : an autobiography / Arthur Foote. — Norwood, Mass. : Plimpton, 1946. — I, 223.

Foote, Henry Wilder. An account of the Bay Psalm Book / Henry Wilder Foote. — New York : Hymn Society of America, 1940. — I, 190.

Foote, Henry Wilder. Musical life in Boston in the eighteenth century / Henry Wilder Foote. — Worcester, Mass. : American Antiquarian Society, 1940. — I, A-30.

Foote, Henry Wilder. Three centuries of American hymnody / Henry Wilder Foote. — Cambridge, Mass. : Harvard University Press, 1940. — I, 66.

Ford, Ira W. Traditional music of America / Ira W. Ford. — New York : Dutton, 1940. — I, 519.

Ford, Tennessee Ernie. This is my story, this is my song / Tennessee Ernie Ford. — Englewood Cliffs, N.J. : Prentice-Hall, 1963. — II, 400.

Fordham, John. Jazz on CD : the essential guide / John Fordham. — London : KC, 1991. — III, 238.

Fordin, Hugh. Getting to know him : a biography of Oscar Hammerstein II / Hugh Fordin. — New York : Random House, 1977. — II, 948.

Fordin, Hugh. Jerome Kern : the man and his music in story, picture and song / Hugh Fordin. — Santa Monica, Calif. : T. B. Harms, 1975. — II, 956.

Fordin, Hugh. The world of entertainment! : Hollywood's greatest musicals / Hugh Fordin. — Garden City, N.Y. : Doubleday, 1975. — I, 1264.

Foreman, Lewis. Discographies : a bibliography of catalogues of recordings / Lewis Foreman. — London : Triad, 1974. — I, 256.

Formento, Don. Rock chronicle : today in rock history / Don Formento. — London : Sidgwick & Jackson, 1983. — II, A-654.

Forrest, Helen. I had the craziest dream / Helen Forrest. — New York : Coward, McCann & Geoghegan, 1982. — II, A-477.

Fors, Luis Ricardo. Gottschalk / Luis Ricardo Fors. — Habana : La Propaganda Literaria, 1880. — I, 227.

Fortas, Alan. Elvis, from Memphis to Hollywood : memories from my twelve years with Elvis Presley / Alan Fortas. — Ann Arbor, Mich. : Popular Culture, Ink., 1992. — III, 821.

Forten, Charlotte L. Journal / Charlotte L. Forten. — New York : Dryden Press, 1953. — I, 736.

Forucci, Samuel L. A folk history of America / Samuel L. Forucci. — Englewood Cliffs, N.J. : Prentice-Hall, 1984. — II, A-174.

Foster, Frank. In defense of be-bop / Frank Foster. — Scarsdale, N.Y. : Foster Fan Club, 1980. — II, 780.

Foster, G. G. New York by gas-light : with here and there a streak of sunshine / G. G. Foster. — New York : Dewitt & Davenport, 1850. — I, 737.

Foster, Morrison. My brother Stephen / Morrison Foster. — Indianapolis : Hollenbeck, 1932. — I, 1208.

Foster, Pops. Pops Foster : the autobiography of a New Orleans jazzman / Pops Foster; as told to Tom Stoppard; discography by Brian Rust. — Berkeley : University of California Press, 1971. — I, 1110.

Foster, Stephen Collins. The music of Stephen C. Foster : a critical edition / Steven Saunders and Deane L. Root. — Washington : Smithsonian Institution Press, 1990. — III, 17.

Fountain, Pete. A closer walk / Pete Fountain; with Bill Neely. — Chicago : Regnery, 1972. — I, 1111.

Fowke, Edith. Lumbering songs from the northern woods / ed. Edith Fowke. — Austin : University of Texas Press, 1970. — II, 461.

Fowke, Edith. Songs of work and freedom / Edith Fowke and Joe Glazer. — Chicago : Roosevelt University, 1960. — I, 586.

Fowler, Gene. Schnozzola : the story of Jimmy Durante / Gene Fowler. — New York : Viking, 1951. — II, 996.

Fowler, Lana Nelson. Willie Nelson family album / Lana Nelson Fowler. — Amarillo, Tex. : Poirot, 1980. — II, 469.

Fox, Charles. Fats Waller / Charles Fox. — London : Cassell, 1960. — I, 1142.

Fox, Charles. Jazz in perspective / Charles Fox. — London : B.B.C., 1969. — I, 1002.

Fox, Charles. Jazz on record : a critical guide / Charles Fox [et al]. — London : Hutchinson, 1960. — I, 958.

Fox, Charles. The jazz scene / Charles Fox. — New York : Hamlyn, 1972. — I, 966.

Fox, Roy. Hollywood, Mayfair, and all that jazz : the Roy Fox story / Roy Fox. — London : Frewin, 1975. — II, 790.

Fox, Ted. In the groove : the men behind the music / Ted Fox; foreword by Doc Pomus. — New York : St. Martin's, 1986. — III, 1241.

Fox, Ted. Showtime at the Apollo / Ted Fox. — New York : Holt, 1983. — II, A-559.

Fox-Cumming, Ray. Stevie Wonder / Ray Fox-Cumming. — London : Mandabrook Books, 1977. — II, 575.

Fox-Sheinwold, Patricia. Too young to die / Patricia Fox-Sheinwold. — Baltimore : Ottenheimer, 1979. — II, 1280.

Foxfire 3. — Garden City, N.Y. : Anchor, 1975. — II, 307.

Foxfire 4. — Garden City, N.Y. : Anchor, 1977. — II, 307.

Foxfire 6. — Garden City, N.Y. : Anchor, 1980. — II, 307.

Frame, Pete. Rock family tree / Pete Frame. — London : Omnibus Press, 1980–1983. — II, 1097.

Franchini, Vittorio. Lester Young / Vittorio Franchini. — Milan : Ricordi, 1961. — II, 791.

Francis, André. Jazz / André Francis. — Rev. ed. — New York : Grove, 1960. — I, A-195.

Francis, Connie. Who's sorry now? / Connie Francis. — New York : St. Martin's, 1984. — II, A-795.

Frank, Alan. Sinatra / Alan Frank. — London : Hamlyn, 1978. — II, 1007.

Frank, Gerold. Judy / Gerold Frank. — New York : Harper & Row, 1975. — I, 1320.

Frank, Leonie C. Musical life in early Cincinnati / Leonie C. Frank. — Cincinnati : Ruter, 1932. — I, A-31.

Frankel, Aaron. Writing the Broadway musical / Aaron Frankel. — New York : Drama Book Specialists, 1977. — II, 917.

Frazier, E. Franklin. The negro church in America / E. Franklin Frazier. — New York : Schocken, 1964. — I, 663.

Frazier, Thomas R. The underside of American history : other readings / Thomas B. Frazier. — New York : Harcourt Brace Jovanovich, 1971. — I, 790.

Fredericks, Jessica M. California composers : biographical notes / Jessica M. Fredericks. — San Francisco : California Federation of Music Clubs, 1934. — I, A-32.

Fredericks, Vic. Who's who in rock 'n' roll / Vic Fredericks. — New York : Fell, 1958. — I, A-288.

Freedland, Michael. Fred Astaire / Michael Freedland. — London : W. B. Allen, 1976. — II, 972.

Freedland, Michael. Irving Berlin / Michael Freedland. — London : Allen, 1974. — I, 1270.

Freedland, Michael. Jerome Kern / Michael Freeland. — London : Robson, 1978. — II, 957.

Frith, Simon. The sociology of rock / Simon Frith. — London : Constable, 1978. — II, 1149.

Frohne, Michael. Subconscious Lee : 35 years of records and tapes : the Lee Konitz discography / Michael Frohne. — Freiburg, Germany : Jazz Realities, 1983. — II, A-378.

Frost, Deborah. ZZ Top : bad and worldwide / Deborah Frost. — New York : Collier Books, 1985. — III, 947.

Frow, George L. The Edison disc phonographs and the Diamond Discs : a history with illustrations / George L. Frow. — Sevenoaks, Kent, England : Author, 1982. — II, A-70.

Fuchs, Walter. Die Geschichte der Country-Music / Walter Fuchs. — Bergish Gladbach, Germany : Lubbe, 1980. — II, 470.

Fuld, James J. 18th-century American secular music manuscripts : an inventory / James J. Fuld. — Philadelphia : Music Library Association, 1980. — II, 134.

Fuld, James J. A pictorial bibliography of the first editions of Stephen C. Foster / James J. Fuld. — Philadelphia : Musical Americana, 1957. — I, 1209.

Fuld, James J. American popular music (reference book) 1875–1950 / James J. Fuld. — Philadelphia : Musical Americana, 1955. — I, 1155.

Fuld, James J. The book of world-famous music / James J. Fuld. — Rev. ed. — New York : Crown, 1971. — I, 1156.

Fuller, John G. Are the kids all right? : the rock generation and its hidden death wish / John G. Fuller. — New York : Times Books, 1981. — II, A-723.

Furia, Philip. The poets of Tin Pan Alley : a history of America's great lyricists / Philip Furia. — New York : Oxford, 1990. — III, 1297.

Furlong, William B. Season with Solti : a year in the life of the Chicago Symphony Orchestra / William B. Furlong. — New York : Macmillan, 1974. — I, A-33.

Fuson, Harvey H. Ballads of the Kentucky highlands / ed. Harvey H. Fuson. — London : Mitre Press, 1931. — II, 309.

Gaar, Gillian G. She's a rebel : the history of women in rock & roll / Gillian G. Gaar. — Seattle, Wash. : Seal, 1992. — III, 419.

Gabin, Jane S. A living minstrelsy : the poetry and music of Sidney Lanier / Jane S. Gabin. — Macon, Ga. : Mercer University Press, 1985. — II, A-84.

Gabree, John. The world of rock / John Gabree. — Greenwich, Conn. : Fawcett, 1968. — I, A-289.

Gagne, Cole. Soundpieces : interviews with American composers / Cole Gagne and Tracy Caras. — Metuchen, N.J. : Scarecrow, 1982. — II, A-101.

Gaillard, Frye. Watermelon wine : the spirit of country music / Frye Gaillard. — New York : St. Martin's Press, 1978. — II, 376.

Gaines, Francis Pendleton. The Southern plantation / Francis Pendleton Gaines. — New York : Columbia University Press, 1924. — I, 664.

Gaines, Steven. Heroes and villains : the true story of the Beach Boys / Steven Gaines. — London : Macmillan, 1986. — III, 897.

Gaisberg, Fred. The music goes round / Fred Gaisberg. — New York : Macmillan, 1942. — II, 132.

Galbreath, Charles Burleigh. Daniel Decatur Emmett, author of "Dixie" / Charles Burleigh Galbreath. — Columbus, Ohio : Fred J. Heer, 1914. — I, 1237.

Gambaccini, Paul. Masters of rock / Paul Gambaccini. — London : BBC, 1982. — II, A-757.

Gambaccini, Paul. Rock critic's choice / Paul Gambaccini. — London : Omnibus, 1978. — II, 1119.

Gambaccini, Peter. Billy Joel : a personal file / Peter Gambaccini. — New York : Quick Fox, 1979. — II, 1210.

Gambaccini, Peter. Bruce Springsteen / Peter Gambaccini. — Rev. ed. — New York : Putnam, 1985. — II, 1243.

Gambaccini, Peter. Bruce Springsteen / Peter Gambaccini. — New York : Perigree, 1985. — II, A-842.

Gambino, Thomas. Nyet : an American rock musician encounters the Soviet Union / Thomas Gambino. — Englewood Cliffs, N.J. : Prentice-Hall, 1976. — II, 1143.

Gamble, Peter. Focus on jazz / Peter Gamble. — New York : St. Martin's, 1988. — III, 61.

Gammond, Peter. A guide to popular music / Peter Gammond and Peter Clayton. — London : Phoenix House, 1960. — I, 1157.

Gammond, Peter. Dictionary of popular music / Peter Gammond and Peter Clayton. — New York : Philosophical Library, 1961. — I, 1157.

Gammond, Peter. Duke Ellington / Peter Gammond. — London : Apollo, 1987. — III, 468a.

Gammond, Peter. Duke Ellington : his life and music / Peter Gammond. — London : Phoenix House, 1958. — I, 1107.

Gammond, Peter. Scott Joplin and the ragtime era / Peter Gammond. — London : Angus & Robertson, 1975. — I, 800.

Gammond, Peter. The big bands / Peter Gammond and Raymond Horricks. — Cambridge, England : Stephens, 1981. — II, A-436.

Gammond, Peter. The Decca book of jazz / Peter Gammond. — London : Muller, 1958. — I, 967.

Gammond, Peter. The music goes round and round : a cool look at the record industry / Peter Gammond and Raymond Horricks. — London : Quartet, 1980. — II, 1157.

Gans, David. Conversations with the Dead : the Grateful Dead interview book / David Gans. — New York : Citadel Underground, 1991. — III, 909.

Gans, David. Playing the band : an oral and visual portrait of the Grateful Dead / David Gans and Peter Simon. — New York : St. Martin's, 1985. — II, A-796.

Gans, David. Talking Heads / David Gans. — New York : Avon, 1985. — II, A-846.

Gans, Terry Alexander. What's new and what is not : Bob Dylan through 1964 : the myth of protest / Terry Alexander Gans. — Munich : Hobo Press, 1983. — II, A-786.

Garbutt, Bob. Rockabilly queens / Bob Garbutt. — Toronto : Ducktail Press, 1979. — II, 1180.

Gardner, Emelyn Elizabeth. Ballads and songs of Southern Michigan / Emelyn Elizabeth Gardner and Geraldine Chickering. / Ann Arbor : University of Michigan Press, 1939. — I, 485.

Gargan, William. Find that tune : an index to rock, folk-rock, disco & soul in collections / William Gargan and Sue Sharma. — New York : Neal-Schuman, 1984–1988. — III, 149.

Garland, Jim. Welcome the traveler home / Jim Garland. — Lexington : University Press of Kentucky, 1983. — II, A-212.

Garland, Peter. Americas : essays on American music and culture, 1973–1980 / Peter Garland. — Santa Fe, N.M. : Soundings, 1982. — II, A-102.

Garland, Peter. Soundings : Ives, Ruggles, Varèse / Peter Garland. — Berkeley, Calif. : Soundings Press, 1974. — II, 169.

Garland, Phyl. Sound of soul / Phyl Garland. — Chicago : Regnery, 1969. — I, 891.

Garodkin, John. Little Richard : king of rock 'n' roll / John Garodkin. — [n.p.] : Danish Rock 'n' Roll Society, 1975. — II, 1216.

Garon, Paul. Blues and the poetic spirit / Paul Garon. — London : Eddison Press, 1975. — II, 552.

Garon, Paul. The devil's son-in-law : the story of Peetie Wheatstraw and his songs / Paul Garon. — London : Studio Vista, 1971. — I, 856.

Garon, Paul. Woman with guitar : Memphis Minnie's blues / Paul Garon and Beth Garon. — New York : Da Capo, 1992. — III, 785.

Garrod, Charles. Artie Shaw and his orchestra / Charles Garrod and Bill Korst. — Zephyrhills, Fla. : Joyce Record Club, 1986. — III, 356.

Garrod, Charles. Ben Bernie and his orchestra / Charles Garrod. — Zephyrhills, Fla. : Joyce Record Club, 1991. — III, 289.

Garrod, Charles. Bob Chester and his orchestra / Charles Garrod and Bill Korst. — Rev. ed. — Zephyrhills, Fla. : Joyce Record Club, 1987. — III, 292.

Garrod, Charles. Bob Crosby and his orchestra / Charles Garrod and Bill Korst. — Zephyrhills, Fla. : Joyce Record Club, 1987. — III, 299.

Garrod, Charles. Bobby Sherwood and his orchestra : plus Randy Brooks and his orchestra / Charles Garrod. — Zephyrhills, Fla. : Joyce Record Club, 1987. — III, 355.

Garrod, Charles. Buddy Clark / Charles Garrod and Bob Gottlieb. — Zephyrhills, Fla. : Joyce Record Club, 1991. — III, 293.

Garrod, Charles. Charlie Barnet and his orchestra / Charles Garrod and Bill Korst. — Zephyrhills, Fla. : Joyce Record Club, 1984. — III, 286.

Garrod, Charles. Charlie Spivak and his orchestra / Charles Garrod. — Zephyrhills, Fla. : Joyce Record Club, 1986. — III, 360.

Garrod, Charles. Chuck Foster and his orchestra / Charles Garrod. — Zephyrhills, Fla. : Joyce Record Club, 1992. — III, 312.

Garrod, Charles. Claude Thornhill and his orchestra / Charles Garrod. — Zephyrhills, Fla. : Joyce Record Club, 1985. — III, 361.

Garrod, Charles. Columbia 78 rpm master listing : Chicago, 501–4999 : January 12, 1933 to February 2, 1949 / Charles Garrod. — Zephyrhills, Fla. : Joyce Record Club, 1990. — III, 203.

Garrod, Charles. Count Basie and his orchestra, 1936–1945. Count Basie and his orchestra, volume two, 1946–1957 / Charles Garrod. — Zephyrhills, Fla. : Joyce Record Club, 1987, 1988. — III, 287.

Garrod, Charles. Decca New York master numbers / Charles Garrod. — Zephyrhills, Fla. : Joyce Record Club, 1992. — III, 205.

Garrod, Charles. Dick Haymes / Charles Garrod and Denis Brown, with special help from Roger Dooner and the Dick Haymes Society. — Zephyrhills, Fla. : Joyce Record Club, 1990. — III, 317.

Garrod, Charles. Dick Jurgens and his orchestra / Charles Garrod. — Zephyrhills, Fla. : Joyce Record Club, 1988. — III, 332.

Garrod, Charles. Eddy Duchin and his orchestra / Charles Garrod. — Zephyrhills, Fla. : Joyce Record Club, 1989. — III, 304.

Garrod, Charles. Erskine Hawkins and his orchestra / Charles Garrod. — Zephyrhills, Fla. : Joyce Record Club, 1992. — III, 316.

Garrod, Charles. Frank Sinatra, 1935–1951. Frank Sinatra 1952–1981 / Charles Garrod. — Zephyrhills, Fla. : Joyce Record Club, 1989, 1990. — III, 358.

Garrod, Charles. Freddy Martin and his orchestra / Charles Garrod. — Zephyrhills, Fla. : Joyce Record Club, 1987. — III, 341.

Garrod, Charles. Gene Krupa and his orchestra (1935–1946) / Charles Garrod and Bill Korst. — Zephyrhills, Fla. : Joyce Record Club, 1984. — III, 338.

Garrod, Charles. Gene Krupa and his orchestra (1947–1973) / Charles Garrod and Bill Korst. — Zephyrhills, Fla. : Joyce Record Club, 1984. — III, 339.

Garrod, Charles. Glen Gray and the Casa Loma Orchestra / Charles Garrod and Bill Korst. — Zephyrhills, Fla. : Joyce Record Club, 1987. — III, 315.

Garrod, Charles. Hal Kemp and his orchestra : plus Art Jarrett and his orchestra / Charles Garrod. — Zephyrhills, Fla. : Joyce Record Club, 1990. — III, 334.

Garrod, Charles. Harry James and his orchestra (1937–1945) / Charles Garrod. — Zephyrhills, Fla. : Joyce Record Club, 1985. — III, 323.

Garrod, Charles. Harry James and his orchestra (1946–1954) / Charles Garrod. — Zephyrhills, Fla. : Joyce Record Club, 1985. — III, 324.

Garrod, Charles. Harry James and his orchestra (1955–1982) / Charles Garrod. — Zephyrhills, Fla. : Joyce Record Club, 1985. — III, 325.

Garrod, Charles. Jimmy Dorsey and his orchestra / Charles Garrod. — Rev. ed. — Zephyrhills, Fla. : Joyce Record Club, 1988. — III, 302.

Garrod, Charles. John Kirby and his orchestra : Andy Kirk and His Orchestra / Charles Garrod. — Zephyrhills, Fla. : Joyce Record Club, 1991. — III, 337.

Garrod, Charles. Kay Kyser and his orchestra / Charles Garrod and Bill Korst. — Zephyrhills, Fla. : Joyce Record Club, 1990. — III, 340.

Garrod, Charles. Larry Clinton and his orchestra / Charles Garrod. — Rev. ed. — Zephyrhills, Fla. : Joyce Record Club, 1990. — III, 295.

Garrod, Charles. MGM 78 rpm master numbers listing, 1946 thru 1952 : working draft / Charles Garrod and Ed Novitsky. — Zephyrhills, Fla. : Joyce Record Club, 1990. — III, 211.

Garrod, Charles. Nat King Cole : his voice and piano / Charles Garrod and Bill Korst. — Zephyrhills, Fla. : Joyce Record Club, 1987. — III, 296.

Garrod, Charles. Ozzie Nelson and his orchestra / Charles Garrod. — Zephyrhills, Fla. : Joyce Record Club, 1991. — III, 346.

Garrod, Charles. Ralph Flanagan and his orchestra / Charles Garrod. — Rev. ed. — Zephyrhills, Fla. : Joyce Record Club, 1990. — III, 311.

Garrod, Charles. Ray Anthony and his orchestra / Charles Garrod and Bill Korst. — Zephyrhills, Fla. : Joyce Record Club, 1988. — III, 285.

Garrod, Charles. Ray Noble and his orchestra / Charles Garrod. — Zephyrhills, Fla. : Joyce Record Club, 1991. — III, 347.

Garrod, Charles. Sam Donahue and his orchestra / Charles Garrod and Bill Korst. — Zephyrhills, Fla. : Joyce Record Club, 1992. — III, 301.

Garrod, Charles. Sammy Kaye and his orchestra / Charles Garrod. — Zephyrhills, Fla. : Joyce Record Club, 1988. — III, 333.

Garrod, Charles. Shep Fields and his orchestra / Charles Garrod. — Zephyrhills, Fla. : Joyce Record Club, 1987. — III, 310.

Garrod, Charles. Spike Jones and the City Slickers / Charles Garrod. — Zephyrhills, Fla. : Joyce Record Club, 1989. — III, 329.

Garrod, Charles. Stan Kenton and his orchestra (1940–1951) / Charles Garrod. — Zephyrhills, Fla. : Joyce Record Club, 1984. — III, 335.

Garrod, Charles. Stan Kenton and his orchestra (1952–1959) / Charles Garrod. — Zephyrhills, Fla. : Joyce Record Club, 1984. — III, 336.

Garrod, Charles. Tommy Dorsey and his orchestra, volume one, 1928–1945; volume two 1946–1956 [bound together] / Charles Garrod, Walter Scott, and Frank Green. — Rev. ed. — Zephyrhills, Fla. : Joyce Record Club, 1988. — III, 303.

Garrod, Charles. Will Osborne and his orchestra / Charles Garrod. — Zephyrhills, Fla. : Joyce Record Club, 1991. — III, 348.

Garrod, Charles. Woody Herman, vol. 1 (1936–1947) / Charles Garrod. — Zephyrhills, Fla. : Joyce Record Club, 1985. — III, 319.

Garrod, Charles. Woody Herman, vol. 2 (1948–1957) / Charles Garrod. — Zephyrhills, Fla. : Joyce Record Club, 1986. — III, 320.

Garrod, Charles. Woody Herman, vol. 3 (1958–1987) / Charles Garrod. — Zephyrhills, Fla. : Joyce Record Club, 1988. — III, 321.

Garrod, Charles. World transcriptions original series, 1–11268 / Charles Garrod, Ken Crawford, and Dave Kressley. — Zephyrhills, Fla. : Joyce Record Club, 1992. — III, 219.

Gart, Galen. ARLD : the American record label directory and dating guide, 1940–1959 / Galen Gart. — Milford, N.H. : Big Nickel, 1989. — III, 195.

Gart, Galen. Duke/Peacock Records : an illustrated history with discography / Galen Gart and Roy C. Ames. — Milford, N.H. : Big Nickel, 1990. — III, 983.

Gart, Galen. First pressings : rock history as chronicled in *Billboard* Magazine / Galen Gart. — Milford, N.H. : Big Nickel, 1986. — III, 1176.

Garwood, Donald. Masters of instrumental blues guitar / Donald Garwood. — New York : Oak, 1968. — I, 869.

Gaskin, L. J. P. A select bibliography of music in Africa / L. J. P. Gaskin. — London : International African Institute, 1965. — I, 720.

Gatti-Casazza, Giulio. Memories of the opera / Giulio Gatti-Casazza. — New York : Scribner's, 1941. — I, 149.

Gaume, Matilda. Ruth Crawford Seeger : memoirs, memories, music / Matilda Gaume. — Metuchen, N.J. : Scarecrow, 1986. III, 516.

Gavin, James. Intimate nights : the golden age of New York cabaret / James Gavin. — New York : Grove Weidenfeld, 1991. — III, 1131.

Gay, Julius. Church music in Farmington in the olden time / Julius Gay. — Hartford, Conn. : Case, Lockwood and Brainard, 1891. — I, A-17.

Gayle, Addison. The black aesthetic / Addison Gayle. — New York : Anchor, 1972. — I, 677.
Gehman, Richard. Sinatra and his rat pack / Richard Gehman. — London : Mayflower, 1961. — II, 1088.
Gelatt, Roland. The fabulous phonograph / Roland Gelatt. — Rev. ed. — New York : Appleton-Century, 1965. — I, 178.
Geller, James J. Famous songs and their stories / James J. Geller. — New York : Macaulay, 1931. — I, 1177.
Geller, Larry. If I can dream : Elvis' own story / Larry Geller and Joel Spector; with Patricia Romanowski. — New York : Simon & Schuster, 1989. — III, 823.
Gellert, Lawrence. "Me and my captain" / Lawrence Gellert. — New York : Hours Press, 1939. — I, 746.
Gellert, Lawrence. — Negro songs of protest / Lawrence Gellert. — New York : American Music League, 1936. — I, 746.
Gelles, George. Teddy Wilson / George Gelles; notes on the music by John Mc-Donough. — Alexandria, Va. : Time-Life Records, 1981. — III, 576.
Gelly, Dave. Lester Young / Dave Gelly; discography by Tony Middleton. — Tunbridge Wells, England : Spellmount; New York : Hippocrene Books, 1984. — III, 677.
Gena, Peter. A John Cage reader / ed. Peter Gena and Jonathan Brent. — New York : Peters, 1982. — II, A-113.
Gennett records of old time tunes : a catalog reprint. — Los Angeles : John Edwards Memorial Foundation, 1975. — II, 360.
Gentry, Linnell. History and encyclopedia of country, western and gospel music / Linnell Gentry. — 2nd ed. — Nashville : Clairmont, 1969. — I, 605.
George, B. The international new wave discography : volume 2 / B. George and Martha Defoe. — London : Omnibus, 1982. — II, A-673.
George, B. Volume : international discography of the new wave / B. George and Martha Defoe. — New York : One Ten Records, 1980. — II, A-673.
George, Don. Sweet man : the real Duke Ellington / Don George. — New York : Putnam, 1981. — II, A-474.
George, Don. The real Duke Ellington / Don George. — London : Robson, 1982. — II, A-474.
George, Nelson. Buppies, B-boys, baps & bohos : notes on post-soul black culture / Nelson George. — New York : HarperCollins, 1992. — III, 1070.
George, Nelson. Cool it now : the authorized biography of New Edition / Nelson George. — Chicago : Contemporary Books, 1986. — III, 929.
George, Nelson. The death of rhythm and blues / Nelson George. — New York : Pantheon, 1988. — III, 1219.
George, Nelson. The Michael Jackson story / Nelson George. — New York : Dell, 1984. — II, A-805.
George, Nelson. Top of the Charts : the most complete listing ever / Nelson George. — Piscataway, N.J. : New Century, 1983. — II, A-674.
George, Nelson. Where did our love go? The rise and fall of the Motown sound / Nelson George; foreword by Quincy Jones; introduction by Robert Christgau. — New York : St. Martin's, 1985. — III, 1203.
Gerard, Charley. Salsa! : the rhythm of Latin music / Charley Gerard and Marty Sheller. — Crown Point, Ind. : White Cliffs Media Co., 1989. — III, 1052.

Gerber, Alain. Le cas Coltrane / Alain Gerber. — Marseilles, France : Editions Parenthèses, 1985. — II, A-465.

Gershwin, Ira. Lyrics on several occasions : a selection of stage and screen lyrics / Ira Gershwin. — New York : Knopf, 1959. — I, 1275.

Gerson, Robert A. Music in Philadelphia / Robert A. Gerson. — Philadelphia : Presser, 1940. — I, 117.

Giannone, Richard. Music in Willa Cather's fiction / Richard Giannone. — Lincoln : University of Nebraska Press, 1968. — II, 510.

Giants of jazz (series). — III, 1114.

Gibble, Kenneth L. Mr. songman : the Slim Whitman story / Kenneth L. Gibble. — Elgin, Ill. : Brethren Press, 1982. — II, A-269.

Gibson, Debbie. Between the lines / Debbie Gibson; with Mark Bego. — Austin, Tex. : Diamond Books, 1989. — III, 726.

Gibson, Robert. Elvis, a king forever / Robert Gibson; with Sid Shaw. — Poole, Dorset, England : Blandford, 1985. — III, 824.

Giddins, Gary. Celebrating Bird : the triumph of Charlie Parker / Gary Giddins. — New York : Beech Tree Books, 1987. — III, 657.

Giddins, Gary. Faces in the crowd : players and writers / Gary Giddins. — New York : Oxford, 1992. — III, 1273a.

Giddins, Gary. Rhythm-a-ning : the jazz tradition and innovation in the 80s / Gary Giddins. — New York : Oxford University Press, 1985. — II, A-427.

Giddins, Gary. Riding on a blue note : jazz and American pop / Gary Giddins. — New York : Oxford, 1981. — III, 1096.

Giddins, Gary. Satchmo / Gary Giddins. — New York : Doubleday, 1988. — III, 598.

Giese, Hannes. Art Blakey : sein Leben, seine Musik, seine Schallplatten / Hannes Giese. — Schaftlach, Germany : Oreos, 1990. — III, 610.

Gilbert, Douglas. American vaudeville : its life and times / Douglas Gilbert. — New York : Whittlesey House, 1940. — I, 1248.

Gilbert, Douglas. Lost chords : the diverting story of American popular songs / Douglas Gilbert. — Garden City, N.Y. : Doubleday, 1942. — I, 1168.

Gilbert, Louis Wolfe. Without rhyme or reason / Louis Wolfe Gilbert. — New York : Vantage, 1956. — II, 1044.

Giles, Ray. Here comes the band! / Ray Giles. — New York : Harper, 1936. — II, 1034.

Gill, Dominic. The book of the piano / Dominic Gill. — Ithaca, N.Y. : Cornell University Press, 1981. — II, A-56.

Gill, Sam D. Sacred words : a study of Navajo religion and prayer / Sam D. Gill. — Westport, Conn. : Greenwood, 1981. — II, A-158.

Gillenson, Lewis N. Esquire's world of jazz / Lewis N. Gillenson. — New York : Grosset & Dunlap, 1962. — I, 968.

Gillespie, Dizzy. Dizzy : the autobiography of Dizzy Gillespie. / Dizzy Gillespie; with Al Fraser. — London : W. H. Allen, 1980. — II, 749.

Gillespie, Dizzy. To be or not to bop : memoirs / Dizzy Gillespie; with Al Fraser. — Garden City, N.Y. : Doubleday, 1979. — II, 749.

Gillespie, Don. George Crumb : profile of a composer / Don Gillespie; introduction by Gilbert Chase. — New York : C. F. Peters, 1986. — III, 464.

Gillespie, John. A bibliography of nineteenth-century American piano music /

John Gillespie and Anna Gillespie. — Westport, Conn. : Greenwood, 1984. — II, A-77.

Gillett, Charlie. Making tracks : Atlantic Records and the growth of a multibillion dollar industry / Charlie Gillett.—New York : Dutton, 1975. — I, 1344.

Gillett, Charlie. Rock file / ed. Charlie Gillett [et al]. — St. Albans, England : Panther, 1972–1978. — II, 1113.

Gillett, Charlie. The sound of the city : the rise of rock and roll / Charlie Gillett. — New York : Outerbridge & Dienstfrey, 1970. — I, 1350.

Gilliam, Dorothy Butler. Paul Robeson, all-American / Dorothy Butler Gilliam. — Washington : New Republic Book Co., 1976. — II, 514.

Gillis, Frank. Ethnomusicology and folk music : an international bibliography of dissertations and theses / Frank Gillis and Alan P. Merriam. — Middletown, Conn. : Wesleyan University Press, 1966. — I, 422.

Gilman, Benjamin Ives. Hopi songs / Benjamin Ives Gilman. — Boston : Houghton Mifflin, 1908. — I, 407.

Gilman, Lawrence. Edward MacDowell : a study / Lawrence Gilman. — New York : Lane, 1908. — I, 236.

Gilman, Samuel. Memories of a New England village choir / Samuel Gilman. — Boston : Goodrich, 1829. — I, A-67.

Ginell, Cary. The Decca hillbilly discography, 1927–1945 / Cary Ginell. — New York : Greenwood, 1989. — III, 225.

Gioia, Ted. The imperfect art : reflections on jazz and modern culture / Ted Gioia. — New York : Oxford, 1988. — III, 1081.

Gioia, Ted. West Coast jazz : modern jazz in California, 1945–1960 / Ted Gioia. — New York : Oxford, 1992. — III, 1125.

Gipson, Richard McCandless. The life of Emma Thursby, 1845–1931 / Richard McCandless Gipson. — New York : New York Historical Society, 1940. — II, 147.

Gitler, Ira. Jazz masters of the forties / Ira Gitler. — New York : Macmillan, 1966. — I, 1048.

Gitler, Ira. Swing to bop : an oral history of the transition in jazz in the 1940s / Ira Gitler. — New York : Oxford, 1985. — III, 1115.

Given, Dave. The Dave Given rock 'n' roll stars handboook / Dave Given. — Smithtown, N.Y. : Exposition, 1980. — II, 1098.

Glass, Paul. Singing soldiers / Paul Glass. — New York : Grosset & Dunlap, 1968. — I, 1189.

Glass, Paul. Songs and stories of the American Indians : with rhythm indications for drum accompaniment / Paul Glass. — New York : Grosset & Dunlap, 1968. — II, 261.

Glass, Paul. Songs of forest and river folk / Paul Glass and Louis C. Singer. — New York : Grosset & Dunlap, 1967. — I, A-106.

Glass, Paul. Songs of the hill and mountain folk / Paul Glass and Louis C. Singer. — New York : Grosset & Dunlap, 1967. — I, A-107.

Glass, Paul. Songs of the sea / Paul Glass and Louis C. Singer. — New York : Grosset & Dunlap, 1966. — I, A-108.

Glass, Paul. Songs of the West / Paul Glass and Louis C. Singer. — New York : Grosset & Dunlap, 1966. — I, A-109.

Glass, Paul. Songs of town and city folk / Paul Glass and Louis C. Singer. — New York : Grosset & Dunlap, 1967. — I, A-110.

Glass, Philip. Music by Philip Glass / Philip Glass. — New York : Harper & Row, 1987. — III, 480.

Glassie, Henry. Folksongs and their makers / Henry Glassie, Edward D. Ives, and John F. Szwed. — Bowling Green, Ohio : Bowling Green State University Popular Press, 1970. — I, 441.

Glazer, Tom. Songs of peace, freedom, and protest / ed. Tom Glazer. — New York : David McKay, 1970. — II, 464.

Gleason, Harold. 20th-century American composers / Harold Gleason and Warren Becker. — 2nd ed. — Bloomington, Ind. : Frangipani, 1980. — II, 165.

Gleason, Ralph J. Celebrating the Duke / Ralph J. Gleason. — Boston : Little, Brown, 1975. — II, 731.

Gleason, Ralph J. The Jefferson Airplane and the San Francisco sound / Ralph J. Gleason. — New York : Ballantine, 1969. — I, 1383.

Gleason, Ralph. Jam sessions : an anthology of jazz / Ralph Gleason. — New York : Putnam, 1958. — I, 1018.

Glickmann, Serge. Judy Garland / Serge Glickmann. — Paris : La Pensée Universelle, 1981. — II, A-626.

Glover, Tony. Blues harp : an instruction method for playing the blues harmonica / Tony Glover. — New York : Oak, 1965. — I, A-177.

Godbolt, Jim. A history of jazz in Britain, 1919–1956 / Jim Godbolt. — London : Quartet, 1984. — II, A-416.

Goddard, Chris. Jazz away from home / Chris Goddard. — New York : Paddington, 1979. — II, 695.

Goffin, Robert. Aux frontières du jazz / Robert Goffin. — Paris : Sagittaire, 1932. — I, 1027.

Goffin, Robert. Horn of plenty : the story of Louis Armstrong / Robert Goffin. — New York : Allen, Towne & Heath, 1947. — I, A-197.

Goffin, Robert. Jazz : from Congo to swing / Robert Goffin. — London : Musician's Press, 1946. — I, 1028.

Goffin, Robert. Louis Armstrong, le roi du jazz / Robert Goffin. — Paris : Seghers, 1947. — I, A-197.

Goggin, Jim. Turk Murphy : just for the record / Jim Goggin. — San Francisco : Traditional Jazz Foundation, 1983. — II, A-492.

Gold, Robert S. Jazz lexicon / Robert S. Gold. — New York : Knopf, 1964. — I, 905.

Gold, Robert S. Jazz talk / Robert S. Gold. — Indianapolis : Bobbs-Merrill, 1975. — I, 905.

Goldberg, Bill. Max Roach discography / Bill Goldberg. — New York : WKCR, 1983. — II, A-382.

Goldberg, Isaac. George Gershwin : a study in American music / Isaac Goldberg. — Rev. ed. — New York : Ungar, 1958. — I, 1281.

Goldberg, Isaac. Tin Pan Alley / Isaac Goldberg. — New ed. — New York : Ungar, 1961. — I, 1169.

Goldberg, Joe. Jazz masters of the fifties / Joe Goldberg. — New York : Macmillan, 1965. — I, 1049.

Goldblatt, Burt. Jazz gallery 1 / Burt Goldblatt. — New York : Newbold, 1982. — II, A-397.

Goldblatt, Burt. Newport jazz festival : the illustrated history / Burt Goldblatt. — New York : Dial, 1977. — II, 674.

Golden, Bruce. The Beach Boys : southern California pastoral / Bruce Golden;
updated by Paul David Seldis. — 2nd ed. — San Bernardino, Calif. : Borgo,
1991. — III, 898.

Golden, Bruce. The Beach Boys : southern California pastoral / Bruce
Golden. — San Bernardino, Calif. : Borgo, 1976. — II, 1185.

Goldin, Milton. The music merchants / Milton Goldin. — New York : Macmillan, 1969. — I, 92.

Goldman, Albert. Elvis / Albert Goldman. — New York : McGraw-Hill,
1981. — III, 825.

Goldman, Albert. Elvis : the last 24 hours / Albert Goldman. — New York : St.
Martin's, 1991. — III, 826.

Goldman, Albert. Freakshow / Albert Goldman. — New York : Atheneum,
1971. — I, A-290.

Goldman, Herbert G. Jolson : the legend comes to life / Herbert G. Goldman. —
New York : Oxford University Press, 1988. — III, 751.

Goldman, Richard Franko. Landmarks of early American music, 1760–1800 /
Richard Franko Goldman. — New York : Schirmer, 1943. — I, A-68.

Goldman, Richard Franko. Selected essays and reviews, 1948–1968 / Richard
Franko Goldman. — Brooklyn : Institute for Studies in American Music,
1980. — II, 170.

Goldman, Richard Franko. The band's music / Richard Franko Goldman. —
New York : Pitman, 1939. — I, 1196.

Goldman, Richard Franko. The concert band / Richard Franko Goldman. —
New York : Rinehart, 1946. — I, 1197.

Goldman, Richard Franko. The wind band : its literature and technique / Richard
Franko Goldman. — Boston : Allyn and Bacon, 1961. — I, 1198.

Goldrosen, John J. Buddy Holly : his life and music / John J. Goldrosen. —
Bowling Green, Ohio : Bowling Green State University Popular Press,
1975. — II, 1208.

Goldrosen, John J. The Buddy Holly story / John J. Goldrosen. — New York :
Quick Fox, 1979. — II, 1208.

Goldrosen, John. Remembering Buddy : the definitive biography of Buddy
Holly / John Goldrosen and John Beecher. — 2nd ed. — New York :
Viking/Penguin; London : Pavilion, 1987. — III, 735.

Goldstein, Malcolm. George S. Kaufman : his life, his theater / Malcolm Goldstein. — New York : Oxford University Press, 1979. — II, 952.

Goldstein, Norm. Frank Sinatra : ol' blue eyes / Norm Goldstein. — New York :
Holt, 1983. — II, A-633.

Goldstein, Richard. Goldstein's greatest hits / Richard Goldstein. — Englewood
Cliffs, N.J. : Prentice-Hall, 1970. — I, A-291.

Goldstein, Richard. The poetry of rock / Richard Goldstein. — New York : Bantam, 1969. — I, 1351.

Goldstein, Stewart. Oldies but goodies : the rock 'n' roll years / Stewart Goldstein. — New York : Mason Charter, 1977. — II, 1110.

Goldstein, Toby. Frozen fire : the story of the Cars / Toby Goldstein; photography by Ebet Roberts. — Chicago : Contemporary Books, 1985. — III, 902.

Gombosi, Marilyn. A day of solemn thanksgiving / Marilyn Gombosi. —
Chapel Hill : University of North Carolina Press, 1977. — II, 44.

Gombosi, Marilyn. Catalog of the Johannes Herbst collection / Marilyn Gombosi. — Chapel Hill, N.C. : University of North Carolina Press, 1970. — I,
79.

Gonzales, Babs. I paid my dues : good times—no bread / Babs Gonzales. —
East Orange, N.J. : Expubidence, 1967. — I, 1113.

Gonzales, Babs. Movin' on down de line / Babs Gonzales. — Newark, N.J. :
Expubidence, 1975. — II, 750.

Gonzalez, Fernando L. Disco-file : the discographical catalog of American rock
& roll and rhythm & blues vocal harmony groups / Fernando L. Gonzalez. —
2nd ed. — Flushing, N.Y. : Author, 1977. — II, 557.

Gooch, Brad. Hall and Oates / Brad Gooch. — New York : Ballantine, 1985. —
III, 918.

Good, Marian Bigler. Some musical backgrounds of Pennsylvania / Marian
Bigler Good. — Carrolltown, Pa. : Carrolltown News Press, 1932. — I, A-34.

Goodenough, Caroline Leonard. High lights on hymnals and their hymns / Caroline Leonard Goodenough. — Rochester, N.Y. : Author, 1931. — II, 29.

Goodfellow, William D. Where's that tune? An index to songs in fakebooks /
William D. Goodfellow. — Metuchen, N.J. : Scarecrow, 1990. — III, 150.

Goodman, Benny. The kingdom of swing / Benny Goodman and Irving
Kolodin. — New York : Stackpole, 1939. — I, 1114.

Goodman, Linda. Music and dance in northwest coast Indian life / Linda Goodman. — Tsaile, Ariz. : Navajo Community College Press, 1977. — II, 249.

Goodspeed, E. J. A full history of the wonderful career of Moody and Sankey,
in Great Britain and America / E. J. Goodspeed. — New York : Goodspeed,
1876. — I, A-18.

Goodwin, Francis. An unfinished history of the Hartford Symphony from
1934–1976 / Francis Goodwin. — [n.p.] 1984. — II, A-35.

Gordon, E. Harrison. Black classical musicians of the 20th century / E. Harrison
Gordon. — Edison, N.J. : MSS Information Corp., 1977. — II, 591.

Gordon, Eric A. Mark the music : the life and work of Marc Blitzstein / Eric A.
Gordon. — New York : St. Martin's, 1989. — III, 456.

Gordon, Joanne Lesley. Art isn't easy : the theater of Stephen Sondheim /
Joanne Lesley Gordon. — New York : Da Capo, 1992. — III, 519.

Gordon, Max. Live at the Village Vanguard / Max Gordon. — New York : St.
Martin's, 1980. — II, 675.

Gordon, Robert. Jazz West Coast : the Los Angeles jazz scene of the 1950s /
Robert Gordon. — London : Quartet, 1986. — III, 1116.

Gordon, Robert Winslow. Folk-songs of America / Robert Winslow Gordon. —
New York : National Service Bureau, 1938. — I, 442.

Goreau, Laurraine. Just Mahalia, baby / Laurraine Goreau. — Waco, Tex. :
Word Books, 1975. — II, 577.

Goreau, Laurraine. Mahalia / Laurraine Goreau. — Berkhampstead, Herts.,
England : Lion, 1976. — II, 577.

Gorer, Geoffrey. Africa dances : a book about West African negroes / Geoffrey
Gorer. — London : Faber, 1935. — I, 721.

Gorman, Clem. Backstage rock : behind the scenes with the bands / Clem Gorman. — London : Pan Books, 1978. — II, 1144.

Goss, Madeleine. Modern music-makers : contemporary American composers / Madeleine Goss. — New York : Dutton, 1952. — I, 286.

Gottfried, Martin. Broadway musicals / Martin Gottfried. — New York : Abrams, 1979. — II, 908.

Gottfried, Martin. In person : the great entertainers / Martin Gottfried. — New York : Abrams, 1985. — II, A-611.

Gottlieb, Jack. Leonard Bernstein : a complete catalogue of his works / Jack Gottlieb. — New York : Amberson, 1978. — II, 175.

Gottlieb, Polly Rose. The nine lives of Billy Rose / Polly Rose Gottlieb. — New York : Crown, 1968. — II, 964.

Gottschalk, Louis Moreau. Notes of a pianist / Louis Moreau Gottschalk. — Philadelphia : Lippincott, 1881. — I, 225.

Götze, Werner. Dizzy Gillespie / Werner Götze. — Wetzlar, Germany : Pegasus Verlag, 1960. — I, A-207.

Gould, Nathaniel D. Church music in America / Nathaniel D. Gould. — Boston : A. N. Johnson, 1853. — I, 58.

Gould, Nathaniel D. History of church music in America / Nathaniel D. Gould. — Boston : Gould & Lincoln, 1853. — I, 58.

Gourse, Leslie. Everyday : the story of Joe Williams / Leslie Gourse. — London : Quartet, 1985. — II, A-326.

Gourse, Leslie. Louis' children : American jazz singers / Leslie Gourse. — New York : Quill, 1984. — II, A-448.

Gourse, Leslie. Unforgettable : the life and mystique of Nat King Cole / Leslie Gourse. — New York : St. Martin's, 1991. — III, 703.

Govenar, Alan B. Living Texas blues / Alan B. Govenar. — Dallas : Dallas Museum of Art, 1985. — II, A-317.

Govenar, Alan B. Meeting the blues / Alan Govenar. — Dallas : Taylor, 1988. — III, 1152.

Graber, Kenneth. William Mason (1829–1908) : an annotated bibliography and catalog of works / Kenneth Graber. — Warren, Mich. : Harmonie Park; published for the College Music Society, 1989. — III, 173.

Gradenwitz, Peter. Leonard Bernstein : unendliche Vielfalt eines Musikers / Peter Gradenwitz. — Zurich : Atlantis, 1984. — II, A-111.

Graf, Herbert. Opera and its future in America / Herbert Graf. — New York : Norton, 1941. — I, 139.

Graf, Herbert. Opera for the people / Herbert Graf. — London : Geoffrey Cumberlege, 1951. — I, 140.

Graf, Herbert. Producing opera for America / Herbert Graf. — Zurich : Atlantis, 1961. — I, A-53.

Graffman, Gary. I really should be practicing / Gary Graffman. — Garden City, N.Y. : Doubleday, 1981. — III, 542.

Grafton, David. Red, hot and rich : an oral history of Cole Porter / David Grafton. — New York : Stein & Day, 1987. — III, 506.

Graham, Albert Powell. Great bands of America / Alberta Powell Graham. — New York : Nelson, 1951. — II, 1035.

Graham, Bill. Bill Graham presents : my life inside rock and out / Bill Graham and Robert Greenfield. — New York : Doubleday, 1992. — III, 978a.

Graham, Philip. Showboats : the history of an American institution / Philip Graham. — Austin : University of Texas Press, 1951. — I, A-253.

Graham, Shirley. Paul Robeson, citizen of the world / Shirley Graham. — New York : Messner, 1946. — I, A-154.

Grame, Theodore C. America's ethnic music / Theodore C. Grame. — Tarpon Springs, Fla. : Cultural Maintenance Associates, 1976. — II, 290.

Grame, Theodore C. Ethnic broadcasting in the United States / Theodore C. Grame. — Washington : American Folklife Center, 1980. — II, 446.

Grandmaster Blast. All you need to know about rappin'/ Grandmaster Blast. — Chicago : Contemporary Books, 1984. — II, A-360.

Graue, Jerald C. Essays on music for Charles Warren Fox / ed. Jerald C. Graue. — Rochester, N.Y. : Eastman School of Music, 1979. — II, 14.

Gray, Andy. Great country music stars / Andy Gray. — London : Hamlyn, 1975. — II, 388.

Gray, Arlene E. Listen to the lambs : a source book of the R. Nathaniel Dett materials in the Niagara Falls Public Library / Arlene E. Gray. — Niagara Falls, N.Y. : Public Library, 1984. — II, A-289.

Gray, Herman. Producing jazz : the experience of an independent record company / Herman Gray. — Philadelphia : Temple University Press, 1988. — III, 1242.

Gray, John. Blacks in classical music : a bibliographical guide to composers, performers, and ensembles / John Gray. — New York : Greenwood, 1988. — III, 113.

Gray, John. Fire music : a bibliography of the new jazz, 1959–1990 / John Gray; foreword by Val Wilmer. — New York : Greenwood, 1991. — III, 128.

Gray, Michael. Song and dance man : the art of Bob Dylan / Michael Gray. — London : Hart-Davis, 1972. — I, 1374.

Gray, Michael. Zappa / Michael Gray. — London : Proteus, 1985. — III, 896.

Gray, Michael H. Bibliography of discographies : vol. 1 : classical music, 1925–1975 / Michael H. Gray and Gerald D. Gibson. — New York : Bowker, 1977. — II, 6.

Gray, Michael H. Bibliography of discographies : volume 3 : popular music / Michael H. Gray. — New York : Bowker, 1983. — II, A-507.

Gray, Roland Palmer. Songs and ballads of the Maine lumberjacks / ed. Roland Palmer Gray. — Cambridge, Mass. : Harvard University Press, 1924. — II, 342.

Green, Abel. Inside stuff on how to write popular songs / Abel Green. — New York : Paul Whiteman Publications, 1927. — I, A-239.

Green, Abel. Show biz, from vaude to video / Abel Green and Joe Laurie. — New York : Holt, 1951. — I, A-254.

Green, Archie. Hear these beautiful sacred selections / Archie Green. — Los Angeles : John Edwards Memorial Foundation, 1972. — I, 545.

Green, Archie. Only a miner : studies in recorded coalmining songs / Archie Green. — Urbana : University of Illinois Press, 1972. — I, 568.

Green, Benny. Blame it on my youth / Benny Green. — London : MacGibbon & Kee, 1967. — I, A-208.

Green, Benny. Drums in my ears / Benny Green. — London : Davis-Poynter, 1973. — I, 1019.

Green, Benny. Fred Astaire / Benny Green. — London : Hamlyn, 1979. — II, 1064.

Green, Benny. Let's face the music : the golden age of popular song / Benny Green. — London : Pavilion, 1989. — III, 412.

Green, Benny. The reluctant art / Benny Green. — New York : Horizon, 1963. — I, 1077.

Green, Douglas B. Country roots : the origins of country music / Douglas B. Green. — New York : Hawthorn, 1976. — II, 368.

Green, Douglas B. Roy Acuff's musical collection at Opryland / Douglas B. Green and George Gruhn. — Nashville : WSM, 1982. — II, A-243.

Green, Jeff. Green book : songs classified by subject / Jeff Green. — Smyrna, Tenn. : Professional Desk References, 1989. — III, 259.

Green, Jeffrey P. Edmund Thornton Jenkins : the life and times of an American composer, 1894–1926 / Jeffrey P. Green. — Westport, Conn. : Greenwood, 1983. — II, A-130.

Green, Jonathan. The book of rock quotes / Jonathan Green. — London : Omnibus, 1977. — II, 1248.

Green, Mildred Denby. Black women composers : a genesis / Mildred Denby Green. — Boston : Twayne, 1983. — II, A-302.

Green, Stanley. Broadway musicals, show by show / Stanley Green. — 3rd ed. — Milwaukee, Wisc. : H. Leonard Books, 1990. — III, 1011.

Green, Stanley. Encyclopedia of the musical film / Stanley Green. — New York : Oxford University Press, 1981. — II, A-587.

Green, Stanley. Encylopedia of the musical theatre / Stanley Green. — New York : Dodd, Mead, 1976. — II, 900.

Green, Stanley. Hollywood musicals year by year / Stanley Green. — Milwaukee : Hal Leonard, 1990. — III, 1281.

Green, Stanley. Ring bells! Sing songs! / Stanley Green. — New Rochelle, N.Y. : Arlington House, 1971. — I, 1255.

Green, Stanley. Starring Fred Astaire / Stanley Green and Burt Goldblatt. — New York : Dodd, Mead, 1973. — I, 1317.

Green, Stanley. The Rodgers and Hammerstein story / Stanley Green. — New York : Day, 1963. — I, 1297.

Green, Stanley. The world of musical comedy / Stanley Green. — 3rd ed. — South Brunswick, N.J. : Barnes, 1974. — I, 1256.

Greenberg, Alan. Love in vain : the life and legend of Robert Johnson / Alan Greenberg, — Garden City, N.Y. : Doubleday, 1983.

Greene, Bob. Billion dollar baby / Bob Greene. — New York : Atheneum, 1974. — II, 1191.

Greene, Herb. Sunshine daydreams : a Grateful Dead journal / Herb Greene. — San Francisco : Chronicle Books, 1991. — III, 910.

Greene, Myrna. — The Eddie Fisher story / Myrna Greene. — Middlebury, Vt. : Eriksson, 1978. — II, 1077.

Greene, Richard M. The hit parade, 1920 to 1970 / Richard M. Greene. — Tustin, Calif. : Author, 1985. — III, 98.

Greene, Victor. A passion for polka : old-time ethnic music in America / Victor Greene. — Berkeley : University of California Press, 1992. — III, 1210.

Greenspoon, Jimmy. One is the loneliest number : on the road and behind the scenes with the legendary rock band, Three Dog Night / Jimmy Greenspoon; with Mark Bego. — New York : Pharos Books, 1991. — III, 942.

Greenwald, Ted. Rock and roll : the music, musicians, and the mania / Ted Greenwald. — New York : Mallard, 1992. — III, 1117.

Greenway, John. American folksongs of protest / John Greenway. — Philadelphia : University of Pennsylvania Press, 1953. — I, 587.

Greenway, John. Folklore of the great West / John Greenway. — Palo Alto, Calif. : American West, 1969. — I, 510.

Greenwood, Earl. Elvis—top secret : the untold story of Elvis Presley's secret FBI files / Earl Greenwood and Kathleen Tracy. — New York : Signet, 1991. — III, 827.

Greenwood, Earl. The boy who would be king / Earl Greenwood and Kathleen Tracy. — New York : Signet, 1990. — III, 828.

Greer, Jim. R.E.M. : behind the mask / Jim Greer; photographs by Laura Levine. — Boston : Little, Brown, 1992. — III, 934.

Gregory, Hugh. Soul music A-Z / Hugh Gregory. — London : Blandford, 1991. — III, 81.

Gregory, Neal. When Elvis died / Neal Gregory and Janice Gregory. — Washington : Communications, 1980. — II, 1224.

Gribin, Anthony. Doo-wop : the forgotten third of rock 'n' roll / Anthony J. Gribin and Matthew M. Schiff. — Iola, Wisc. : Krause, 1992. — III, 1166.

Grider, Rufus A. Historical notes on music in Bethlehem, Pennsylvania, from 1741 to 1871 / Rufus A. Grider. — Philadelphia : John L. Pile for J. Hill Martin, 1873. — I, 80.

Gridley, Mark C. Concise guide to jazz / Mark C. Gridley. — Englewood Cliffs, N.J. : Prentice-Hall, 1992. — III, 1082.

Gridley, Mark C. How to teach jazz history / Mark Gridley. — Manhattan, Kans. : National Association of Jazz Educators, 1984. — II, A-401.

Gridley, Mark C. Jazz styles : history & analysis / Mark C. Gridley. — 3rd ed. — Englewood Cliffs, N.J. : Prentice-Hall, 1991. — III, 1083.

Gridley, Mark C. Jazz styles / Mark C. Gridley. — 2nd ed. — Englewood Cliffs, N.J. : Prentice-Hall, 1985. — II, 664.

Grieb, Lyndal. The operas of Gian Carlo Menotti, 1937–1972 : a selective bibliography / Lyndal Grieb. — Metuchen, N.J. : Scarecrow, 1974. — I, 339.

Griffin, Sid. Gram Parsons : a music biography / Sid Griffin. — Pasadena : Sierra Records and Books, 1985. — II, A-815.

Griffis, Ken. Hear my song : the story of the celebrated Sons of the Pioneers / Ken Griffis. — Los Angeles : John Edwards Memorial Foundation, 1974. — I, 641.

Griffiths, Paul. Cage / Paul Griffiths. — London : Oxford University Press, 1981. — II, A-114.

Griffiths, Paul. Modern music : the avant garde since 1945 / Paul Griffiths. — London : Dent, 1981. — II, A-90.

Griffiths, Paul. Stravinsky / Paul Griffiths. — London : Dent, 1992. — III, 527.

Griggs, Bill. Buddy Holly : a collector's guide / Bill Griggs and Jim Black. — Sheboygan, Wisc. : Red Wax, 1983. — II, A-803.

Grime, Kitty. Jazz at Ronnie Scott's / Kitty Grime. — London : Robert Hale, 1979. — II, 676.

Grime, Kitty. Jazz voices / Kitty Grime. — London : Quartet, 1983. — II, A-449.

Grissim, John. Country music : white man's blues / John Grissim. — New York : Paperback Library, 1970. — I, A-129; II, 377.

Grissom, Mary Allen. The negro sings a new heaven / Mary Allen Grissom. — Chapel Hill : University of North Carolina Press, 1930. — I, 775.

Groce, Nancy. Musical instrument makers of New York : a directory of eighteenth- and nineteenth-century urban craftsmen / Nancy Groce. — Stuyvesant, N.Y. : Pendragon, 1991. — III, 447.

Groce, Nancy. The hammered dulcimer in America / Nancy Groce. — Washington : Smithsonian Institution Press, 1983. — II, A-206.

Groia, Philip. They all sang on the corner : New York City's rhythm and blues vocal groups of the 1950s / Philip Groia. — Setauket, N.Y. : Edmond, 1973. — I, 884.

Gronow, Pekka. Studies in Scandinavian-American discography / Pekka Gronow. — Helsinki : Finnish Institute of Recorded Sound, 1977. — II, 299.

Gronow, Pekka. The Columbia 33000-F Irish series : a numerical listing / Pekka Gronow. — Los Angeles : John Edwards Memorial Foundation, 1979. — II, 298.

Groom, Bob. The blues revival / Bob Groom. — London : Studio Vista, 1971. — I, 814.

Gross, Michael. Bob Dylan : an illustrated history / Michael Gross. — London : Elm Tree Books, 1978. — II, 1197.

Grossman, Alan. Diamond : a biography / Alan Grossman, Bill Truman, and Roy Oki Yamanaka. — Chicago : Contemporary Books, 1987. — III, 708.

Grossman, Alan. Funnywoman : the life and times of Fanny Brice / Barbara Grossman. — Bloomington : Indiana University Press, 1991. — III, 1292.

Grossman, F. Karl. A history of music in Cleveland / F. Karl Grossman. — Cleveland : Case Western Reserve University, 1972. — II, 58.

Grossman, Lloyd. A social history of rock music / Lloyd Grossman. — New York : McKay, 1976. — S-1150.

Grossman, Stefan. Country blues guitar / Stefan Grossman. — New York : Oak, 1968. — I, 870.

Grossman, Stefan. Country blues songbook / Stefan Grossman [et al]. — New York : Oak, 1973. — I, 871.

Grossman, Stefan. Delta blues guitar / Stefan Grossman. — New York : Oak, 1969. — I, 872.

Grossman, Stefan. Ragtime blues guitar / Stefan Grossman. — New York : Oak, 1970. — I, 873.

Grossman, William L. The heart of jazz / William L. Grossman and Jack W. Farrell. — New York : New York University Press, 1958. — I, 992.

Grosz, Marty. The guitarists / Marty Grosz and Lawrence Cohn. — Alexandria, Va. : Time-Life Records, 1980. — III, 431.

Groves, Alan. Bud Powell / Alan Groves. — Tunbridge Wells, England : Spellmount, 1987. — III, 569.

Groves, Alan. The glass enclosure : the life of Bud Powell / Alan Groves and Alyn Shipton. — Angleton, Tex. : Bayou Press, 1992. — III, 568.

Grubbs, John W. Current thought in musicology / ed. John W. Grubbs. — Austin : University of Texas Press, 1976. — II, 15.

Gruen, John. Menotti : a biography / John Gruen. — New York : Macmillan, 1978. — II, 195.

Gruen, John. The private world of Leonard Bernstein / John Gruen; photographs by Ken Heyman. — New York : Viking, 1968. — I, 304.

Grushkin, Paul. Grateful Dead : the official book of the Dead Heads / Paul Grushkin. — New York : Morrow, 1983. — II, A-797.

Guernsey, Otis L., Jr. Broadway song and story : playwrights/lyricists/composers discuss their hits / Otis L. Guernsey, Jr. — New York : Dodd, Mead, 1985. — III, 1290.

Guernsey, Otis L. Playwrights, lyricists, composers on the theater / Otis L. Guernsey. — New York : Dodd, Mead, 1974. — I, 1257.

Guerry, Jack. Silvio Scionti : remembering a master pianist and teacher / Jack Guerry. — Denton : University of North Texas Press, 1991. — III, 570.

Guida, Louis. Blues music in Arkansas / Louis Guida. — Philadelphia : Portfolio Associates, 1983. — II, A-318.

Guinness encyclopedia of popular music / ed. Colin Larkin. — London : Guinness, 1992. — III, 76.

Guntharp, Matthew G. Learning the fiddler's ways / Matthew G. Guntharp. — University Park : Pennsylvania State University Press, 1980. — II, 326.

Guralnick, Peter. Feel like going home : portraits in blues and rock 'n' roll / Peter Guralnick. — New York : Outerbridge & Dienstfrey, 1971. — I, 830.

Guralnick, Peter. Listener's guide to the blues / Peter Guralnick. — New York : Quarto, 1982. — II, A-311.

Guralnick, Peter. Lost highway : journeys and arrivals of American musicians / Peter Guralnick. — Boston : Godine, 1979. — II, 389.

Guralnick, Peter. Searching for Robert Johnson / Peter Guralnick. — New York : Dutton, 1989. — III, 750.

Guralnick, Peter. Sweet soul music : rhythm and blues and the southern dream of freedom / Peter Guralnick. — New York : Harper & Row, 1986. — III, 1154.

Gusikoff, Lynne. Guide to musical America / Lynne Gusikoff. — New York : Facts on File, 1984. — II, A-145.

Guterman, Jimmy. Rockin' my life away : listening to Jerry Lee Lewis / Jimmy Guterman. — Nashville : Rutledge Hill, 1991. — III, 766.

Guthrie, Woody. American folksong / Woody Guthrie. — New York : Oak, 1961. — I, 595.

Guthrie, Woody. Ballads of Sacco and Vanzetti / Woody Guthrie. — New York : Oak, 1960. — I, A-112.

Guthrie, Woody. Born to win / Woody Guthrie. — New York : Macmillan, 1965. — I, 596.

Guthrie, Woody. Bound for glory / Woody Guthrie. — New York : Dutton, 1943. — I, 597.

Guthrie, Woody. California to the New York island / Woody Guthrie. — New York : Guthrie Children's Trust Fund, 1960. — I, 598.

Guthrie, Woody. Pastures of plenty : a self-portrait / Woody Guthrie; ed. Dave Marsh and Harold Leventhal. — New York : Harper & Row, 1990. — III, 482.

Guthrie, Woody. Seeds of man : an experience lived and dreamed / Woody Guthrie. — New York : Dutton, 1976. — II, 347.

Gutman, Bill. Duke : the musical life of Duke Ellington / Bill Gutman. — New York : Random House, 1977. — II, 792.

Guttridge, Leonard F. Jack Teagarden / Leonard F. Guttridge. — Alexandria, Va. : Time-Life Records, 1979. — III, 670.

Haas, Oscar. A chronological history of the singers of German songs in Texas / Oscar Haas. — New Brunfels, Tex. : Author, 1948. — I, 128.

Haas, Robert Bartlett. William Grant Still and the fusion of cultures in American music / ed. Robert Bartlett Haas [et al]. — Los Angeles : Black Sparrow, 1972. — I, 348.

Hackett, Karleton. The beginning of grand opera in Chicago (1850–1859) / Karleton Hackett. — Chicago : Laurentian Publishers, 1913. — I, A-54.

Hadlock, Richard. Jazz masters of the twenties / Richard Hadlock. — New York : Macmillan, 1965. — I, 1029.

Haefer, J. Richard. Papago music and dance / J. Richard Haefer. — Tsaile, Ariz. : Navajo Community College Press, 1977. — II, 250.

Haeussler, Armin. The story of our hymns / Armin Haeussler. — St. Louis : Eden, 1952. — II, 30.

Hagan, Chet. Country music legends in the Hall of Fame / Chet Hagan. — Nashville : Country Music Foundation, 1982. — II, A-241.

Hagan, Chet. Grand Ole Opry / Chet Hagan. — New York : Holt, 1989. — III, 1162.

Hagan, Chet. The great country music book / Chet Hagan. — New York : Pocket Books, 1983. — II, A-220.

Hagarty, Britt. The day the world turned blue : a biography of Gene Vincent / Britt Hagarty. — Vancouver : Talon, 1983. — II, A-851.

Hagen, Earle. Scoring for films : a complete text / Earle Hagen. — New York : Criterion, 1971. — II, 938.

Hager, Steven. Hip hop : the illustrated history of break dancing, rap music, and graffiti / Steven Hager. — New York : St. Martin's, 1984. — II, A-361.

Haggard, Merle. Sing me back home / Merle Haggard and Peggy Russell. — New York : Times Books, 1981. — II, A-251.

Haglund, Urban. A listing of bluegrass LP's / Urban Haglund and Lillies Ohlsson. — Vasteras, Sweden : Kountry Korral, 1971. — I, 624.

Hague, Eleanor. Spanish-American folk songs / Eleanor Hague. — Lancaster, Pa. : American Folk-lore Society, 1917. — I, 473.

Haines, Connie. For once in my life / Connie Haines; as told to Robert B. Stone. — New York : Warner, 1976. — II, 751.

Hainsworth, Brian. Songs by Sinatra / Brian Hainsworth. — Bramhope, Leeds, England : Author, 1973. — I, 1334.

Hale, Philip. Philip Hale's Boston Symphony programme notes / Philip Hale. — Garden City, N.Y. : Doubleday, 1935. — I, A-35.

Haley, John W. Sound and glory : the incredible story of Bill Haley, the father of rock 'n' roll and the music that shook the world / John W. Haley and John von Hoelle. — Wilmington, Del. : Dyne-American, 1990. — III, 728.

Halker, Clark. For democracy, workers, and God : labor song-poems and labor protest, 1865–95 / Clark D. Halker. — Urbana : University of Illinois Press, 1991. — III, 1211.

Hall, Douglas Kent. Rock : a world as bold as love / Douglas Kent Hall and Sue C. Clark. — New York : Cowles, 1970. — I, 1352.

Hall, Fred. Dialogues in swing : intimate conversations with the stars of the big band era / Fred Hall; foreword by Artie Shaw. — Ventura, Calif. : Pathfinder, 1989. — III, 1136.

Hall, Fred. More dialogues in swing : intimate conversations with the stars of the big band era / Fred Hall; foreword by Jo Stafford and Paul Weston. — Ventura, Calif. : Pathfinder, 1991. — III, 1137.

Hall, George. Jan Savitt and his orchestra / George Hall. — Zephyrhills, Fla. : Joyce Record Club, 1985. — III, 354.

Hall, Harry H. A Johnny Reb band from Salem / Harry H. Hall. — Raleigh, N.C. : North Carolina Confederate Centennial Commission, 1963. — II, 876.

Hall, J. H. Biography of gospel song and hymn writers / J. H. Hall. — New York : Fleming H. Revell, 1914. — I, 72.

Hall, Ruth K. A place of her own : the story of Elizabeth Garrett / Ruth K. Hall. — Rev. ed. — Santa Fe, N.M. : Sunstone, 1983. — III, 474.

Hall, Ruth K. A place of her own : the story of Elizabeth Garrett / Ruth K. Hall. — Santa Fe, N.M. : Sunstone, 1976. — II, 865.

Hall, Stuart. The popular arts / Stuart Hall and Paddy Whannel. — London : Hutchinson Educational, 1964. — I, 1164.

Hall, Tom T. The storyteller's Nashville / Tom T. Hall. — Garden City, N.Y. : Doubleday, 1979. — II, 401.

Halloran, Mark. The musician's business and legal guide / Mark Halloran. — 4th ed. — Englewood Cliffs, N.J. : Prentice-Hall, 1991. — III, 1243.

Hallowell, Emily. Calhoun plantation songs / Emily Hallowell. — 2nd ed. — Boston : C. W. Thompson, 1907. — I, 776.

Hallowell, John. Inside Creedence / John Hallowell. — New York : Bantam, 1971. — I, A-292.

Hames, Mike. Albert Ayler, Sunny Murray, Cecil Taylor, Byard Lancaster, and Kenneth Terroade on disc and tape / Mike Hames. — Ferndown, Dorset, England : Author, 1983. — II, A-374.

Hamilton, Virginia. Paul Robeson : the life and times of a free black man / Virginia Hamilton. — New York : Harper & Row, 1974. — II, 515.

Hamlisch, Marvin. The way I was / Marvin Hamlisch; with Gerald Gardner. — New York : Scribner's, 1992. — III, 484.

Hamm, Charles. Afro-American music, South Africa, and apartheid / Charles Hamm. — Brooklyn : Institute for Studies in American Music, 1988. — III, 1220.

Hamm, Charles. Contemporary music and music cultures / Charles Hamm [et al]. — Englewood Cliffs, N.J. : Prentice-Hall, 1975. — II, 158.

Hamm, Charles. Music in the new world / Charles Hamm. — New York : Norton, 1983. — II, A-12.

Hamm, Charles. Yesterdays : popular song in America / Charles Hamm. — New York : Norton, 1979. — II, 835.

Hammerstein, Oscar, II. Lyrics / Oscar Hammerstein II. — Milwaukee : Hal Leonard Books, 1985. — II, A-602.

Hammerstein, Oscar, II. Lyrics / Oscar Hammerstein II. — New York : Simon & Schuster, 1949. — I, 1287.

Hammond, John. John Hammond on record : an autobiography / John Hammond; with Irving Townsend. — New York : Ridge Press, 1977. — II, 669.

Hammontree, Patsy Guy. Elvis Presley : a bio-bibliography / Patsy Guy Hammontree. — Westport, Conn. : Greenwood, 1985. — III, 829.

Hampton, Lionel. Hamp : an autobiography / Lionel Hampton; with James Haskins. — New York : Warner Books, 1989. — III, 640.

Hampton, Wayne. Guerilla minstrels : John Lennon, Joe Hill, Woody Guthrie, and Bob Dylan / Wayne Hampton. — Knoxville : University of Tennessee Press, 1986. — III, 1057.

Handel and Haydn Society, Boston. History of the Handel and Haydn Society of Boston, Massachusetts. — Boston : Mudge [varies], 1883–1934. — I, 96.

Handel's national directory for the performing arts. — 5th ed. — New York : Bowker, 1992. — III, 39.

Handy, D. Antoinette. Black music : opinions and reviews / D. Antoinette Handy. — Ettrick, Va. : BM & M, 1974. — II, 499.

Handy, D. Antoinette. Black women in American bands and orchestras / D. Antoinette Handy. — Metuchen, N.J. : Scarecrow, 1981. — II, A-297.

Handy, D. Antoinette. The International Sweethearts of Rhythm / D. Antoinette Handy. — Metuchen, N.J. : Scarecrow, 1983. — II, A-483.

Handy, W. C. Blues : an anthology / W. C. Handy. — Rev. ed. — New York : Macmillan, 1972. — I, 874.

Handy, W. C. Father of the blues : an autobiography / W. C. Handy. — New York : Macmillan, 1941. — I, 838.

Handy, W. C. Negro authors and composers of the United States / W. C. Handy. — New York : Handy Brothers, 1938. — I, 703.

Hanel, Ed. The essential guide to rock books / Ed Hanel. — London : Omnibus, 1983. — II, A-646.

Hannerz, Ulf. Soulside : inquiries into ghetto culture and community / Ulf Hannerz. — New York : Columbia University Press, 1969. — I, 665.

Hanson, Howard. Music in contemporary American civilization / Howard Hanson. — Lincoln : University of Nebraska Press, 1951. — I, 294.

Haralambos, Michael. Right on : from blues to soul in black America / Michael Haralambos. — London : Eddison Press, 1974. — I, 892.

Haraszti, Zoltan. The enigma of the Bay Psalm Book / Zoltan Haraszti. — Chicago : University of Chicago Press, 1956. — I, 191.

Harbinson, W. A. Elvis Presley : an illustrated biography / W. A. Harbinson. — London : Michael Joseph, 1975. — II, 1225.

Harbinson, W. A. The life and death of Elvis Presley / W. A. Harbinson. — London : Michael Joseph, 1977. — II, 1225.

Hardy, Phil. The encyclopedia of rock / Phil Hardy and Dave Laing. — St. Albans, England : Panther, 1976. — II, 1099.

Hardy, Phil. The encyclopedia of rock 1955–1975 / Phil Hardy and Dave Laing. — London : Aquarius, 1977. — II, 1099.

Hare, Walter Ben. The minstrel encyclopedia / Walter Ben Hare. — Boston : Baker, 1921. — I, A-256.

Harker, Dave. One for the money : politics and popular song / Dave Harker. — London : Hutchinson, 1980. — II, 1151.

Harkreader, Sidney J. Fiddlin' Sid's memoirs / Sidney J. Harkreader. — Los Angeles : John Edwards Memorial Foundation, 1976. — II, 402.

Harlow, Frederick Pease. Chanteying aboard American ships / Frederick Pease Harlow. — Barre, Mass. : Barre Gazette, 1962. — I, A-113.

Harmetz, Aljean. The making of "The Wizard of Oz" / Aljean Harmetz. — New York : Knopf, 1978. — II, 929.

Harper, Francis. Okefinokee album / Francis Harper and Delma E. Presley. — Athens : University of Georgia Press, 1981. — II, A-188.

Harper, Michael S. Chant of saints : a gathering of Afro-American literature, art, and scholarship / Michael S. Harper and Robert B. Stepto. — Urbana : University of Illinois Press, 1979. — II, 495.

Harris, Charles K. After the ball : forty years of melody : an autobiography / Charles K. Harris. — New York : Frank-Maurice, 1926. — I, 1215.

Harris, Charles W. The cowboy : six-shooters, songs, and sex / Charles W. Harris and Buck Rainey. — Norman : University of Oklahoma Press, 1976. — II, 338.

Harris, Craig. The new folk music / Craig Harris. — Crown Point, N.Y. : White Cliffs Media, 1991. — III, 403.

Harris, Michael W. The rise of gospel blues : the music of Thomas Andrew Dorsey in the urban church / Michael W. Harris. — New York : Oxford, 1992. — III, 1040.

Harris, Rex. Enjoying jazz / Rex Harris. — London : Phoenix House, 1961. — I, A-109.

Harris, Rex. Jazz / Rex Harris. — 4th ed. — Harmondsworth, England : Penguin, 1956. — I, 1003.

Harris, Rex. Recorded jazz : a critical guide / Rex Harris and Brian Rust. — Harmondsworth, England : Penguin, 1958. — I, 957.

Harris, Sheldon. Blues who's who / Sheldon Harris. — New Rochelle, N.Y. : Arlington House, 1979. — II, 538.

Harris, Steve. Film, television, and stage music on phonograph records : a discography / Steve Harris. — Jefferson, N.C. : McFarland, 1988. — III, 243.

Harris, Steve. Jazz on compact disc : a critical guide to the best recordings / Steve Harris. — New York : Harmony Books/Crown, 1987. — III, 239.

Harris, Thomas J. Children's live-action musical films : a critical survey and filmography / Thomas J. Harris. — Jefferson, N.C. : McFarland, 1990. — III, 1282.

Harrison, Conrad B. Five thousand concerts : a commemorative history of the Utah Symphony / Conrad B. Harrison. — Salt Lake City : Utah Symphony Society, 1986. — III, 1002.

Harrison, Daphne Duvall. Black pearls : blues queens of the 1920s / Daphne Duvall Harrison. — New Brunswick, N.J. : Rutgers University Press, 1988. — III, 1155.

Harrison, Hank. The Dead / Hank Harrison. — Milbrae, Calif. : Celestial Arts, 1980. — II, 1206.

Harrison, Hank. The Dead book : a social history of the Grateful Dead / Hank Harrison. — New York : Links Books, 1973. — I, A-293.

Harrison, Lou. About Carl Ruggles : section four of a book on Ruggles / Lou Harrison; with a note by Henry Cowell. — Yonkers, N.Y. : Oscar Baradinsky at the Alicat Bookshop, 1946. — I, 344.

Harrison, Lou. Music primer : various items about music to 1970 / Lou Harrison. — New York : Peters, 1971. — I, 322.

Harrison, Max. A jazz retrospect / Max Harrison. — Boston : Crescendo, 1976. — II, 704.

Harrison, Max. Charlie Parker / Max Harrison. — London : Cassell, 1960. — I, 1133.

Harrison, Max. Modern jazz : the essential records / Max Harrison [et al]. — London : Aquarius, 1975. — I, 959.

Harrison, Max. The essential jazz records. Volume 1, Ragtime to swing / Max Harrison, Charles Fox and Eric Thacker. — Westport, Conn. : Greenwood, 1984. — III, 240.

Harrison, William P. The gospel among the slaves / William P. Harrison. — Nashville : M. E. Church, 1893. — I, A-165.

Harry, Debbie. Making tracks : the rise of Blondie / Debbie Harry [et al]. — New York : Dell, 1982. — II, A-770.

Hart, Dorothy. Thou swell, thou witty : the life and lyrics of Lorenz Hart / Dorothy Hart. — New York : Harper & Row, 1976. — II, 949.

Hart, Kitty Carlisle. Kitty : an autobiography / Kitty Carlisle Hart. — New York : Doubleday, 1988. — III, 697.

Hart, Lorenz. The complete lyrics of Lorenz Hart / ed. Dorothy Hart and Robert Kimball. — New York : Knopf, 1986. — III, 50.

Hart, Mary L. The blues : a bibliographic guide / Mary L. Hart, Brenda M. Eagles, and Lisa N. Howorth; introduction by William Ferris. — New York : Garland, 1989. — III, 119.

Hart, Mickey. Drumming at the edge of magic : a journey into the spirit of percussion / Mickey Hart; with Jay Stevens and Fredric Lieberman. — San Francisco : Harper, 1990. — III, 432.

Hart, Moss. Act one : an autobiography / Moss Hart. — New York : Random House, 1959. — II, 950.

Hart, Philip. Orpheus in the new world : the symphony orchestra as an American cultural institution / Philip Hart. — New York : Norton, 1973. — II, 46.

Hartley, Kenneth R. Bibliography of theses and dissertations in sacred music / Kenneth R. Hartley. — Detroit : Information Coordinators, 1966. — I, 59.

Hartman, Charles O. Jazz text : voice and improvisation in poetry, jazz, and song / Charles O. Hartman. — Princeton, N.J. : Princeton University Press, 1991. — III, 1084.

Hartsock, Ralph. Otto Luening : a bio-bibliography / Ralph Hartsock. — New York : Greenwood, 1991. — III, 171.

Hartzell, Lawrence W. Ohio Moravian music / Lawrence W. Hartzell. — Winston-Salem, N.C. : Moravian Music Foundation Press, 1988. — III, 1035.

Harvey, Eddie. Jazz piano / Eddie Harvey. — London : English Universities Press, 1974. — I, 982.

Harvey, Jacques. Monsieur Sinatra / Jacques Harvey. — Paris : Albin Michel, 1976. — II, 1089.

Harvey, Stephen. Fred Astaire / Stephen Harvey. — New York : Pyramid, 1975. — II, 1065.

Harwell, Richard B. Confederate music / Richard B. Harwell. — Chapel Hill : University of North Carolina Press, 1950. — I, 168.

Hasebe, Koh. Music life rock photo gallery / Koh Hasebe. — New York : Sire / Chappell, 1976. — II, 1273.

Haselgrove, J. R. Readers' guide to books on jazz / J. R. Haselgrove and Donald Kennington. — 2nd ed. — London : Library Association, 1965. — I, 913.

Haskins, James. Donna Summer / James Haskins and J. M. Stifle. — Boston : Little, Brown, 1983. — II, A-845.

Haskins, James. Ella Fitzgerald : a life through jazz / Jim Haskins. — London : New English Library, 1991. — III, 721.

Haskins, James. I'm gonna make you love me : the story of Diana Ross / James Haskins. — New York : Dial, 1980. — II, 572.

Haskins, James. Lena : a personal and professional biography of Lena Horne / James Haskins; with Kathleen Benson. — New York : Stein & Day, 1984. — II, A-629.

Haskins, James. Mabel Mercer : a life / James Haskins. New York : Atheneum, 1987. — III, 786.

Haskins, James. Nat King Cole / James Haskins. — New York : Stein & Day, 1984. — II, A-622.

Haskins, James. Queen of the blues : a biography of Dinah Washington / James Haskins. — New York : Morrow, 1987. — III, 884.

Haskins, James. Scatman : an authorized biography of Scatman Crothers / Jim Haskins; with Helen Crothers. — New York : Morrow, 1991. — III, 707.

Haskins, James. Scott Joplin / James Haskins. — Garden City, N.Y. : Doubleday, 1978. — II, 536.

Haskins, James. The Cotton Club / James Haskins. — New York : Random House, 1977. — II, 677.

Haskins, James. The story of Stevie Wonder / James Haskins. — New York : Lothrop, Lee & Shepard, 1976. — II, 576.

Hasse, John Edward. Ragtime : its history, composers, and music / John Edward Hasse. — New York : Schirmer, 1985. — II, A-310.

Hastings, George Everett. The life and works of Francis Hopkinson / George Everett Hastings. — Chicago : University of Chicago Press, 1926. — I, 203.

Hastings, Thomas. Dissertation on musical taste / Thomas Hastings. — New York : Mason, 1853. — I, 213.

Hastings, Thomas. History of forty choirs / Thomas Hastings. — New York : Mason, 1854. — I, 60.

Hatch, James V. Black image on the American stage / James V. Hatch. — New York : Drama Book Specialists, 1971. — I, 1231.

Hatfield, Edwin F. The poets of the church / Edwin F. Hatfield. — New York : Randolph, 1884. — I, A-19.

Hatfield, Edwin Francis. Freedom's lyre / Edwin Francis Hatfield. — New York : S. W. Benedict, 1840. — II, 604.

Hauser, William. The Hesperian harp / William Hauser. — Philadelphia, 1848. — I, 533.

Havlice, Patricia Pate. Popular song index / Patricia Pate Havlice. — Metuchen, N.J. : Scarecrow, 1975. — 1st supplement, 1978; 2nd supplement, 1984. — II, 804.

Hawes, Hampton. Raise up off me : a portrait of Hampton Hawes / Hampton Hawes and Don Asher. — Reprint with new introduction by Gary Giddins. — New York : Da Capo, 1979. — II, 752.

Hay, George D. Story of the Grand Ole Opry / George D. Hay. — Nashville : Author, 1953. — I, 620.

Haydon, Geoffrey. Repercussions : a celebration of Afro-American music / Geoffrey Haydon and Dennis Marks. — London : Century, 1985. — II, A-294.

Hayes, Cedric. Discography of gospel records, 1937–1971 / Cedric Hayes. — Copenhagen : Knudsen, 1973. — I, 896.

Haywood, Charles. Bibliography of North American folklore and folksong / Charles Haywood. — 2nd ed. — New York : Dover, 1961. — I, 429.

Hazen, Margaret Hindle. The music men : an illustrated history of brass bands in America, 1800–1920 / Margaret Hindle Hazen and Robert M. Hazen. — Washington : Smithsonian Institution Press, 1987. — III, 1003.

Head, Heno. America's favorite janitor : the life story of country songwriter Johnny Mullins / Heno Head, Jr.; foreword by Emmylou Harris. — Independence, Mo. : International University Press, 1986. — III, 503.

Heaps, Willard A. The singing sixties : the spirit of Civil War days drawn from the music of the times / Willard A. Heaps and Porter W. Heaps. — Norman : University of Oklahoma Press, 1960. — I, 1190.

Heard, Priscilla S. American music 1698–1800 : an annotated bibliography / Priscilla S. Heard. — Waco, Tex. : Markham Press Fund, Baylor University Press, 1975. — II, 135.

Hearn, Lafcadio. American miscellany / Lafcadio Hearn. — New York : Dodd, Mead, 1924. — I, A-166.

Heartz, Daniel. Report of the twelfth congress of the International Musicological Society / Daniel Heartz and Bonnie Wade. — Kassel : Bärenreiter, 1981. — II, A-15.

Hebey, Jean-Bernard. Encyclopédie illustrée du rock / Jean-Bernard Hebey. — Paris : R.T.L. Editions, 1981. — II, A-656.

Hedges, Dan. Eddie VanHalen / Dan Hedges. — New York : Vintage, 1985. — III, 593.

Hefele, Bernhard. Jazz-Bibliographie / Bernhard Hefele. — Munich : Saur, 1981. — II, A-364.

Hefley, James C. How sweet the sound / James C. Hefley. — Wheaton, Ill. : Tyndale House, 1981. — II, A-26.

Heilbut, Tony. — Gospel sound : good news and bad times / Tony Heilbut. — New York : Simon & Schuster, 1971. — I, 897.

Heintze, James R. American music before 1865 in print and on records / James R. Heintze. — 2nd ed. — Brooklyn : Institute for Studies in American Music, 1990. — III, 95.

Heintze, James R. American music studies : a classified bibliography of master's theses / James R. Heintze. — Detroit : Information Coordinators, 1984. — II, A-2.

Heintze, James R. Early American music : a research and information guide / James R. Heintze. — New York : Garland Publishing, 1990. — III, 99.

Heintze, James R. Esther Williamson Ballou : a bio-bibliography / James R. Heintze. — New York : Greenwood, 1987. — III, 157.

Heintze, James R. Scholars' guide to Washington, D.C., for audio resources / James R. Heintze. — Washington : Smithsonian Institution Press, 1985. — III, 33.

Heisley, Micahel. An annotated bibliography of Chicano folklore from the Southwestern United States / Michael Heisley. — Los Angeles : University of California, 1977. — II, 434.

Helander, Brock. The rock who's who : a biographical dictionary and critical discography including rhythm-and-blues, soul, rockabilly, folk, country, easy listening, punk, and new wave / Brock Helander. — New York : Schirmer, 1982. — III, 80.

Hellhund, Hubert. Cool jazz / Hubert Hellhund. — Mainz, Germany : Schott, 1985. — II, A-439.

Helm, MacKinley. Angel Mo' and her son, Roland Hayes / MacKinley Helm. — Boston : Little, Brown, 1944. — I, 708.

Hemming, Roy. Discovering great singers of classic pop : a new listener's guide to the sounds and lives of the top performers and their recordings, movies, and videos / Roy Hemming and David Hajdu. — New York : Newmarket, 1991. — III, 440.

Hemming, Roy. The melody lingers on : the great songwriters and their movie musicals / Roy Hemming. — New York : Newmarket, 1986. — III, 1283.

Hemphill, La Breeska Rogers. La Breeska : an autobiography / La Breeska Rogers Hemphill. — Nashville : Hemphill Music Co., 1976. — II, 40.

Hemphill, Paul. The good old boys / Paul Hemphill. — New York : Simon & Schuster, 1974. — II, 471.

Hemphill, Paul. — The Nashville sound : bright lights and country music / Paul Hemphill. — New York : Simon & Schuster, 1970. — I, 631.

Henderson, Clayton W. The Charles Ives tunebook / Clayton W. Anderson. — Warren, Mich. : Harmonie Park, 1990. — III, 168.

Henderson, David. Jimi Hendrix : voodoo child of the Aquarian age / David Henderson. — Garden City, N.Y. : Doubleday, 1978. — II, 1207.

Henderson, David. 'Scuse me while I kiss the sky : the life of Jimi Hendrix / David Henderson. — New York : Bantam, 1981. — II, 1207.

Henderson, Stephen. Understanding the new black poetry / Stephen Henderson. — New York : Morrow, 1973. — II, 490.

Hendler, Herb. Year by year in the rock era / Herb Hendler. — Westport, Conn. : Greenwood, 1983. — II, A-658.

Hennessee, Don A. Samuel Barber : a bio-bibliography / Don A. Hennessee. — Westport, Conn. : Greenwood, 1985. — II, A-109.

Hennessey, Mike. Klook : the Kenny Clarke story / Mike Hennessey. — London : Quartet, 1990. — III, 616.

Henry Mancini : an American Film Institute seminar on his work. — Glen Rock, N.J. : Microfilming Corp. of America, 1977. — II, 1054.

Henry, Mellinger Edward. A bibliography for the study of American folksongs / Mellinger Edward Henry. — London : Mitre, 1936. — I, 430.

Henry, Mellinger Edward. Folk-songs from the Southern Highlands / Mellinger Edward Henry. — New York : Augustin, 1938. — I, A-114.

Henry, Mellinger Edward. Songs sung in the Southern Appalachians / Mellinger Edward Henry. — London : Mitre, 1934. — I, A-115.

Henry, Robert E. The jazz ensemble / Robert E. Henry. — Englewood Cliffs, N.J. ; Prentice-Hall, 1981. — II, A-402.

Henry, Tricia. Break all rules! : punk rock and the making of a style / Tricia Henry. — Ann Arbor, Mich. : UMI Research Press, 1989. — III, 1178.

Hensel, Octavia. Life and letters of Louis Moreau Gottschalk / Octavia Hensel. — Boston : Ditson, 1870. — I, 228.

Hentoff, Nat. Boston boy / Nat Hentoff. — New York : Knopf, 1986. — III, 1302.

Hentoff, Nat. Jazz is / Nat Hentoff. — New York : Random House, 1976. — II, 732.

Hentoff, Nat. The jazz life / Nat Hentoff. — New York : Dial, 1961. — I, 973.

Hentoff, Nat. Jazz : new perspectives on the history of jazz / Nat Hentoff and Albert J. McCarthy. — New York : Rinehart, 1959. — I, 1020.

Herbst, Peter. The Rolling Stone interviews, 1967–1980 : talking with the legends of rock & roll / ed. Peter Herbst. — New York : St. Martin's, 1981. — II, A-758.

Herdman, John. Voice without restraint : a study of Dylan's lyrics and their background / John Herdman. — Edinburgh : Paul Harris, 1982. — II, A-787.

Herman, Gary. Rock 'n' roll Babylon / Gary Herman. — London : Plexus, 1982. — II, A-724.

Herman, Woody. The woodchoppers ball : the autobiography of Woody Herman. — New York : Dutton, 1990. — III, 644.

Herndon, Marcia. Native American music / Marcia Herndon. — Darby, Pa. : Norwood Editions, 1980. — II, 239.

Hershey, Geri. Nowhere to run : the story of soul music / Geri Hershey. — New York : Times Books, 1984. — II, A-351.

Herskovits, Melville J. The myth of the negro past / Melville J. Herskovits. — Rev. ed. — Boston : Beacon, 1958. — I, 666.

Herzhaft, Gérard. Encyclopedia of the blues / Gérard Herzhaft. — Fayetteville : University of Arkansas Press, 1992. — III, 66.

Herzhaft, Gérard. Encyclopédie du blues / Gérard Herzhaft. — Lyon, France : Fédérop, 1979. — II, 539.

Herzog, George. Research in primitive and folk music in the United States : a survey / George Herzog. — Washington : American Council of Learned Societies, 1936. — I, 431.

Heskes, Irene. Resource book of Jewish music / Irene Heskes. — Westport, Conn. : Greenwood, 1985. — II, A-3.

Heskes, Irene. Yiddish American popular songs, 1895 to 1950 : a catalog based on the Lawrence Marwick roster of copyright entries / Irene Heskes. — Washington : Library of Congress, 1992. — III, 129.

Hester, Mary Lee. Going to Kansas City / Mary Lee Hester. — Sherman, Tex. : Early Bird, 1980. — II, 726.

Heth, Charlotte. Sharing a heritage : American Indian arts / Charlotte Heth. — Los Angeles : American Indian Studies Center, 1984. — II, A-159.

Hewitt, John Hill. Shadows on the wall / John Hill Hewitt. — Baltimore : Turnbull, 1877. — I, 1217.

Heylin, Clinton. Bob Dylan : behind the shades : a biography / Clinton Heylin. — New York : Summit Books, 1991. — III, 712.

Heylin, Clinton. Rain unravelled tales / Clinton Heylin. — Sale, Cheshire, England : Ashes & Sand, 1982. — II, A-788.

Heyman, Barbara B. Samuel Barber : the composer and his music / Barbara B. Heyman. — New York : Oxford, 1992. — III, 450.

Hibbard, Don. The role of rock / Don Hibbard and Carol Kaleialoha. — Englewood Cliffs, N.J. : Prentice-Hall, 1983. — II, A-730.

Hibbert, Tom. Rare records : wax trash and vinyl treasures / Tom Hibbert. — London : Proteus, 1982. — II, A-675.

Hibbert, Tom. The dictionary of rock terms / Tom Hibbert. — London : Omnibus, 1982. — II, A-659.

Hicks, Daryl. God comes to Nashville / Daryl Hicks. — Harrison, Ark. : New Leaf, 1979. — II, 472.

Hicks, Michael. Mormonism and music : a history / Michael Hicks. — Urbana : University of Illinois Press, 1989. — III, 45.

Hicks, Val. Heritage of harmony / Val Hicks. — Kenosha, Wisc. : Society for the Preservation and Encouragement of Barbershop Singing in America, 1988. — III, 45.

Higgins, Dick. Computers for the arts / Dick Higgins. — Somerville, Mass. : Abyss Publications, 1970. — I, A-78.

Higgins, Dick. Postface / Dick Higgins. — New York : Something Else Press, 1964. — I, 323.

Higginson, J. Vincent. Handbook for American Catholic hymnals. / J. Vincent Higginson. — New York : Hymn Society of America, 1976. — II, 31.

Higginson, J. Vincent. Hymnody in the American Indian missions / J. Vincent Higginson. — New York : Hymn Society of America, 1954. — II, 32.

Higginson, Thomas Wentworth. Army life in a black regiment / Thomas Wentworth Higginson. — New ed. — Boston : Houghton Mifflin, 1900. — I, 791.

High, Ellen Clay. Past Titan Rock : journeys into an Appalachian valley / Ellen Clay High. — Lexington : University Press of Kentucky, 1984. — II, A-192.

Higham, Charles. Ziegfeld / Charles Higham. — London : W. H. Allen, 1973. — II, 1045.

Highwater, Jamake. Ritual of the wind : North American Indian ceremonies, music, and dances / Jamake Highwater. — New York : Viking, 1977. — II, 240.

Hilbert, Robert. Pee Wee speaks : a discography of Pee Wee Russell / Robert Hilbert; with David Niven. — Metuchen, N.J. : Scarecrow, 1992. — III, 353.

Hilburn, Robert. Bruce Springsteen : born in the U.S.A. / Robert Hilburn. — London : Sidgwick & Jackson, 1985. — III, 865.

Hill, Dave. Prince : a pop life / Dave Hill. — London : Faber & Faber, 1989. — III, 848.

Hill, Fred. Grass roots : illustrated history of bluegrass and mountain music / Fred Hill. — II, 372.

Hill, Joe. Songs of Joe Hill / Joe Hill. — New York : People's Artists, 1955. — I, 591.

Hill, Michael. Jelly Roll Morton : a microgroove discography and musical analysis / Michael Hill and Eric Bryce. — Salisbury East, South Australia : Salisbury College of Advanced Education, 1977. — II, 763.

Hill, Randall C. The official price guide to collectible rock records / Randall C. Hill. — Orlando, Fla. : House of Collectibles, 1979. — II, 1251.

Hiller, Lejaren. Experimental music : composition with an electronic computer / Lejaren Hiller and Leonard M. Isaacson. — New York : McGraw-Hill, 1959. — I, 281.

Hillman, Christopher. Bunk Johnson : his life & times / Christopher Hillman. — New York : Universe, 1988. — III, 649   .

Hillman, Joseph. The revivalist / Joseph Hillman. — Rev. ed. — Troy, N.Y. : Author, 1872. — I, 536.

Hines, Robert Stephan. The composer's point of view / Robert Stephan Hines. — Norman : University of Oklahoma Press, 1963. — I, 260.

Hines, Robert Stephan. The orchestral composer's point of view / Robert Stephan Hines. — Norman : University of Oklahoma Press, 1970. — I, 261.

Hinks, Donald R. Brethren hymn books and hymnals, 1720–1884 / Donald R. Hinks. — Gettysburg, Pa. : Heritage, 1986. — III, 1033.

Hinton, Milt. Bass line : the stories and photographs of Milt Hinton / Milt Hinton and David G. Berger; foreword by Dan Morgenstern. — Philadelphia : Temple University Press, 1988. — III, 585.

Hippenmeyer, Jean-Roland. Jazz sur films / Jean-Roland Hippenmeyer. — Yverdon, France : Éditions de la Thièle, 1973. — II, 631.

Hippenmeyer, Jean-Roland. Sidney Bechet / Jean-Roland Hippenmeyer. — Geneva : Tribune Editions, 1980. — II, 738.

Hipsher, Edward Ellsworth. American opera and its composers / Edward Ellsworth Hipsher. — Philadelphia : Presser, 1927. — I, 53.

Hirsch, Abby. The photography of rock / Abby Hirsch. — New York : Bobbs-Merrill, 1972. — II, 1163.

Hirsch, Foster. Harold Prince and the American musical theatre / Foster Hirsch. — Cambridge, England : Cambridge University Press, 1989. — III, 981.

Hirsch, Paul. The structure of the popular music industry / Paul Hirsch. — Ann Arbor, Mich. : Institute of Social Research, 1970. - — I, 1345.

Hirschhorn, Clive. Gene Kelly : a biography / Clive Hirschhorn. — Rev. ed. — London : W. H. Allen, 1984. — II, 976.

Hirschhorn, Clive. The Hollywood musical / Clive Hirschhorn. — London : Octopus 1981. — II, A-588.

Hischak, Thomas S. Word crazy : Broadway lyricists from Cohan to Sondheim / Thomas S. Hischak. — New York : Praeger, 1991. — III, 1298.

Historical Records Survey, District of Columbia. Bio-bibliographical index of musicians in the United States of America since colonial times. — 2nd ed. — Washington : Pan American Union, Music Section, 1956. — I, 14.

Hitchcock, H. Wiley. After 100 (!) years : the editorial side of Sonneck / H. Wiley Hitchcock. — Washington : Library of Congress, 1975. — II, 211.

Hitchcock, H. Wiley. An Ives celebration / ed. H. Wiley Hitchcock and Vivian Perlis. — Urbana : University of Illinois Press, 1977. — II, 190.

Hitchcock, H. Wiley. Ives / H. Wiley Hitchcock. — London : Oxford University Press, 1977. — II, 189.

Hitchcock, H. Wiley. Music in the United States : a historical introduction / H. Wiley Hitchcock. — 3rd ed. — Englewood Cliffs, N.J. : Prentice-Hall, 1988. — III, 368.

Hitchcock, H. Wiley. Music in the United States : a historical introduction / H. Wiley Hitchcock. — 2nd ed. — Englewood Cliffs, N.J. : Prentice-Hall, 1974. — I, 30.

Hitchcock, H. Wiley. The phonograph and our musical life / ed. H. Wiley Hitchcock. — Brooklyn : Institute for Studies in American Music, 1980. — II, 105.

Hixon, Donald L. Music in early America : a bibliography of music in Evans / Donald L. Hixon. — Metuchen, N.J. : Scarecrow, 1970. — I, 1.

Hixon, Donald L. Women in music : a bio-bibliography / Don L. Hixon and Don Hennessee. — Metuchen, N.J. : Scarecrow, 1975. — I, 45.

Hoare, Ian. The soul book / ed. Ian Hoare. — London : Eyre Methuen, 1975. — II, 567.

Hobson, Wilder. American jazz music / Wilder Hobson. — Rev. ed. — London : Dent, 1941. — I, 1030.

Hodeir, André. Hommes et problèmes du jazz / André Hodeir. — Paris : Portulan, 1954. — I, 993.

Hodeir, André. Jazz : its evolution and essence / André Hodeir. — New York : Grove, 1956. — I, 993.

Hodeir, André. Les mondes du jazz / André Hodeir. — Paris : Union Générale, 1970. — I, 995.

Hodeir, André. The worlds of jazz / André Hodeir. — New York : Grove, 1972. — I, 995.

Hodeir, André. Toward jazz / André Hodeir. — New York : Grove, 1962. — I, 994.

Hodes, Art. Hot man : the life of Art Hodes / Art Hodes; with Chadwick Hansen; discography by Howard Rye. — Urbana : University of Illinois Press, 1992. — III, 545.

Hodes, Art. Selections from the gutter : jazz portraits from *The Jazz Record* / ed. Art Hodes and Chadwick Hansen. — Berkeley : University of California Press, 1977. — II, 733.

Hodge, Charlie. Me 'n' Elvis / Charlie Hodge; with Charles Goodman. — Memphis : Castle Books, 1988. — III, 830.

Hodge, Frederick Webb. Handbook of American Indians north of Mexico / Frederick Webb Hodge. — Washington : Smithsonian Institution, 1907–1910. — I, 385.

Hodgins, Gordon W. The Broadway musical : a complete LP discography / Gordon W. Hodgins. — Metuchen, N.J. : Scarecrow, 1980. — II, 901.

Hoffman, Richard. Some musical recollections of fifty years / Richard Hoffman. — New York : Scribner, 1910. — I, 244.

Hoffmann, Frank W. The literature of rock, 1954–1978 / Frank W. Hoffmann. — Metuchen, N.J. : Scarecrow, 1981. — II, A-647.

Hoffmann, Frank. The Cash Box album charts, 1955–1974 / Frank Hoffmann and George Albert; with the assistance of Lee Ann Hoffmann. — Metuchen, N.J. : Scarecrow, 1988. — III, 260.

Hoffmann, Frank. The *Cash Box* album charts, 1975–1985 / Frank Hoffmann and George Albert; with Lee Ann Hoffmann. — Metuchen, N.J. : Scarecrow, 1987. — III, 261.

Hoffmann, Frank. The *Cash Box* black contemporary album charts, 1975–1987 / Frank Hoffmann and George Albert. — Metuchen, N.J. : Scarecrow, 1989. — III, 262.

Hoffmann, Frank. The *Cash Box* black contemporary singles charts, 1960–1984 / Frank Hoffmann and George Albert; with the assistance of Lee Ann Hoffmann. — Metuchen, N.J. : Scarecrow, 1986. — III, 249.

Hoffmann, Frank. The *Cash Box* country album charts, 1964–1988 / Frank Hoffmann and George Albert. — Metuchen, N.J. : Scarecrow, 1989. — III, 226.

Hoffmann, Frank. The literature of rock, II : including an exhaustive survey of the literature from 1979–1983 and incorporating supplementary material from 1954–1978 not covered in the first volume / Frank Hoffmann and B. Lee Cooper; with the assistance of Lee Ann Hoffmann. — Metuchen, N.J. : Scarecrow, 1986. — III, 145.

Hoffmann, Gerhard. Das amerikanische Drama / Gerhard Hoffmann. — Bern, Switzerland : Francke, 1984. — II, A-556.

Hofmann, Charles. American Indians sing / Charles Hofmann; drawings by Nicholas Amorosi. — New York : John Day, 1967. — I, 397.

Hofmann, Charles. Frances Densmore and American Indian music : a memorial volume / ed. Charles Hofmann. — New York : Museum of the American Indian, 1968. — I, 398.

Hofmann, Charles. Sounds for silents / Charles Hofmann. — New York : DBS Publications, 1970. — I, A-257.

Hofmann, Charles. War hoops and medicine songs / Charles Hofmann. — Boston : Boston Music Co., 1952. — II, 241.

Hofmann, Coen. Man of many parts : a discography of Buddy Collette / Coen Hofmann; foreword by Lyle Murphy. — Amsterdam : Micrography, 1985. — III, 297.

Hofmann, Coen. Shorty Rogers : a discography / Coen Hofmann and Erik M. Bakker. — Amsterdam : Micrography, 1983. — III, 352.

Hofstein, Francis. Au miroir du jazz / Francis Hofstein. — Paris : Pierre, 1985. — II, A-406.

Hoggard, Stuart. Bob Dylan : an illustrated discography / Stuart Hoggard and Jim Shields. — Warborough, Oxon., England : Transmedia Express, 1978. — II, 1198.

Holden, Dorothy J. Life and work of Ernest M. Skinner / Dorothy J. Holden. — Richmond, Va. : Organ Historical Society, 1985. — III, 973.

Holiday, Billie. Lady sings the blues / Billie Holiday. — Rev. ed. — London : Sphere Books, 1973. — I, 1118.

Holiday, Chico. Holiday in hell / Chico Holiday and Bob Owen. — Anaheim, Calif. : Melodyland Productions, 1974. — II, 403.

Holland, James R. Tanglewood / James R. Holland. — Barre, Mass. : Barre, 1973. — II, 51.

Hollander, A. N. J. den. American civilization : an introduction / ed. A. N. J. den Hollander and Sigmund Skard. — London : Longmans, 1968. — I, 35.

Hollaran, Carolyn. Meet the stars of country music / Carolyn Hollaran. —
  Nashville : Aurora, 1977–1978. — II, 473.
Hollaran, Carolyn. Your favorite country music stars / Carolyn Hollaran. —
  New York : Popular Library, 1975. — II, 474.
Holm, Dallas. This is my story / Dallas Holm. — Nashville : Impact Books,
  1980. — II, 41.
Holmes, Lowell D. Jazz greats : getting better with age / Lowell D. Holmes and
  John W. Thomson. — New York : Holmes & Meier, 1986. — III, 428.
Holmes, Thomas B. Electronic and experimental music / Thomas B Holmes. —
  New York : Scribner's, 1985. — II, A-93.
Holmes, Tim. John Cougar Mellencamp / Tim Holmes. — New York : Ballan-
  tine, 1986. — III, 783.
Holtzman, Will. Judy Holiday : only child / Will Holtzman. — New York : Put-
  nam, 1982. — II, A-617.
Holyoke, Samuel. The Christian harmonist / Samuel Holyoke. — Salem, Mass. :
  Joshua Cushing, 1804. — I, 521.
Holz, Ronald W. Heralds of victory : a history celebrating the 100th anniversary
  of the New York Staff Band & Male Chorus, 1887–1987 / Ronald W. Holz. —
  New York : Salvation Army Literary Department, 1986. — III, 1004.
Holzer, Hans. Elvis Presley speaks / Hans Holzer. — New York : Manor Books,
  1978. — II, 1296.
Homer, Sidney. My wife and I : the story of Louis and Sidney Homer / Sidney
  Homer. — New York : Macmillan, 1939. — II, 187.
Hood, George. A history of music in New England / George Hood. — Boston :
  Wilkins, Carter, 1846. — I, 181.
Hood, Mantle. The ethnomusicologist / Mantle Hood. — New York : McGraw-
  Hill, 1971. — I, 423.
Hood, Phil. Artists of American folk music : the legends of traditional folk, the
  stars of the sixties, the virtuosi of new acoustic music / Phil Hood. — New
  York : Morrow, 1986. — III, 441.
Hoogerwerf, Frank. Confederate sheet-music imprints / Frank W. Hoogerwerf. —
  Brooklyn : Institute for Studies in American Music, 1984. — II, A-547.
Hoogerwerf, Frank. John Hill Hewitt : sources and bibliography / Frank
  Hoogerwerf. — Atlanta : Emory University Libraries, 1981. — II, A-83.
Hoogerwerf, Frank. Music in Georgia / Frank Hoogerwerf. — New York : Da
  Capo, 1984. — II, A-36.
Hoogeveen, Gerard J. Meet Mr. Gordon : a discography of Bob Gordon / Ger-
  ard J. Hoogeveen. — Amsterdam : Micrography, 1987. — III, 314.
Hooper, William Lloyd. Church music in transition / William Lloyd Hooper. —
  Nashville : Broadman Press, 1963. — II, 27.
Hoover, Cynthia A. Music machines, American style / Cynthia A. Hoover. —
  Washington : Smithsonian Institution Press, 1971. — II, 99.
Hoover, Cynthia A. The history of music machines / Cynthia A. Hoover. —
  New York : Drake, 1975. — II, 99.
Hoover, Kathleen. Virgil Thomson : his life and music / Kathleen Hoover and
  John Cage. — New York : Yoseloff, 1959. — I, 350.
Hopkins, Jerry. Elvis : a biography / Jerry Hopkins. — New York : Simon &
  Schuster, 1971. — I, 1386.

Hopkins, Jerry. Elvis : the final years / Jerry Hopkins. — New York : St. Martin's, 1980. — II, 1226.

Hopkins, Jerry. Festival! : the book of American music celebrations / Jerry Hopkins. — New York : Macmillan, 1970. — I, 1353.

Hopkins, Jerry. Hit and run : the Jimi Hendrix story / Jerry Hopkins. — New York : Putnam, 1982. — II, A-801.

Hopkins, Jerry. No one here gets out alive / Jerry Hopkins and Daniel Sugarman. — New York : Warner, 1980. — II, 1219.

Hopkins, Jerry. The lizard king : the essential Jim Morrison / Jerry Hopkins. — New York : Scribner's, 1992. — III, 792.

Hopkins, Jerry. The rock story / Jerry Hopkins. — New York : New American Library, 1970. — I, 1354.

Horgan, Paul. Ernst Bacon : a contemporary tribute / Paul Horgan. — Orinda, Calif. : 1974. — II, 173.

Horn, Barbara Lee. The age of *Hair* : evolution and impact of Broadway's first rock musical / Barbara Lee Horn. — New York : Greenwood, 1991. — III, 496.

Horn, David. Popular music perspectives : papers from the First International Conference on Popular Music Research, Amsterdam, June 1981 / ed. David Horn and Philip Tagg. — Göteborg, Sweden : IASPM, 1982. — II, A-530.

Horn, David. Popular music perspectives 2 : papers from the Second International Conference on Popular Music Research, Reggio Emilia, September 19–24, 1983 / ed. David Horn. — Göteborg, Sweden : IASPM, 1985. — II, A-531.

Horn, Dorothy. Sing to me of heaven / Dorothy Horn. — Gainesville : University of Florida Press, 1970. — I, 546.

Horn, Paul. Inside Paul Horn : the spiritual odyssey of a universal traveler / Paul Horn; with Lee Underwood. — San Francisco : Harper, 1990. — III, 647.

Horne, Aaron. Keyboard music of black composers : a bibliography / Aaron Horne. — Westport, Conn. : Greenwood, 1992. — III, 114.

Horne, Aaron. String music of black composers : a bibliography / Aaron Horne; foreword by Dominique-René DeLerma. — New York : Greenwood, 1991. — III, 115.

Horne, Aaron. Woodwind music of black composers / Aaron Horne; foreword by Samuel A. Floyd, Jr. — New York : Greenwood, 1990. — III, 116.

Horne, Lena. In person : Lena Horne / Lena Horne; as told to Helen Arstein and Carlton Moss. — New York : Greenberg, 1950. — II, 1001.

Horne, Lena. Lena / Lena Horne and Richard Schickel. — Garden City, N.Y. : Doubleday, 1965. — I, 1329; II, 1002.

Horne, Marilyn. Marilyn Horne : my life / Marilyn Horne; with James Scovell. — New York : Atheneum, 1983. — II, A-43.

Horowitz, Joseph. Understanding Toscanini : how he became an American culture-god and helped create a new audience for old music / Joseph Horowitz. — New York : Knopf, 1987. — III, 964.

Horricks, Raymond. Count Basie and his orchestra / Raymond Horricks. — New York : Citadel, 1957. — I, 1088.

Horricks, Raymond. Dizzy Gillespie and the be-bop revolution / Raymond Horricks. — New York : Hippocrene, 1984. — II, A-479.

Horricks, Raymond. Gerry Mulligan's ark / Raymond Horricks; discography by Tony Middleton. — London : Apollo, 1986. — III, 654.

Horricks, Raymond. Profiles in jazz : from Sidney Bechet to John Coltrane / Raymond Horricks. — New Brunswick, N.J. : Transaction, 1991. — III, 420.

Horricks, Raymond. Quincy Jones / Raymond Horricks; discography by Tony Middleton. — Tunbridge Wells, England : Spellmount, 1985. — III, 494.

Horricks, Raymond. Svengali : or the orchestra called Gill [sic] Evans / Raymond Horricks. — London : Apollo, 1984. — III, 951.

Horricks, Raymond. The importance of being Eric Dolphy / Raymond Horricks; discography by Tony Middleton. — Tunbridge Wells, England : D. J. Costello, 1989. — III, 632.

Horricks, Raymond. These jazzmen of our time / Raymond Horricks. — London : Gollancz, 1959. — I, 1050.

Horstmann, Dorothy. Sing your heart out, country boy / Dorothy Horstmann. — New York : Dutton, 1975. — II, 366.

Hoskins, Robert. Louis Armstrong : biography of a musician / Robert Hoskins. — Los Angeles : Holloway House, 1979. — II, 793.

Hounsome, Terry. New rock record : a collector's directory of rock albums and musicians / Terry Hounsome and Tim Chambre. — Rev. ed. — Poole, Dorset, England : Blandford, 1983. — II, A-677.

Hounsome, Terry. Rock record : a collector's directory of rock albums and musicians / Terry Hounsome. — 3rd ed. — New York : Facts on File, 1987. — III, 281.

Houseman, John. Run-through : a memoir / John Houseman. — New York : Simon & Schuster, 1972. — I, 141.

Housewright, Wiley L. A history of music and dance in Florida, 1565–1865 / Wiley L. Housewright. — Tuscaloosa : University of Alabama Press, 1991. — III, 380.

Hovland, Michael A. Musical settings of American poetry : a bibliography / Michael A. Hovland. — Westport, Conn. : Greenwood, 1986. — III, 156.

Howard, Brett. Lena / Brett Howard. — Los Angeles : Holloway House, 1981. — II, A-630.

Howard, James H. Choctaw music and dance / James H. Howard and Victoria Lindsay Levine. — Norman : University of Oklahoma Press, 1990. — III, 1231.

Howard, James H. Shawnee! : the ceremonialism of a native Indian tribe and its cultural background / James H. Howard. — Athens, Ohio : Ohio University Press, 1981. — II, 160.

Howard, Jan. Sunshine and shadow / Jan Howard. — New York : Richardson & Steirman, 1987. — III, 737.

Howard, Jean. Travels with Cole Porter / Jean Howard; introduction by George Eells. — New York : Abrams, 1991. — III, 507.

Howard, John Tasker. Ethelbert Nevin / John Tasker Howard. — New York : Crowell, 1935. — I, 241.

Howard, John Tasker. Music of George Washington's time / John Tasker Howard. — Washington : United States George Washington Bicentennial Commission, 1931. — I, 209.

Howard, John Tasker. Our American music : a comprehensive history from 1620 to the present / John Tasker Howard. — 4th ed. — New York : Crowell, 1965. — I, 24.

Howard, John Tasker. Our contemporary composers : American music in the twentieth century / John Tasker Howard. — New York : Crowell, 1941. — I, 287.

Howard, John Tasker. Short history of music in America / John Tasker Howard and George Kent Bellows. — 2nd ed. — New York : Crowell, 1967. — I, 26.

Howard, John Tasker. Stephen Foster : America's troubadour / John Tasker Howard. — 2nd ed. — New York : Crowell, 1953. — I, 1210.

Howard, John Tasker. Studies of contemporary American composers / John Tasker Howard. — New York : Fischer, 1925–1940. — I, 295.

Howard University Library. Dictionary catalog of the Arthur B. Spingarn Collection of negro authors. — Boston : G. K. Hall, 1970. — I, 687.

Howe, M. A. De Wolfe. The Boston Symphony Orchestra, 1881–1931 / M. A. De Wolfe Howe and John N. Burk. — Boston : Houghton Mifflin, 1931. — I, 96a.

Howe, M. A. DeWolfe. The tale of Tanglewood / M. A. DeWolfe Howe. — New York : Vanguard, 1946. — II, 52.

Howe, Mabel Almy. Music publishers in New York City before 1850 / Mabel Almy Howe. — New York : New York Public Library, 1917. — I, A-36.

Howell, John. David Byrne / John Howell. — New York : Thunder's Mouth, 1992. — III, 458.

Howlett, John. Frank Sinatra / John Howlett. — London : Plexus, 1980. — II, 1008.

Hoyt, Edwin P. Paul Robeson, the American Othello / Edwin P. Hoyt. — Cleveland : World, 1967. — I, 709.

Hubbard, John. An essay on music / John Hubbard. — Boston : Manning & Loring, 1808. — I, 214.

Hubbard, Lester A. Ballads and songs from Utah / Lester A. Hubbard. — Salt Lake City : University of Utah Press, 1961. — I, 516.

Hubbard, W. L. History of American music / W. L. Hubbard; introductions by George W. Chadwick and Frank Damrosch. — Toledo, Ohio : Irving Squire, 1908. — I, 22.

Hubler, Richard G. The Cole Porter story / Richard G. Hubler, — Cleveland : World, 1965. — I, 1293.

Huddleston, Judy. This is the end : my only friend : living and dying with Jim Morrison / Judy Huddleston. — New York : Shapolsky, 1991. — III, 793.

Hudson, Arthur Palmer. Folk tunes from Mississippi / Arthur Palmer Hudson. — New York : National Play Bureau, 1937. — I, 497.

Hudson, Arthur Palmer. Folksongs of Mississippi and their background / Arthur Palmer Hudson. — Chapel Hill : University of North Carolina Press, 1936. — I, 496.

Huenemann, Lynn. Songs and dances of native America / Lynn Huenemann. — Tsaile, Ariz. : Education House, 1978. — II, 262.

Huggins, Nathan Irvin. Harlem renaissance / Nathan Irvin Huggins. — New York : Oxford University Press, 1971. — I, 667.

Hughbanks, Leroy. Talking wax : or the story of the phonograph, simply told for general readers / Leroy Hughbanks. — New York : Hobson Book Press, 1945. - — I, A-37.

Hughes, Charles W. American hymns old and new / Charles W. Hughes. — New York : Columbia University Press, 1980. — II, 33.

Hughes, Langston. Black magic : a pictorial history of the negro in American entertainment / Langston Hughes and Milton Meltzer. — Englewood Cliffs, N.J. : Prentice-Hall, 1967. — I, 1232.

Hughes, Langston. Famous negro music makers / Langston Hughes. — New York : Dodd, Mead, 1955. — I, 704.

Hughes, Robert. Songs from the hills of Vermont / Robert Hughes and Edith B. Sturges. — New York : Schirmer, 1919. — I, A-116.

Hughes, Rupert. American composers / Rupert Hughes. — Boston : Page, 1914. — I, 219.

Hughes, Rupert. Contemporary American composers / Rupert Hughes. — Boston : Page, 1900. — I, 219.

Hugill, Stan. Shanties from the seven seas / Stan Hugill. — London : Routledge & Kegan Paul, 1961. — I, 575.

Hume, Martha. Kenny Rogers : gambler, dreamer, lover / Martha Hume. — New York : New American Library, 1980. — III, 851.

Hume, Martha. You're so cold I'm turning blue / Martha Hume. — New York : Viking, 1982. — II, A-221.

Hummel, David. The collector's guide to the American musical theatre / David Hummel. — 3rd ed. — Metuchen, N.J. : Scarecrow, 1983. — II, 902.

Humphries, Patrick. Absolutely Dylan : illustrated with more than 200 photographs / Patrick Humphries and John Bauldie. — New York : Viking, 1991. — III, 713.

Humphries, Patrick. Bruce Springsteen : blinded by the light / Patrick Humphries and Chris Hunt. — New York : Holt, 1986. — III, 866.

Humphries, Patrick. Paul Simon, still crazy after all these years / Patrick Humphries. — New York : Doubleday, 1989. — III, 857.

Huneker, James Gibbons. Steeplejack / James Gibbons Huneker. — New York : Scribner's, 1920. — I, 374.

Huneker, James Gibbons. The Philharmonic Society of New York and its seventy-fifth anniversary : a retrospect / James Gibbons Huneker. — New York : Philharmonic-Society of New York, 1917. — I, 113.

Hungerford, James. The old plantation, and what I gathered there in an autumn month / James Hungerford. — New York : Harper, 1859. — I, A-167.

Hurst, Jack. Nashville's Grand Ole Opry / Jack Hurst. — New York : Abrams, 1975. — II, 378.

Hurst, Richard Maurice. Republic Studios : between poverty row and the majors / Richard Maurice Hurst. — Metuchen, N.J. : Scarecrow, 1979. — II, 930.

Hurst, Walter E. The music industry book / Walter E. Hurst. — Hollywood : Seven Arts, 1981. — II, A-740.

Hurston, Zora Neale. Mules and men / Zora Neale Hurston. — Philadelphia : Lippincott, 1935. — I, 747.

Hurston, Zora Neale. The sanctified church / Zora Neale Hurston. — Berkeley, Calif. : Turtle Island, 1983. — III, 1.

Hutchinson Family. Excelsior : journals of the Hutchinson Family Singers, 1842–1846 / ed. Dale Cockrell. — Stuyvesant, N.Y. : Pendragon, 1989. — III, 919.

Hutchinson, John W. Story of the Hutchinsons / John W. Hutchinson. — Boston : Lee & Shepard, 1896. — I, 1218.

Hutchinson, Sean. Crying out loud / Sean Hutchinson. — Santa Barbara, Calif. : J. Daniel, 1988. — III, 648.

Hyman, Laurence J. Going to Chicago : a year on the Chicago blues scene / ed. Laurence J. Hyman; photographs by Stephen Green. — San Francisco : Woodford, 1990. — III, 1153.

Ilson, Carol. Harold Prince : from *Pajama Game* to *Phantom of the Opera* / Carol Ilson; foreword by Sheldon Harnick. — Ann Arbor, Mich. : UMI Research Press, 1989. — III, 1294.

Index of the recorded anthology of American music (New World Records). — Brooklyn : Institute for Studies in American Music, 197–?. — II, 2.

Indiana University. Archives of Traditional Music. A catalog of phonorecordings of music and oral data held by the Archives of Traditional Music. — Boston : G. K. Hall, 1975. — II, 273.

Ingalls, Jeremiah. The Christian harmony / Jeremiah Ingalls. — Exeter, N.H. : Author, 1805. — I, 522.

Inge, M. Thomas. Handbook of American popular culture : volume 3 / M. Thomas Inge. — Westport, Conn. : Greenwood, 1981. — II, A-508.

Ingram, Adrian. Wes Montgomery / Adrian Ingram. — Gateshead, England : Ashley Mark, 1985. — II, A-489.

Insana, Tino. The authorized Al / Tino Insana. — Chicago : Contemporary Books, 1985. — III, 675.

Inserra, Lorraine. The music of Henry Ainsworth's psalter (Amsterdam, 1612) / Lorraine Inserra and H. Wiley Hitchcock. — Brooklyn : Institute for Studies in American Music, 1981. — II, A-73.

International Congress of Americanists, 29th, New York, 1949. Selected papers, vol. 2 : Acculturation in the Americas. — Chicago : University of Chicago Press, 1952. — I, 678.

Ireland, Joseph N. Records of the New York stage / Joseph N. Ireland. — New York : Morrell, 1866–1867. — I, A-62.

Irwin, John. Instruments of the southern Appalachian mountains / John Irwin. — Norris, Tenn. : Museum of Appalachia Press, 1979. — II, 458.

Irwin, John Rice. Musical instruments of the southern Appalachian mountains / John Rice Irwin. — 2nd ed. — Exton, Pa. : Schiffer, 1983. — III, 987.

Isaacs, Edith J. R. The negro in the American theatre / Edith J. R. Isaacs. — New York : Theatre Arts, 1947. — I, 1233.

Isman, Felix. Weber and Fields / Felix Isman. — New York : Boni and Liveright, 1924. — II, 890.

Ives, Burl. Wayfaring stranger / Burl Ives. — New York : Whittlesey House, 1948. — I, 443.

Ives, Charles. Essays before a sonata / Charles Ives. — New York : Norton, 1964. — I, 324.

Ives, Charles. Memos / Charles Ives; ed. John Kirkpatrick. — New York : Norton, 1972. — I, 325.

Ives, Edward D. Larry Gorman, the man who made the songs / Edward D. Ives. — Bloomington : Indiana University Press, 1964. — I, 444.

Ivey, William. A dose of reality therapy : university musicianship in a commercial world / William Ivey. — Nashville : Country Music Foundation, 1973. — I, 171.

Iwamoto, Shin-ichi. Have you met mister Jones : Hank Jones : a discography / Shin-ichi Iwamoto. — Rev. ed. — Tokyo : Sun Copy Center, 1989. — III, 328.

Iwaschkin, Roman. Popular music : a reference guide / Roman Iwaschkin. — New York : Garland, 1986. — III, 141.

Jablonski, Edward. Encyclopedia of American music / Edward Jablonski. — Garden City, N.Y. : Doubleday, 1981. — II, A-9.

Jablonski, Edward. Gershwin / Edward Jablonski. — Garden City, N.Y. : Doubleday, 1987. — III, 141.

Jablonski, Edward. Gershwin remembered / Edward Jablonski. — London : Faber & Faber; Portland, Ore. : Amadeus, 1992. — III, 477.

Jablonski, Edward. Harold Arlen : happy with the blues / Edward Jablonski. — Garden City, N.Y. : Doubleday, 1961. — I, 1269.

Jablonski, Edward. The Gershwin years / Edward Jablonski and Lawrence D. Stewart. — 2nd ed. — Garden City, N.Y. : Doubleday, 1973. — I, 1282.

Jackson, Arthur. The book of musicals : from *Show Boat* to *Chorus Line* / Arthur Jackson. — London : Mitchell Beazley, 1977. — II, 909.

Jackson, Arthur. The world of big bands : the sweet and swinging years / Arthur Jackson. — Newton Abbot, England : David & Charles, 1977. — II, 781.

Jackson, Blair. Goin' down the road : a Grateful Dead traveling companion / Blair Jackson. — New York : Harmony Books, 1992. — ML421 .G72 J2. — III, 911.

Jackson, Blair. Grateful Dead / Blair Jackson. — New York : Delilah, 1983. — II, A-798.

Jackson, Bruce. Folklore & society : essays in honor of Ben. A. Botkin / ed. Bruce Jackson. — Hatboro, Pa. : Folklore Associates, 1966. — II, 280.

Jackson, Bruce. The negro and his folk-lore in 19th century periodicals / Bruce Jackson. — Austin : University of Texas Press, 1967. — I, 757.

Jackson, Bruce. Wake up dead men : Afro-American worksongs from Texas prisons / Bruce Jackson. — Cambridge, Mass. : Harvard University Press, 1972. — I, 748.

Jackson, Clyde Owen. Songs of our years : a study of negro folk music / Clyde Owen Jackson. — New York : Exposition, 1968. — I, 758.

Jackson, George Pullen. Another sheaf of white spirituals / George Pullen Jackson. — Gainesville : University of Florida Press, 1952. — I, 542.

Jackson, George Pullen. Down-East spirituals and others / George Pullen Jackson. — Locust Valley : Augustin, 1939. — I, 541.

Jackson, George Pullen. Spiritual folk songs of early America / George Pullen Jackson. — New York : Augustin, 1937. — I, 540.

Jackson, George Pullen. The story of the Sacred Harp, 1844–1944 / George Pullen Jackson. — Nashville : Vanderbilt University Press, 1944. — I, 531.

Jackson, George Pullen. White and negro spirituals : their life span and kinship / George Pullen Jackson. — Locust Valley : Augustin, 1943. — I, 548.

Jackson, George Pullen. White spirituals in the southern uplands / George Pullen Jackson. — Chapel Hill : University of North Carolina Press, 1933. — I, 547.

Jackson, Irene V. Afro-American religious music : a bibliography and a catalogue of gospel music / Irene V. Jackson. — Westport, Conn. : Greenwood, 1979. — III, 153.

Jackson, Irene V. Afro-American gospel music and its social setting, with special attention to Roberta Martin / Irene V. Jackson. — Dissertation, Wesleyan University, 1974. — II, 626.

Jackson, Irene V. Afro-American religious music : a bibliogrphy and a catalogue of gospel music / Irene V. Jackson. — Westport, Conn. : Greenwood, 1979. — II, 578.

Jackson, Jesse. Make a joyful noise unto the Lord! / Jesse Jackson. — New York : Crowell, 1974. — I, 898.

Jackson, John A. Big beat heat : Alan Freed and the early years of rock & roll / John A. Jackson. — New York : Schirmer, 1991. — III, 978.

Jackson, Judge. The colored sacred harp / ed. Judge Jackson. — Rev. ed. — Montgomery, Ala. : Paragon, 1973. — II, 524.

Jackson, LaToya. LaToya : growing up in the Jackson family / LaToya Jackson; with Patricia Romanowski. — New York : Dutton, 1991. — III, 740.

Jackson, Mahalia. Movin' on up / Mahalia Jackson. — New York : Hawthorn, 1974. — I, 899.

Jackson, Michael. Moonwalk / Michael Jackson. — New York : Doubleday, 1988. — III, 742.

Jackson, Paul. Saturday afternoons at the old Met : the Metropolitan Opera broadcasts, 1931–1950 / Paul Jackson. — Portland, Ore. : Amadeus, 1992. — III, 1019.

Jackson, Richard. Democratic souvenirs : an historical anthology of nineteenth-century American music / selected, with introduction and commentary by Richard Jackson; foreword by Virgil Thomson. — New York : published for the New York Public Library by C. F. Peters, 1988. — III, 19.

Jackson, Richard. U.S. Bicentennial music 1 / Richard Jackson. — Brooklyn : Institute for Studies in American Music, 1977. — II, 3.

Jackson, Richard. United States music : sources of bibliography and collective biography / Richard Jackson. — Brooklyn : Institute for Studies in American Music, 1973. — I, 5.

Jacobi, Hugh. Contemporary American composers based at American colleges and universities / Hugh Jacobi. — Paradise, Calif. : Paradise Arts, 1975. — I, 288.

Jacobs, Dick. Who wrote that song? / Dick Jacobs. — White Hall, Va. : Betterway, 1988. — III, 100.

Jacobson, Robert. Magnificence : onstage at the Met / Robert Jacobson. — New York : Simon & Schuster, 1985. — II, A-44.

Jaffe, Andrew. Jazz theory / Andrew Jaffe. — Dubuque, Iowa : Brown, 1983. — II, A-403.

Jahn, Janheinz. Blues and work songs / Janheinz Jahn. — Frankfurt : Fischer, 1964. — I, 875.

Jahn, Mike. Jim Morrison and the Doors / Mike Jahn. — New York : Grosset & Dunlap, 1969. — I, 1385.

Jahn, Mike. Rock : from Elvis Presley to the Rolling Stones / Mike Jahn. — New York : Quadrangle, 1973. — I, 1355.

Jairazbhoy, Nazir. Asian music in North America / Nazir Jairazbhoy and Sue Carole DeVale. — Los Angeles : Department of Music, University of California at Los Angeles, 1985. — III, 1207.

Jakubowski, Maxim. The rock album : a good rock guide / Maxim Jakubowski. — London : Zomba Books, 1984. — II, A-686.

James, Burnett. Billie Holiday / Burnett James. — New York : Hippocrene, 1984. — II, A-482.

James, Burnett. Bix Beiderbecke / Burnett James. — London : Cassell, 1959. — I, 1090.

James, Burnett. Coleman Hawkins / Burnett James. — Tunbridge Wells, England : Spellmount; New York : Hippocrene Books, 1984. — III, 642.

James, Burnett. Essays on jazz / Burnett James. — London : Sidgwick & Jackson, 1961. — I, 1021.

James, Helga. A catalog of the musical works of Philip James (1890–1975) / Helga James. — Southampton, N.Y. : Author, 1980. — II, 193.

James, Michael. Dizzy Gillespie / Michael James. — London : Cassell, 1959. — I, 1112.

James, Michael. Miles Davis / Michael James. — London : Cassell, 1961. — I, 1100.

James, Michael. Ten modern jazzmen / Michael James. — London : Cassell, 1960. — I, 1051.

James, Otis. Dolly Parton : a personal portrait / Otis James. New York : Quick Fox, 1978. — II, 411.

Jameson, Gladys V. Wake and sing : a miniature anthology of the music of Appalachian America / ed. Gladys V. Jameson. — New York : BMI, 1955. — II, 303.

Jameson, Gladys. Sweet rivers of song / Gladys Jameson. — Berea, Ky. : Berea College, 1967. — II, 427.

Jan, Ramona. Bon Jovi / Ramona Jan. — Toronto : PaperJacks, 1988. — III, 901.

Janssens, Eddy. Art Ensemble of Chicago discography / Eddy Janssens and Hugo de Craen. — Brussels : New Think Publications, 1984. — II, A-373.

Janta, Aleksander. A history of nineteenth century American Polish music / Aleksander Janta. — New York : Kosciuszko Foundation, 1982. — II, A-183.

Jarman, Douglas. Kurt Weill : an illustrated biography / Douglas Jarman. — Bloomington : Indiana University Press, 1982. — III, 533.

Jarman, Harry E. Old-time dance tunes / ed. Harry E. Jarman. — New York : BMI, 1951. — II, 459.

Jasen, David A. Rags and ragtime : a musical history / David A. Jasen and Trebor Jay Richenor. — New York : Seabury, 1978. — II, 532.

Jasen, David A. Recorded ragtime, 1897–1958 / David A. Jasen. — Hamden, Conn. : Archon, 1973. — I, 801.

Jasen, David A. The theatre of P. G. Wodehouse / David A. Jasen. — London : Batsford, 1979. — II, 970.

Jasen, David A. Tin Pan Alley : the composers, the songs, the performers, and their times : the golden age of American popular music from 1886 to 1956 / David Jasen. — New York : Donald I. Fine, 1988. — III, 1058.

Jasper, Tony. The international encyclopedia of hard rock and heavy metal / Tony Jasper. — New York : Facts on File, 1983. — II, A-660.

Jasper, Tony. Tony Bennett / Tony Jasper. — London : W. H. Allen, 1984. — II, A-621.

Jay, Dave. Jolsonography / Dave Jay. — 2nd ed. — Bournemouth, England : Anderton, 1974. — I, 1331.

Jay, Dave. The Irving Berlin songography, 1907–1966 / Dave Jay. — New Rochelle, N.Y. : Arlington House, 1969. — I, 1270a.

Jazz guitarists : collected interviews from *Guitar Player* magazine. — Saratoga, N.Y. : Guitar Player Books, 1975. — II, 734.

Jazz life and times (series). — III, 1117.

Jazz masters (series). — III, 1118.

Jazz on 78's. London : Decca Record Co., 1954. — I, 955.

Jazz on LP's. London : Decca Record Co., 1955. — I, 955.

Jazzforschung / Jazz research. — Graz, Austria : Universal Edition, 1969. — I, 996.

Jeambar, Denis. George Gershwin / Denis Jeambar. — Paris : Mazarine, 1982. — II, A-599.

Jefferson, Blind Lemon. Blind Lemon Jefferson / Blind Lemon Jefferson. — Knutsford, England : Blues World, 1970. — I, 839.

Jenkinson, Philip. Celluloid rock : twenty years of movie rock / Philip Jenkinson and Alan Warner. — London : Lorrimer, 1974. — II, 1164.

Jensen, Jamie. Grateful Dead : built to last : 25th anniversary album, 1965–1990 / Jamie Jensen. — New York : Plume, 1990. — III, 912.

Jepsen, Jorgen Grunnet. Discography of Billie Holiday / Jorgen Grunnet Jepsen. — Copenhagen : Knudsen, 1969. — I, 944.

Jepsen, Jorgen Grunnet. Discography of Charlie Parker / Jorgen Grunnet Jepsen. — Copenhagen : Knudsen, 1968. — I, 944.

Jepsen, Jorgen Grunnet. Discography of Count Basie / Jorgen Grunnet Jepsen. — Copenhagen : Knudsen, 1969. — I, 944.

Jepsen, Jorgen Grunnet. Discography of Dizzy Gillespie / Jorgen Grunnet Jepsen. — Copenhagen : Knudsen, 1969. — I, 944.

Jepsen, Jorgen Grunnet. Discography of John Coltrane / Jorgen Grunnet Jepsen. — Copenhagen : Knudsen, 1969. — I, 944.

Jepsen, Jorgen Grunnet. Discography of Lester Young / Jorgen Grunnet Jepsen. — Copenhagen : Knudsen, 1968. — I, 944.

Jepsen, Jorgen Grunnet. Discography of Louis Armstrong / Jorgen Gurnnet Jepsen. — Copenhagen : Knudsen, 1968. — I, 944.

Jepsen, Jorgen Grunnet. Discography of Miles Davis / Jorgen Grunnet Jepsen. — Copenhagen : Knudsen, 1969. — I, 944.

Jepsen, Jorgen Grunnet. Discography of Thelonious Monk and Bud Powell / Jorgen Grunnet Jepsen. — Copenhagen : Knudsen, 1969. — I, 944.

Jepsen, Jorgen Grunnet. Jazz records : a discography / Jorgen Grunnet Jepsen. — Copenhagen : Knudsen, 1963–1970. — I, 931.

Jepsen, Jorgen Grunnet. Louis Armstrong : the Tsumura collection / J. G. Jepsen; discography by Akira Tsumura. — Tokyo : Author, 1989. — II, 285a.

Jerrentrup, Ansgar. Entwicklung der Rockmusik vom den Anfängen bis zum Beat / Ansgar Jerrentrup. — Regensburg, Germany : Bosse, 1981. — II, A-694.

Jessye, Eva A. My spirituals / Eva A. Jessye. — New York : Robbins-Engel, 1927. — II, 605.

Jewell, Derek. Duke : a portrait of Duke Ellington / Derek Jewell. — Rev. ed. — London : Sphere Books, 1978. — II, 746.

Jewell, Derek. Frank Sinatra : a celebration / Derek Jewell. — London : Pavilion Books, 1985. — II, A-634.

Jewell, Derek. The popular voice : a musical record of the 60s and 70s / Derek Jewell. — London : Andre Deutsch, 1980. — II, 836.

Jezic, Diane Peacock. The musical migration and Ernst Toch / Diane Peacock Jezic; with worklist and discography by Alyson McLamore. — Ames : Iowa State University Press, 1989. — III, 531.

Jobson, Richard. The golden trade / Richard Jobson. — London : N. Okes, 1623. — I, 716.

John Edwards Memorial Foundation. The Carter family on border radio. — Los Angeles : The Foundation, 1972. — I, 635.

John Edwards Memorial Foundation. The early recording career of Ernest V. "Pop" Stoneman : a bio-discography. — Los Angeles : The Foundation, 1968. — I, 642.

Johns, Clayton. Reminiscences of a musician / Clayton Johns. — Cambridge, Mass. : Washburn & Thomas, 1929. — II, 148.

Johnson, Carl. Paul Whiteman : a chronology (1890–1967) / Carl Johnson. — Rev. ed. — Williamstown, Mass. : Williams College, 1979. — II, 771.

Johnson, Charles A. The frontier camp meeting : religion's harvest time / Charles A. Johnson. — Dallas : Southern Methodist University Press, 1955. — I, 549.

Johnson, Charles S. Shadow of the plantation / Charles S. Johnson. — Chicago : University of Chicago Press, 1934. — I, 815.

Johnson, Edward. Bernard Herrmann, Hollywood's music-dramatist / Edward Johnson. — Rickmansworth, Herts., England : Triad, 1977. — II, 951.

Johnson, Frances Hall. Musical memories of Hartford : drawn from records public and private / Frances Hall Johnson. — Hartford, Conn. : Witkower's, 1931. — I, 101.

Johnson, Guy B. Folk culture on St. Helena Island, South Carolina / Guy B. Johnson. — Chapel Hill : University of North Carolina Press, 1930. — I, 759.

Johnson, Guy B. John Henry : tracking down a negro legend / Guy B. Johnson. — Chapel Hill : University of North Carolina Press, 1929. — I, 760.

Johnson, H. Earle. First performances in America to 1900 : works with orchestra / H. Earle Johnson. — Detroit : Information Coordinators, 1979. — II, 143.

Johnson, H. Earle. Hallelujah, Amen! : the story of the Handel and Haydn Society of Boston / H. Earle Johnson. — Boston : Bruce Humphries, 1965. — I, 97.

Johnson, H. Earle. Music in America before 1825 / H. Earle Johnson and Bonnie Hedges. — New York : Da Capo, 1985. — II, A-74.

Johnson, H. Earle. Musical interludes in Boston, 1795–1830 / H. Earle Johnson. — New York : Columbia University Press, 1943. — I, 98.

Johnson, H. Earle. Operas on American subjects / H. Earle Johnson. — New York : Coleman-Ross, 1964. — I, 54.

Jones, Louis M. Everybody's grandpa / Louis M. Jones. — Knoxville : University of Tennessee Press, 1984. — II, A-255.
Jones, Loyal. Minstrel of the Appalachians : the story of Bascom Lamar Lunsford / Loyal Jones. — Boone, N.C. : Appalachian Consortium Press, 1984. — II, A-256.
Jones, Loyal. Radio's "Kentucky Mountain Boy," Bradley Kincaid / Loyal Jones. — Berea, Ky. : Appalachian Center, Berea College, 1980. — II, 405.
Jones, Matt B. Bibliographical notes on Thomas Walter's "Grounds and rules of musick explained" / Matt B. Jones. — Worcester, Mass. : American Antiquarian Society, 1933. — I, 198.
Jones, Matt B. Some bibliographical notes on Cotton Mather's "The accomplished singer" / Matt B. Jones. — Boston, 1933. — I, 195.
Jones, Max. A tribute to Huddie Ledbetter / Max Jones and Albert McCarthy. — London : Jazz Music Books, 1946. — I, 845.
Jones, Max. Louis : the Louis Armstrong story, 1900–1971 / Max Jones and John Chilton. — London : Studio Vista, 1971. — I, 1084.
Jones, Max. Salute to Satchmo / Max Jones, John Chilton, and Leonard Feather. — London : IPC, 1970. — I, 1085.
Jones, Max. Talking jazz / Max Jones. — New York : Norton, 1988. — III, 420a.
Jones, Morley. Jazz / Morley Jones. — New York : Simon & Schuster, 1980. — II, 659.
Jones, Peter. Elvis / Peter Jones. — London : Octopus, 1976. — II, 1297.
Jones, Reginald M., Jr. The mystery of the masked man's music : a search for the music used on "The Lone Ranger" radio program, 1933–1954 / Reginald M. Jones, Jr. — Metuchen, N.J. : Scarecrow, 1987. — III, 58.
Jones, Steve. Rock formation : music, technology, and mass communication / Steve Jones. — Newbury Park, Calif. : Sage, 1992. — III, 1179.
Joplin, Laura. Love, Janis / Laura Joplin. — New York : Villard, 1992. — III, 755.
Joplin, Scott. The collected works / Scott Joplin; ed. Vera Brodsky Lawrence; ed. consultant Richard Jackson. — New York : New York Public Library, 1971. — I, 802.
Jordan, Philip D. Singin' Yankees / Philip D. Jordan. — Minneapolis : University of Minnesota Press, 1946. — I, 1220.
Jordan, René. Streisand : an unauthorized biography / René Jordan. — London : W. H. Allen, 1976. — II, 1015.
Jordan, René. The greatest star : the Barbra Streisand story / René Jordan. — New York : Putnam, 1975. — II, 1015.
Jordan, Steve. Rhythm man : fifty years in jazz / Steve Jordan, with Tom Scanlan. — Ann Arbor : University of Michigan Press, 1991. — III, 586.
Jorgenson, Ernest. Elvis recording sessions / Ernest Jorgenson. — Stenlose, Denmark : JEE Productions, 1977. — II, 1311.
Jörgensen, John. Mosaik jazz lexicon / John Jörgensen and Erik Wiedemann. — Hamburg : Mosaik, 1966. — I, 906.
Joseph, Pleasant. Cousin Joe : blues from New Orleans / Pleasant ("Cousin Joe") Joseph and Harriet J. Ottenheimer. — Chicago : University of Chicago Press, 1987. — III, 705.

Jost, Ekkehard. Free jazz / Ekkehard Jost. — Graz, Austria : Universal Edition, 1974. — I, 1053.

Jost, Ekkehard. Jazzmusiker / Ekkehard Jost. — Berlin : Ullstein, 1981. — II, A-392.

Jost, Ekkehard. Sozialgeschichte des Jazz in den USA / Ekkehard Jost. — Frankfurt, Germany : Fischer, 1982. — II, A-393.

Joyner, Charles W. Folk song in South Carolina / Charles W. Joyner. — Columbia : University of South Carolina Press, 1971. — I, 502.

Jubilee and plantation songs. — Boston : Ditson, 1887. — II, 608.

Judd, Naomi. Love can build a bridge / Naomi Judd and Wynonna Judd; with Bud Schaetzle. — New York : Villard, 1992. — III, 920.

Juge, Pascale. Rockeuses : les héroines de jukebox / Pascale Juge. — Paris : Grancher, 1982. — II, A-764.

Junchen, David L. Encyclopedia of the American theatre organ. Volume 1 / David L. Junchen. — Pasadena, Calif. : Showcase, 1985. — III, 990.

Kahn, E. J. The merry partners : the age and stage of Harrigan and Hart / E. J. Kahn. — New York : Random House, 1955. — II, 891.

Kahn, E. J. The voice : the story of an American phenomenon / E. J. Kahn. — New York : Harper, 1947. — I, 1335.

Kahn, Ed. Hillbilly music : source and resource / Ed Kahn. — Los Angeles : John Edwards Memorial Foundation, 1966. — I, 614.

Kalet, Beth. Kris Kristofferson / Beth Kalet. — New York : Quick Fox, 1979. — II, 406.

Kalinak, Kathryn Marie. Settling the score : music and the classical Hollywood film / Kathryn Marie Kalinak. — Madison : University of Wisconsin Press, 1992. — III, 1028.

Kamin, Philip. Cyndi Lauper / Philip Kamin and Peter Goddard. — New York : McGraw-Hill, 1986. — III, 760.

Kamin, Philip. VanHalen / Philip Kamin and Peter Goddard. — New York : Beaufort, 1984. — III, 945.

Kaminsky, Max. My life in jazz / Max Kaminsky; with V. E. Hughes. — New York : Harper & Row, 1963. — I, 1121.

Kanaharis, Richard. Linda Ronstadt : a portrait / Richard Kanaharis. — Los Angeles : L.A. Pop Publishing, 1972. — II, 1241.

Kanahele, George S. Hawaiian music and musicians : an illustrated history / George S. Kanahele. — Honolulu : University of Hawaii Press, 1979. — II, 447.

Kanter, Kenneth Aaron. The Jews in Tin Pan Alley / Kenneth Aaron Kanter. — New York : KTAV, 1982. — II, A-540.

Kapell, William. William Kapell : a documentary life history of the American pianist / compiled by Tim Page. — College Park, Md. : International Piano Archives at the University of Maryland, 1992. — III, 555.

Kaplan, E. Ann. Rocking around the clock : music television, post modernism and consumer culture / E. Ann Kaplan. — New York : Methuen, 1987. — III, 1278.

Kaplan, Mike. Variety's directory of major show business awards / Mike Kaplan. — 2nd ed. — New York : Bowker, 1989. — III, 1288.

Kappler, Frank K. Benny Goodman / Frank K. Kappler. — Alexandria, Va. : Time-Life Records, 1979. — III, 955.

Kappler, Frank K. James P. Johnson / Frank K. Kappler. — Alexandria, Va. : Time-Life Records, 1981. — III, 554.

Kappler, Frank K. Sidney Bechet / Frank K. Kappler. — Alexandria, Va. : Time-Life Records, 1980. — III, 603.

Karpeles, Maud. Cecil Sharp : his life and work / Maud Karpeles. — Chicago : University of Chicago Press, 1967. — I, 470.

Karpp, Phyllis. Ike's boys : the story of the Everly Brothers / Phyllis Karpp. — Ann Arbor, Mich. : Pierian, 1988. — III, 907.

Karson, Burton. Festival essays for Pauline Alderman / ed. Burton Karson. — Salt Lake City, Utah : Brigham Young University Press, 1976. — II, 331.

Kartsonakis, Dino. Dino : beyond the glitz and glamour : an autobiography / Dino Kartsonakis; with Cecil Murphey. — Nashville : T. Nelson, 1990. — III, 556.

Kasem, Casey. Casey Kasem's American top 40 yearbook / Casey Kasem. — New York : Grosset & Dunlap, 1979. — II, 1252.

Kash, Murray. Murray Kash's book of country / Murray Kash. — London : Star Books, 1981. — II, A-222.

Kasha, Al. Notes on Broadway : intimate conversations with Broadway's greatest songwriters / Al Kasha. — Chicago : Contemporary Books, 1985. — III, 404.

Katkov, Norman. The fabulous Fanny : the story of Fanny Brice / Norman Katkov. — New York : Knopf, 1953. — II, 973.

Katz, Bernard. The social implications of early negro music in the United States / Bernard Katz. — New York : Arno, 1969. — I, 792.

Katz, Israel J. Libraries, history, diplomacy, and the performing arts : essays in honor of Carleton Sprague Smith / ed. Israel J. Katz. — Stuyvesant, N.Y. : Pendragon, 1991. — III, 54.

Katz, Susan. Superwomen of rock / Susan Katz. — New York : Grosset & Dunlap, 1978. — II, 1181.

Kaufman, Charles H. Music in New Jersey, 1655–1860 / Charles H. Kaufman. — Rutherford, N.J. : Fairleigh Dickinson University Press, 1982. — II, A-37.

Kaufman, Fredrick. The African roots of jazz / Fredrick Kaufman and John P. Guckin. — Sherman Oaks, Calif. : Alfred Publishing, 1979. — II, 710.

Kaufmann, Helen L. From Jehova to jazz : music in America from psalmody to the present day / Helen L. Kaufmann. — New York : Dodd, Mead, 1937. — I, A-5.

Kaye, Joseph. Victor Herbert : the biography of America's greatest composer of romantic music / Joseph Kaye. — New York : G. Howard Watt, 1931. — I, 1288.

Kearns, William K. Horatio Parker, 1863–1919 / William K. Kearns. — Metuchen, N.J. : Scarecrow, 1990. — III, 504.

Kebede, Ashenofi. Roots of black music / Ashenofi Kebede. — Englewood Cliffs, N.J. : Prentice-Hall, 1982. — II, A-296.

Keck, George R. Feel the spirit : studies in nineteenth-century Afro-American music / ed. George R. Keck and Sherrill V. Martin. — New York : Greenwood, 1988. — III, 1218.

Keefer, Lubov. Baltimore's music : the haven of the American composer / Lubov Keefer. — Baltimore : J. H. Furst, 1962. — I, 118.

Keele University. First American music conference, Friday, April 18–21, 1975. — Keele, Staffs., England : Keele University Music Department, 1978. — II, 171.

Keeling, Richard. A guide to early field recordings (1900–1949) at the Lowie Museum of Anthropology / Richard Keeling. — Berkeley : University of California Press, 1991. — III, 190a.

Keeling, Richard. Cry for luck : sacred song and speech among the Yurok, Hupa, and Karok Indians of northwestern California / Richard Keeling. — Berkeley : University of California Press, 1992. — III, 1232.

Keeling, Richard. Women in North American Indian music : six essays / Richard Keeling. — Bloomington, Ind. : Society for Ethnomusicology, 1989. — III, 1235.

Keene, James A. A history of music education in the United States / James A. Keene. — Hanover, N.H. : University of New England, 1982. — II, A-66.

Keepnews, Orrin. Pictorial history of jazz / Orrin Keepnews and Bill Grauer. — New York : Crown, 1955. — I, 907.

Keepnews, Orrin. The view from within : jazz writings, 1948–1987 / Orrin Keepnews. — New York : Oxford, 1988. — III, 1098.

Keil, Charles. Urban blues / Charles Keil. — Chicago : University of Chicago Press, 1966. — I, 860.

Keller, Kate van Winkle. Popular secular music in America through 1800 / Kate van Winkle Keller. — Philadelphia : Music Library Association, 1981. — II, A-75.

Keller, Kate Van Winkle. The national tune index : 18th-century secular music / Kate Van Winkle Keller. — New York : University Music Editions, 1980. — II, 136.

Keller, Keith. Oh Jess! a jazz life : the Jess Stacy story / Keith Keller. — New York : Mayan Music, 1989. — III, 571.

Kellner, Bruce. The Harlem renaissance : a historical dictionary for the era / Bruce Kellner. — Westport, Conn. : Greenwood, 1984. — II, A-277.

Kellogg, Clare Louise. Memoirs of an American prima donna / Clare Louise Kellogg. — New York : Putnam, 1913. — II, 69.

Kelly, Kitty. His way : the unauthorized biography of Frank Sinatra / Kitty Kelly. — Toronto : Bantam, 1986. — III, 860.

Kelly, Michael Bryan. The Beatle myth : the British invasion of American popular music, 1956–1969 / Michael Bryan Kelly. — Jefferson, N.C. : McFarland, 1991. — III, 1180.

Kelpius, Johannes. The diarium of Magister Johannes Kelpius / Johannes Kelpius. — Lancaster, Pa. : New Era Printing Co., 1917. — I, A-20.

Kemble, Frances Anne. Journal of a residence on a Georgian plantation, 1836–1839 / Frances Anne Kemble. — London : Longman, Green, 1863. — I, 738.

Kemp, Robert. Father Kemp and his old folks / Robert Kemp. — Boston : Author, 1868. — I, 211.

Kendall, Alan. George Gershwin : a biography / Alan Kendall. — New York : Universe, 1987. — III, 478.

Kennealy, Patricia. Strange days : my life with and without Jim Morrison / Patricia Kennealy. — New York : Dutton, 1992. — III, 795.

Kennedy, Peter. Films on traditional music and dance : a first international catalogue / Peter Kennedy. — Paris : Unesco, 1970. — I, 424.

Kennedy, R. Emmet. Black cameos / R. Emmet Kennedy. — New York : Boni, 1924. — I, A-179.

Kennedy, R. Emmet. Mellows : a chronicle of unknown singers / R. Emmet Kennedy. — New York : Boni, 1925. — I, 778.

Kennedy, R. Emmet. More mellows / R. Emmet Kennedy. — New York : Dodd, Mead, 1931. — I, 779.

Kennington, Donald. The literature of jazz : a critical guide / Donald Kennington and Danny L. Read. — 2nd ed. — Chicago : American Library Association, 1980. — III, 127.

Kennington, Donald. Literature of jazz : a critical guide / Donald Kennington. — London : Library Association, 1970. — I, 914.

Kenny, Nick. How to write and sell popular songs / Nick Kenny. — New York : Hermitage, 1946. — II, 1027.

Kent, Jeff. The rise and fall of rock / Jeff Kent. — Stoke-on-Trent, England : Witan Books, 1983. — II, A-695.

Kerschbaumer, Franz. Miles Davis / Franz Kerschbaumer. — Graz, Austria : Akademische Druck und Verlagsanstalt, 1978. — II, 744.

Kershaw, Alan Roy. The rock reader / Alan Roy Kershaw. — Leura, New South Wales, Australia : Afloat Press, 1982. — II, A-714.

Kester, Marian. Dead Kennedys : the unauthorized version / Marian Kester. — Berkeley, Calif. : Last Gasp of San Francisco, 1983. — II, A-777.

Kienzle, Rich. Great guitarists / Rich Kienzle. — New York : Facts on File, 1985. — II, A-58.

Kiersh, Edward. Where are you now, Bo Diddley? : the stars who made us rock and where they are now / Edward Kiersh. — Garden City, N.Y. : Doubleday, 1986. — III, 421.

Killion, Ronald G. A treasury of Georgia folklore / Ronald G. Killion and Charles T. Waller. — Atlanta : Cherokee, 1972. — II, 308.

Kilpatrick, Jack Frederick. Muskogean charm songs among the Oklahoma Cherokees / Jack Frederick Kilpatrick and Anna Gritts Kilpatrick. — Washington : Smithsonian Press, 1967. — I, 408.

Kimball, Robert. Cole / Robert Kimball. — New York : Holt, Rinehart & Winston, 1971. — I, 1294.

Kimball, Robert. Reminiscing with Sissle and Blake / Robert Kimball and William Bolcom. — New York : Viking, 1973. — I, 1234.

Kimball, Robert. The Gershwins / Robert Kimball and Alfred Simon. — New York : Atheneum, 1973. — I, 1283.

Kimberling, Victoria J. David Diamond : a bio-bibliography / Victoria J. Kimberling; foreword by David Diamond. — Metuchen, N.J. : Scarecrow, 1987. — III, 466.

Kimbrell, James. Barbra : an actress who sings / James Kimbrell and Cheri Kimbrell. — Boston : Brandell, 1992. — III, 869.

Kiner, Larry F. Al Jolson : a bio-discography / Larry F. Kiner; foreword by Leonard Maltin. — Metuchen, N.J. : Scarecrow, 1992. — III, 327.

Kiner, Larry F. Basic musical library, "P" series, 1–1000 / Larry F. Kiner and Harry Mackenzie; foreword by Richard S. Sears. — New York : Greenwood, 1990. — III, 198.

Kiner, Larry F. Nelson Eddy : a bio-discography / Larry F. Kiner; foreword by Sharon Rich. — Metuchen, N.J. : Scarecrow, 1992. — III, 305.

Kiner, Larry F. The Cliff Edwards discography / Larry F. Kiner. — New York : Greenwood, 1987. — III, 306.

Kiner, Larry F. The Rudy Vallee discography / Larry F. Kiner. — Westport, Conn. : Greenwood, 1985. — II, A-645.

Kinezle, Rich. Papa's jumpin' : the MGM years of Bob Wills. — Rich Kinzele. — Bremen : Bear Family Records, 1985. —

King, B. B. B. B. King : the blues, the wellspring of today's American popular music / B. B. King. — New York : Amsco, 1970. — I, A-180.

King, Larry L. The whorehouse papers / Larry L. King. — New York : Viking, 1982. — II, A-580.

King, Norman. Madonna : the book / Norman King. — New York : Quill, 1991. — III, 771.

Kingman, Daniel. American music : a panorama / Daniel Kingman. — 2nd ed. — New York : Schirmer, 1990. — III, 369.

Kingman, Daniel. American music : a panorama / Daniel Kingman. — New York : Schirmer, 1979. — A-11.

Kinkle, Roger D. The complete encyclopedia of popular music and jazz, 1900–1950 / Roger D. Kinkle. — New Rochelle, N.Y. : Arlington House, 1974. — I, 1158.

Kinscella, Hazel Gertrude. History sings : backgrounds of American music / Hazel Gertrude Kinscella. — Lincoln, Nebr. : University Publishing Co., 1940. — I, A-6.

Kirby, Edward. From Africa to Beale Street / Edward Kirby. — Memphis : Musical Management, 1983. — II, A-316.

Kirby, Edward. Memories of Beale Street / Edward Kirby. — Memphis, Tenn. : Penny Pincher Sales, 1979. — II, 618.

Kirk, Andy. Twenty years on wheels / Andy Kirk; as told to Amy Lee; discography by Howard Rye. — Ann Arbor : University of Michigan Press, 1989. — III, 651.

Kirk, Elise K. Music at the White House : a history of the American spirit / Elise K. Kirk. — Urbana : University of Illinois Press, 1986. — III, 398.

Kirkeby, W. T. Ain't misbehavin' : the story of Fats Waller / W. T. Kirkeby. — London : Davies, 1966. — I, 1143.

Kirkpatrick, John. A temporary mimeographed catalogue of the music manuscripts and related materials of Charles Edward Ives, 1875–1954, given by Mrs. Ives to the Library of the Yale School of Music / compiled by John Kirkpatrick. — New Haven, Conn. : Yale University, School of Music, 1960. — I, 330.

Kirkpatrick, Ralph. Early years / Ralph Kirkpatrick; epilogue by Frederick Hammond. — New York : Peter Lang, 1985. — III, 557.

Kirsch, Don R. Rock 'n' roll obscurities / Don R. Kirsch. — 2nd ed. — Tacoma, Wash. : Author, 1981. — II, A-687.

Kirsten, Dorothy. A time to sing / Dorothy Kirsten; discography by Stanley A. Bowker. — Garden City, N.Y. : Doubleday, 1982. — III, 756.

Kislan, Richard. Hoofing on Broadway : a history of show dancing / Richard Kislan. — New York : Prentice-Hall, 1987. — III, 9.

Kislan, Richard. The musical / Richard Kislan. — Englewood Cliffs, N.J. : Prentice-Hall, 1980. — II, 910.

Kitt, Eartha. Alone with me : a new autobiography / Eartha Kitt. — Chicago : Regnery, 1976. — II, 1081.

Kitt, Eartha. Confessions of a sex kitten / Eartha Kitt. — New York : Barricade Books, 1991. — III, 757.

Kitt, Eartha. Thursday's child / Eartha Kitt. — New York : Duell, Sloan & Pearce, 1956. — I, A-278.

Klah, Hasteen. Navajo creation myth : the story of the emergence / Hasteen Klah and Mary C. Wheelwright. — Santa Fe, N.M. : Museum of Navajo Ceremonial Art, 1942. — I, 409.

Klamkin, Marian. Old sheet music : a pictorial history / Marian Klamkin. — New York : Hawthorn, 1975. — II, 843.

Klaren, J. H. Edgar Varèse : pioneer of new music in America / J. H. Klaren. — Boston : Birchard, 1928. — I, 352.

Klauber, Bruce H. World of Gene Krupa : that legendary drummin' man / Bruce H. Klauber; with an introduction by Mel Tormé. — Ventura, Calif. : Pathfinder, 1990. — III, 653.

Klein, Hermann. Unmusical New York : a brief criticism of triumphs, failures, and abuses / Hermann Klein. — New York : John Lane, 1910. — I, 107.

Klein, Joe. Woody Guthrie : a life / Joe Klein. — New York : Knopf, 1980. — II, 348.

Klein, Mary Justina. The contribution of Daniel Gregory Mason to American music / Mary Justina Klein. — Washington : Catholic University of America Press, 1957. — I, 338.

Kleinhout, Henk. The Wallace Bishop story / Henk Kleinhout and Wim van Eyle. — Alphen aan de Rijn, Netherlands : Micrography, 1981. — II, A-461.

Kliment, Bud. Billie Holiday / Bud Kliment. — New York : Chelsea House, 1990. — III, 731.

Klinkowitz, Jerome. Listen : Gerry Mulligan : an aural narrative in jazz / Jerome Klinkowitz. — New York : Schirmer, 1991. — III, 655.

Kluckhohn, Clyde. An introduction to Navaho chant practice / Clyde Kluckhohn and Leland C. Wyman. — Menasha, Wisc. : American Anthropological Association, 1940. — I, 410.

Klussmeier, Gerhard. Benny Goodman und Deutschland / Gerhard Klussmeier. — Frankfurt am Main : H. A. Eisenbletter & B. S. M. Naumann, 1989. — III, 956.

Kmen, Henry A. Music in New Orleans : the formative years, 1791–1841 / Henry A. Kmen. — Baton Rouge : Louisiana State University Press, 1966. — I, 134.

Kneif, Tibor. Rock music / Tibor Kneif. — Reinbek, Germany : Rowohlt, 1982. — II, A-661.

Kneif, Tibor. Sachlexikon Rockmusik / Tibor Kneif. — Rev. ed. — Reinbek bei Hamburg : Rowohlt, 1980 — II, 1100.

Knight, Curtis. Jimi : an intimate biography of Jimi Hendrix / Curtis Knight. — New York : Praeger, 1974. — I, 1380.

Knippers, Ottis J. Who's who among Southern singers and composers / Ottis J. Knippers. — Lawrenceburg, Tenn. : James D. Vaughan, 1937. — I, 73.

Knockin' on Dylan's door. New York : Pocket Books, 1974. — II, 1199.

Knowles, Eleanor. The films of Jeanette MacDonald and Nelson Eddy / Eleanor Knowles. — South Brunswick, N.J. : Barnes, 1975. — II, 979.

Knox, Donald. The magic factory : how MGM made *An American in Paris* / Donald Knox. — New York : Praeger, 1973. — II, 1055.

Kobal, John. Gotta sing gotta dance : a pictorial history of film musicals / John Kobal. — London : Hamlyn, 1970. — I, 1265.

Kobbe, Gustav. Famous American songs / Gustav Kobbe. — New York : Crowell, 1906. — I, 1185.

Koch, Frederick. Reflections on composing : four American composers : Elwell, Shepherd, Rogers, Cowell / Frederick Koch. — Pittsburgh : Carnegie-Mellon University Press, 1983. — II, A-103.

Koch, Lawrence O. Yardbird suite : a compendium of the music and life of Charlie Parker / Lawrence O. Koch. — Bowling Green, Ohio : Bowling Green State University Popular Press, 1988. — III, 349.

Kochman, Marilyn. The big book of bluegrass / Marilyn Kochman. — New York : Morrow, 1984. — II, A-231.

Kodish, Debora. Good friends and bad enemies : Robert Winslow Gordon and the study of American folksong / Debora Kodish. — Urbana : University of Illinois Press, 1986. — III, 967.

Koenigsberg, Allen. Edison cylinder records, 1889–1912 : with an illustrated history of the phonograph / Allen Koenigsberg. — 2nd ed. — Brooklyn : APM Press, 1987. — III, 206.

Koenigsberg, Allen. Edison cylinder records, 1889–1912 : with an illustrated history of the phonograph / Allen Koenigsberg. — New York : Stellar Productions, 1969. — II, 811.

Koenigsberg, Allen. The patent history of the phonograph, 1877–1912 / Allen Koenigsberg. — Brooklyn : APM Press, 1990. — III, 1244.

Kofsky, Frank. Black nationalism and the revolution in music / Frank Kofsky. — New York : Pathfinder, 1970. — I, 1054.

Kogan, Judith. Nothing but the best : the struggle for perfection at the Juilliard School / Judith Kogan. — New York : Random House, 1987. — III, 1265.

Kolar, Walter W. A history of the tamburs / Walter W. Kolar. — Pittsburgh : Duquesne University, 1975. — II, 448.

Kolar, Walter W. Duquesne University Tamburitzans : the first fifty years remembered / Walter W. Kolar. — Pittsburgh : Tamburitza Press, 1986. — III, 422.

Kolodin, Irving. Metropolitan Opera, 1883–1966 / Irving Kolodin. — New York : Knopf, 1967. — I, 150.

Konkle, B. A. Joseph Hopkinson, 1770–1842 / B. A. Konkle. — Philadelphia : University of Pennsylvania, 1931. — II, 152.

Koon, George William. Hank Williams : a bio-bibliography / George William Koon. — Westport, Conn. : Greenwood, 1983. — II, A-271.

Koopal, Grace G. Miracle of music : the history of the Hollywood Bowl / Grace G. Koopal. — Los Angeles : W. Ritchie, 1972. — II, 67.

Kooper, Al. Backstage passes : rock 'n' roll life in the sixties / Al Kooper. — New York : Stein & Day, 1977. — II, 1214.

Korall, Burt. Drummin' men : the heartbeat of jazz : the swing years / Burt Korall; foreword by Mel Tormé. — New York : Schirmer, 1990. — III, 433.

Korda, Marion. Louisville music publications of the 19th century / Marion Korda. — Louisville, Ky. : Music Library, University of Louisville, 1991. — III, 90.

Korf, William E. The orchestral music of Louis Moreau Gottschalk / William E. Korf. — Henryville, Pa. : Institute of Mediaeval Music, 1983. — II, A-81.

Kornbluh, Joyce L. Rebel voices : an I.W.W. anthology / Joyce L. Kornbluh. — Ann Arbor : University of Michigan Press, 1964. — I, 593.

Korngold, Luzi. Erich Wolfgang Korngold : ein Lebensbild / Luzi Korngold. — Vienna : Lafite, 1967. — I, 1308.

Kornick, Rebecca Hodell. Recent American opera : a production guide / Rebecca Hodell Kornick. — New York : Columbia University Press, 1991. — III, 1269.

Korson, George. Black rock : mining folklore of the Pennsylvania Dutch / George Korson. — Baltimore : Johns Hopkins Press, 1960. — I, A-117.

Korson, George. Coal dust on the fiddle : songs and stories of the bituminous industry / George Korson. — Philadelphia : University of Pennsylvania Press, 1943. — I, 569.

Korson, George. Minstrels of the mine patch : songs and stories of the anthracite industry / George Korson. — Philadelphia : University of Pennsylvania Press, 1938. — I, 570.

Korson, George. Pennsylvania songs and legends / George Korson. — Philadelphia : University of Pennsylvania Press, 1949. — I, 482.

Korst, Bill. Elite, Hit, and Majestic master listing / Bill Korst [et al]. — Zephyrhills, Fla. : Joyce Record Club, 1989. — III, 208.

Koshgarian, Richard. American orchestral music : a performance catalog / Richard Koshgarian. — Metuchen, N.J. : Scarecrow, 1992. — III, 138.

Kosht, R. M. A & M records discography : including associated labels and alphanumeric index / R. M. Kosht. — Anaheim, Calif. : A & Mania, 1986. — III, 196.

Kosser, Michael. Those bold and beautiful country girls / Michael Kosser. — Leicester, England : Mayflower, 1979. — II, 475.

Kostelanetz, Andre. Echoes : memoirs of Andre Kostelanetz / Andre Kostelanetz and Gloria Hammond. — New York : Harcourt Brace Jovanovich, 1981. — II, A-147.

Kostelanetz, Richard. John Cage / Richard Kostelanetz. — New York : Praeger, 1970. — I, 310.

Kostelanetz, Richard. The new American arts / Richard Kostelanetz. — New York : Collier Books, 1967. — I, 272.

Kostelanetz, Richard. The theatre of mixed means / Richard Kostelanetz. — New York : Dial, 1968. — I, 273.

Koster, Piet. Charlie Parker / Piet Koster and Dick Bakker. — Vols. 3 and 4. — Alphen aan den Rijn, Netherlands : Micrography, 1975. — II, 773.

Koster, Piet. Charlie Parker / Piet Koster and Dick M. Bakker. — Alphen aan den Rijn, Netherlands : Micrography, 1974–1975. — I, 945.

Kotschenreuther, Helmut. Kurt Weill / Helmut Kotschenreuther. — Berlin : Hesse, 1962. — II, 1049.

Kozak, Roman. This ain't no disco : the story of CBGB / Roman Kozak; photographs by Ebet Roberts. — Boston : Faber & Faber, 1988. — III, 1181.

Kozinn, Allan. The guitar : the history, the music, the players / Allan Kozinn [et al]. — New York : Morrow, 1984. — II, A-59.

Kramarz, Volkmar. Harmonieanalyse der Rockmusik / Volkmar Kramarz. — Mainz, Germany : Schott, 1983. — II, A-715.

Kramer, Daniel. Bob Dylan / Daniel Kramer. — New York : Citadel, 1967. — I, A-294.

Kramer, Lawrence. Music and poetry : the 19th century and after / Lawrence Kramer. — Berkeley : University of California Press, 1984. — II, A-104.

Krasker, Tommy. Catalog of the American musical : musicals of Irving Berlin, George and Ira Gershwin, Cole Porter, Richard Rodgers, and Lorenz Hart / Tommy Krasker and Robert Kimball. — Washington : National Institute for Opera and Musical Theater, 1988. — III, 132.

Krassen, Miles. Appalachian fiddle / Miles Krassen. — New York : Oak, 1973. — I, A-136.

Kraut, Eberhard. George Lewis / Eberhard Kraut. — Menden, Germany : Der Jazzfreund, 1980. — II, 794.

Krehbiel, Henry Edward. Afro-American folksongs : a study in racial and national music / Henry Edward Krehbiel. — New York : Schirmer, 1914. — I, 761.

Krehbiel, Henry Edward. Chapters of opera / Henry Edward Krehbiel. — 3rd ed. — New York : Holt, 1911. — I, 151.

Krehbiel, Henry Edward. More chapters of opera / Henry Edward Krehbiel. — New York : Holt, 1919. — I, 152.

Krehbiel, Henry Edward. Notes on the cultivation of choral music and the Oratorio Society of New York / H. E. Krehbiel. — New York : Schuberth, 1884. — I, 108.

Krehbiel, Henry Edward. Reviews of the New York musical seasons 1885–1890 / Henry Edward Krehbiel. — London : Novello, Ewer, 1886–1890. — I, A-38.

Krehbiel, Henry Edward. The Philharmonic Society of New York : a memorial / Henry Edward Krehbiel. — London : Novello, 1892. — I, 114.

Kreitner, Kenneth. Discoursing sweet music : town bands and community life in turn-of-the-century Pennsylvania / Kenneth Kreitner. — Urbana : University of Illinois Press, 1990. — III, 1006.

Kreitner, Kenneth. Robert Ward : a bio-bibliography / Kenneth Kreitner. — Westport, Conn. : Greenwood, 1988. — III, 184.

Kreitzer, Jack. A living tradition : South Dakota songwriter's songbook : vol. 1 / Jack Kreitzer and Susan Braunstein. — Sioux Falls, S.D. : George B. German Music Archives, 1983. — II, A-197.

Krenek, Ernst. Exploring music : essays / Ernst Krenek. — London : Calder & Boyars, 1966. — I, A-79.

Krenek, Ernst. Music here and now / Ernst Krenek. — New York : Russell & Russell, 1967. — I, A-80.

Kreuger, Miles. *Show Boat* : the story of a classic American musical / Miles Kreuger. — New York : Oxford University Press, 1977. — II, 925.

Kreuger, Miles. The movie musical from Vitaphone to 42nd Street, as reported in a great fan magazine / Miles Kreuger. — New York : Dover, 1975. — I, 1266.

Kriebel, Howard Wiegner. The Schwenkfelders in Pennsylvania : a historical sketch / Howard Wiegner Kriebel. — Lancaster, Pa. : New Era Printing Co., 1904. — I, 21.

Krieger, Susan. Hip capitalism / Susan Krieger. — Beverly Hills, Calif. : Sage, 1979. — II, 1267.

Kriss, Eric. Barrelhouse and boogie piano / Eric Kriss. — New York : Oak, 1974. — I, 876.

Kriss, Eric. Six blue-roots pianists / Eric Kriss. — New York : Oak, 1973. — I, 877.

Krivine, John. Juke box Saturday night / John Krivine. — Secaucus, N.J. : Chartwell Books, 1971. — II, 100.

Kroeger, Karl. Catalog of the musical works of William Billings / Karl Kroeger. — New York : Greenwood, 1991. — III, 159.

Krogsgaard, Michael. Twenty years of recording : the Bob Dylan reference book / Michael Krogsgaard. — Copenhagen : Scandinavian Institute for Rock Research, 1981. — II, A-789.

Krohn, Ernst C. A century of Missouri music / Ernst C. Krohn. — St. Louis : Author, 1924. — I, 135.

Krohn, Ernst C. Missouri music / Ernst C. Krohn. — New York : Da Capo, 1971. — I, 135.

Krohn, Ernst C. Music publishing in St. Louis / Ernst C. Krohn; completed and ed. by J. Bunker Clark; foreword by Lincoln Bunce Spiess. — Warren, Mich. : Harmonie Park, 1988. — III, 91.

Krohn, Ernst C. Music publishing in the Middle Western states before the Civil War / Ernst C. Krohn. — Detroit : Information Coordinators, 1972. — I, 169.

Krueger, Karl. The musical heritage of the United States : the unknown portion / Karl Krueger. — New York : Society for the Preservation of the American Musical Heritage, 1973. — I, 36.

Krummel, Donald W. Bibliographic inventory to the early music in Newberry Library, Chicago, Illinois / Donald W. Krummel. — Boston : G. K. Hall, 1977. — II, 4.

Krummel, Donald W. Bibliographical handbook of American music / Donald William Krummel. — Urbana : University of Illinois Press, 1987. — III, 101.

Krummel, Donald W. Resources of American music history : a directory of source materials from colonial times to World War II / Donald W. Krummel [et al]. — Urbana : University of Illinois Press, 1981. — II, A-11.

Kubik, Gerhard. Mehrstimmigkeit und Tonsysteme in Zentral- und Ostafrika / Gerhard Kubik. — Vienna : Böhlau, 1968. — I, 723.

Kuehl, Linda. Billie Holiday remembered / Linda Kuehl and Ellie Schokert. — New York : New York Jazz Museum, 1973. — I, 1120.

Kuhn, Dieter. Josephine / Dieter Kuhn. — Frankfurt : Suhrkamp, 1976. — II, 1068.

Kuhnke, Klaus. Geschichte der Pop-Musik / Klaus Kuhnke [et al]. — Bremen : Archiv für Populäre Musik, 1977. — II, 1259.

Kuhnke, Klaus. Schriften zur populären Musik / Klaus Kuhnke [et al]. — Bremen : Archiv für Populäre Musik, 1975–1977. — II, 1249.

Kukla, Barbara J. Swing city : Newark nightlife, 1925–50 / Barbara J. Kukla. — Philadelphia : Temple University Press, 1991. — III, 1132.

Kupferberg, Herbert. Tanglewood / Herbert Kupferberg. — New York : Mc-Graw-Hill, 1976. — II, 53.

Kupferberg, Herbert. Those fabulous Philadelphians : the life and times of a great orchestra / Herbert Kupferberg. — New York : Scribner's, 1969. — I, 119.

Music in homes and churches / ed. Barbara Lambert — Boston : Colonial Society of Massachusetts, 1985. — II, A-38.

Lambert, Constant. Music ho! A study of music in decline / Constant Lambert. — 3rd ed. — London : Faber, 1966. — I, 974.

Lambert, Dennis. Producing hit records / Dennis Lambert and Ronald Zalkind. — New York : Schirmer, 1980. — II, 1158; III, 1245.

Lambert, G. E. Duke Ellington / G. E. Lambert. — London : Cassell, 1959. — I, 1108.

Lambert, G. E. Johnny Dodds / G. E. Lambert. — New York : Barnes, 1971. — I, 1101.

Lambert, Jake. The good things in life outweigh the bad : a biography of Lester Flatt / Jake Lambert. — Rev. ed. — Hendersonville, Tenn. : Jay-Lyn, 1982. — II, A-249.

Landau, Deborah. Janis Joplin : her life and times / Deborah Landau. — New York : Paperback Library, 1971. — II, 1212.

Landau, Jon. It's too late to stop now : a rock and roll journal / Jon Landau. — San Francisco : Straight Arrow Books, 1972. — I, 1366.

Landeck, Beatrice. Echoes of Africa in the folksongs of the Americas / Beatrice Landeck. — 2nd ed. — New York : McKay, 1969. — I, 690.

Landon, John W. Behold the mighty Wurlitzer : the history of the theatre pipe organ / John W. Landon. — Westport, Conn. : Greenwood, 1983. — III, 989.

Landowska, Wanda Alice L. La musique américaine / Wanda Alice L. Landowska. — Paris : Horay, 1952. — I, A-7.

Landrum, Larry N. American popular culture : a guide to information sources / Larry N. Landrum. — Detroit : Gale, 1982. — II, A-509.

Landy, Elliott. Woodstock vision / Elliott Landy. — Reinbek, Germany : Rowohlt, 1984. — II, A-725.

Lang, Iain. Background of the blues / Iain Lang. — London : Workers' Music Association, 1943. — I, 997.

Lang, Iain. Jazz in perspective / Iain Lang. — London : Hutchinson, 1947. — I, 997.

Lang, Paul Henry. One hundred years of music in America / Paul Henry Lang. — New York : Schirmer, 1961. — I, 94.

Lang, Paul Henry. Problems of modern music / Paul Henry Lang. — New York : Norton, 1962. — I, 262.

Lange, Francisco Curt. Vida y muerte de Louis Moreau Gottschalk / Francisco Curt Lange. — Mendoza, Argentina : Universidad Nacional de Cuyo, 1951. — I, 229.

Lange, Horst H. The fabulous fives / Horst H. Lange. — Rev. ed. — Chigwell, England : Storyville, 1978. — II, 641.

Langridge, Derek. Your jazz collection / Derek Langridge. — London : Bingley, 1970. — I, 908.

Lanier, Sidney. Music and poetry / Sidney Lanier. — New York : Scribner, 1898. — I, 233.

Laplace, Michel. Jabbo Smith : the misunderstood and the "modernistic" / Michel Laplace; trans. by Denis Egan. — Menden, Germany : Jazzfreund, 1988. — III, 668.

Larkin, Margaret. Singing cowboy / Margaret Larkin. — New York : Knopf, 1931. — I, 560.

Larkin, Philip. All what jazz / Philip Larkin. — London : Faber, 1970. — I, A-210.

Larkin, Philip. All what jazz / Philip Larkin. — Rev. ed. — London : Faber & Faber, 1985. — II, 705.

Larkin, Philip. Required writing / Philip Larkin. — London : Faber & Faber, 1983. — II, A-429.

Larkin, Rochelle. Soul music! / Rochelle Larkin. — New York : Lancer Books, 1970. — II, 568.

LaRochelle, Réal. Callas : la diva et le vinyl / Réal LaRochelle. — Montreal : Éditions Triptyque, 1987. — III, 692.

Larsen, John. Riley Puckett (1894–1946) : discography / John Larsen [et al]. — Bremen, Germany : Archiv für Populäre Musik, 1977. — II, 414.

Larson, Peter H. Turn on the stars : Bill Evans : the complete discography / Peter H. Larsen. — Holte, Denmark : Author, 1984. — III, 309.

Larson, Randall D. Musique fantastique : a survey of film music in the fantastic cinema / Randall D. Larson. — Metuchen, N.J. : Scarecrow, 1985. — III, 1029.

Latham, Caroline. E is for Elvis : an A-Z illustrated guide to the king of rock and roll / Caroline Latham and Jeannie Sakol. — New York : Penguin, 1990. — III, 832.

Latham, Caroline. Priscilla and Elvis : the Priscilla Presley story / Caroline Latham. — New York : New American Library, 1985. — III, 1293.

Laubich, Arnold. Art Tatum : a guide to his recorded music / Arnold Laubich and Ray Spencer. — Metuchen, N.J. : Scarecrow, 1982. — II, A-386.

Laufe, Abe. Broadway's greatest musicals / Abe Laufe. — Rev. ed. — New York : Funk & Wagnalls, 1973. — I, 1258.

Laurie, Joe. Vaudeville : from the honky-tonks to the Palace / Joe Laurie. — New York : Holt, 1953. — I, 1249.

Lavignac, Albert. Music and musicians / Albert Lavignac. — New York : Holt, 1899. — I, A-8.

Law, Andrew. Essays on music / Andrew Law. — Philadelphia : Author, 1814. — I, 205.

Law, Andrew. The musical primer : containing the rules of psalmody, newly revised and improved / Andrew Law. — Cheshire, Conn. : William Law, 1793. — I, 206.

Lawhead, Steve. Rock reconsidered : a Christian looks at contemporary music / Steve Lawhead. — Downers Grove, Ill. : Intervarsity Press, 1981. — II, A-716.

Lawless, Ray M. Folksingers and folksongs in America / Ray M. Lawless. — 2nd ed. — New York : Meredith, 1965. — I, 432.

Lawrence, Vera Brodsky. Music for patriots, politicians, and presidents / Vera Brodsky Lawrence. — New York : Macmillan, 1975. — II, 860.

Lawrence, Vera Brodsky. Strong on music : the New York music scene in the days of George Templeton Strong / Vera Brodsky Lawrence. — New York: Oxford, 1987- . — III, 395.

Lawrenz, Marguerite Martha. Bibliography and index of negro music / Marguerite Martha Lawrenz. — Detroit : Board of Education, 1969. — I, A-148.

Laws, G. Malcolm. American balladry from British broadsides / Malcolm G. Laws. — Philadelphia : American Folklore Society, 1957. — I, 467.

Laws, G. Malcolm. Native American balladry / G. Malcolm Laws. — 2nd ed. — Philadelphia : American Folklore Society, 1964. — I, 445.

Lax, Roger. The great song thesaurus / Roger Lax and Frederick Smith. — New York : Oxford University Press, 1984. — II, A-513.

Layne, Maude Wanzer. The negro's contribution to music / Maude Wanzer Layne. — Charleston, W.Va. : Mathews, 1942. — II, 587.

Lazarus, Lois. Country is my music! / Lois Lazarus. — New York : Messner, 1980. — II, 364.

Leach, MacEdward. Guide for collectors of oral traditions and folk material in Pennsylvania / MacEdward Leach and Henry Glassie. — Harrisburg : Pennsylvania Historical and Museum Commission, 1968. — I, 483.

Leadbitter, Mike. Blues records : 1942–1970 / Mike Leadbitter and Neil Slaven. — London : Record Information Services, 1987. — III, 221.

Leadbitter, Mike. Blues records, January 1943–December 1966 / Mike Leadbitter and Neil Slaven. — London : Hanover, 1968. — I, 808.

Leadbitter, Mike. Crowley, Louisiana blues / Mike Leadbitter. — Bexhill-on-Sea, England : Blues Unlimited, 1968. — I, 822.

Leadbitter, Mike. Delta country blues / Mike Leadbitter. — Bexhill-on-Sea, England : Blues Unlimited, 1968. — I, 823.

Leadbitter, Mike. French Cajun music / Mike Leadbitter. — Bexhill-on-Sea, England : Blues Unlimited, 1968. — I, 648.

Leadbitter, Mike. From the bayou : the story of Goldband Records / Mike Leadbitter and Eddie Shuler. — Bexhill-on-Sea, England : Blues Unlimited, 1969. — I, 649.

Leadbitter, Mike. Nothing but the blues / Mike Leadbitter. — London : Hanover, 1971. — I, 831.

Leaf, David. The Beach Boys and the California myth / David Leaf. — New York : Grosset & Dunlap, 1978. — II, 1186.

LeBrew, Arthur R. Black musicians of the colonial period / Arthur R. LaBrew. — 2nd ed. — Detroit : Author, 1981. — II, 517.

Leckrone, Michael. Popular music in the U.S. (1920–1950) : class outline : the big bands / Michael Leckrone. — Rev. ed. — Dubuque, Iowa : Eddie Bowers, 1986. — III, 1138.

Ledbetter, Huddie. Leadbelly legend: a collection of world famous songs / Huddie Ledbetter; ed. John A. Lomax and Alan Lomax. — 2nd ed. — New York : Folkways, 1965. — I, 844.

Ledbetter, Huddie. Leadbelly songbook / Huddie Ledbetter; ed. Moses Asch and Alan Lomax. — New York : Oak, 1962. — I, 844.

Ledbetter, Steven. 100 years of the Boston Pops / Steven Ledbetter. — Boston : Boston Symphony Orchestra, 1985. — II, A-39.

Ledbetter, Steven. Sennets & tuckets : a Bernstein celebration / ed. Steven Ledbetter. — Boston : Boston Symphony Orchestra, in association with D. R. Godine, 1988. — III, 454.

Lederman, Minna. The life and death of a small magazine : *Modern Music*, 1924–1946 / Minna Lederman. — Brooklyn : Institute for Studies in American Music, 1983. — II, A-148.

Ledford, Lily May. Coon Creek girl / Lily May Ledford. — Berea, Ky. : Appalachian Center, Berea College, 1980. — II, 476.

Leduc, Jean-Marie. Le rock de A à Z / Jean-Marie Leduc. — Paris : Michel, 1984. — II, A-662.

Lee, Bill. Jazz dictionary / Bill Lee. — New York : Shattinger International Music Corp., 1979. — II, 632.

Lee, Dorothy Sara. Native North American music and oral data : a catalogue of sound recordings 1893–1976 / Dorothy Sara Lee. — Bloomington : Indiana University Press, 1979. — II, 235.

Lee, George W. Beale Street : where the blues began / George W. Lee. — New York : Ballou, 1934. — I, 816.

Lee, Johnny. Lookin' for love / Johnny Lee; with Randy Wyles. — Austin, Tex. : Diamond Books, 1989. — III, 762.

Lee, Katie. Ten thousand goddam cattle : a history of the American cowboy in song, story and verse / Katie Lee. — Flagstaff, Ariz. : Northland, 1976. — II, 339.

Lee, Peggy. Miss Peggy Lee : an autobiography / Peggy Lee. — New York : Donald I. Fine, 1989. — III, 763.

Lee, William F. Stan Kenton : artistry in rhythm / William F. Lee. — Los Angeles : Creative Press of Los Angeles, 1980. — II, 757.

Lees, Gene. Inventing champagne : the worlds of Lerner and Loewe / Gene Lees. — New York : St. Martin's, 1990. — III, 495.

Lees, Gene. Meet me at Jim & Andy's : jazz musicians and their world / Gene Lees. — New York : Oxford, 1988. — III, 423.

Lees, Gene. Oscar Peterson : the will to swing / Gene Lees. — Rocklin, Calif. : Prima Publishing & Communications, 1990. — III, 565.

Lees, Gene. Singers and the song / Gene Lees; foreword by Grover Sales. — New York : Oxford, 1987. — III, 1059.

Lees, Gene. Waiting for Dizzy / Gene Lees. — New York : Oxford, 1991. — III, 1099.

Lefcowitz, Eric. The Monkees tale / Eric Lefcowitz. — Rev. ed. — Berkeley, Calif. : Last Gasp, 1989. — III, 925.

Lefton, Mark. Approaches to deviance / Mark Lefton. — New York : Appleton-Century-Crofts, 1968. — II, 782.

Leggett, Carol. Reba McEntire : the queen of country / Carol Leggett. — New York : Fireside, 1992. — III, 782.

Lehmann, Theo. Blues and trouble / Theo Lehmann. — Berlin : Henschel, 1966. — I, 861.

Lehmann, Theo. Negro spirituals : Geschichte und Theologie / Theo Lehmann. — Berlin : Eckhart, 1965. — I, 793.

Leibovitz, Annie. Shooting stars / Annie Leibovitz. — San Francisco : Straight Arrow Books, 1973. — II, 1274.

Leiby, Bruce R. Gordon MacRae : a bio-bibliography / Bruce R. Leiby. — New York : Greenwood, 1991. — III, 186.

Leichtentritt, Hugo. Serge Koussevitzky, the Boston Symphony Orchestra and the new American music / Hugo Leichtentritt. — Cambridge, Mass. : Harvard University Press, 1946. — I, 364.

Leichter, Albert. A discography of rhythm & blues and rock & roll, circa 1946–1964 / Albert Leichter. — Staunton, Va. : Author, 1975. — II, 558.

Leigh, Robert. Index to song books : a title index to over 11,000 copies of almost 6,800 songs in 111 song books published between 1933 and 1962 / Robert Leigh. — Stockton, Calif. : Author, 1964. — II, 805.

Leigh, Spencer. Paul Simon now and then / Spencer Leigh. — Liverpool : Raven Books, 1973. — I, 1387.

Leigh, Spencer. Stars in my eyes : personal interviews with pop music stars / Spencer Leigh. — Liverpool : Raven Books, 1980. — II, 1172.

Leiser, Willie. I'm a road runner baby / Willie Leiser. — Bexhill-on-Sea, England : Blues Unlimited, 1969. — I, 862.

Leiter, Robert D. The musicians and Petrillo / Robert D. Leiter. — New York : Bookman Associates, 1953. — I, 365.

Lemay, J. A. Leo. "New England's arrogances" : American's first folk song / J. A. Leo Lemay. — Cranbury, N.J. : Associated University Presses for the University of Delaware Press, 1985. — II, A-193.

Lemlich, Jeffrey M. Savage lost : Florida garage bands : the 60s and beyond / Jeffrey M. Lemlich. — Florida Plantation, Fla. : Distinctive Publishing, 1991. — III, 1183.

Lenz, Günter H. History and tradition in Afro-American culture / ed. Günter H. Lenz. — Frankfurt : Campus Verlag, 1984. — II, A-281.

Leon, Ruth. Applause : New York's guide to the performing arts / Ruth Leon. — New York : Applause Books, 1991. — III, 1291.

Leonard, Neil. Jazz and the white Americans / Neil Leonard. — Chicago : University of Chicago Press, 1962. — I, 975.

Leonard, Neil. Jazz : myth and religion / Neil Leonard. — New York : Oxford, 1987. — III, 1086.

Leonard, William Torbert. Broadway bound : a guide to the shows that died aborning / William Torbert Leonard. — Metuchen, N.J. : Scarecrow, 1983. — II, A-570.

LePage, Jane W. Women composers, conductors and musicians of the twentieth century. Volume III. / Jane W. LePage. — Metuchen, N.J. : Scarecrow, 1988. — III, 84.

LePage, Jane Weiner. Women composers, conductors, and musicians of the twentieth century : selected biographies / Jane Weiner LePage. — Metuchen, N.J. : Scarecrow, 1980–1983. — II, 22.

Lerner, Alan Jay. A hymn to him : the lyrics of Alan Jay Lerner. — New York : Limelight, 1987. — III, 1299.

Lerner, Alan Jay. The musical theatre : a celebration / Alan Jay Lerner. — New York : McGraw-Hill, 1986. — III, 1022.

Lester, Julius. The 12-string guitar as played by Leadbelly : an instruction manual / Julius Lester and Pete Seeger. — New York : Oak, 1965. — I, A-181.

Levant, Oscar. A smattering of ignorance / Oscar Levant. — Garden City, N.Y. : Doubleday, 1959. — I, 366.

Levine, Joseph A. Synagogue song in America / Joseph A. Levine. — Crown Point, Ind. : White Cliffs Media, 1988. — III, 1044.

Levine, Lawrence W. Black culture and black consciousness / Lawrence W. Levine. — New York : Oxford University Press, 1977. — II, 491.

Levine, Lawrence W. Highbrow/lowbrow : the emergence of cultural hierarchy in America / Lawrence W. Levine. — Cambridge, Mass. : Harvard University Press, 1988. — III, 4.

Levine, Michael. The music address book : how to reach anyone who's anyone in music / Michael Levine. — New York : Harper, 1989. — III, 35.

Levitt, Ellen. Land of a thousand bands : the current American independent label rock 'n' roll band experience / Ellen Levitt. — Brooklyn : Midwood, 1987. — III, 1182.

Levy, Alan Howard. Musical nationalism : American composers' search for identity / Alan Howard Levy. — Westport, Conn. : Greenwood, 1984. — II, A-105.

Levy, Alan. Operation Elvis / Alan Levy. — London : Deutsch, 1960. — II, 1298.

Levy, Joseph. The jazz experience : a guide to appreciation / Joseph Levy. — Englewood Cliffs, N.J. : Prentice-Hall, 1983. — II, A-389.

Levy, Lester S. Flashes of merriment : a century of humorous songs in America, 1805–1905 / Lester S. Levy. — Norman : University of Oklahoma Press, 1971. — I, 1178.

Levy, Lester S. Give me yesterday : American history in song, 1890–1920 / Lester S. Levy. — Norman : University of Oklahoma Press, 1975. — II, 861.

Levy, Lester S. Grace notes in American history / Lester S. Levy. — Norman : University of Oklahoma Press, 1967. — I, 1170.

Levy, Lester S. Picture the songs / Lester S. Levy. — Baltimore : Johns Hopkins University Press, 1976. — II, 844.

Lewine, Richard. Songs of the American theater : a comprehensive listing of more than 12,000 songs / Richard Lewine and Alfred Simon. — New York : Dodd, Mead, 1973. — I, 1259.

Lewine, Richard. Songs of the theater / Richard Lewine and Alfred Simon. — New York : H. W. Wilson, 1984. — III, 152.

Lewis, David Levering. When Harlem was in vogue / David Levering Lewis. — New York : Knopf, 1981. — II, A-282.

Lewis, Laurie. The concerts / Laurie Lewis. — New York : A & W Visual Library, 1979. — II, 1275.

Lewis, Myra. Great balls of fire : the uncensored story of Jerry Lee Lewis / Myra Lewis. — New York : Morrow, 1982. — II, A-809.

Leydi, Roberto. Sarah Vaughan / Roberto Leydi. — Milan : Ricordi, 1961. — I, A-211.

Liberace. The wonderful private world of Liberace / Liberace. — New York : Harper, 1986. — III, 559.

Libin, Laurence. American musical instruments in the Metropolitan Museum of Art / Laurence Libin. — New York : Metropolitan Museum of Art and W. W. Norton, 1985. — III, 988.

Lichtenwanger, William. Oscar Sonneck and American music / William Lichtenwanger. — Urbana : University of Illinois Press, 1983. — II, A-149.

Lichtenwanger, William. The music of Henry Cowell : a descriptive catalog / William Lichtenwanger. — Brooklyn : Institute for Studies in American Music, 1986. — III, 161.

Lichter, Paul. The boy who dared to rock : the definitive Elvis / Paul Lichter. — Garden City, N.Y. : Doubleday, 1978. — II, 1228.

Lieb, Sandra. Mother of the blues : a study of Ma Rainey / Sandra Lieb. — Amherst : University of Massachusetts Press, 1981. — II, A-323.

Lieberman, Robbie. "My song is my weapon" : people's songs, American communism, and the politics of culture, 1930–50 / Robbie Lieberman. — Urbana : University of Illinois Press, 1989. — III, 1212.

Lifton, Sarah. The listener's guide to folk music / Sarah Lifton. — New York : Facts on File, 1983. — II, A-167.

Lightfoot, Robert M. The Chicago Symphony Orchestra / Robert M. Lightfoot and Thomas Willis. — Chicago : Rand McNally, 1974. — I, A-39.

Lightner, Helen. Class voice and the American art song : a source book and anthology / Helen Lightner. — Metuchen, N.J. : Scarecrow, 1991. — III, 1268.

Lilje, Hanns. Das Buch der Spirituals und Gospel Songs / Hanns Lilje. — Hamburg : Furche, 1961. — II, 609.

Limbacher, James L. Film music : from violins to video / James L. Limbacher. — Metuchen, N.J. : Scarecrow, 1974. — I, 1309.

Limbacher, James L. Keeping score : film and television music, 1980–1988 : with additional coverage of 1921–1979 / James L. Limbacher and H. Stephen Wright, Jr. — Metuchen, N.J. : Scarecrow, 1991. — III, 130.

Limbacher, James L. Keeping score : film music 1972–1979 / James L. Limbacher. — Metuchen, N.J. : Scarecrow, 1981. — II, A-594.

Lincoln, Harry B. The computer and music / Harry B. Lincoln. — Ithaca, N.Y. : Cornell University Press, 1970. — I, 282.

Lindenmaier, H. Lukas. The man who never sleeps : the Charles Mingus discography 1945–1978 / H. Lukas Lindenmaier and Horst J. Salewski. — Freiburg, Germany : Jazz Realities, 1983. — II, A-379.

Lindquist, Emory Kempton. Hagbard Brase : beloved music master / Emory Lindquist. — Lindsborg, Kans. : Bethany College Press, 1984. — III, 950.

Lindsay, Joe. Picture discs of the world : price guide / Joe Lindsay. — Scottsdale, Ariz. : Biodisc, 1990. — III, 210.

Linedecker, Cliff. Country music stars and the supernatural / Cliff Linedecker. — New York : Dell, 1979. — II, 477.

Lingenfelter, Richard E. Songs of the American West / Richard E. Lingenfelter [et al]. — Berkeley : University of California Press, 1968. — I, 511.

Lingg, Ann M. John Philip Sousa / Ann M. Lingg. — New York : Holt, 1954. — II, 1036.

Linn, Karen. That half-barbaric twang : the banjo in American popular culture / Karen Linn. — Urbana : University of Illinois Press, 1991. — III, 995.

Linscott, E. H. Folk songs of old New England / E. H. Linscott. — New York : Macmillan, 1939. — I, A-118.

Lipman, Samuel. Arguing for music, arguing for culture / Samuel Lipman. — Boston : D. R. Godine, in association with the American Council for the Arts, 1990. — III, 56.

Lipmann, Eric. L'Amérique de George Gershwin / Eric Lipmann. — Paris : Messine, 1981. — II, A-600.

Lipscomb, Mance. I say me for a parable / Mance Lipscomb and A. Glenn Myers. — El Rito, N.M. : Possum Heard, 1982. — II, A-321.

Lipsitz, George. Class and culture in cold war America / George Lipsitz. — South Hadley, Mass. : Bergin & Garvey, 1982. — II, A-731.

Lisciandro, Frank. An hour for magic : a photojournal of Jim Morrison and the Doors / Frank Lisciandro. — New York : Delilah, 1982. — II, A-778.

Lisciandro, Frank. Morrison : a feast of friends / ed. Frank Lisciandro. — New York : Warner Books, 1991. — III, 796.

Lissauer, Robert. Lissauer's encyclopedia of popular music in America, 1888 to the present / Robert Lissauer. — New York : Paragon House, 1991. — III, 142.

List, George. Music in the Americas / ed. George List and Juan Orrego-Salas. — Bloomington, Ind. : Indiana Research Center in Anthropology, Folklore, and Liguistics, 1967. — I, 37.

List, George. Singing about it : folk song in southern Indiana / transcribed by George List. — Indianapolis : Indiana Historical Society, 1991. — III, 24.

Little, William. The easy instructor : or a new method of teaching sacred harmony / William Little and William Smith. — Rev. ed. — Albany, N.Y. : Websters & Skinners and Daniel Steele, 1831. — I, 523.

Litweiler, John. Ornette Coleman : the harmolodic life / John Litweiler. — London : Quartet, 1992. — III, 619.

Litweiler, John. The freedom principle : jazz after 1958 / John Litweiler. — New York : Morrow, 1984. — II, A-440.

Livingston, Robert Allen. Livingstone's complete music industry business and law reference book / Robert Allen Livingston. — Cardiff by the Sea, Calif. : La Costa, 1981. — III, 14.

Livingston's complete music business directory. — Cardiff by the Sea, Calif. : La Costa, 1991. — III, 28.

Lloyd's church musicians directory (1910) / Frederic E. J. Lloyd. — Chicago : Ritzmann, Brookes, 1910. — I, A-22.

Lock, Graham. Forces in motion : the music and thoughts of Anthony Braxton / Graham Lock; photographs by Nick White; foreword by Anthony Braxton. — London : Quartet, 1988. — III, 612.

Locke, Alain Leroy. The negro and his music / Alain Leroy Locke. — Washington : Associates in Negro Folk Education, 1936. — I, 691.

Loesser, Arthur. Humor in American song / Arthur Loesser. — New York : Howell, Soskin, 1942. — I, 1179.

Loesser, Arthur. Men, women and pianos : a social history / Arthur Loesser. — New York : Simon & Schuster, 1954. — I, 161.

Loewen, Alice. Exploring the Mennonite hymnal / Alice Loewen. — Newton, Kans. : Faith & Life Press, 1983. — II, A-28.

Logan, Nick. The illustrated encyclopedia of rock / Nick Logan and Bob Woffinden. — 3rd ed. — London : Salamander, 1982. — II, 1101.

Logan, William A. Road to heaven : twenty-eight negro spirituals / ed. William A. Logan. — University : University of Alabama Press, 1955. — II, 526.

Loggins, Vernon. Where the word ends : the life of Louis Moreau Gottschalk / Vernon Loggins. — Baton Rouge : Louisiana State University Press, 1958. — I, 230.

Logsdon, Guy. The whorehouse bells were ringing, and other songs cowboys sing / ed. Guy Logsdon. — Urbana : University of Illinois Press, 1989. — III, 21.

Lomax, Alan. American folk song and folk lore : a regional bibliography / Alan Lomax and Sidney Robertson Cowell. — New York : Progressive Education Association, 1942. — I, 434.

Lomax, Alan. Folk song style and culture / Alan Lomax. — Washington : American Association for the Advancement of Science, 1968. — I, 425.

Lomax, Alan. Folk songs of North America in the English language / Alan Lomax. — London : Cassell, 1960. — I, 455.

Lomax, Alan. Hard hitting songs for hard-hit people / Alan Lomax. — New York : Oak, 1967. — I, 588.

Lomax, Alan. Mister Jelly Roll / Alan Lomax. — 2nd ed. — Berkeley : University of California Press, 1973. — I, 1128.

Lomax, Alan. Penguin book of American folk songs / Alan Lomax. — Harmondsworth, England : Penguin, 1964. — I, 456.

Lomax, Alan. The rainbow sign : a southern documentary / Alan Lomax. — New York : Duell, Sloan & Pearce, 1959. — II, 522.

Lomax, John A. Adventures of a ballad hunter / John A. Lomax. — New York : Macmillan, 1947. — I, 446.

Lomax, John A. American ballads and folk songs / John A. Lomax and Alan Lomax. — New York : Macmillan, 1934. — I, 457.

Lomax, John A. Cowboy songs and other frontier ballads / John A. Lomax. — Rev. ed. — New York : Macmillan, 1938. — I, 561.

Lomax, John A. Folk song U.S.A. / John A. Lomax and Alan Lomax. — New York : Meredith, 1947. — I, 459.

Lomax, John A. Negro folk songs as sung by Lead Belly / John A. Lomax and Alan Lomax. — New York : Macmillan, 1936. — I, 846.

Lomax, John A. Our singing country / John A. Lomax and Alan Lomax. — New York : Macmillan, 1949. — I, 458.

Lomax, John A. Songs of the cattle trail and cow camp / John A. Lomax. — New York : Macmillan, 1919. — I, 562.

Lomax, John, III. Nashville : music city, USA / John Lomax III. — New York : Abrams, 1985. — II, A-235.

Lombardo, Guy. Auld acquaintance / Guy Lombardo; with Jack Altschul. — Garden City, N.Y. : Doubleday, 1975. — II, 759.

London, Herbert I. Closing the circle : a cultural history of rock / Herbert I. London. — Chicago : Nelson-Hall, 1984. — II, A-732.

London, Kurt. Film music / Kurt London. — London : Faber, 1936. — I, 1310.

Loney, Glenn. Musical theatre in America : papers and proceedings of the conference on the Musical Theatre in America / ed. Glenn Loney. — Westport, Conn. : Greenwood, 1984. — II, A-575.

Longolius, Christian. George Gershwin / Christian Longolius. — Berlin : Hesse, 1959. — I, A-259.

Longstreet, Stephen. Knaurs Jazz-lexikon / Stephen Longstreet and Alfons M. Dauer. — Munich : Knaur, 1957. — I, 909.

Longstreet, Stephen. Sportin' house : a history of New Orleans sinners and the birth of jazz / Stephen Longstreet. — Los Angeles : Sherbourne, 1965. — I, 1066.

Longstreet, Stephen. Storyville to Harlem : fifty years in the jazz scene / Stephen Longstreet. — New Brunswick, N.J. : Rutgers University Press, 1986. — III, 62.

Longworth, Mike. Martin guitars : a history / Mike Longworth. — Cedar Knolls, N.J. : Colonial Press, 1975. — II, 96.

Lonstein, Albert I. Sinatra / Albert I. Lonstein. — New York : Musicprint, 1983. — II, A-635.

Lonstein, Albert I. The compleat Sinatra / Albert I. Lonstein and Vito R. Marino. — Monroe, N.Y. : Library Research Associates, 1970. — I, 1336.

Lord, Bobby. Hit the glory road! / Bobby Lord. — Nashville : Broadman, 1969. — I, A-131.

Lord, Francis A. Bands and drummer boys of the Civil War / Francis A. Lord and Arthur Wise. — New York : Yoseloff, 1966. — I, 1199.

Lord, Tom. Clarence Williams / Tom Lord. — Chigwell, Essex, England : Storyville, 1976. — II, 656.

Lord, Tom. The jazz discography / Tom Lord. — Redwood, N.Y. : Cadence Jazz Books, 1992- . — III, 241.

Lorenz, Ellen Jane. Glory, hallelujah! : the story of the campmeeting spiritual / Ellen Jane Lorenz. — Nashville : Abingdon, 1980. — II, 332.

Lorenz, Kenneth M. Two-minute brown wax and XP cylinder records of the Columbia Phonograph Company : numerical catalog, August 1896-ca. March 1909 / Kenneth M. Lorenz. — Wilmington, Del. : Kastlemusick, 1981. — III, 204.

Lorenz, Wolfgang. Robert Nighthawk : complete discography, 1936–1967 / Wolfgang Lorenz. — Bonn : Author, 1963. — II, A-322.

Loring, William C. Music of Arthur Bird / William C. Loring. — Washington : Author, 1974. — I, 222.

Lornell, Kip. "Happy in the service of the Lord" : Afro-American gospel quartets in Memphis / Kip Lornell. — Urbana : University of Illinois Press, 1988. — III, 1041.

Lornell, Kip. Virginia's blues : country & gospel records, 1902–1943 : an annotated discography / Kip Lornell. — Lexington : University Press of Kentucky, 1989. — III, 222.

Loucks, Richard. Arthur Shepherd, American composer / Richard Loucks. — Provo, Utah : Brigham Young University Press, 1980. — II, 199.

Lourie, Arthur. Sergei Koussevitzky and his epoch / Arthur Lourie. — New York : Knopf, 1931. — II, 212.

Lovell, John. Black song : the forge and the flame / John Lovell. — New York : Macmillan, 1972. — I, 794.

Lovingood, Penman. Famous modern negro musicians / Penman Lovingood. — Brooklyn : Press Forum Co., 1921. — I, 705.

Lowe, David A. Callas as they saw her / David A. Lowe. — New York : Ungar, 1986. — III, 693.

Lowe, Leslie. Directory of popular music, 1900–1965 / Leslie Lowe. — Droitwich, Worcestershire, England : Peterson, 1975. — II, 806.

Lowenberg, Carlton. Musicians wrestle everywhere : Emily Dickinson and music / Carlton Lowenberg; foreword by Richard B. Sewall. — Berkeley, Calif. : Fallen Leaf, 1992. — III, 185.

Lowens, Irving. A bibliography of songsters printed in America before 1821 / Irving Lowens. — Worcester, Mass. : American Antiquarian Society, 1976. — II, 137.

Lowens, Irving. Music and musicians in early America / Irving Lowens. — New York : Norton, 1964. — I, 38.

Lowens, Irving. Music in America and American music : two views of the scene / Irving Lowens. — Brooklyn : Institute for Studies in American Music, 1978. — II, 16.

Lubbock, Mark. The complete book of light opera / Mark Lubbock. — London : Putnam, 1962. — I, 1224.

Lucas, G. W. Remarks on musical conventions in Boston / G. W. Lucas. — Northampton, Mass. : Author, 1844. — I, 216.

Luckert, Karl W. Coyoteway : a Navajo Holyway healing ceremonial / Karl W. Luckert. — Tucson : University of Arizona Press, 1979. — II, 251.

Luening, Otto. The odyssey of an American composer / Otto Luening. — New York : Scribner's, 1980. — II, 194.

Lummis, Charles F. Spanish songs of old California / Charles F. Lummis. — Los Angeles : Author, 1923. — I, 474.

Lumpkin, Ben Gray. Folksongs on records / Ben Gray Lumpkin. — Denver : Alan Swallow, 1950. — II, 274.

Lunsford, Bascom Lamar. 30 and 1 folksongs / Bascom Lamar Lunsford and Lamar Stringfield. — New York : Fischer, 1929. — II, 428.

Lust, Patricia. American vocal chamber music, 1915–1980 : an annotated bibliography / Patricia Lust. — Westport, Conn. : Greenwood, 1985. — II, A-96.

Lustig, Milton. Music editing for motion pictures / Milton Lustig. — New York : Hastings House, 1980. — II, 939.

Luther, Frank. Americans and their songs / Frank Luther. — New York : Harper, 1942. — I, 1180.

Luzzi, Mario. Charles Mingus / Mario Luzzi. — Rome : Lato Side, 1983. — II, A-486.

Lydon, Michael. Boogie lightning / Michael Lydon. — New York : Dial, 1974. — I, A-182.

Lydon, Michael. Boogie lightning : how music became electric / Michael Lydon. — Reprinted with a new foreword by B. B. King. — New York : Da Capo, 1980. — II, 559.

Lydon, Michael. Rock folk / Michael Lydon. — New York : Dial, 1971. — I, 1368.

Lyle, Katie Letcher. Scalded to death by the steam / Katie Letcher Lyle. — Chapel Hill, N.C. : Algonquin Books, 1983. — II, A-214.

Lynch, Richard Chigley. Broadway on record : a directory of New York cast recordings of musical shows, 1931–1986 / Richard Chigley Lynch. — Westport, Conn. : Greenwood, 1987. — III, 1023.

Lynch, Richard Chigley. Movie musicals on record : a directory of recordings of motion picture musicals, 1927–1987 / Richard Chigley Lynch. — New York : Greenwood, 1989. — III, 244.

Lynch, Richard Chigley. Musicals! : a directory of musical properties available for production / Richard Chigley Lynch. — Chicago : American Library Association, 1984. — II, A-579.

Lynch, Richard Chigley. TV and studio cast musicals on record : discography of television musicals and studio recordings of stage and film musicals / Richard Chigley Lynch. — Westport, Conn. : Greenwood, 1990. — III, 245.

Lynch, Vincent. Jukeboxes : the golden age / Vincent Lynch and Bill Henkin. — Berkeley, Calif. : Lancaster-Miller, 1981. — II, A-65.

Lynes, Russell. The lively audience : a social history of the visual and performing arts in America, 1890–1950 / Russell Lynes. — New York : Harper & Row, 1985. — II, A-13.

Lynn, Loretta. Coal miner's daughter / Loretta Lynn. — Chicago : Regnery, 1976. — II, 407.

Lyon, Hugh Lee. Leontyne Price : highlights of a prima donna / Hugh Lee Lyon. — New York : Vantage, 1973. — II, 70.

Lyons, Jimmy. Dizzy, Duke, the Count and me : the story of the Monterey Jazz Festival / Jimmy Lyons. — San Francisco : California Living Books, 1978. — II, 678.

Lyons, Len. Jazz portraits : the lives and music of the jazz masters / Len Lyons and Don Perlo. — New York : Morrow, 1989. — III, 424.

Lyons, Len. The 101 best jazz albums : a history of jazz on records / Len Lyons. — New York : Morrow, 1980. — II, 660.

Lyons, Len. The great jazz pianists / Len Lyons. — New York : Morrow, 1983. — II, A-450.

Lyttelton, Humphrey. Basin Street to Harlem : jazz masters and masterpieces, 1917–1930 / Humphrey Lyttelton. — New York : Taplinger, 1982. — III, 1119.

Lyttelton, Humphrey. Enter the giants, 1931–1944 / Humphrey Lyttelton. — New York : Taplinger, 1982. — III, 1120.

Lyttelton, Humphrey. The best of jazz : Basin Street to Harlem / Hymphrey Lyttelton. — London : Robson Books, 1978. — II, 711.

Mabey, Richard. The pop process / Richard Mabey. — London : Hutchinson Educational, 1969. — I, A-296.

MacDougall, Hamilton C. Early New England psalmody : an historical appreciation, 1620–1820 / Hamilton C. MacDougall. — Brattleboro, Vt. : Daye, 1940. — I, 182.

MacDowell, Edward. Critical and historical essays / Edward MacDowell. — Boston : Schmidt, 1912. — I, 235.

MacDowell, Marian. Random notes on Edward MacDowell / Marian MacDowell. — Boston : Schmidt, 1950. — I, 237.

Machlin, Milt. The Michael Jackson catalog : a comprehensive guide to records, videos, clothing, posters, toys and millions of collectible souvenirs / Milt Machlin. — New York : Arbor House, 1984. — III, 745.

Machlin, Paul. Stride : the music of Fats Waller / Paul Machlin. — Boston : G. K. Hall, 1985. — II, A-501.

Machlis, Joseph. American composers of our time / Joseph Machlis. — New York : Crowell, 1963. — I, 289.

Machlis, Joseph. Introduction to contemporary music / Joseph Machlis. — New York : Norton, 1961. — I, 274.

MacInnis, Craig. Bruce Springsteen here & now / Craig MacInnis. — New York : Barron's, 1988. — III, 867.

Macken, Bob. The rock music source book / Bob Macken [et al]. — Garden City, N.Y. : Anchor, 1980. — II, 1139.

Mackenzie, Harry. One Night Stand series, 1–1001 / Harry Mackenzie and Lothar Polomski. — New York : Greenwood, 1991. — III, 215.

Mackenzie, Harry. The Johnny Mercer Chesterfield music shop, with A.F.R.S. additions featuring Johnny Mercer, Jo Stafford, Pied Pipers, Paul Weston and his orchestra / Harry Mackenzie. — Zephyrhills, Fla. : Joyce Record Club, 1986. — III, 265.

MacMinn, George R. The theater of the golden era in California / George R. MacMinn. — Caldwell, Idaho : Caxton, 1941. — II, 65.

Maddocks, Melvin. Billie Holiday / Melvin Maddocks. — Alexandria, Va. : Time-Life Records, 1979. — III, 732.

Madeira, Louis C. Annals of music in Philadelphia / Louis C. Madeira. — Philadelphia : Lippincott, 1896. — II, 59.

Madonna. Sex / Madonna; ed. Glenn O'Brien. — New York : Warner Books, 1992. — III, 767.

Magriel, Paul D. Chronicles of the American dance / Paul D. Magriel. — New York : Holt, 1948. — II, 610.

Mahan, Katherine. Showboats to soft shoes : a century of music development in Columbus, Ga., 1828–1928 / Katherine Mahan. — Columbus, Ga. : Columbus Office Supply, 1969. — I, A-41.

Mahanna, John G. W. Music under the moon : a history of the Berkshire Symphonic Festival, Inc. / John G. W. Mahanna. — Pittsfield, Mass. : Eagle Printing and Binding, 1955. — II, 54.

Mahony, Dan. The Columbia 13/14000-D series : a numerical listing / Dan Mahony. — 2nd ed. — Stanhope, N.J. : Walter C. Allen, 1966. — I, 809.

Maisel, Edward. Charles T. Griffes : the life of an American composer / Edward Maisel. — Rev. ed. — New York : Knopf; distributed by Random House, 1984. — III, 481.

Maisel, Edward M. Charles T. Griffes : the life of an American composer / Edward M. Maisel. — New York : Knopf, 1943. — I, 321.

Major, Clarence. Black slang : a dictionary of Afro-American talk / Clarence Major. — New York : International Publishers, 1970. — London : Routledge & Kegan Paul, 1971. — I, 652.

Makower, Joel. Woodstock : the oral history / Joel Makower. — New York : Doubleday, 1989. — III, 49.

Malcolm X. The autobiography of Malcolm X / Malcolm X. — New York : Grove, 1965 — I, 976.

Malone, Bill C. Country music, U.S.A. / Bill Malone. — Rev. ed. — Austin : University of Texas Press, 1985. — III, 498.

Malone, Bill C. Country music U.S.A. / Bill C. Malone. — Austin : University of Texas Press, 1968. / I, 606.

Malone, Bill C. Southern music, American music / Bill C. Malone. — Lexington : University Press of Kentucky, 1979. — II, 837.

Malone, Bill C. Stars of country music / Bill C. Malone and Judith McCulloh. — Urbana : University of Illinois Press, 1975. — II, 390.

Malson, Lucien. Des musiques de jazz / Lucien Malson. — Paris : Éditions Parenthèses, 1983. — II, A-407.

Malson, Lucien. Histoire du jazz / Lucien Malson. — Lausanne : Éditions Rencontre, 1967. — I, 1004.

Malson, Lucien. Histoire du jazz moderne / Lucien Malson. — Paris : La Table Ronde, 1961. — I, 1056.

Malson, Lucien. Les maitres du jazz / Lucien Malson. — 6th ed. — Paris : Presses Universitaires de France, 1972. — I, 1078.

Mancini, Henry. Did they mention the music? / Henry Mancini; with Gene Lees. — Chicago : Contemporary Books, 1989. — III, 498.

Mancini, Henry. Sounds and scores : a practical guide to professional orchestration / Henry Mancini. — Northridge, Calif. : Northridge Music, 1975. — II, 1057.

Mandelbaum, Ken. Not since Carrie : forty years of Broadway musical flops / Ken Mandelbaum. — New York : St. Martin's, 1991. — III, 1017.

Mandrell, Barbara. Get to the heart : my story. — Barbara Mandrell; with George Vecsey. — New York : Bantam, 1991. — III, 777.

Mandrell, Louise. The Mandrell family album / Louise Mandrell and Ace Collins. — New York : New American Library, 1983. — II, A-258.

Mangler, Joyce Ellen. Rhode Island music and musicians, 1753–1850 / Joyce Ellen Mangler. — Detroit : Information Service, 1965. — I, 104.

Manilow, Barry. Sweet life : adventures on the way to paradise / Barry Manilow. — New York : McGraw-Hill, 1987. — III, 779.

Manion, Martha L. Writings about Henry Cowell : an annotated bibliography / Martha L. Manion. — Brooklyn : Institute for Studies in American Music, 1982. — II, A-120.

Mann, May. Elvis and the colonel / May Mann. — New York : Drake, 1975. — II, 1299.

Mann, May. Private Elvis / May Mann. — New York : Pocket Books, 1977. — II, 1299.

Mann, Woody. Six black blues guitarists / Woody Mann. — New York : Oak, 1973. — I, 878.

Mannering, Derek. Mario Lanza : a biography / Derek Mannering. — London : Hale, 1991. — III, 758.

Mannes, David. Music is my faith : an autobiography / David Mannes. — New York : Norton, 1938. — II, 213.

Manning, Peter. Electronic and computer music / Peter Manning. — Oxford : Clarendon Press, 1985. — II, A-94.

Manone, Wingy. Trumpet on the wing / Wingy Manone and Paul Vandervoort. — New York : Doubleday, 1948. — I, 1123.

Manvell, Roger. The technique of film music / Roger Manvell and John Huntley. — Rev. ed. — London : Focal Press, 1975. — I, 1312.

Manzano, Alberto. Jackson Browne / Alberto Manzano. — Madrid : Jucar, 1982. — II, A-772.

Mapleson, James Henry. The Mapleson memoirs, 1848–1888 / James Henry Mapleson. — London : Remington, 1888. — II, 71.

Mapp, Edward C. Directory of blacks in the performing arts / Edward C. Mapp; foreword by Earle Hyman. — 2nd ed. — Metuchen, N.J. : Scarecrow, 1990. — III, 1277.

Mapp, Edward. Directory of blacks in the performing arts / Edward Mapp. — Metuchen, N.J. : Scarecrow, 1978. — II, 503.

Marchbank, Pearce. The illustrated rock almanac / Pearce Marchbank. — New York : Paddington, 1977. — II, 1102.

Marco, Guy A. Information on music : a handbook of reference sources in European languages / Guy A. Marco [et al]. — Littleton, Colo. : Libraries Unlimited, 1975– . — II, 7.

Marco, Guy A. Opera : a research and information guide / Guy A. Marco. — New York : Garland, 1984. — II, A-22.

Marcosson, Isaac F. Charles Frohman : manager and man / Isaac F. Marcosson and Daniel Frohman. — New York : Harper, 1916. – II, 882.

Marcus, Greil. Dead Elvis : a chronicle of a cultural obsession / Greil Marcus. — New York : Doubleday, 1991. — III, 833.

Marcus, Greil. Mystery train : images of America in rock 'n' roll music / Greil Marcus. — 3rd ed. — New York : Dutton, 1990. — III, 1184.

Marcus, Greil. Mystery train : images of America in rock and roll music / Greil Marcus. — New York : Dutton, 1975. — I, 1369.

Marcus, Greil. Rock and roll will stand / Greil Marcus. — Boston : Beacon, 1969. — I, 1357.

Marcus, Greil. Stranded : rock and roll for a desert island / Greil Marcus. — New York : Knopf, 1979. — II, 1135.

Marcuse, Maxwell F. Tin Pan Alley in gaslight / Maxwell F. Marcuse. — Watkins Glen, N.Y. : Century House, 1959. — I, A-240.

Maretzek, Max. Crotchets and quavers : or, revelations of an opera manager in America / Max Maretzek. — New York : French, 1855. — I, 153.

Maretzek, Max. Sharps and flats : a sequel to Crotchets and quavers / Max Maretzek. — New York : American Musician Publishing Co., 1890. — I, 153.

Mark, Michael L. A history of American music education / Michael L. Mark and Charles Gary. — New York : Schirmer, 1992. — III, 1262.

Markewich, Reese. Bibliography of jazz and pop tunes sharing the chord progressions of other compositions / Reese Markewich. — 2nd ed. — New York : Author, 1974. — I, 910.

Markewich, Reese. Jazz publicity / Reese Markewich. — 2nd ed. — New York : Author, 1974. — I, 911.

Marks, Edward B. They all had glamour : from the Swedish Nightingale to the naked lady / Edward B. Marks. — New York : Messner, 1944. — I, 1225.

Marks, Edward B. They all sang : from Tony Pastor to Rudy Vallee / Edward B. Marks. — New York : Viking, 1934. — I, 1226.

Marks, J. Rock and other four-letter words : music of the electric generation / J. Marks. — New York : Bantam, 1968. — I, A-297.

Marothy, János. Music and the bourgeois / János Marothy. — Budapest : Akadémiai Kiadó, 1974. — I, 998.

Marquis, Donald M. Finding Buddy Bolden, first man of jazz / Donald M. Marquis. — Goshen, Ind. : Pinchpenny Press, Goshen College, 1978. — II, 739.

Marquis, Donald M. In search of Buddy Bolden, first man of jazz / Donald M. Marquis. — Baton Rouge : Louisiana State University Press, 1978. — II, 740.

Marre, Jeremy. Beats of the heart : popular music of the world / Jeremy Marre and Hannah Charlton. — London : Pluto, 1985. — II, A-532.

Marrocco, W. Thomas. Music in America / W. Thomas Marrocco and Harold Gleason. — New York : Norton, 1964. — I, A-10.

Marschall, Richard. The encyclopedia of country and western music / Richard Marschall. — Greenwich, Conn. : Brompton, 1990. — III, 67.

Marsh, Dave. Born to run : the Bruce Springsteen story / Dave Marsh. — Garden City, N.Y. : Doubleday, 1979. — II, 1244.

Marsh, Dave. Elvis / Dave Marsh. — New York : Rolling Stone Press, 1982. — II, A-829.

Marsh, Dave. Fortunate son : essays and criticism by America's best known rock writer / Dave Marsh. — New York : Random House, 1985. — II, A-720.

Marsh, Dave. Glory days : Bruce Springsteen in the 1980s / Dave Marsh. — New York : Pantheon, 1987. — III, 868.

Marsh, Dave. Paul Simon / Dave Marsh. — New York : Quick Fox, 1978. — II, 1316.

Marsh, Dave. Springsteen : born to run / Dave Marsh. — London : Omnibus, 1981. — II, 1244.

Marsh, Dave. Sun city, by artists united against apartheid / Dave Marsh. — New York : Penguin, 1985. — II, A-733.

Marsh, Dave. The book of rock lists / Dave Marsh and Kevin Stein. — New York : Dell, 1981. — II, A-663.

Marsh, Dave. The first rock & roll confidential report / Dave Marsh [et al]. — New York : Pantheon, 1985. — II, A-719.

Marsh, Dave. The new *Rolling Stone* record guide / Dave Marsh and John Swenson. — Rev. ed. — New York : Random House, 1983. — II, 1120.

Marsh, Dave. Trapped : Michael Jackson and the crossover dream / Dave Marsh. — New York : Bantam, 1985. — III, 746.

Marsh, Graham. Blue Note : the album cover art / Graham Marsh, Glyn Callingham, and Felix Cromey. — San Francisco : Chronicle Books, 1991. — III, 1271.

Marsh, Graham. California cool : West Coast jazz of the 50s & 60s : the album cover art / Graham Marsh and Glyn Callingham; foreword by William Claxton. — San Francisco : Chronicle Books, 1992. — III, 1272.

Marsh, J. B. T. Story of the Jubilee Singers / J. B. T. Marsh. — Rev. ed. — Cleveland : Cleveland Printing & Publishing Co., 1892. — I, 782.

Marsh, Robert C. The Cleveland Orchestra / Robert C. Marsh. — Cleveland, World, 1967. — I, 136.

Marshall Cavendish history of popular music. — Freeport, Long Island, N.Y. : Marshall Cavendish, 1990. — III, 1047.

Marshall, Howard Wight. "Keep on the sunny side of life" / Howard Wight Marshall. — Los Angeles : John Edwards Memorial Foundation, 1974. — I, 625.

Martens, Frederick H. Leo Ornstein : the man, his ideas, his work / Frederick H. Martens. — New York : Breitkopf & Härtel, 1918. — II, 196.

Martin, Bernice. A sociology of contemporary cultural change / Bernice Martin. — Oxford : Blackwell, 1981. — II, A-734.

Martin, George. The Damrosch dynasty / George Martin. — Boston : Houghton Mifflin, 1983. — II, A-151.

Martin, James. John Denver : Rocky Mountain wonderboy / James Martin. — London : Everest, 1977. — II, 1289.

Martin, Linda. Anti-rock : the opposition to rock 'n' roll / Linda Martin and Kerry Segrave. — Hamden, Conn. : Archon Books, 1988. — III, 1185.

Martin, Mary. My heart belongs / Mary Martin. — New York : Morrow, 1976. — II, 982.

Martin, William R. Music of the twentieth century / William R. Martin and Julius Drossin. — Englewood Cliffs, N.J. : Prentice-Hall, 1980. — II, 159.

Martinez, Raymond J. Portraits of New Orleans jazz : miscellaneous notes / Raymond J. Martinez. — New Orleans : Hope Publications, 1971. — I, 1067.

Martorella, Rosanne. The sociology of opera / Rosanne Martorella. — New York : Praeger, 1982. — II, A-46.

Marx, Henry. Weill-Lenya / Henry Marx. — New York : Goethe House, 1976. — II, 1047.

Marx, Samuel. Rodgers & Hart : bewitched, bothered, bedeviled / Samuel Marx and Jan Clayton. — New York : Putnam's, 1976. — II, 960.

Mason, Daniel Gregory. Music in my time, and other reminiscences / Daniel Gregory Mason. — New York : Macmillan, 1938. — I, 337.

Mason, Daniel Gregory. The dilemma of American music, and other essays / Daniel Gregory Mason. — New York : Macmillan, 1928. — I, 375.

Mason, Daniel Gregory. Tune in America : a study of our coming musical independence / Daniel Gregory Mason. — New York : Knopf, 1931. — I, 376.

Mason, Henry L. Hymn-tunes of Lowell Mason : a bibliography / Henry L. Mason. — Cambridge, Mass. : Harvard University Press, 1944. — I, 67.

Mason, Henry Lowell. Lowell Mason : an appreciation of his life and work / Henry Lowell Mason. — New York : Hymn Society of America, 1941. — I, 217.

Mason, Lowell. A Yankee musician in Europe : the 1837 journals of Lowell Mason / Lowell Mason; ed. Michael Broyles. — Ann Arbor, Mich. : UMI Research Press, 1990. — III, 499.

Mason, Lowell. Musical letters from abroad / Lowell Mason. — New York : Mason, 1854. — I, 215.

Mason, Lowell. The sacred harp : or eclectic harmony / Lowell Mason and Timothy B. Mason. — Cincinnati : Truman, 1934. — I, 526.

Mason, Michael. The country music book / Michael Mason. — New York : Scribner's, 1985. — II, A-223.

Mason, William. Memories of a musical life / William Mason. — New York : Century, 1901. — I, 245.

Massagli, Luciano. Duke Ellington's story on records / Luciano Massagli [et al]. — Vols. 10–16. — Milan : Raretone, 1976–1983. — II, 774.

Massagli, Luciano. Duke Ellington's story on records / Luciano Massagli [et al]. — Milan : Musica Jazz, 1966. — I, 946.

Massey, Ellen Gray. Bittersweet country / Ellen Gray Massey. — Garden City, N.Y. : Doubleday, 1978. — II, 454.

Masson, Alain. Comédie musicale / Alain Masson. — Paris : Stock, 1981. — II, A-576.

Mast, Gerald. Can't help singin' : the American musical on stage and screen / Gerald Mast. — Woodstock, N.Y. : Overlook, 1987. — III, 1012.

Mates, Julian. America's musical stage : two hundred years of musical theatre / Julian Mates. — Westport, Conn. : Greenwood, 1985. — II, A-557.

Mates, Julian. The American musical stage before 1800 / Julian Mates. — New Brunswick, N.J. : Rutgers University Press, 1962. — I, 1227.

Matesich, Ken. Jimi Hendrix : a discography / Ken Matesich and Dave Armstrong. — Rev. ed. — Tucson, Ariz. : J.H. Discography, 1982. — III, 318.

Mather, Cotton. The accomplished singer / Cotton Mather. — Boston : S. Gerrish, 1721. — I, 194.

Mathews, W. S. B. A hundred years of music in America / W. S. B. Mathews. — Chicago : Howe, 1889. — I, 220.

Matlaw, Myron. American popular entertainment / ed. Myron Matlaw. — Westport, Conn. : Greenwood, 1979. — II, 838.

Mattfeld, Julius. A hundred years of grand opera in New York, 1825–1925 / Julius Mattfeld. — New York : New York Public Library, 1927. — I, 154.

Mattfeld, Julius. Folk music of the Western hemisphere : a list of references in the New York Public Library / Julius Mattfeld. — New York : New York Public Library, 1925. — I, 435.

Mattfeld, Julius. Handbook of American operatic premieres, 1731–1862 / Julius Mattfeld. — Detroit : Information Service, 1963. — I, 143.

Mattfeld, Julius. Variety music cavalcade, 1620–1969 / Julius Mattfeld. — 3rd ed. — Englewood Cliffs, N.J. : Prentice-Hall, 1971. — I, 17.

Matthew-Walker, Robert. Elvis Presley : a study in music / Robert Matthew-Walker. — Tunbridge Wells, England : Midas Books, 1979. — II, 1229.

Matthew-Walker, Robert. Simon & Garfunkel / Robert Matthew-Walker. — Tunbridge Wells, England : Baton, 1984. — II, A-840.

Matthews, Washington. Navaho myths, prayers, and songs with texts and translations / Washington Matthews. — Berkeley : University of California Press, 1907. — I, A-93.

Mauerer, Hans J. Discography of Sidney Bechet / Hans J. Mauerer. — Copenhagen : Knudsen, 1968. — I, 947.

Mauerer, Hans J. The Pete Johnson story / Hans J. Mauerer. — Bremen, Germany : Humburg, 1965. — I, 840.

Maultsby, Portia K. Afro-American religious music, 1610–1861 / Portia K. Maultsby. — Dissertation, University of Wisconsin, 1974. — II, 627.

Mauro, Walter. Louis Armstrong, il re del jazz / Walter Mauro. — Milan : Rusconi, 1979. — II, 795.

Mawhinney, Paul C. MusicMaster : the 45 rpm record directory : 1947 to 1982 / Paul C. Mawhinney. — Allison Park, Pa. : Record-Rama, 1983. — III, 264.

Maxwell, Gilbert. Helen Morgan : her life and legend / Gilbert Maxwell. — New York : Hawthorn, 1974. — II, 984.

May, Elizabeth. Music of many cultures / ed. Elizabeth May. — Berkeley : University of California Press, 1980. — S. 243.

Mayer, Martin. The Met : one hundred years of grand opera / Martin Mayer. — London : Thames & Hudson, 1983. — II, A-47.

Mays, Benjamin E. The negro's God as reflected in his literature / Benjamin E. Mays. — Boston : Chapman & Grimes, 1938. — I, 795.

McAllester, David P. Enemy way music : a study of social and esthetic values as seen in Navaho music / David P. McAllester. — Cambridge, Mass. : Peabody Museum, 1954. — I, 413.

McAllester, David P. Indian music in the Southwest / David P. McAllester. — Colorado Springs, Colo. : Taylor Museum, 1961. — I, 414.

McAllester, David P. Peyote music / David P. McAllester. — New York : Viking Fund, 1949. — I, 415.

McAllester, David P. Readings in ethnomusicology / ed. David P. McAllester. — New York : Johnson Reprint, 1971. — II, 242.

McBrier, Vivian Flagg. R. Nathaniel Dett : his life and works / Vivian Flagg McBrier. — Washington : Associated Publishers, 1977. — II, 508.

McCabe, John. George M. Cohan : the man who owned Broadway / John Mc-
Cabe. — Garden City, N.Y. : Doubleday, 1973. — II, 974.

McCall, Adeline. Music in America / Adeline McCall. — Chapel Hill : University of North Carolina Press, 1944. — I, A-9.

McCall, Michael. Garth Brooks : a biography / Michael McCall. — New York :
Bantam, 1991. — III, 687.

McCalla, James. Jazz : a listener's guide / James McCalla. — Englewood Cliffs,
N.J. : Prentice-Hall, 1982. — II, A-390.

McCarthy, Albert J. Big band jazz / Albert McCarthy. — London : Barrie &
Jenkins, 1974. — I, 1042.

McCarthy, Albert J. Coleman Hawkins / Albert J. McCarthy. — London : Cassell, 1963. — I, 1116.

McCarthy, Albert J. Jazz discography 1 / Albert J. McCarthy. — London : Cassell, 1960. — I, 928.

McCarthy, Albert J. Jazz on record : a critical guide to the first 50 years,
1917–1967 / Albert McCarthy [et al]. — London : Hanover, 1968. — I, 958.

McCarthy, Albert J. Louis Armstrong / Albert J. McCarthy. — London : Cassell, 1960. — I, 1086.

McCarthy, Albert J. The dance band era / Albert McCarthy. — London : Studio
Vista, 1971. — I, 1043.

McCarthy, Albert J. The trumpet in jazz / Albert McCarthy. — London : Citizen
Press, 1945. — I, 1031.

McCarthy, Margaret William. More letters of Amy Fay : the American years,
1879–1916 / Selected and ed. by Margaret William McCarthy. — Detroit :
Information Coordinators, 1986. — III, 541.

McCarty, Clifford. Film composers in America : a checklist of their work / Clifford McCarty. — Glendale, N.Y. : J. Valentine, 1953. — I, 1311.

McClelland, Doug. Blackface to blacklist : Al Jolson, Larry Parks, and "The Jolson Story" / Doug McClelland. — Metuchen, N.J. : Scarecrow, 1987. — III,
1287.

McClure, Dorothy May. The world famous cowboy band, 1923–1973 / Dorothy
May McClure. — Abilene, Tex. : Hardin-Simmons University, 1983. — II,
A-210.

McColm, Bruce. Where have they gone? : rock 'n' roll stars / Bruce McColm
and Doug Payne. — New York : Grosset & Dunlap, 1979. — II, 1281.

McCorkle, Donald M. Collegium musicum Salem : its music, musicians and importance / Donald M. McCorkle. — Winston-Salem, N.C. : Moravian Music
Foundation, 1956. — I, 81.

McCorkle, Donald M. John Antes, American dilettante / Donald M. McCorkle. —
Winston-Salem, N.C. : Moravian Music Foundation, 1956. — I, 82.

McCorkle, Donald M. Moravian contribution to American music / Donald M.
McCorkle. — Winston-Salem, N.C. : Moravian Music Foundation, 1956. —
I, 83.

McCoy, Judy. Rap music in the 1980s : a reference guide / Judy McCoy. —
Metuchen, N.J. : Scarecrow, 1992. — III, 144.

McCoy, Meredith. Catalog of the John D. Reid Collection of Early American
Jazz / Meredith McCoy and Barbara Parker. — Little Rock : Arkansas Arts
Center, 1975. — II, 637.

McCue, George. Music in American society, 1776–1976 / ed. George McCue. — New Brunswick, N.J. : Transaction Books, 1977. — II, 17.

McCulloh, Judith. Hillbilly records and tune transcriptions / Judith McCulloh. — Los Angeles : John Edwards Memorial Foundation, 1968. — I, 615.

McCulloh, Judith. Some Child ballads and hillbilly records / Judith McCulloh. — Los Angeles : John Edwards Memorial Foundation, 1967. — I, 616.

McCurry, John G. The social harp / John G. McCurry. — Philadelphia : T. K. Collins, 1855. — I, 534.

McCutchan, Robert Guy. Our hymnody : a manual of the Methodist hymnal / Robert Guy McCutchan. — New York : Methodist Book Concern, 1937. — II, 34.

McCutcheon, Lynn Ellis. Rhythm and blues / Lynn Ellis McCutcheon. — Arlington, Va. : Beatty, 1971. — I, A-183.

McDaniel, William R. Grand Ole Opry / William R. McDaniel and Harold Seligman. — New York : Greenberg, 1952. — I, 621.

McDermott, John. Hendrix : setting the record straight / John McDermott, Mark Lewisohn, and Eddie Kramer. — New York : Warner Books, 1992. — III, 580.

McDonald, Arlys L. Ned Rorem : a bio-bibliography / Arlys L. McDonald. — Westport, Conn. : Greenwood, 1989. — III, 179.

McDonald, William F. Federal relief administration and the arts / William F. McDonald. — Columbus : Ohio State University Press, 1969. — I, 367.

McDonough, Jack. San Francisco rock / Jack McDonough. — San Francisco : Chronicle Books, 1985. — II, A-706a.

McDonough, John. Coleman Hawkins / John McDonough. — Alexandria, Va. : Time-Life Records, 1979. — III, 643.

McDonough, John. Lester Young / John McDonough. — Alexandria, Va. : Time-Life Records, 1980. — II, 772.

McDonough, John. Pee Wee Russell / John McDonough. — Alexandria, Va. : Time-Life Records, 1981. — III, 667.

McDowell, L. L. Songs of the old camp ground / L. L. McDowell. — Ann Arbor, Mich. : Edwards, 1937. — I, 543.

McEwen, Joe. Sam Cooke : a biography in words and pictures / Joe McEwen. — New York : Sire Books/Chappell, 1977. — II, 571.

McGeary, Thomas. The music of Harry Partch : a descriptive catalog / Thomas McGeary. — Brooklyn : Institute for Studies in American Music, 1991. — III, 174.

McGee, Mark Thomas. The rock & roll movie encyclopedia of the 1950s / Mark Thomas McGee. — Jefferson, N.C. : McFarland, 1990. — III, 1283a.

McGhee, Brownie. Guitar styles of Brownie McGhee / Brownie McGhee. — New York : Oak, 1971. — I, 847.

McGill, Josephine. Folk songs of the Kentucky mountains / Josephine McGill. — New York : Boosey, 1917. — I, A-119.

McGowan, R. The significance of Stephen Collins Foster / R. McGowan. — Indianapolis : Author, 1932. — II, 1038.

McGregor, Craig. Bob Dylan : a retrospective / Craig McGregor. — New York : Morrow, 1972. — I, 1375.

McGregor, Craig. Pop goes the culture / Craig McGregor. — London : Pluto, 1984. — II, A-717.

McGregor, Craig. Soundtrack for the eighties / Craig McGregor. — Sydney : Hodder & Stoughton, 1983. — II, A-718.

McGuire, Patricia. Lullaby of Broadway : a biography of Al Dubin / Patricia McGuire. — Secaucus, N.J. : Citadel, 1983. — II, A-598.

McIlhenny, E. A. Befo' de war spirituals / E. A. McIlhenny. — Boston : Christopher, 1933. — I, 780.

McIntosh, David S. Folk songs and singing games of the Illinois Ozarks / David S. McIntosh. — Carbondale : Southern Illinois University Press, 1974. — II, 252.

McIntosh, Ruskin. Helen Rice : the great lady of chamber music / Ruskin McIntosh. — Burlington, Vt. : George Little, 1983. — II, A-150.

McKay, David. William Billings of Boston / David McKay and Richard Crawford. — Princeton, N.J. : Princeton University Press, 1975. — I, 202.

McKee, Margaret. Beale black and blue / Margaret McKee and Fred Chisenhall. — Baton Rouge : Louisiana State University Press, 1981. — II, A-319.

McKenna, Harold J. New York City Opera sings : stories and productions of the New York City Opera, 1944–79 / Harold J. McKenna. — New York : Richards Rosen, 1981. — II, A-45.

McKenzie, Michael. Madonna : lucky star / Michael McKenzie. — Chicago : Contemporary Books, 1985. — III, 773.

McLaurin, Melton. You wrote my life : lyrical themes in country music / Melton McLaurin and Richard Peterson. — Philadelphia : Gordon & Breach, 1992. — III, 1164.

McLendon, James W. Biography as theology : how life stories can remake today's theology / James W. McLendon. — Nashville : Abingdon, 1974. — II, 230.

McNamara, Brooks. Step right up / Brooks McNamara. — Garden City, N.Y. : Doubleday, 1976. — II, 888.

McNeil, W. K. Southern folk ballads / comp. W. K. McNeil. — Little Rock, Ark. : August House, 1987. — III, 23.

McNutt, Randy. We wanna boogie : an illustrated history of the American rockabilly movement / Randy McNutt. — 2nd ed. — Hamilton, Ohio : HHP Books, 1988. — III, 1202.

McPartland, Marian. All in good time / Marian McPartland. — New York : Oxford, 1987. — III, 1100.

McPherson, James M. Blacks in America : bibliographical essays / James M. McPherson [et al]. — Garden City, N.Y. : Doubleday, 1971. — I, 651.

McRae, Barry. Dizzy Gillespie : his life and times / Barry McRae. — New York : Universe, 1988. — III, 637.

McRae, Barry. Miles Davis / Barry McRae. — London : Apollo, 1988. — III, 628.

McRae, Barry. Ornette Coleman / Barry McRae; selected discography by Tony Middleton. — London : Apollo, 1988. — III, 620.

McRae, Barry. The jazz cataclysm / Barry McRae. — London : Dent, 1967. — I, 1055.

McRae, Barry. The jazz handbook / Barry McRae. — Burnt Mill, Harlow, Essex, England : Longman; Boston : G. K. Hall, 1987. — III, 72.

McSpadden, J. Walker. Operas and musical comedies / J. Walker McSpadden. — Rev. ed. — New York : Crowell, 1951. — I, 55.

McVay, J. Douglas. The musical film / J. Douglas McVay. — London : Zwemmer, 1967. — I, A-260.

Mead, Rita H. American music before 1865 in print and on records : a bibliodiscography / Rita H. Mead. — Brooklyn : Institute for Studies in American Music, 1976. — II, 1.

Mead, Rita H. Doctoral dissertations in American music : a classified bibliography / Rita H. Mead. — Brooklyn : Institute for Studies in American Music, 1974. — I, 6.

Mead, Rita H. Henry Cowell's "New Music" / Rita H. Mead. — Ann Arbor, Mich. : UMI Research Press, 1981. — II, A-121.

Meadows Eddie S. Jazz reference and research materials : a bibliography / Eddie S. Meadows. — New York : Garland, 1981. — II, A-365.

Meadows, Eddie S. Theses and dissertations on black American music / Eddie S. Meadows. — Beverly Hills, Calif. : Theodore Front, 1980. — II, 497.

Mecklenburg, Carl Gregor, Herzog zu. 1970 supplement to International jazz bibliography / Carl Gregor, Herzog zu Mecklenburg. — Graz, Austria : Universal Edition, 1971. — I, 916.

Mecklenburg, Carl Gregor, Herzog zu. 1971/72/73 supplement to International jazz bibliography / Carl Gregor, Herzog zu Mecklenburg. — Graz, Austria : Universal Edition, 1975. — I, 917.

Mecklenburg, Carl Gregor, Herzog zu. Die Theorie des Blues im modernen Jazz / Carl Gregor, Herzog zu Mecklenburg and Waldemar Scheck. — Strasbourg : Heitz, 1963. — I, 1057.

Mecklenburg, Carl Gregor, Herzog zu. International jazz bibliography / Carl Gregor, Herzog zu Mecklenburg. — Strasbourg : Heitz, 1969. — I, 915.

Meckna, Michael. Virgil Thomson: a bio-bibliography / Michael Meckna. — New York : Greenwood, 1986. — III, 182.

Meek, Bill. Songs of the Irish in America / ed. Bill Meek. — Cublin : Gilbert Dalton, 1978. — II, 449.

Meeker, David. Jazz in the movies : a tentative index to the work of jazz musicians for the cinema / David Meeker. — London : British Film Institute, 1972. — I, 921.

Meggett, Joan M. Music periodical literature : an annotated bibliography of indexes and bibliographies / Joan M. Meggett. — Metuchen, N.J. : Scarecrow, 1978. — II, 8.

Megill, Donald D. Introduction to jazz history / Donald D. Megill and Richard S. Demory. — 3rd ed. — Englewood Cliffs, N.J. : Prentice-Hall, 1993. — III, 1087.

Megill, Donald D. Introduction to jazz history / Donald D. Megill and Richard Demory. — Englewood Cliffs, N.J. : Prentice-Hall, 1984. — II, A-417.

Mehegan, John. Jazz improvisation / John Mehegan. — New York : Watson, Guptill, 1958–1965. — I, 983.

Mehr, Linda Harris. Motion pictures, television, and radio : a union catalog of manuscript and special collections in the western United States / Linda Harris Mehr. — Boston : G. K. Hall, 1977. — II, 1058.

Mellers, Wilfrid. A darker shade of pale : a backdrop to Bob Dylan / Wilfrid Mellers. — London : Faber & Faber, 1984. — II, A-790.

Mellers, Wilfrid. Angels of the night : popular female singers of our time / Wildrid Mellers. — New York : B. Blackwell, 1986. — III, 442.

Mellers, Wilfrid. Caliban reborn : renewal in twentieth-century music / Wilfrid Mellers. — New York : Harper & Row, 1967. — I, A-212.

Mellers, Wilfrid. Music in a new found land : themes and developments in the history of American music / Wilfrid Mellers. — London : Barrie & Rockliff, 1964. — I, 27.

Mellquist, Jerome. Paul Rosenfeld, voyager in the arts / Jerome Mellquist and Lucie Wiese. — New York : Creative Age, 1948. — I, 378.

Meltzer, R. The aesthetics of rock / R. Meltzer. — New York : Something Else Press, 1970. — I, 1358.

Memorial tribute : Mahalia Jackson. — [no place; no publisher] 1972. — I, 900.

Memphis Housing Authority. Beale Street, U.S.A. : where the blues began. — Bexhill-on-Sea, England : Blues Unlimited [no date]. — I, 812.

Mencken, H. L. H. L. Mencken on music / H. L. Mencken. — New York : Knopf, 1961. — I, A-42.

Mendheim, Beverly. Ritchie Valens, the first Latino rocker / Beverly Mendheim. — Tempe : Arizona State University Press/Bilingual Press, 1987. — III, 881.

Mendl, R. W. S. The appeal of jazz / R. W. S. Mendl. — London : Philip Allan, 1927. — I, 1032.

Mercer, Johnny. Our huckleberry friend : the life, times and lyrics of Johnny Mercer / Johnny Mercer; ed. Bob Bach and Ginger Mercer. — Secaucus, N.J. : Lyle Stuart, 1982. — II, A-605.

Meredith, Scott. George S. Kaufman and his friends / Scott Meredith. — Garden City, N.Y. : Doubleday, 1974. — II, 953.

Meredith, Scott. George S. Kaufman and the Algonquin round table / Scott Meredith. — London : Allen & Unwin, 1977. — II, 953.

Meriwether, Doug. We don't play requests : a musical biography/discography of Buddy Rich / Doug Meriwether. — Chicago : K.A.R., 1984. — II, A-497.

Merman, Ethel. Don't call me madam / Ethel Merman. — London : Allen, 1955. — I, 1321.

Merman, Ethel. Merman / Ethel Merman; with George Eells. — New York : Simon and Schuster, 1978. — II, 983.

Merman, Ethel. Who could ask for anything more / Ethel Merman. — Garden City, N.Y. : Doubleday, 1955. — I, 1321.

Merriam, Alan P. African music on LP : an annotated discography / Alan P. Merriam. — Evanston, Ill. : Northwestern University Press, 1970. — I, A-160.

Merriam, Alan P. Bibliography of jazz / Alan P. Merriam. — Philadelphia : American Folklore Society, 1954. — I, 918.

Merriam, Alan P. Ethnomusicology of the Flathead Indians / Alan P. Merriam. — Chicago : Aldine, 1967. — I, 416.

Merrill, Hugh. The blues route / Hugh Merrill. — New York : Morrow, 1990. — III, 1156.

Mertens, Wim. American minimal music : La Monte Young, Terry Riley, Steve Reich, Philip Glass / Wim Mertens; trans by J. Hautekiet; preface by Michael Nyman. — London : Kahn and Averill; New York : Alexander Broude, 1983. — III, 374.

Mertens, Wim. Amerikaanse repetitive muziek / Wim Mertens. — Bierbeck, Belgium : W. Vergaelen, 1980. — II, 172.

Messiter, A. H. History of the choir and music of Trinity Church, New York, from its organization to the year 1897 / A. H. Messiter. — New York : Edwin S. Gorham, 1906. — I, 61.

Metcalf, Frank J. American psalmody / Frank J. Metcalf. — New York : Charles F. Heartman, 1917. — I, 183.

Metcalf, Frank J. American writers and compilers of sacred music / Frank J. Metcalf. — New York : Abingdon, 1925. — I, 62.

Metfessel, Milton. Phonophotography in folk music : American negro songs in new notation/ Milton Metfessel. — Chapel Hill : University of North Carolina Press, 1928. — I, 762.

Metzger, Heinz-Klaus. Edgard Varèse / Heinz-Klaus Metzger and Rainer Riehn. — Munich : Text & Kritik, 1978. — II, 200.

Metzger, Heinz-Klaus. John Cage / Heinz-Klaus Metzger and Rainer Riehn. — Munich : Text & Kritik, 1978. — II, 180.

Meyer, Hazel. The gold in Tin Pan Alley / Hazel Meyer. — Philadelphia : Lippincott, 1958. — II, 826.

Meyer, John. Heartbreaker / John Meyer. — Garden City, N.Y. : Doubleday, 1983. — SA 627.

Meyer, Raymond. Backwoods jazz in the twenties / Raymond F. "Peg" Meyer; edited with an introduction by Frank Nickell. — Cape Girardeau, Mo. : Center for Regional History and Cultural Heritage, Southeast Missouri State University, 1989. — III, 958.

Mezzrow, Milton. Really the blues / Milton Mezzrow and Bernard Wolfe. — New York : Random House, 1946. — I, 1124.

Middleton, Richard. — Pop music and the blues / Richard Middleton. — London : Gollancz, 1972. — I, 863.

Midler, Bette. A view from a broad / Bette Midler. — New York : Simon & Schuster, 1980. — II, 1217.

Milburn, George. The hobo's hornbook : a repertory for a gutter jongleur / George Milburn. — New York : Ives Washburn, 1930. — I, 578.

Miles, William. Songs, odes, glees and ballads : a bibliography of American presidential campaign songsters / William Miles. — New York : Greenwood, 1990. — III, 120.

Millar, Bill. The Coasters / Bill Millar. — London : Star Books, 1975. — I, 885.

Millar, Bill. The Drifters / Bill Millar. — London : Studio Vista, 1971. — I, 886.

Millard, Bob. The Judds : a biography / Bob Millard. — New York : Doubleday, 1988. — III, 921.

Miller, Douglas T. The fifties : the way we really were / Douglas T. Miller and Marion Nowak. — Garden City, N.Y. : Doubleday, 1975. — II, 1261.

Miller, Elizabeth W. The negro in America / Elizabeth W. Miller. — Cambridge, Mass. : Harvard University Press, 1966. — I, A-149.

Miller, Jack. Born to sing : a discography of Billie Holiday / Jack Miller. — Copenhagen : Jazzmedia, 1979. — II, 650.

Miller, Jim. The *Rolling Stone* illustrated history of rock & roll / Jim Miller. — Rev. ed. — London : Picador, 1981. — II, 1122.

Miller, Paul Eduard. *Down Beat's* yearbook of swing / Paul Eduard Miller. — Chicago : Down Beat, 1939. — II, 714.

Miller, Terry E. Folk music in America : a reference guide / Terry E. Miller. — New York : Garland, 1986. — III, 123.

Miller, William Robert. The world of pop music and jazz / William Robert Miller. — St. Louis : Concordia, 1965. — I, A-298.

Milligan, Harold Vincent. Stephen Collins Foster : a bibliography of America's folk-song composer / Harold Vincent Milligan. — New York : Schirmer, 1920. — I, 1211.

Mills, Bart. Tina / Bart Mills. — New York : Warner Books, 1985. — II, A-847.

Mills, Earl. Dorothy Dandridge : a portrait in black / Earl Mills. — Los Angeles : Holloway House, 1970. — II, 1076.

Milsap, Ronnie. Almost like a song / Ronnie Milsap. — New York : McGraw-Hill, 1990. — III, 789.

Milstein, Nathan. From Russia to the West : the musical memoirs and reminiscences of Nathan Milstein / Nathan Milstein and Solomon Volkov : trans. from Russian by Antonina W. Bovis. — New York : Holt, 1990. — III, 589.

Milstein, Silvina. Arnold Schoenberg : notes, sets, forms / Silvina Milstein. — New York : Cambridge University Press, 1992. — III, 512.

Milword, John. Beach Boys : silver anniversary / John Milword. – Garden City, N.Y. : Doubleday, 1985. — III, 899.

Mims, Edwin. Sidney Lanier / Edwin Mims. — Boston : Houghton Mifflin, 1908. — I, 234.

Mingus, Charlie. Beneath the underdog : his world as composed by Mingus / Charlie Mingus; ed. Nel King. — New York : Knopf, 1971. — I, 1127.

Miron, Charles. Rock gold : all the hit charts from 1955 to 1976 / Charles Miron. — New York : Drake, 1977. — II, 1253.

Mirtle, Jack. Thank you, music lovers : a bio-discography of Spike Jones and his City Slickers / Jack Mirtle and Ted Hering; foreword by Peter Schickele. — Westport, Conn. : Greenwood, 1986. — III, 330.

Mitchell, Frank. Navajo Blessingway Singer : the autobiography of Frank Mitchell, 1881–1967 / Frank Mitchell. — Tucson : University of Arizona Press, 1978. — II, 253.

Mitchell, George. Blow my blues away / George Mitchell. — Baton Rouge : Louisiana State University Press, 1971. — I, 824.

Mitchell, Mitch. Jimi Hendrix : inside the Experience / Mitch Mitchell; with John Platt. — New York : Harmony Books, 1990. — III, 581.

Mitsui, Toru. Bluegrass ongaku / Toru Mitsui. — 2nd ed. — Tokyo : Bronze-sha, 1975. — II, 373.

Mitsui, Toru. Eikei Amerika minzoku-ongaku no gakki / Toru Mitsui. — Toyo Rashi, Japan : Traditional Song Society, 1970. — II, 327.

Mitsui, Toru. Kantori ongaku no redishi / Toru Mitsui. — Tokyo : Ongaku-no-Tomo Sha, 1971. — II, 369.

Mitsui, Toru. Rock no bigaku / Toru Mitsui. — Tokyo : Bronze-sha, 1976. — II, 1136.

Mix annual directory of recording industry facilities and services, 1988. — Emeryville, Calif. : Mix Publications, 1988. — III, 13.

Mize, J. T. H. Bing Crosby and the Bing Crosby style / J. T. H. Mize. — Chicago : Who Is Who in Music, 1946. — I, A-279.

Moline, Karen. Streisand through the lens / Karen Moline. — New York : Delilah, 1982. — II, A-642.

Monaco, Bob. The platinum rainbow : how to succeed in the music business without selling your soul / Bob Monaco and James Riordan. — Sherman Oaks, Calif. : Swordsman, 1980. — II, 1159.

Mongan, Norman. A history of the guitar in jazz / Norman Mongan. — New York : Oak, 1983. — II, A-418.

Monk, Thelonious. Thelonious Monk / Thelonious Monk. — London : Apollo, 1987. — III, 562.

Montell, William Lynwood. Singing the glory down : amateur gospel music in south central Kentucky, 1900–1990 / William Lynwood Montell. — Lexington : University Press of Kentucky, 1991. — III, 1042.

Moody, Richard. Ned Harrigan : from Corlear's Hook to Herald Square / Richard Moody. — Chicago : Nelson-Hall, 1980. — II, 892.

Moon, Pete. Bibliography of jazz discographies published since 1960 / Pete Moon. — 2nd ed. — South Harrow, England : British Institute of Jazz Studies, 1972. — I, 919.

Mooney, James. The ghost-dance religion and the Sioux outbreak of 1890 / James Mooney. — Washington : Government Printing Office, 1896. — I, A-94.

Moore, Carman. Somebody's angel child : the story of Bessie Smith / Carman Moore. — New York : Crowell, 1969. — I, 852.

Moore, Edward C. Forty years of opera in Chicago / Edward C. Moore. — New York : Liveright, 1930. — II, 78.

Moore, Ethel. Ballads and folksongs of the Southwest / Ethel Moore and Chauncey D. Moore. — Norman : University of Oklahoma Press, 1964. — I, 514.

Moore, John W. A dictionary of musical information / John W. Moore. — Boston : Ditson, 1876. — I, A-11.

Moore, Macdonald Smith. Yankee blues : musical culture and American identity / Macdonald Smith Moore. — Bloomington : Indiana University Press, 1985. — II, A-106.

Moore, Mary Ellen. The Linda Ronstadt scrapbook / Mary Ellen Moore. — New York : Sunridge, 1978. — II, 1314.

Moore, Thurston. Hank Williams : the legend / Thurston Moore. — Denver : Heather Enterprises, 1972. — I, 643.

Moravian Music Foundation. Moravian music for the bicentennial. — Winston-Salem, N.C. : Moravian Music Foundation, 1975. — II, 108.

Mordden, Ethan. Better foot forward : the history of American musical theatre / Ethan Mordden. — New York : Grossman, 1976. — II, 911.

Mordden, Ethan. Broadway babies : the people who made the American musical / Ethan Mordden. — New York : Oxford University Press, 1983. — II, A-577.

Mordden, Ethan. Rodgers and Hammerstein / Ethan Mordden. — New York : Abrams, 1992. — III, 508.

Mordden, Ethan. The Hollywood musical / Ethan Mordden. — New York : St. Martin's, 1982. — II, A-589.

Morehouse, Ward. George M. Cohan, prince of the American theater / Ward Morehouse. — Philadelphia : Lippincott, 1943. — I, 1318.

Morell, Parker. Lillian Russell : the era of plush / Parker Morell. — New York : Random House, 1940. — II, 893.

Morella, Joe. Simon and Garfunkel : old friends / Joe Morella and Patricia Barey. — New York : Birch Lane Press, 1991. ML420 .S563 M7. — III, 856.

Morella, Joe. The films and career of Judy Garland / Joe Morella and Edward Z. Epstein. — New York : Citadel, 1969. — II, 1079.

Morgan, Alun. Count Basie / Alun Morgan. — Tunbridge Wells, England : Spellmount, 1984. — II, A-458.

Morgan, Alun. Modern jazz : a survey of developments since 1939 / Alun Morgan and Raymond Horricks. — London : Gollancz, 1956. — II, 720.

Morgan, Thomas L. From cakewalks to concert halls : an illustrated history of African American popular music from 1895 to 1930 / Thomas L. Morgan and William Barlow. — Washington : Elliott & Clark, 1992. — III, 1071.

Morgenstern, Dan. Bird and Diz : a bibliography / Dan Morgenstern, Ira Gitler, and Jack Bradley. — New York : New York Jazz Museum, 1973. — I, 1134.

Morgereth, Timothy A. Bing Crosby : a discography, radio program list and filmography / Timothy A. Morgereth. — Jefferson, N.C. : McFarland, 1987. — III, 298.

Morneweck, Evelyn Foster. Chronicles of Stephen Foster's family / Evelyn Foster Morneweck. — Pittsburgh : University of Pittsburgh Press, 1944. — I, 1212.

Morrill, Dexter. Woody Herman : a guide to the big band recordings, 1936–1987 / Dexter Morrill. — New York : Greenwood, 1990. — III, 322.

Morris, Alton C. Folksongs of Florida / Alton C. Morris. — Gainesville : University of Florida Press, 1950. — I, 492.

Morris, Edward. Alabama / Edward Morris. — Chicago : Contemporary Books, 1985. — II, A-244.

Morris, Ronald L. Wait until dark : jazz and the underworld 1880–1940 / Ronald L. Morris. — Bowling Green, Ohio : Bowling Green State University Popular Press, 1980. — II, 670.

Morrison, Jim. American night / Jim Morrison. — New York : Villard, 1990. — III, 791.

Morrison, Jim. Wilderness : the lost writings of Jim Morrison / Jim Morrison. — New York : Villard, 1989. — III, 790.

Morrissey, Steven. New York Dolls / Steven Morrissey. — Manchester : Babylon Books, 1980. — II, 1292.

Morrow, Cousin Bruce. Cousin Brucie! My life in rock 'n' roll radio / Cousin Bruce Morrow and Laura Baudo; introduction by Neil Sedaka. — New York : Beech Tree Books, 1987. — III, 979.

Morse, David. Motown and the arrival of black music / David Morse. — London : Studio Vista, 1971. — I, 893.

Morthland, John. The best of country music / John Morthland. — Garden City, N.Y. : Doubleday, 1984. — II, A-224.

Morton, David C. DeFord Bailey : a black star in early country music / David C. Morton; with Charles K. Wolfe. — Knoxville : University of Tennessee Press, 1991. — III, 600.

Morton, Jelly Roll. The collected piano music / Jelly Roll Morton; ed. James Dapogny. — Washington : Smithsonian Institution Press, 1982. — II, A-491.

Moses, Julian Morton. Collectors' guide to American recordings, 1895–1925 / Julian Morton Moses. — New York : American Record Collectors' Exchange, 1949. — I, A-12.

Moses, Montrose J. The life of Heinrich Conried / Montrose J. Moses. — New York : Crowell, 1916. — I, A-57.

Mueller, John. Astaire dancing : the musical films / John Mueller. — New York : Knopf, 1985. — II, A-614.

Mueller, John H. The American symphony orchestra : a social history of musical taste / John H. Mueller. — Bloomington : Indiana University Press, 1951. / I, 368.

Mueller, Kate Hevner. — Twenty-seven major American symphony orchestras / Kate Hevner Mueller. — Bloomington : Indiana University Press, 1973. — II, 47.

Mugridge, Donald H. A guide to the study of the United States of America / Donald H. Mugridge and Blanche P. McCrum. — Washington : Library of Congress, 1960. — I, 7.

Muir, John. The life and times of Captain Beefheart / John Muir. — Manchester : Babylon Books, 1980. — II, 1286.

Muller, Joseph. The Star Spangled Banner / Joseph Muller. — New York : Baker, 1935. — I, 1186.

Munn, Robert F. The southern Appalachians : a bibliography and guide to studies / Robert F. Munn. — Morgantown : West Virginia University Library, 1961. — II, 429.

Murdock, George Peter. Ethnographic bibliography of North America / George Peter Murdock. — 3rd ed. — New Haven, Conn. : Human Relations Area Files, 1960. — I, 386.

Murie, James R. Ceremonies of the Pawnee / James R. Murie. — Washington : Smithsonian Institution Press, 1981. — II, A-162.

Murray, Albert. Stomping the blues / Albert Murray. — New York : McGraw-Hill, 1976. — II, 553.

Murray, Charles Shaar. Crosstown traffic : Jimi Hendrix and the post-war rock 'n' roll revolution / Charles Shaar Murray. — New York : St. Martin's, 1989. — III, 582.

Murrells, Joseph. Million selling records, 1903–1983 / Joesph Murrells. — London : Batsford, 1984. — II, 812.

Murrells, Joseph. The book of golden discs / Joseph Murrells. — Rev. ed. — London : Barrie & Jenkins, 1978. — II, 812.

Music education the United States : contemporary issues : based on proceedings of symposia sponsored by the Alabama Project : Music, Society and Education in America / ed. J. Terry Gates. — Tuscaloosa : University of Alabama Press, 1988. — III, 1263.

Music industry directory : formerly the *Musician's Guide*. — 7th ed. — Chicago : Marquis Professional Publications, 1983. — III, 30.

Music librarianship in America / ed. Michael Ochs. — Cambridge, Mass. : Eda Kuhn Loeb Music Library, Harvard University, 1991. — III, 89.

Musical America international directory of the performing arts, 1992 edition. — New York : Musical America Publications, 1992. — III, 29.

Mussulman, Joseph A. Dear people . . . Robert Shaw : a biography / Joseph A. Mussulman. — Bloomington : Indiana University Press, 1979. — II, 214.

Mussulman, Joseph A. Music in the cultured generation : a social history of music in America, 1870–1900 / Joseph A. Mussulman. — Evanston, Ill. : Northwestern University Press, 1971. — I, 221.

Mussulman, Joseph A. The uses of music : an introduction to music in contemporary American life / Joseph A. Mussulman. — Englewood Cliffs, N.J. : Prentice-Hall, 1974. — I, 39.

Myers, Rollo H. Twentieth century music / Rollo H. Myers. — London : Calder, 1960. — I, A-82.

Myrus, Donald. Ballads, blues, and the big best / Donald Myrus. — New York : Macmillan, 1966. — II, 345.

Nance, Scott. New Kids on the Block / Scott Nance. — Las Vegas : Pioneer Books, 1990. — III, 930.

Nance, Scott. Recycling the blues : ZZ Top / Scott Nance. — Las Vegas : Pioneer Books, 1991. — III, 948.

Nanry, Charles. American music : from Storyville to Woodstock / Charles Nanry. — New Brunswick, N.J. : Transaction Books, 1972. — I, 1022.

Nanry, Charles. The jazz text / Charles Nanry and Edward Berger. — New York : Van Nostrand, 1979. — II, 665.

Napier, Simon A. Back woods blues / Simon A. Napier. — Bexhill-on-Sea, England : Blues Unlimited, 1968. — I, 832.

Nash, Alanna. Dolly / Alanna Nash. — Los Angeles : Read Books, 1978. — II, 412.

Nash, Elizabeth. Always first class : the career of Geraldine Farrar / Elizabeth Nash. — Lanham, Md. : University Press of America, 1981. — II, A-48.

Nash, Roderick. From these beginnings / Roderick Nash. — 3rd ed. — New York : Harper & Row, 1984. — II, 1200.

Nassour, Ellis. Patsy Cline / Ellis Nassour. — New York : Tower, 1981. — II, A-248.

Nathan, Hans. Dan Emmett and the rise of early negro minstrelsy / Hans Nathan. — Norman : University of Oklahoma Press, 1962. — I, 1238.

Nathan, Hans. William Billings : data and documents / Hans Nathan. — Detroit : Information Coordinators, 1976. — II, 141.

Nazel, Joseph. Paul Robeson : biography of a proud man / Joseph Nazel. — Los Angeles : Holloway House, 1980. — II, 516.

Neal, James H. Music research in Tennessee : a guide to special collections / James H. Neal. — Murfreesboro : Middle Tennessee State University, Center for Popular Music, 1989. — III, 109.

Near, Holly. Fire in the rain . . . singer in the storm : an autobiography / Holly Near; with Derk Richardson. — New York : Morrow, 1990. — III, 798.

Neeser, Robert W. American naval songs & ballads / ed. Robert W. Neeser. — New Haven, Conn. : Yale University Press, 1938. — II, 344.

Neff, Robert. Blues / Robert Neff and Anthony Connor. — London : Latimer, 1976. — II, 546.

Neilson, Francis. My life in two worlds, 1867–1952 / Francis Neilson. — Appleton, Wisc. : Nelson, 1952–1953. — II, 1048.

Neilson, Kenneth P. The world of Langston Hughes music / Kenneth P. Neilson. — Hollis, N.Y. : All Seasons Art, 1982. — II, A-283.

Nelson, Havelock. Bring the noise : a guide to rap music and hip-hop culture /

Havelock Nelson and Michael A. Gonzales. — New York : Harmony Books, 1991. — III, 443.

Nelson, Stephen. "Only a paper moon" : the theatre of Billy Rose / Stephen Nelson. — Ann Arbor, Mich. : UMI Research Press, 1987. — III, 1295.

Nelson, Susie. Heart worn memories : a daughter's personal biography of Willie Nelson / Susie Nelson. — Austin, Tex. : Eakin, 1987. — III, 803.

Nelson, Willie. Willie : an autobiography / Willie Nelson; with Bud Shrake. — New York : Pocket Books, 1989. — III, 802.

Nesbitt, Jim. Inside Buddy Rich / Jim Nesbitt; with Buddy Rich. — Delevan, N.Y. : Kendor, 1984. — II, A-498.

Nettl, Bruno. Blackfoot musical thought : comparative perspectives / Bruno Nettl. — Kent, Ohio : Kent State University Press, 1989. — III, 1233.

Nettl, Bruno. Eight urban musical cultures : tradition and change / Bruno Nettl. — Urbana : University of Illinois Press, 1978. — II, 300.

Nettl, Bruno. Folk and traditional music of the Western continents / Bruno Nettl. — 2nd ed. — Englewood Cliffs, N.J. : Prentice-Hall, 1973. — I, 426.

Nettl, Bruno. Introduction to folk music in the United States / Bruno Nettl. — 2nd ed. — Detroit : Wayne State University Press, 1962. — I, 447.

Nettl, Bruno. North American Indian musical styles / Bruno Nettl. — Philadelphia : American Folklore Society, 1954. — I, 399.

Nettl, Bruno. Reference materials in ethnomusicology : a bibliographic essay / Bruno Nettl. — 2nd ed. — Detroit : Information Coordinators, 1967. — I, 427.

Neumeyer, David. The music of Paul Hindemith / David Neumeyer. — New Haven, Conn. : Yale University Press, 1986. — III, 486.

Nevell, Richard. A time to dance : American country dancing from hornpipes to hot hash / Richard Nevell. — New York : St. Martin's, 1977. — II, 281.

New Grove dictionary of American music / ed. H. Wiley Hitchcock and Stanley Sadie. — New York : Grove's Dictionaries of Music, 1986. — III, 65.

New Grove dictionary of jazz / ed. Barry Kernfeld. — London : Macmillan; New York : Grove's Dictionaries of Music, 1988. — III, 73.

New Lost City Ramblers. The New Lost City Ramblers song book. — New York : Oak, 1964. — I, 617.

New perspectives on jazz : report on a national conference held at Wingspread, Racine, Wisconsin, September 8–10, 1986 / ed. David N. Baker. — Washington : Smithsonian Institution Press, 1990. — III, 1073.

New York Public Library. Dictionary catalog of the Schomburg collection of negro literature and history. — Boston : G. K. Hall, 1962. — I, A-150.

New York Public Library. Elliott Carter : sketches and scores in manuscript / New York Public Library. — New York : The Library, 1973. — I, 313.

New York Singing Teachers' Association. 20 years of the New York Singing Teachers' Association / Philadelphia : Presser, 1928. — II, 121.

New York Women Composers, Inc. Catalog : compositions of concert music. — North Tarrytown, N.Y. : New York Women Composers, Inc., 1991. — III, 106.

Newlin, Dika. Schoenberg remembered : diaries and recollections (1938–76) / Dika Newlin. — New York : Pendragon, 1980. — III, 513.

Newman, Richard. Black access : a bibliography of Afro-American bibliographies / Richard Newman. — Westport, Conn. : Greenwood, 1984. — II, A-278.

Newman, Shirlee P. Marian Anderson : lady from Philadelphia / Shirlee P. Newman. — Philadelphia : Westminster Press, 1965. — I, A-155.

Newman, Shirlee P. Mary Martin on stage / Shirlee P. Newman. — Philadelphia : Westminster, 1969. — II, 1082.

Newsom, Iris. Wonderful inventions : motion pictures, broadcasting, and recorded sound at the Library of Congress / ed. Iris Newsom; introduction by Erik Barnouw. — Washington : Library of Congress, 1985. — III, 1246.

Newsom, Jon. Perspectives on John Philip Sousa / ed. Jon Newsom. — Washington : Library of Congress, 1983. — II, A-554.

Newton, Francis. The jazz scene / Francis Newton. — London : Macgibbon & Kee, 1959. — I, 977.

Newton, Wayne. Once before I go / Wayne Newton; with Dick Maurice. — New York : Morrow, 1989. — III, 804.

Nicholas, A. X. The poetry of soul / A. X. Nicholas. — New York : Bantam, 1971. — I, 894.

Nicholas, A. X. Woke up this morning : poetry of the blues / A. X. Nicholas. — New York : Bantam, 1973. — II, 555.

Nicholls, David. American experimental music, 1890–1940 / David Nicholls. — London : Cambridge University Press, 1990. — III, 375.

Niles, John Jacob. Singing soldiers / John Jacob Niles. — New York : Scribner's, 1927. — I, A-242.

Niles, John Jacob. The songs my mother never taught me / John Jacob Niles. — New York : Macaulay, 1929. — I, A-243.

Ninde, Edward S. The story of the American hymn / Edward S. Ninde. — New York : Abingdon, 1921. — I, 68.

Nininger, Ruth. Church music comes of age / Ruth Nininger. — New York : Fischer, 1957. — II, 109.

Nisenson, Eric. 'Round about midnight : a portrait of Miles Davis / Eric Nisenson. — New York : Dial, 1982. — II, A-471.

Nite, Norm N. Rock on almanac / Norm N. Nite; foreword by Dick Clark. — 2nd ed. — New York : HarperCollins, 1992. — III, 1186.

Nite, Norm N. Rock on : the illustrated encyclopedia of rock 'n' roll / Norm N. Nite. — New York : Crowell; Harper & Row, 1974–1985. — II, 1103.

Nketia, J. H. Kwabena. African music in Ghana / J. H. Kwabena Nketia. — Accra, Ghana : Longmans, 1963. — I, 724.

Nketia, J. H. Kwabena. Drumming in Akan communities of Ghana / J. H. Kwabena Nketia. — Edinburgh : Nelson, 1963. — I, 725.

Nketia, J. H. Kwabena. Music in African cultures / J. H. Kwabena Nketia. — Legon, Ghana : University of Ghana, 1966. — I, 726.

Nketia, J. H. Kwabena. Music of Africa / J. H. Kwabena Nketia. — New York : Norton, 1974. — I, 727.

Noble, Gurre Ploner. Hula blues : the story of Johnny Noble, Hawaii, its music and musicians / Gurre Ploner Noble. — Honolulu : E. D. Noble, 1984. — III, 381.

Noblitt, Thomas. Music east and west : essays in honor of Walter Kaufman / ed. Thomas Noblitt. — New York : Pendragon, 1981. — II, A-82.

Noebel, David A. The Marxist minstrels : a handbook on communist subversion of music / David A. Noebel. — Tulsa, Okla. : American Christian College Press, 1974. — II, 1268.

Obermanns, Norbert. Zappalog / Norbert Obermanns. — Los Angeles : Rhino Books, 1982. — II, A-853.

Obrecht, Jan. Blues guitar : the men who made the music / ed. Jan Obrecht. — San Francisco : Miller Freeman, 1990. — III, 430.

Obst, Lynda Rosen. The sixties : the decade remembered now by the people who lived it then / Lynda Rosen Obst. — New York : Rolling Stone Press, 1977. — II, 1126.

Ochs, Michael. Rock archives : a photographic journey through the first two decades of rock & roll / Michael Ochs. — Garden City, N.Y. : Doubleday, 1984. — II, A-752.

Ochse, Orpha. The history of the organ in the United States / Orpha Ochse. — Bloomington : Indiana University Press, 1975. — I, 162.

Odell, George C. D. Annals of the New York stage / George C. D. Odell. — New York : Columbia University Press, 1927–1949. — I, A-63.

Odum, Howard W. Negro workaday songs / Howard W. Odum and Guy B. Johnson. — Chapel Hill : University of North Carolina Press, 1926. — I, 764.

Odum, Howard W. The negro and his songs : a study of typical negro songs in the South / Howard W. Odum and Guy B. Johnson. — Chapel Hill : University of North Carolina Press, 1925. — I, 763.

Oermann, Robert K. The listener's guide to country music / Robert K. Oermann. — New York : Facts on File, 1983. — II, A-225.

Offen, Carol. Country music : the poetry / Carol Offen. — New York : Ballantine, 1977. — II, 478.

Offergeld, Robert. Centennial catalogue of the published and unpublished compositions of Louis Moreau Gottschalk / Robert Offergeld. — New York : Ziff-Davis, 1970. — I, 231.

Ogasapian, John. Henry Erben : portrait of a nineteenth-century American organ builder / John Ogasapian. — Braintree, Mass. : Organ Literature Foundation, 1980. — II, 131.

Ogasapian, John. Organ building in New York City, 1700–1900 / John Ogasapian. — Braintree, Mass. : Organ Literature Foundation, 1977. — II, 84.

Ogren, Kathy J. The jazz revolution : twenties America and the meaning of jazz / Kathy J. Ogren. — New York : Oxford, 1989. — III, 1121.

Ohrlin, Glenn. The hell-bound train : a cowboy songbook / Glenn Ohrlin. — Urbana : University of Illinois Press, 1973. — I, 563.

Oja, Carol J. American music recordings : a discography of 10th-century U.S. composers / Carol J. Oja. — Brooklyn : Institute for Studies in American Music, 1982. — II, A-97.

Oja, Carol J. Colin McPhee : composer in two worlds / Carol J. Oja. — Washington : Smithsonian Institution Press, 1990. — III, 501.

Oja, Carol J. Stravinsky in "Modern music" 1924–1946 / ed. Carol J. Oja; foreword by Aaron Copland. — New York : Da Capo, 1982. — III, 528.

Okun, Milton. Something to sing about / Milton Okun. — New York : Macmillan, 1968. — I, 460.

Oliver, Paul. Aspects of the blues tradition / Paul Oliver. — New York : Oak, 1970. — I, 866.

Oliver, Paul. Bessie Smith / Paul Oliver. — London : Cassell, 1959. — I, 853.

Oliver, Paul. Blues fell this morning : meaning in the blues / Paul Oliver; foreword by Richard Wright. — 2nd ed. — Cambridge, England : Cambridge University Press, 1990. — III, 1157.

Oliver, Paul. Blues fell this morning : the meaning of the blues / Paul Oliver. — London : Cassell, 1960. — I, 864.

Oliver, Paul. Conversations with the blues / Paul Oliver. — London : Cassell, 1965. — I, 865.

Oliver, Paul. Meaning of the blues / Paul Oliver. — New York : Collier, 1963. — I, 864.

Oliver, Paul. Savannah syncopators : African retentions in the blues / Paul Oliver. — London : Studio Vista, 1970. — I, 817.

Oliver, Paul. Screening the blues : aspects of the blues tradition / Paul Oliver. — London : Cassell, 1968. — I, 866.

Oliver, Paul. Story of the blues / Paul Oliver. — London : Barrie & Rockliff, 1969. — I, 818.

Oliver, Paul. The New Grove gospel, blues, and jazz, with spirituals and ragtime / Paul Oliver, Max Harrison, and William Bolcom. — New York : Norton, 1988. — III, 1221.

Olmstead, Andrea. Conversations with Roger Sessions / Andrea Olmstead. — Boston : Northeastern University Press, 1987. — III, 517.

Olmstead, Andrea. Roger Sessions and his music / Andrea Olmstead. — Ann Arbor, Mich. : UMI Research Press, 1985. — II, A-138.

Olmstead, Andrea. The correspondence of Roger Sessions / Andrea Olmstead. — Boston : Northeastern University Press, 1992. — III, 518.

Olmsted Frederick Law. The cotton kingdom / Frederick Law Olmsted. — New York : Mason, 1861. — I, 739.

Olsen, Kenneth E. Music and musket : bands and bandsmen of the American Civil War / Kenneth E. Olsen. — Westport, Conn. : Greenwood, 1981. — II, A-555.

Olsson, Bengt. Memphis blues and jug bands / Bengt Olsson. — London : Studio Vista, 1970. — I, 825.

Open University. Popular culture : form and meaning 2. — Milton Keynes, England : Open University Press, 1982. — II, A-534.

Open University. Popular culture : politics, ideology and popular culture 1. — Milton Keynes, England : Open University Press, 1981. — II, A-535.

Open University. Popular culture : science, technology and popular culture 1. — Milton Keynes, England : Open University Press, 1982. — II, A-741.

Open University. The rise of jazz. — Milton Keynes, England : Open University Press, 1979. — II, 712.

Opera annual, U.S. 1984–85 / ed. by Jerome S. Ozer. — Englewood, N.J. : Author, 1988. — III, 1008.

Orgill, Michael. Anchored in love : the Carter family story / Michael Orgill. — Old Tappan, N.J. : Fleming H. Revell, 1975. — II, 395.

Orloff, Katherine. Rock 'n' roll woman / Katherine Orloff. — Los Angeles : Nash Publishing, 1974. — II, 1182.

Orman, John M. The politics of rock music / John M. Orman. — Chicago : Nelson-Hall, 1984. — II, A-735.

Ortiz, Simon. Song, poetry and language : expression and perception / Simon Ortiz. — Tsaile, Ariz. : Navajo Community College Press, 1977. — II, 254.

Osborne, Jerry. 33 1/3 and 45 extended play record album price guide / Jerry Osborne. — Phoenix, Ariz. : O'Sullivan Woodside, 1977. — II, 1256.

Osborne, Jerry. 55 years of recorded country/western music / Jerry Osborne. — Phoenix, Ariz. : O'Sullivan Woodside, 1976. — II, 361.

Osborne, Jerry. A guide to record collecting / Jerry Osborne and Bruce Hamilton. — Phoenix, Ariz. : O'Sullivan Woodside, 1979. — II, 1254.

Osborne, Jerry. Popular and rock price guide for 45's / Jerry Osborne. — Phoenix, Ariz. : O'Sullivan Woodside, 1979. — II, 1255.

Osborne, Jerry. Popular and rock records 1948–1978 / Jerry Osborne. — Phoenix, Ariz. : O'Sullivan Woodside, 1978. — II, 1225.

Osborne, Jerry. Presleyana : the complete Elvis guide / Jerry Osborne and Bruce Hamilton. — Phoenix, Ariz. : O'Sullivan Woodside, 1980. — II, 1312.

Osborne, Jerry. Record albums 1948–1978 / Jerry Osborne. — Phoenix, Ariz. : O'Sullivan Woodside, 1978. — II, 1256.

Osborne, Jerry. Record collector's price guide / Jerry Osborne. — Phoenix, Ariz. : O'Sullivan Woodside, 1976. — II, 1255.

Osborne, Jerry. Rockin' records buyers-sellers reference book and price guide 1991 edition / Jerry Osborne. — Boyne Falls, Mich. : Jellyroll, 1991. — III, 263.

Osborne, Jerry. The Elvis Presley record price guide / Jerry Osborne. — 3rd ed. — Port Townsend, Wash. : Jellyroll, 1992. — III, 350.

Osborne, Jerry. The official price guide to movie and TV soundtracks and original cast albums / Jerry Osborne; ed. Ruth Maupin. — New York : House of Collectibles, 1991. — III, 246.

Osburn, Mary Hubbell. Ohio composers and musical authors / Mary Hubbell Osburn. — Columbus, Ohio : F. J. Heer, 1942. — I, 137.

Osgood, Henry O. So this is jazz / Henry O. Osgood. — Boston : Little, Brown, 1926. — I, 1033.

Ostendorf, Berndt. Black literature in white America / Berndt Ostendorf. — Brighton, England : Harvester Press, 1982. — II, A-284.

Ostendorf, Berndt. Ethnicity and popular music / Berndt Ostendorf. — Exeter, England : IASPM/UK, 1984. — II, A-541.

Oster, Harry. Living country blues / Harry Oster. — Detroit : Folklore Associates, 1969. — I, 879.

Ostransky, Leroy. Jazz city : the impact of our cities on the development of jazz / Leroy Ostransky. — Englewood Cliffs, N.J. : Prentice-Hall, 1978. — II, 671.

Ostransky, Leroy. The anatomy of jazz / Leroy Ostransky. — Seattle : University of Washington Press, 1960. — I, 999.

Ostransky, Leroy. Understanding jazz / Leroy Ostransky. — Englewood Cliffs, N.J. : Prentice-Hall, 1977. — II, 690.

Otis, Johnny. Listen to the lambs / Johnny Otis. — New York : Norton, 1968. — II, 560.

Otis, Philo Adams. The Chicago Symphony Orchestra : its organization, growth and development, 1891–1924. — Chicago : Summy, 1924. — I, 126.

Ottley, Roi. The negro in New York : an informal social history / Roi Ottley and William J. Weatherby. — New York : New York Public Library, 1967. — I, 668.

Ouellette, Fernand. Edgard Varèse. — Fernand Ouellette; trans. Derek Coltman. — New York : Orion, 1968. — I, 353.

Overmyer, Grace. Famous American composers / Grace Overmyer. — New York : Crowell, 1944. — I, A-13.

Owen, Barbara. E. Power Biggs, concert organist / Barbara Owen; discography by Andrew Kazdin. — Bloomington : Indiana University Press, 1987. — III, 535.

Owen, Barbara. The Mormon Tabernacle organ, an American classic / Barbara Owen. — Salt Lake City : Church of Latter Day Saints, 1990. — III, 990a.

Owen, Barbara. The organ in New England / Barbara Owen. — Raleigh, N.C. : Sunbury, 1979. — II, 85.

Owens, William A. Tell me a story, sing me a song : a Texas chronicle / William A. Owens. — Austin : University of Texas Press, 1983. — II, A-201.

Owens, William A. Texas folk songs / William A. Owens — Austin : Texas Folklore Society, 1950. — I, 515.

Oyer, Mary. Exploring the Mennonite hymnal / Mary Oyer. — Newton, Kans. : Faith and Life Press, 1980. — II, 110.

Page, Drew. Drew's blues : a sideman's life with the big bands / Drew Page. — Baton Rouge : Louisiana State University Press, 1980. — II, 764.

Page, Elizabeth Fry. Edward MacDowell : his work and ideals / Elizabeth Fry Page. — New York : Dodge, 1910. — I, 238.

Page, Tim. Music from the road : views and reviews, 1978–1992 / Tim Page. — New York : Oxford, 1992. — III, 57.

Page, Tim. William Kapell : a documentary life history of the American pianist / Tim Page. — College Park : International Piano Archives at Maryland, University of Maryland Press, 1992. — III, 555.

Paige, Harry W. Songs of the Teton Sioux / Harry W. Paige. — Los Angeles : Westernlore, 1970. — I, 416a.

Paley, William S. As it happened : a memoir / William S. Paley. — Garden City, N.Y. : Doubleday, 1979. — II, 133.

Palmer, Christopher. Dimitri Tiomkin : a portrait / Christopher Palmer. — London : T. E. Books, 1984. — II, A-607.

Palmer, Christopher. Miklos Rozsa : a sketch of his life and work / Christopher Palmer. — London : Breitkopf & Härtel, 1975. — I, 1313.

Palmer, Christopher. The composer in Hollywood / Christopher Palmer. — London : Marion Boyars, 1989. — III, 1030.

Palmer, Larry. Harpsichord in America : a twentieth-century revival / Larry Palmer. — Bloomington : Indiana University Press, 1989. — III, 991.

Palmer, Myles. New wave explosion / Myles Palmer. — London : Proteus, 1981. — II, A-699.

Palmer, Richard. Oscar Peterson / Richard Palmer. — Tunbridge Wells, England : Spellmount; New York : Hippocrene Books, 1984. — III, 566.

Palmer, Richard. Stan Getz / Richard Palmer. — London : Apollo, 1988. — III, 635.

Palmer, Robert. A tale of two cities : Memphis rock and New Orleans roll / Robert Palmer. — Brooklyn : Institute for Studies in American Music, 1979. — II, 1130.

Palmer, Robert. Baby, that was rock & roll : the legendary Leiber & Stoller / Robert Palmer. — New York : Harcourt Brace Jovanovich, 1978. — II, 1215.

Palmer, Robert. Jerry Lee Lewis rocks! / Robert Palmer. — New York : Delilah, 1982. — II, A-810.

Palmer, Tony. All you need is love : the story of popular music / Tony Palmer. — New York : Grossman, 1976. — II, 839.

Palmieri, Robert. Sergei Vasil'evich Rachmaninoff : a guide to research / Robert Palmieri. — New York : Garland, 1985. — III, 177.

Pan American Union. Composers of the Americas : biographical data and catalogs of their works. — Washington : Organization of American States, 1955–. — I, 290.

Panassié, Hugues. Dictionary of jazz / Hugues Panassié. — London : Cassell, 1956. — I, 912.

Panassié, Hugues. Dictionnaire du jazz / Hugues Panassié. — Paris : Laffont, 1954. — I, 912.

Panassié, Hugues. Guide to jazz / Hugues Panassié. — Boston : Houghton Mifflin, 1956. — I, 912.

Panassié, Hugues. Histoire des disques swing enregistrés à New York par Tommy Ladnier, Mezz Mezzrow, Frank Newton / Hugues Panassié. — Geneva : Grasset, 1944. — I, A-214.

Panassié, Hugues. Hot jazz : the guide to swing music / Hugues Panassié. — New York : Witmark, 1936. — I, 1034.

Panassié, Hugues. Le jazz hot / Hugues Panassié. — Paris : Correa, 1934. — I, 1034.

Panassié, Hugues. Louis Armstrong / Hugues Panassié. — Paris : Nouvelles Éditions Latines, 1969. — I, 1087.

Panassié, Hugues. Quand Mezzrow enregistre / Hugues Panassié. — Paris : Laffont, 1952. — I, A-215.

Panassié, Hugues. The real jazz / Hugues Panassié. — Rev. ed. — Paris : Laffont, 1952. — I, 1035.

Panta, Ilona. Elvis Presley : the king of kings / Ilona Panta. — New York : Exposition, 1979. — II, 1230.

Panzeri, Louis. Louisiana composers / Louis Panzeri. — New Orleans : Dinstuhl, 1972. — II, 61.

Paparelli, Frank. Leeds' eight to the bar / New York : Leeds Music, 1941. — I, A-185.

Paparelli, Frank. The blues and how to play 'em / Frank Paparelli. — New York : Leeds Music, 1942. — I, A-184.

Pape, Uwe. Organs in America : vol. 1 / Uwe Pape. — Berlin : Author, 1982. — II, A-55.

Papich, Stephen. Remembering Josephine / Stephen Papich. — Indianapolis : Bobbs-Merrill, 1976. — II, 1069.

Paredes, Américo. A Texas-Mexican cancionero / Américo Paredes. — Urbana : University of Illinois Press, 1976. — II, 293.

Pareles, John. The *Rolling Stone* encyclopedia of rock & roll / John Pareles and Patricia Romanowski. — New York : Rolling Stone Press, 1983. — II, A-664.

Paris, Leonard A. Men and melodies / Leonard A. Paris. — New York : Crowell, 1954. — II, 903.

Paris, Mike. Jimmie the kid : the life of Jimmie Rodgers / Mike Paris and Chris Comber. — London : Eddison Press, 1977. — II, 417.

Parish, James Robert. Hollywood songsters / James Robert Parish and Michael R. Pitts. — New York : Garland, 1991. — III, 44.

Parish, James Robert. Liza : her Cinderella nightmare / James Robert Parish and Jack Ano. — London : W. H. Allen, 1975. — II, 1005.

Parish, James Robert. Liza! : an unauthorized biography / James Robert Parish and Jack Ano. — New York : Pocket Books, 1975. — II, 1005.

Parish, James Robert. The Elvis Presley scrapbook / James Robert Parish. — Rev. ed. — New York : Ballantine, 1977. — II, 1300.

Parish, James Robert. The great Hollywood musical pictures / James Robert Parish and Michael R. Pitts. — Metuchen, N.J. : Scarecrow, 1992. — III, 1284.

Parish, James Robert. The Jeanette MacDonald story / James Robert Parish. — New York : Mason Charter, 1976. — II, 980.

Park, Mungo. Travels in the interior districts of Africa / Mungo Park. — London, 1799. — I, 717.

Parker, Chan. To Bird with love / Chan Parker. — Poitiers, France : Wizlov, 1981. — II, A-494.

Parker, Edmund K. Inside Elvis / Edmund K. Parker. — Orange, Calif. : Rampart House, 1978. — II, 1301.

Parrish, Lydia. Slave songs of the Georgia Sea Islands / Lydia Parrish. — New York : Creative Age, 1942. — I, 751.

Partch, Harry. Bitter music : collected journals, essays, introductions, and librettos / Harry Partch; ed., with introduction by Thomas McGeary. — Champaign : University of Illinois Press, 1991. — III, 505.

Partch, Harry. Genesis of a music / Harry Partch. — 2nd ed. — New York : Da Capo, 1974. — I, 341.

Pascall, Jeremy. The illustrated history of rock music / Jeremy Pascall. — Rev. ed. — London : Hamlyn, 1984. — II, 1123.

Pascall, Jeremy. The stars and superstars of black music / Jeremy Pascall and Rob Burt. — London : Phoebus, 1977. — II, 622.

Paschedag, Theodore. The music came first : the memoirs of Theodore Paschedag; as told to Thomas J. Hatton. — Carbondale : Southern Illinois University Press, 1988. — III, 960.

Paskman, Dailey. Gentlemen be seated! / Dailey Paskman and Sigmund Spaeth. — Garden City, N.Y. : Doubleday, 1928. — I, 1239.

Passman, Arnold. The deejays / Arnold Passman. — New York : Macmillan, 1971. — II, 1269.

Passman, Donald S. All you need to know about the music business / Donald S. Passman. — New York : Simon & Schuster, 1991. — III, 1247.

Pasteur, Alfred B. Roots of soul : the psychology of black expressiveness / Alfred B. Pasteur and Ivory I. Toldson. — Garden City, N.Y. : Anchor, 1982. — III, 5.

Patterson, Daniel W. Gift drawing and gift song : a study of two forms of Shaker inspiration / Daniel W. Patterson. — Sabbathday Lake, Maine : United Society of Shakers, 1983. — II, A-207.

Patterson, Daniel W. Nine Shaker spirituals / Daniel W. Patterson. — Old Chatham, N.J. : Shaker Museum Foundation, 1964. — I, 555.

Patterson, Daniel W. The Shaker spiritual / Daniel W. Patterson. — Princeton, N.J. : Princeton University Press, 1979. — II, 333.

Patterson, Donald L. Vincent Persichetti : a bio-bibliography / Donald L. Patterson and Janet L. Patterson. — Westport, Conn. : Greenwood, 1988. — III, 175.

Patterson, Lindsay. The negro in music and art / Lindsay Patterson. — 2nd ed. — New York : Publishers Co., 1969. — I, 692.

Pattison, Robert. The triumph of vulgarity : rock music in the mirror of romanticism / Robert Pattison. — New York : Oxford, 1987. — III, 1187.

Paul, Elliot. That crazy American music / Elliot Paul. — Indianapolis : Bobbs-Merrill, 1957. — I, A-216.

Paul, Elliot. The story of North American jazz / Elliot Paul. — London : Muller, 1957. — I, A-216.

Pavlakis, Christopher. The American music handbook / Christopher Pavlakis. New York : Free Press, 1974. — I, 369.

Pavletich, Aida. Rock-a-bye baby / Aida Pavletich. — Garden City, N.Y. : Doubleday, 1980. — II, 1183.

Pawlowska, Harriet M. Merrily we sing : 105 Polish folksongs / Harriet M. Pawlowska. — Detroit : Wayne State University Press, 1961. — II, 301.

Paymer, Marvin E. Facts behind the songs : a handbook of American popular music from the nineties to the '90s / Marvin E. Paymer. — New York : Garland, 1993. — III, 75.

Payne, Daniel Alexander. Recollections of seventy years / Daniel Alexander Payne. — Nashville : A.M.E. Sunday School Union, 1888. — I, 740.

Payne, Robert. Gershwin / Robert Payne. — New York : Pyramid Books, 1960. — I, 1284.

Pearl, Minnie. Minnie Pearl : an autobiography / Minnie Pearl and Joan Dew. — New York : Simon & Schuster, 1980. — II, 413.

Pearson, Barry Lee. Virginia Piedmont blues : the lives and art of two Virginia bluesmen / Barry Lee Pearson. — Philadelphia : University of Pennsylvania Press, 1990. — III, 406.

Pearson, Nathan W., Jr. Goin' to Kansas City / Nathan W. Pearson, Jr. — Urbana : University of Illinois Press, 1987. — III, 1127.

Peavy, Charles D. Afro-American literature and culture since World War II : a guide to information sources / Charles D. Peavy. — Detroit : Gale, 1979. — II, 485.

Pebworth, James R. A directory of 132 Arkansas composers / James R. Pebworth. — Fayetteville : University of Arkansas Press, 1979. — II, 62.

Peel, David. Oooh, well, well, it's the Peetie Wheatstraw stomps / David Peel. — Burlington, Ontario : Belltower Books, 1972. — I, 857.

Peelaert, Guy. Rock dreams / Guy Peelaert and Nik Cohn. — London : Pan Books, 1974. — II, 1165.

Peisch, Jeffrey. Stevie Wonder / Jeffrey Peisch. — New York : Ballantine, 1984. — III, 891.

Pemberton, Carol A. Lowell Mason : a bio-bibliography / Carol A. Pemberton. — Westport, Conn. : Greenwood, 1988. — III, 172.

Pemberton, Carol A. Lowell Mason : his life and work / Carol A. Pemberton. — Ann Arbor, Mich. : UMI Research Press, 1985. — II, A-85.

Pennebaker, D. A. Bob Dylan : don't look back / D. A. Pennebaker. — New York : Ballantine, 1968. — I, A-299.

Peña, Manuel H. The Texas-Mexican conjunto / Manuel H. Peña. — Austin : University of Texas Press, 1985. — II, A-182.

Pepper, Art. Straight life : the story of Art Pepper / Art Pepper and Laurie Pepper. — New York : Schirmer, 1979. — II, 766.

Peretti, Burton W. The creation of jazz : music, race, and culture in urban America / Burton W. Peretti. — Urbana : University of Illinois Press, 1992. — III, 1122.

Performing arts books 1876–1981. — New York : Bowker, 1981. — II, A-4.

Perkins, Carl. Discipline in blue suede shoes / Carl Perkins; with Ron Rendleman. — Grand Rapids, Mich. : Zondervan, 1978. — II, 1221.

Perlis, Vivian. Charles Ives papers / Vivian Perlis. — New Haven, Conn. : Yale University Music Library, 1983. — II, A-128.

Perlis, Vivian. Charles Ives remembered : an oral history / Vivian Perlis. — New Haven, Conn. : Yale University Press, 1974. — I, 331.

Perlis, Vivian. Two men for modern music : E. Robert Schmitz and Herman Langinger / Vivian Perlis. — Brooklyn : Institute for Studies in American Music, 1978. — II, 215.

Perone, Karen. Lukas Foss : a bio-bibliography / Karen Perone. — New York : Greenwood, 1988. — III, 163.

Perry, Charles. The Haight-Ashbury : a history / Charles Perry. — New York : Random House, 1984. — II, A-706b.

Perry, Hamilton Derby. Libby Holman : body and soul / Hamilton Derby Perry. — Boston : Little, Brown, 1983. — II, A-619.

Perry, Jeb H. Variety obits : an index to obituaries in Variety, 1905–1978 / Jeb H. Perry. — Metuchen, N.J. : Scarecrow, 1980. — II, 824.

Perry, Rosalie Sandra. Charles Ives and the American mind / Rosalie Sandra Perry. — Kent, Ohio : Kent State University Press, 1974. — I, 332.

Pescatello, Ann M. Charles Seeger : a life in American music / Ann M. Pescatello. — Pittsburgh : University of Pittsburgh Press, 1992. — III, 970.

Peters, Richard. Barry Manilow : an illustrated biography / Richard Peters. — New York : Delilah, 1983. — II, A-813.

Peters, Richard. Elvis : the golden anniversary tribute / Richard Peters. — London : Pop Universal, 1984. — II, A-830.

Peters, Richard. Elvis : the music lives on : the recording sessions 1954–1976 / Richard Peters. — London : Pop Universal/Souvenir Press, 1992. — III, 834.

Peters, Richard. The Barry Manilow scrapbook / Richard Peters. — London : Pop Universal, 1982. — II, A-813.

Peters, Richard. The Frank Sinatra scrapbook / Richard Peters. — New York : St. Martin's, 1983. — II, A-636.

Peterson, John W. The miracle goes on / John W. Peterson; with Richard Engquist. — Grand Rapids, Mich. : Zondervan, 1976. — II, 111.

Peterson, Richard A. Single-industry firm to conglomerate synergistics / Richard A. Peterson. — Los Angeles : John Edwards Memorial Foundation, 1975. — II, 379.

Petrie, Gavin. Black music / ed. Gavin Petrie. — London : Hamlyn, 1974. — II, 569.

Petrie, Gavin. Rock life / Gavin Petrie. — London : Hamlyn, 1974. — II, 1173.

Petrik, Hanns E. Bill Evans / Hanns E. Petrik. — Waakirchen, Germany : Oreos, 1989. — III, 539.

Peyser, Ethel. The house that music built : Carnegie Hall / Ethel Peyser. — New York : McBride, 1936. — I, 109.

Peyser, Joan. Bernstein : a biography / Joan Peyser. — New York : Beech Tree Books, 1987. — III, 455.

Philbin, Marianne. Give peace a chance : music and the struggle for peace / Marianne Philbin. — Chicago : Chicago Review Press, 1983. — II, A-216.

Phillips, John. Papa John : an autobiography / John Phillips; with Jim Jerome. — Garden City, N.Y. : Doubleday, 1986. — III, 813.

Phillips, Michelle. California dreamin' : the true story of the Mamas and the Papas / Michelle Phillips. — New York : Warner Books, 1986. — III, 923.

Phimster, William. American piano concertos : a bibliography / William Phimster. — Detroit : College Music Society, 1985. — II, A-5.

Pichaske, David R. A generation in motion : popular music and culture in the sixties / David R. Pichaske. — New York : Schirmer, 1979. — II, 1127.

Pichaske, David R. The poetry of rock : the golden years / David R. Pichaske. — Peoria, Ill. : Ellis Press, 1981. — II, A-722.

Pichierri, Louis. Music in New Hampshire, 1623–1800 / Louis Pichierri. — New York : Columbia University Press, 1960. — I, 103.

Pickering, Stephen. Dylan : a commemoration / Stephen Pickering. — Berkeley, Calif. : Book People, 1971. — I, 1376.

Pickering, Stephen. Praxis one : existence, men and realities / Stephen Pickering. — Berkeley, Calif. : Book People, 1971. — I, 1377.

Pierce, Frank H. The Washington Saengerbund : a history of German song and culture in the nation's capital / Frank H. Pierce. — Washington : The Saengerbund, 1981. — II, A-40.

Pike, Bob. The genius of Busby Berkeley / Bob Pike. — Reseda, Calif. : Creative Film Society, 1973. — II, 931.

Pike, Gustavus D. The Jubilee Singers and their campaign for twenty thousand dollars / Gustavus D. Pike. — Boston : Lee & Shepard, 1873. — I, 783.

Pincus, Andrew L. Scenes from Tanglewood / Andrew L. Pincus; foreword by Seiji Ozawa. — Boston : Northeastern University Press, 1992. — III, 387.

Pincus, Lee. The songwriter's success manual / Lee Pincus. — New York : Music Press, 1974. — II, 1270.

Pinfold, Mike. Louis Armstrong : his life & times / Mike Pinfold. — London : Omnibus, 1988. — III, 599.

Pino, Giuseppe. From spirituals to swing / Giuseppe Pino [et al]. — Montreux, Switzerland : International Booking Agency, 1979. — II, 682.

Pinza, Ezio. Ezio Pinza : an autobiography / Ezio Pinza. — New York : Rinehart, 1958. — II, 1083.

Pirie, Christopher A. Artistry in Kenton / Christopher A. Pirie and Siegfried Mueller. — 3rd ed. — Vienna : Mueller, 1972. — I, 948.

Pitts, Michael R. Hollywood on record : the film stars' discography / Michael R. Pitts and Louis H. Harrison. — Metuchen, N.J. : Scarecrow, 1978. — II, 830.

Pitts, Michael R. Kate Smith : a bio-bibliography / Michael R. Pitts. — Westport, Conn. : Greenwood, 1988. — III, 190.

Pitts, Michael R. Radio soundtracks : a reference guide / Michael R. Pitts. — Metuchen, N.J. : Scarecrow, 1976. — II, 813.

Placksin, Sally. American women in jazz, 1900 to the present / Sally Placksin. — New York : Seaview Books, 1982. — II, A-453.

Plaskin, Glenn. Horowitz : a biography of Vladimir Horowitz / Glenn Plaskin; discography by Robert McAlear. — New York : Morrow, 1983. — III, 549.

Pleasants, Henry. Death of a music? / Henry Pleasants. — London : Gollancz, 1961. — I, 1000.

Pleasants, Henry. Serious music—and all that jazz! / Henry Pleasants. — New York : Simon & Schuster, 1969. — I, 1001.

Pleasants, Henry. The great American popular singers / Henry Pleasants. — New York : Simon & Schuster, 1974. — I, 1323.

Plutzik, Roberta. Lionel Richie / Robert Plutzik. — New York : Dell, 1985. — II, A-838.

Podell, Janet. Rock music in America / Janet Podell. — New York : H. W. Wilson, 1987. — III, 1191.

Polic, Edward F. The Glenn Miller Army Air Force Band / Edward F. Polic; foreword by George T. Simon. — Metuchen, N.J. : Scarecrow, 1989. — III, 1139.

Polillo, Arrigo. Jazz : la vicenda e i protagonisti della musica afro-americana / Arrigo Polillo. — Milan : Mondadori, 1983. — II, A-408.

Polillo, Arrigo. Jazz : la vicenda e i protagonisti della musica afro-americana / Arrigo Polillo. — Milan : Mondadori, 1975. — I, 1005.

Pollack, Howard. Harvard composers : Walter Piston and his students, from Elliott Carter to Frederic Rzewski / Howard Pollack. — Metuchen, N.J. : Scarecrow, 1992. — III, 413.

Pollack, Howard. Walter Piston / Howard Pollack. — Ann Arbor, Mich. : UMI Research Press, 1982. — II, A-133.

Pollock, Bruce. In their own words / Bruce Pollock. — New York : Macmillan, 1975. — II, 1174.

Pollock, Bruce. The face of rock & roll : images of a generation / Bruce Pollock. — New York : Holt, Rinehart & Winston, 1978. — II, 1167.

Pollock, Bruce. When rock was young / Bruce Pollock. — New York : Holt, Rinehart & Winston, 1981. — II, A-701.

Pollock, Bruce. When the music mattered : rock in the 1960s / Bruce Pollock. — New York : Holt, Rinehart & Winston, 1984. — II, A-700.

Ponselle, Rosa. Ponselle, a singer's life / Rosa Ponselle; with James A. Drake; discography by Bill Park. — Garden City, N.Y. : Doubleday, 1982. — III, 814.

Pop, Iggy. I need more : the Stooges and other stories / Iggy Pop; with Anne Wehre. — Princeton, N.J. : Karz-Cohl, 1982. — II, A-816.

Popa, Jay. Cab Calloway and his orchestra, 1925–1958 / Jay Popa. — Rev. ed. — Zephyrhills, Fla. : Joyce Record Club, 1987. — III, 291.

Popular music : an annotated index of American popular songs / ed. Nat Shapiro and Bruce Pollock. — Detroit : Gale, 1984- . — III, 102.

Popular song index. 3rd supplement / ed. Patricia Pate Havlice. — Metuchen, N.J. : Scarecrow, 1989. — III, 151.

Porte, J. F. Edward MacDowell : a great American tone poet, his life and music / J. F. Porte. — London : Kegan, Paul, Trench, Trübner, 1922. — I, 239.

Porter, Andrew. A musical season : a critic from abroad in America / Andrew Porter. — New York : Viking, 1974. — II, 216.

Porter, Andrew. Music of three more seasons : 1977–1980 / Andrew Porter. — New York : Knopf, 1981. — III, 397.

Porter, Andrew. Music of three seasons : 1974–1977 / Andrew Porter. — New York : Farrar, Straus & Giroux, 1978. — II, 217.

Porter, Bob. Signature Record Company master listing / Bob Porter. —
Zephyrhills, Fla. : Joyce Record Club, 1989. — III, 217.
Porter, Cole. 103 lyrics / Cole Porter; selected with an introduction and commentary by Fred Lounsberry. — New York : Random House, 1954. — I, 1291.
Porter, Dorothy B. The negro in the United States : a selected bibliography /
Dorothy B. Porter. — Washington : Library of Congress, 1970. — I, 653.
Porter, Ellen Jane. Two early American tunes : fraternal twins? / Ellen Jane
Porter. — New York : Hymn Society of America, 1975. — II, 35.
Porter, Grace Cleveland. Negro folk singing games and folk games of the habitants / ed. Grace Cleveland Porter. — London : Curwen, 1914. — II, 519.
Porter, James. The ballad image : essays presented to Bertrand Harris Bronson /
ed. James Porter. — Los Angeles : Center for the Study of Comparative Folklore & Mythology, 1983. — II, A-177.
Porter, Lewis. A Lester Young reader / Lewis Porter. — Washington : Smithsonian Institution Press, 1991. — III, 678.
Porter, Lewis. Lester Young / Lewis Porter. — Boston : G. K. Hall, 1985. — II,
A-504.
Porter, Roy. There and back : the Roy Porter story / Roy Porter; with David
Keller. — Baton Rouge : Louisiana State University Press, 1991. — III, 659.
Porter, Susan L. With an air debonair : musical theatre in America, 1785–1815 /
Susan L. Porter. — Washington : Smithsonian Institution Press, 1992. — III,
1013.
Porterfield, Nolan. Jimmie Rodgers : the life and times of America's blue yodeler / Nolan Porterfield. — Urbana : University of Illinois Press, 1979. — II,
418.
Postgate, John. A plain man's guide to jazz / John Postgate. — London :
Hanover, 1973. — I, 969.
Potter, Hugh M. False dawn : Paul Rosenfeld and art in America, 1916–1946 /
Hugh M. Potter. — Ann Arbor, Mich. : UMI Research Press, 1980. — II,
224.
Pound, Ezra. Antheil and the Treatise on harmony / Ezra Pound. — Paris : Three
Mountains, 1924. — I, 301.
Pound, Ezra. Ezra Pound and music : the complete criticism / Ezra Pound; ed. R.
Murray Schafer. — New York : New Directions, 1977. — II, 225.
Pound, Louise. American ballads and songs / Louise Pound. — New York :
Scribner's, 1922. — I, 461.
Pound, Louise. Folk-song of Nebraska and the central West / Louis Pound. —
Lincoln : Nebraska Academy of Sciences, 1915. — I, A-120.
Powell, John. Twelve folk hymns from the old shape note hymnals and from oral
tradition / John Powell. — New York : Fischer, 1934. — I, 544.
Pratt, Ray. Rhythm and resistance : explorations in the political uses of popular
music / Ray Pratt. — New York : Praeger, 1990. — III, 1049.
Pratt, Waldo Selden. Grove's dictionary of music and musicians : American supplement / ed. Waldo Selden Pratt. — Philadelphia : Presser, 1927. — I, 13.
Pratt, Waldo Selden. The music of the Pilgrims / Waldo Selden Pratt. — Boston :
Ditson, 1921. — I, 187.
Preiss, Byron. The Beach Boys / Byron Preiss. — New York : Ballantine,
1979. — II, 1187.

Prendergast, Curtis. Bix Beiderbecke / Curtis Prendergast. — Alexandria, Va. : Time-Life Records, 1979. — III, 605.

Prendergast, Roy. A neglected art : a critical study of music in film / Roy Prendergast. — New York : New York University Press, 1977. — II, 940.

Prendergast, Roy. Film music : a neglected art / Roy Prendergast. — New York : Norton, 1977. — II, 940.

Presley, Dee. Elvis, we love you tender / Dee Presley [et al]. — New York : Delacorte, 1980. — II, 1231.

Presley, Elvis. Elvis in his own words / Elvis Presley; comp. Mick Farren. — London : Omnibus, 1977. — II, 1232.

Presley, Priscilla Beaulieu. Elvis and me / Priscilla Beaulieu Presley; with Sandra Harmon. — New York : Putnam, 1985. — III, 835.

Preston, Denis. Mood indigo / Denis Preston. — Egham, England : Citizen Press, 1946. — I, A-217.

Preston, Katherine K. Music for hire : a study of professional musicians in Washington (1877–1900) / Katherine K. Preston. — Stuyvesant, N.Y. : Pendragon, 1992. — III, 661.

Previn, André. No minor chords : my days in Hollywood / André Previn. — New York : Doubleday, 1991. — III, 961.

Previn, Dory. Bog-Trotter : an autobiography with lyrics / Dory Previn. — Garden City, N.Y. : Doubleday, 1980. — II, 1237.

Previn, Dory. Midnight baby : an autobiography / Dory Previn. — New York : Macmillan, 1976. — II, 1238.

Price, Sammy. Boogie-woogie land / Sammy Price. — New York : Marks, 1944. — I, A-186.

Price, Sammy. What do they want? a jazz autobiography / Sammy Price; ed. Caroline Richmond. — Urbana : University of Illinois Press, 1990. — III, 567.

Price, Steven D. Old as the hills : the story of bluegrass music / Steven D. Price. — New York : Viking, 1975. — I, 626.

Price, Steven D. Take me home : the rise of country and western music / Steven D. Price. — New York : Praeger, 1974. — I, 607.

Priest, Daniel B. American sheet music / Daniel B. Priest. — Des Moines, Iowa : Wallace-Homestead, 1978. — II, 855.

Priestley, Brian. Charlie Parker / Brian Priestley. — New York : Hippocrene, 1984 — II, A-495.

Priestley, Brian. Jazz on record : a history / Brian Priestley. — New York : Billboard Books, 1991. — III, 1088.

Priestley, Brian. John Coltrane / Brian Priestley. — London : Apollo, 1987. — III, 623.

Priestley, Brian. Mingus : a critical biography / Brian Priestley. — London : Quartet, 1982. — II, A-487.

Propes, Steve. Golden goodies : a guide to 50s and 60s popular rock & roll record collecting / Steve Propes. — Radnor, Pa. : Chilton, 1975. — II, 1121.

Propes, Steve. Golden oldies : a guide to '60s record collecting / Steve Propes. — Radnor, Pa. : Chilton, 1974. — I, 887.

Propes, Steve. Those oldies but goodies : a guide to '50s record collecting / Steve Propes. — New York : Macmillan, 1973. — I, 888.

Pruett, Barbara J. Marty Robbins : fast cars and country music / Barbara J. Pruett. — Metuchen, N.J. : Scarecrow, 1990. — III, 189.

Pruter, Robert. Chicago soul : making black music Chicago style / Robert Pruter. — Urbana : University of Illinois Press, 1991. — III, 1204.

Psalms hymns and spiritual songs of the Old and New Testament [Bay psalm book, 9th ed.]. Boston : B. Green and J. Allen, 1698. — I, 188.

Psalms hymns and spiritual songs of the Old and New Testament [Bay psalm book, 3rd ed.]. Cambridge, Mass. : Samuel Green, 1651. — I, 188.

Publications of the Texas Folk-Lore Society. II, 321.

Pudlo, Van. Chicago's local rock / Van Pudlo and Joe Ziemba. — Merrillville, Ind. : Toris Productions, 1982. — III, 1200.

Purchaser's guide to the music industries. — Englewood, N.J. : Music Trades, 1897– . — III, 40.

Purdy, Claire Lee. Victor Herbert, American music master / Claire Lee Purdy. — New York : Messner, 1945. — I, A-261.

Purple Haze Archives. Jimi Hendrix : a discography. — Tucson, Ariz. : Purple Haze Archives, 1981. — II, A-802.

Quain, Kevin. The Elvis reader : texts and sources on the king of rock 'n' roll / Kevin Quain. — New York : St. Martin's, 1992. — III, 836.

Quarles, Benjamin. The negro in the making of America / Benjamin Quarles. — 2nd ed. — New York : Collier, 1969. — I, 669.

Quinn, Jennifer Post. An index to the field recordings in the Flanders Ballad Collection at Middlebury College, Middlebury, Vermont / Jennifer Post Quinn. — Middlebury, Vt. : Middlebury College, 1983. — III, 191.

Quirin, Jim. Chartmasters' rock 100 : an authoritative ranking of the 100 most popular songs for each year, 1956 through 1986 / Jim Quirin and Barry Cohen. — 4th ed. — Covington, La. : Chartmasters, 1986. — III, 266.

Quirk, Lawrence J. Totally uninhibited : the life and wild times of Cher / Lawrence J. Quirk. — New York : Morrow, 1991. — III, 702.

Raben, Erik. Jazz records 1942–80 : a discography / Erik Raben. — Copenhagen : JazzMedia, 1987– . — III, 240a.

Rabin, Carol Price. A guide to music festivals / Carol Price Rabin. — Stockbridge, Mass. : Berkshire Traveller Press, 1979. — II, 218.

Rabin, Carol Price. Music festivals in America: classical, opera, jazz, pops, country, old-time fiddlers, folk, bluegrass, Cajun / Carol Price Rabin. — Rev. ed. — Great Barrington, Mass. : Berkshire Traveller, 1990. — III, 46.

Rabson, Carolyn. Songbook of the American Revolution / ed. Carolyn Rabson. — Peaks Island, Maine : NEO Press, 1974. — II, 871.

Rachlin, Harvey. The encyclopedia of the music business / Harvey Rachlin. — New York : Harper & Row, 1981. — III, 74.

Radzitzky, Carlos de. A 1960–1967 Clark Terry discography / Carlos de Radzitzky. — Antwerp, Belgium : United Hot Club of Europe, 1968. — II, 654.

Rael, Juan B. The New Mexican alabado / Juan B. Rael. — Stanford, Calif. : Stanford University Press, 1951. — II, 435.

Raichelson, Richard M. Black religious folksong : a study in generic and social change / Richard M. Raichelson. — Dissertation, University of Pennsylvania, 1975. — II, 628.

Railsback, Thomas C. The drums would roll : a pictorial history of US Army bands on the American frontier, 1866–1900 / Thomas C. Railsback and John P. Langellier. — Poole, Dorset, England : Arms & Armour Press; New York : Sterling, 1987. — III, 1005.

Raine, James Watt. Mountain ballads for social singing / ed. James Watt Raine. — Berea, Ky. : Berea College Press, 1923. — II, 430.

Rammel, Hal. Nowhere in America : the Big Rock Candy Mountain and other comic utopias / Hal Rammel. — Urbana : University of Illinois Press, 1990. — III, 7.

Ramsey, Dan. How to be a disc jockey / Dan Ramsey. — Blue Ridge Summit, Pa. : Tab Books, 1981. — II, A-742.

Ramsey, Doug. Jazz matters : reflections on the music and some of its makers / Doug Ramsey. — Fayetteville : University of Arkansas Press, 1989. — III, 1101.

Ramsey, Frederic. A guide to longplay jazz records / Frederic Ramsey. — New York : Long Player Publications, 1954. — I, 956.

Ramsey, Frederic. Been here and gone / Frederic Ramsey. — New Brunswick, N.J. : Rutgers University Press, 1960. — I, 765.

Ramsey, Frederic. Chicago documentary : portrait of a jazz era / Frederic Ramsey. — London : Jazz Music Books, 1944. — I, 1073.

Ramsey, Frederic. Jazzmen / Frederic Ramsey and Charles Edward Smith. — New York : Harcourt, Brace, 1939. — I, 1036.

Ramsey, Frederic. Where the music started : a photographic essay / Frederic Ramsey. — New Brunswick, N.J. : Rutgers University, Institute of Jazz Studies, 1970. — I, 766.

Randall, Lee. Madonna scrapbook / Lee Randall. — New York : Citadel, 1992. — III, 774.

Randle, Bill. The American popular music discography, 1920–1930 / Bill Randle. — Vol. 3. — Bowling Green, Ohio : Bowling Green State University Popular Press, 1974. — II, 814.

Randolph, Vance. Ozark folksongs / Vance Randolph. — Columbia : State Historical Society of Missouri, 1946–1950. — I, 499.

Randolph, Vance. Ozark folksongs / Vance Randolph; ed. and abridged by Norman Cohen. — Urbana : University of Illinois Press, 1982. — III, 22.

Rapaport, Diane Sward. How to make and sell your own record / Diane Sward Rapaport. — New York : Quick Fox, 1979. — II, 1160.

Rapee, Erno. Encyclopedia of music for films / Erno Rapee. — New York : Belwin, 1925. — I, A-262.

Rasaf, Henry. The folk, country and bluegrass musician's catalogue / Henry Rasaf. — New York : St. Martin's, 1982. — II, A-171.

Rasmussen, Jane. Musical taste as a religious question in nineteenth-century America / Jane Rasmussen. — Lewiston, N.Y. : Edwin Mellen, 1986. — III, 1034.

Rasmusson, Ludwig. Blues / Ludwig Rasmusson. — Stockholm : Almqvist & Wiksell, 1979. — II, 619.

Ratcliffe, Ronald V. Steinway / Ronald V. Ratcliffe; foreword by Henry Z. Steinway. — San Francisco : Chronicle Books, 1989. — III, 974.

Rattenbury, Ken. Duke Ellington, jazz composer / Ken Rattenbury. — New Haven, Conn. : Yale University Press, 1991. — III, 469.

Rau, Albert G. Catalogue of music by American Moravians 1742–1842 / Albert G. Rau and Hans T. David. — Bethlehem, Pa. : Moravian Seminary and College for Women, 1938. — I, 84.

Ravinia : the festival at its half century. — [n.p.] : Ravinia Festival Association, 1985. — III, 47.

Raymond, Al. Swinging big bands . . . into the 90's / Al Raymond. — Broomall, Pa. : Harmony Press, 1992. — III, 1140.

Raymond, Jack. Numerical list of Liberty records / Jack Raymond. — Falls Church, Va. : Author, 1993. — III, 209.

Raymond, Jack. Show music on record : from the 1890s to the 1980s / Jack Raymond. — New York : Ungar, 1982. — II, A-571.

Raymond, Jack. Show music on record : the first 100 years / Jack Raymond. — Rev. ed. — Washington : Smithsonian Institution Press, 1992. — III, 248.

Read, Oliver. From tin foil to stereo : evolution of the phonograph / Oliver Read and Walter L. Welch. — Indianapolis : Howard W. Sams, 1959. — I, 179.

Reagon, Bernice. We'll understand it better by and by : pioneering African American gospel composers / Bernice Johnson Reagon. — Washington : Smithsonian Institution Press, 1992. — III, 416.

Reavy, Joesph M. The music of Corktown / Joseph M. Reavy. — Melrose Park, Pa. : Author, 1979. — II, 450.

Reclams Jazzführer. — 2nd ed. — Stuttgart : Reclam, 1977. — II, 633.

Recording industry sourcebook 1993. — Los Angeles : Ascona Communications, 1993. — III, 36.

Reda, Jacques. Anthologies des musiciens de jazz / Jacques Reda. — Paris : Stock, 1981. — II, A-409.

Reda, Jacques. Jouer le jeu : improviste 2 / Jacques Reda. — Paris : Gallimard, 1985. — II, A-411.

Redd, Laurence N. Rock is rhythm and blues / Laurence N. Redd. — East Lansing : Michigan State University Press, 1974. — II, 1161.

Redding, Noel. Are you experienced? the inside story of Jimi Hendrix / Noel Redding and Carol Appleby. — London : Fourth Estate, 1990. — III, 583.

Redfern, David. David Redfern's jazz album / David Redfern. — London : Eel Pie, 1980. — II, 683.

Redway, Virginia Larkin. Music directory of early New York City / Virginia Larkin Redway. — New York : New York Public Library, 1941. — I, 110.

Reed, Joseph W. Three American originals : John Ford, William Faulkner and Charles Ives / Joseph W. Reed. — Middletown, Conn. : Wesleyan University Press, 1984. — II, A-129.

Rees, Dafydd. Rock movers & shakers / Dafydd Rees and Luke Crampton. — Rev. ed. — New York : Billboard Books, 1991. — III, 1189.

Rees, Tony. Rare rock : a collector's guide / Tony Rees. — Poole, Dorset, England : Blandford, 1985. — III, 282.

Reese, Gustave. Birthday offering to Carl Engel / ed. Gustave Reese. — New York : Schirmer, 1943. — I, 40.

Reese, Gustave. Essays in musicology in honor of Dragan Plamenac on his 70th birthday / ed. Gustave Reese and Robert J. Snow. — Pittsburgh : University of Pittsburgh Press, 1969. — II, 244.

Reggero, John. Elvis in concert / John Reggero. — New York : Dell, 1979. — II, 1302.

Rehrauer, George. The Macmillan film bibliography / George Rehrauer. — New York : Macmillan, 1982. — II, A-595.

Reich, Charles. Garcia : the Rolling Stone interview / Charles Reich and Jann Wenner. — San Francisco : Straight Arrow Books, 1972. — I, 1379.

Reich, Steve. Writings about music / Steve Reich. — Halifax, Nova Scotia : Nova Scotia College of Art and Design, 1974. — I, 342.

Reichardt, Uwe. Like a human voice : the Eric Dolphy discography / Uwe Reichardt. — Schmitten, Germany : Ruecker, 1986. — III, 300.

Reid, Gary B. Stanley Brothers : a preliminary discography / Gary B. Reid. — Roanoke, Va. : Copper Creek Publications, 1984. — II, A-265.

Reid, Jan. The improbable rise of redneck rock / Jan Reid. — Austin, Tex. : Heidelberg, 1973. — II, 383.

Reiff, Carole. Nights in Birdland : jazz photographs, 1954–1960 / Carole Reiff; with an essay by Jack Kerouac. — New York : Simon & Schuster, 1987. — III, 63.

Reig, Teddy. Reminiscing in tempo : the life and times of a jazz hustler / Teddy Reig; with Edward M. Berger. — Metuchen, N.J. : Scarecrow, 1990. — III, 982.

Reilly, Edward. The Monkees : a manufactured image : the ultimate reference guide to Monkee memories & memorabilia / Edward Reilly, Maggie McManus, and William Chadwick. — Ann Arbor, Mich. : Pierian, 1987. — III, 926.

Reinbach, Edna. Music and musicians in Kansas / Edna Reinbach. — Topeka : Kansas State Historical Society, 1930. — I, A-43.

Reiner, David. Anthology of fiddle styles / ed. David Reiner. — Pacific, Mo. : Mel Bay, 1979. — II, 460.

Reis, Claire R. Composers, conductors and critics / Claire R. Reis. — New York : Oxford University Press, 1955. — I, 296.

Reis, Claire R. Composers in America : biographical sketches of living composers with a record of their works / Claire R. Reis. — Rev. ed. — New York : Macmillan, 1947. — I, 291.

Reisfeld, Randi. Debbie Gibson : electric star / Randi Reisfeld. — New York : Bantam, 1990. — III, 727.

Reisfeld, Randi. Nelson : double play / Randi Reisfeld. — New York : Bantam, 1991. — III, 928.

Reisner, R. G. Bird : the legend of Charlie Parker / R. G. Reisner. — New York : Bonanza Books, 1962. — I, 1135.

Reisner, Robert G. Literature of jazz / Robert G. Reisner. — 2nd ed. — New York : New York Public Library, 1959. — I, 920.

Reisner, Robert G. The jazz titans / Robert G. Reisner. — Garden City, N.Y. : Doubleday, 1960. — I, A-218.

Renaud, Henri. Jazz classique et jazz moderne / Henri Renaud. — Paris : Casterman, 1971. — II, 783.

Renshaw, Jeffrey H. The American Wind Symphony commissioning project : a descriptive catalog of published editions, 1957–1991 / Jeffrey H. Renshaw; foreword by Warren Benson. — New York : Greenwood, 1991. — III, 110.

Restum, Willie. They all came to see me / Willie Restum; as told to Paul Willistein. — Allentown, Pa. : W. Restum, 1986. — III, 662.

Reuss, Richard A. A Woody Guthrie bibliography, 1912–1967 / Richard A. Reuss. — New York : Guthrie Children's Trust Fund, 1968. — I, 599.

Reuss, Richard A. Songs of American labor / ed. Richard A. Reuss. — Ann Arbor : University of Michigan, Labor Studies Center, 1983. — II, A-208.

Revill, David. The roaring silence : John Cage : a life / David Revill. — New York : Little, Brown, 1992. — III, 460.

Revitt, Paul J. The George Pullen Jackson collection of southern hymnody : a bibliography / Paul J. Revitt. — Los Angeles : University of California Library, 1964. — I, 550.

Rey, Luise King. Those swinging years / Luise King Rey. — Salt Lake City, Utah : Olympus, 1983. — II, A-485.

Reyman, Randall G. An analysis of melodic improvisational practices of Miles Davis / Randall G. Reyman. — Decatur, Ill. : Millikin University, 1986. — III, 629.

Reynolds, Simon. Blissed out : the raptures of rock / Simon Reynolds. — London : Serpent's Tail, 1990. — III, 1190.

Rhodes, Robert. Hopi music and dance / Robert Rhodes. — Tsaile, Arizona : Navajo Community College Press, 1977. — II, 155.

Ribakove, Sy. Folk-rock : the Bob Dylan story / Sy Ribakove and Barbara Ribakove. — New York : Dell, 1966. — I, A-301.

Ribowsky, Mark. He's a rebel : the truth about Phil Spector, rock and roll's legendary madman / Mark Ribowsky. — New York : Dutton, 1989. — III, 984.

Rice, Edward Le Roy. Monarchs of minstrelsy from "Daddy" Rice to date / Edward Le Roy Rice. — New York : Kenny, 1911. — I, 1240.

Rice, Michael E. Folk songs of central West Virginia / ed. Michael E. Bush. — Ravenswood, W.Va. : Author, 1969–1970. — II, 319.

Rich, Arthur Lowndes. Lowell Mason : "the father of singing among the children" / Arthur Lowndes Rich. — Chapel Hill : University of North Carolina Press, 1946. — I, 218.

Richards, Dick. Ginger : salute to a star / Dick Richards. — Brighton, England : Clifton Books, 1969. — II, 1085.

Richards, Stanley. Great musicals of the American theatre / ed. Stanley Richards. — Radnor, Pa. : Chilton, 1976. — II, 905.

Richards, Stanley. Great rock musicals / ed. Stanley Richards. — New York : Stein & Day, 1979. — II, 906.

Richards, Stanley. Ten great musicals of the American theatre / ed. Stanley Richards. — Radnor, Pa. : Chilton, 1973. — II, 904.

Richardson, Ethel Park. American mountain songs / Ethel Park Richardson. — New York : Greenberg, 1927. — I, 489.

Richman, Harry. A hell of a life / Harry Richman and Richard Gehman. — New York : Duell, Sloan & Pearce, 1956. — II, 1006.

Richmond, Mary L. Shaker literature : a bibliography / Mary L. Richmond. — Hancock, Mass. : Shaker Community, 1977. — II, 334.

Rickaby, Franz. Ballads and songs of the shanty-boys / ed. Franz Rickaby. — Cambridge, Mass. : Harvard University Press, 1926. — II, 343.

Ricks, George Robinson. Some aspects of the religious music of the United States negro / George Robinson Ricks. — New York : Arno, 1977. — II, 579.

Riddle, Almeda. A singer and her songs / Almeda Riddle. — Baton Rouge : Louisiana State University Press, 1970. — I, 500.

Riddle, Ronald. Flying dragons, flowing streams : music in the life of San Francisco's Chinese / Ronald Riddle. — Westport, Conn. : Greenwood, 1983. — II, A-184.

Ridge, Millie. The Elvis album / Millie Ridge. — London : Grange, 1991. — III, 837.

Ridgway, John. The Sinatrafile / John Ridgway. — Birmingham, England : John Ridgway Books, 1977–1980. — II, 1009.

Riedel, Johannes. Soul music black and white : the influence of black music on the churches / Johannes Riedel. — Minneapolis : Augsburg, 1975. — I, 693.

Riefler, Wolfgang. Jazz : eine improvisierte Musik / Wolfgang Riefler. — Menden, Germany : Der Jazzfreund, 1984. — II, A-412.

Riesco, José Francisco. El jazz clásico y Johnny Dodds / José Francisco Riesco. — Santiago, Chile : Imprenta Mueller, 1972. — II, 796.

Riese, Randall. Nashville Babylon : the uncensored truth and private lives of country music's stars / Randall Riese. — New York : Congdon & Weed (Contemporary Books), 1988. — III, 407.

Riis, Thomas Laurence. Just before jazz : black musical theater in New York, 1890–1915 / Thomas Laurence Riis. — Washington : Smithsonian Institution Press, 1989. — III, 1020.

Riis, Thomas Laurence. More than just minstrel shows : the rise of black musical theatre at the turn of the century / Thomas Laurence Riis. — Brooklyn : Institute for Studies in American Music, 1992. — III, 1014.

Rijff, Ger. Elvis : long lonely highway / Ger Rijff. — Amsterdam : Tutti Frutti, 1985. — II, A-831.

Rijff, Ger. Long lonely highway : a 1950's Elvis scrapbook / Ger Rijff. — Reprinted with additions. — Ann Arbor, Mich. : Pierian, 1988. — III, 838.

Riker, Charles. The Eastman School of Music : its first quarter century, 1921–1946 / Charles Riker. — Rochester, N.Y. : University of Rochester Press, 1946. — I, 172.

Riley, Jeannie C. From Harper Valley to the mountain top / Jeannie C. Riley. — Lincoln, Va. : Chosen Books, 1981. — II, A-264.

Riley, Tim. Hard rain : a Dylan commentary / Tim Riley. — New York : Knopf, 1992. — III, 714.

Riley, Tim. Madonna illustrated / Tim Riley. — New York : Hyperion, 1992. — III, 775.

Rimler, Walter. A Gershwin companion : a critical inventory & discography, 1916–1984 / Walter Rimler. — Ann Arbor, Mich. : Popular Culture, Ink., 1991. — III, 165.

Rimler, Walter. Not fade away / a comparison of jazz age with rock era pop song composers / Walter Rimler. — Ann Arbor, Mich. : Pierian Press, 1984. — II, A-542.

Ring the banjar : the banjo in American folklore to factory. — Cambridge, Mass. : Massachusetts Institute of Technology Museum, 1984. — III, 997.

Ringel, Harvey. History of the National Association of Teachers of Singing /

Harvey Ringel. — Jacksonville, Fla. : National Association of Teachers of Singing, 1990. — III, 44.

Ringgold, Gene. The films of Frank Sinatra / Gene Ringgold and Clifford Mc-Carty. — New York : Citadel, 1971. — II, 1010.

Rinzler, Ralph. Uncle Dave Macon : a bio-discography / Ralph Rinzler and Norm Cohen. — Los Angeles : John Edwards Memorial Foundation, 1970. — I, 638.

Riordan, James. Break on through : the life and death of Jim Morrison / James Riordan and Jerry Prochnicky. — New York : Morrow, 1991. — III, 797.

Ritchie, Jean. Folk songs of the southern Appalachians as sung by Jean Ritchie / Jean Ritchie. — New York : Oak, 1965. — I, 490.

Ritchie, Jean. Jean Ritchie's dulcimer people / Jean Ritchie. — New York : Oak, 1975. — II, 328.

Ritchie, Jean. Singing family of the Cumberlands / Jean Ritchie. — New York : Oxford University Press, 1955. — II, 310.

Ritchie, Jean. The dulcimer book / Jean Ritchie. — New York : Oak, 1963. — I, A-137.

Ritter, Frederic Louis. Music in America / Frederic Louis Ritter. — New ed. — New York : Scribner's, 1890. — I, 20.

Ritz, David. Divided soul : the life of Marvin Gaye / David Ritz. — New York : McGraw-Hill, 1985. — II, A-354.

Rivadue, Barry. Mary Martin : a bio-bibliography / Barry Rivadue. — Westport, Conn. : Greenwood, 1991. — III, 187.

Rivelli, Pauline. Giants of black music / Pauline Rivelli and Robert Levin. — New York : Da Capo, 1979. — II, 721.

Rivelli, Pauline. Rock giants / Pauline Rivelli and Robert Levin. — New York : World, 1970. — I, 1370.

Rivelli, Pauline. The black giants / Pauline Rivelli and Robert Levin. — New York : World, 1970. — II, 721.

Rivers, Jerry. Hank Williams : from life to legend / Jerry Rivers; ed. Thurston Moore. — Denver : Heather Enterprises, 1967. — I, 644.

Roach, Dusty. Patti Smith : rock & roll madonna / Dusty Roach. — South Bend, Ind. : And Books, 1979. — II, 1317.

Roach, Hildred. Black American music : past and present / Hildred Roach. — Boston : Crescendo, 1973. — I, 694.

Roads, Curtis. Composers and the computer / Curtis Roads. — Los Altos, Calif. : William Kaufman, 1985. — II : A-95.

Robb, John Donald. Hispanic folk songs of New Mexico / ed. John Donald Robb. — Albuquerque : University of New Mexico Press, 1954. — II, 294.

Robb, John Donald. Hispanic folk music of New Mexico and the Southwest / ed. John Donald Robb. — Norman : University of Oklahoma Press, 1980. — II, 294.

Robbin, Edward. Woody Guthrie and me : an intimate reminiscence / Edward Robbin. — Berkeley, Calif. : Lancaster-Miller, 1979. — II, 349.

Roberts, Helen H. Form in primitive music / Helen H. Roberts. — New York : Norton, 1933. — I, 417.

Roberts, Helen H. Musical areas in aboriginal North America / Helen H. Roberts. — New Haven, Conn. : Yale University Press, 1936. — I, 400.

Roberts, John Storm. Black music of two worlds / John Storm Roberts. — New York : Praeger, 1972. — I, 695.

Roberts, John Storm. The Latin tinge : the impact of Latin American music on the United States / John Storm Roberts. — New York : Oxford University Press, 1979. — II, 840.

Roberts, Leonard. In the pines : selected Kentucky folksongs / ed. Leonard Roberts. — Pikeville, Ky. : Pikeville College Press, 1978. — II, 311.

Roberts, Leonard. Sang Branch settlers : folksongs and tales of a Kentucky mountain family / ed. Leonard Roberts. — Austin : University of Texas Press, 1974. — II, 312.

Robeson, Eslanda Goode. Paul Robeson, negro / Eslanda Goode Robeson. — New York : Harper, 1930. — I, A-156.

Robeson, Susan. The whole world in his hands : a pictorial biography of Paul Robeson / Susan Robeson. — Secaucus, N.J. : Citadel, 1985. — II, A-306.

Robinette, Richard. Historical perspectives on popular music / Richard Robinette. — Dubuque, Iowa : Kendall/Hunt, 1980. — II, 841.

Robinson, Albert F. The bicentennial tracker / ed. Albert F. Robinson. — Washington, Ohio : Organ Historical Society, 1976. — II, 83.

Robinson, Barbara J. The Mexican American : a critical guide to research aids / Barbara J. Robinson and J. Cordell Robinson. — Greenwich, Conn. : Jai Press, 1980. — II, 295.

Robinson, Charles Seymour. Annotations upon popular hymns / Charles Seymour Robinson. — New York : Hunt & Eaton, 1893. — II, 36.

Robinson, Francis. Celebration : the Metropolitan Opera / Francis Robinson. — Garden City, N.Y. : Doubleday, 1979. — II, 74.

Robinson, Paul. Bernstein / Paul Robinson. — New York : Vanguard, 1982. — II, A-112.

Robinson, Paul. Stokowski / Paul Robinson. — New York : Vanguard, 1977. — II, 232.

Robinson, Smokey. Smokey : inside my life. / Smokey Robinson. — New York : McGraw-Hill, 1988. — III, 850.

Rochberg, George. The aesthetics of survival : a composer's view of twentieth-century music / George Rochberg. — Ann Arbor : University of Michigan Press, 1984. — II, A-136.

Rock guitarists : from the pages of *Guitar Player* magazine. — Saratoga, N.Y. : Guitar Player Magazine, 1975–1977. — II, 1175.

Rockmore, Noel. Preservation Hall portraits / Noel Rockmore [et al]. — Baton Rouge : Louisiana State University Press, 1968. — I, 1068.

Rockwell, John. All American music : composition in the late 20th century / John Rockwell. — New York : Knopf, 1983. — II, A-107.

Rockwell, John. Sinatra : an American classic / John Rockwell. — New York : Random House, 1983. — II, A-637.

Rodeheaver, Homer. Singing black : twenty thousand miles with a music missionary / Homer Rodeheaver. — Chicago : Rodeheaver Co., 1936. — II, 580.

Rodgers & Hammerstein Archives of Recorded Sound, New York Public Library. Dictionary catalog. — Boston : G. K. Hall, 1981. — II, A-6.

Rodgers and Hammerstein fact book, with supplement. — New York : Lynn Farnol Group, 1968. — I, 1298.

Rodgers, Dorothy. A person book / Dorothy Rodgers. — New York : Harper & Row, 1977. — II, 961.

Rodgers, Mrs. Jimmie. My husband, Jimmie Rodgers / Mrs. Jimmie Rodgers. — San Antonio : Southern Literary Institute, 1935. — I, 640.

Rodgers, Richard. Musical stages : an autobiography / Richard Rodgers. — New York : Random House, 1975. — I, 1295.

Rodnitsky, Jerome L. Minstrels of the dawn : the folk-protest singer as a cultural hero / Jerome L. Rodnitsky. — Chicago : Nelson-Hall, 1976. — II, 346.

Roell, Craig H. The piano in America, 1890–1940 / Craig H. Roell. — Chapel Hill : University of North Carolina Press, 1989. — III, 991a.

Rogal, Samuel J. Guide to the hymns and tunes of American Methodism / Samuel J. Rogal. — New York : Greenwood, 1986. — III, 2.

Rogal, Samuel J. Sisters of sacred song : a selected listing of women hymnodists in Great Britain and America / Samuel J. Rogal. — New York : Garland, 1981. — II, A-25.

Rogal, Samuel J. The children's jubilee / Samuel J. Rogal. — Westport, Conn. : Greenwood, 1983. — II, A-24.

Rogan, John. Timeless flight : the definitive biography of the Byrds / John Rogan. — London : Scorpion, 1981. — II, A-774.

Rogan, Johnny. Neil Young : the definitive story of the musical career / Johnny Rogan. — London : Proteus, 1982. — II, A-852.

Roger Reynolds : profile of a composer. — New York : Peters, 1982. — II, A-134.

Rogers, Alice. Dance bands and big bands / Alice Rogers. — Tempe, Ariz. : Jelly Roll Productions, 1986. — III, 268.

Rogers, Dave. Rock 'n' roll / Dave Rogers. — London : Routledge & Kegan Paul, 1982. — II, A-696.

Rogers, Jimmie N. The country music message : revisited / Jimmie N. Rogers. — 2nd ed. — Fayetteville : University of Arkansas Press, 1989. — III, 1165.

Rogers, Jimmie N. The country music message / Jimmie N. Rogers. — Englewood Cliffs, N.J. : Prentice-Hall, 1983. — II, A-228.

Rohrer, Gertrude Martin. Music and musicians of Pennsylvania / Gertrude Martin Rohrer. — Philadelphia : Presser, 1940. — I, 121.

Rolling Stone (periodical). *Rolling Stone* interviews. — New York : Warner, 1971–1973. — I, 1371.

Rolling Stone album guide : completely new reviews : every essential album, every essential artist / ed. Anthony DeCurtis and James Henke; with Holly George-Warren. — New York : Random House, 1992. — III, 267.

Rolling Stone rock almanac. New York : Macmillan, 1983. — II, A-665.

Rollini, Arthur. Thirty years with the big bands / Arthur Rollini. — London : Macmillan; Urbana : University of Illinois Press, 1987. — III, 1141.

Rollins, Sonny. Sonny Rollins / Sonny Rollins. — London : Apollo, 1988. — III, 664.

Roman, Zoltan. Gustav Mahler's American years, 1907–1911 : a documentary history / Zoltan Roman. — Stuyvesant, N.Y. : Pendragon, 1989. — III, 497.

Rome, Florence. The Scarlett letters / Florence Rome. — New York : Random House, 1971. — II, 962.

Roncaglia, Gian Carlo. Una storia del jazz / Gian Carlo Roncaglia. — Venice : Marsilio, 1979. — II, 784.

Rooney, James. Bossmen : Bill Monroe and Muddy Waters / James Rooney. — New York : Dial, 1971. — I, 627.

Root, Deane L. American popular stage music, 1860–1880 / Deane L. Root. — Ann Arbor, Mich. : UMI Research Press, 1981. — II, A-565.

Root, George F. The story of a musical life : an autobiography / George F. Root. — Cincinnati : Church, 1891. — I, 1216.

Rorem, Ned. An absolute gift : a new diary / Ned Rorem. — New York : Simon & Schuster, 1978. — II, 197.

Rorem, Ned. Critical affairs : a composer's journal / Ned Rorem. — New York : Braziller, 1970. — I, 343.

Rorem, Ned. Final diary / Ned Rorem. — New York : Holt, Rinehart & Winston, 1974. — I, 343.

Rorem, Ned. Music and people / Ned Rorem. — New York : Braziller, 1968. — I, 343.

Rorem, Ned. Music from inside out / Ned Rorem. — New York : Braziller, 1967. — I, 343.

Rorem, Ned. New York diary / Ned Rorem. — New York : Braziller, 1967. — I, 343.

Rorem, Ned. Paris diary / Ned Rorem — New York : Braziller, 1966. — I, 343.

Rorem, Ned. Pure contraption : a composer's essays / Ned Rorem. — New York : Holt, Rinehart & Winston, 1974. — I, 343.

Rorem, Ned. Setting the tone : essays and a diary / Ned Rorem — New York : Coward, McCann & Geoghegan, 1983. — II, A-137.

Rorem, Ned. The Nantucket diary / Ned Rorem. — San Francisco : North Point, 1987. — III, 509.

Rorer, Clifford Kinney. Charlie Poole and the North Carolina Ramblers / Clifford Kinney Rorer. — Reidsville, N.C. : Reidsville Printing Co., 1968. — I, 639.

Rorer, Clifford Kinney. Rambling blues : the life and songs of Charlie Poole / Clifford Kinney Rorer. — London : Old Time Music, 1982. — II, A-263.

Rose, Al. Eubie Blake / Al Rose. — New York : Schirmer, 1979. — II, 535.

Rose, Al. I remember jazz : six decades among the great jazzmen / Al Rose. — Baton Rouge : Louisiana State University Press, 1987. — III, 1089.

Rose, Al. New Orleans jazz : a family album / Al Rose and Edmond Souchon. — Baton Rouge : Louisiana State University Press, 1967 — I, 1069.

Rose, Billy. Wine, women and words / Billy Rose. — New York : Simon & Schuster, 1948. — II, 963.

Rose, Cynthia. Living in America : the soul saga of James Brown / Cynthia Rose. — London : Serpent's Tail; distributed by Consortium Book Sales and Distribution, 1990. — III, 689.

Rose, Phyllis. Jazz Cleopatra : Josephine Baker in her time / Phyllis Rose. — New York : Doubleday, 1989. — III, 11.

Rosen, Charles. The musical language of Elliott Carter / Charles Rosen. — Washington : Library of Congress, 1984. — II, A-115.

Rosen, David M. Protest songs in America / David M. Rosen. — Westlake Village, Calif. : Aware, 1972. — I, 589.

Rosenbaum, Art. Folk visions and voices : traditional music and song in North Georgia / Art Rosenbaum and Margo Newark Rosenbaum. — Athens : University of Georgia Press, 1983. — II, A-189.

Rosenbaum, Art. Old-time mountain banjo / Art Rosenbaum. — New York : Oak, 1968. — I, A-138.

Rosenberg, Bruce A. The art of the American folk preacher / Bruce A. Rosenberg. — New York : Oxford University Press, 1970. — II, 581.

Rosenberg, Bruce A. The folksongs of Virginia / Bruce A. Rosenberg. — Charlottesville : University Press of Virginia, 1969. — I, 505.

Rosenberg, Deena. Fascinating rhythm : the collaboration of Geroge and Ira Gershwin / Deena Rosenberg. — New York : Dutton, 1991. — III, 479.

Rosenberg, Neil V. Bill Monroe and his Blue Grass Boys : an illustrated discography / Neil V. Rosenberg. — Nashville : Country Music Foundation Press, 1974. — I, 628.

Rosenberg, Neil V. Bluegrass : a history / Neil V. Rosenberg. — Urbana : University of Illinois Press, 1985. — II, A-232.

Rosenberg, Neil V. From sound to style : the emergence of bluegrass / Neil V. Rosenberg. — Los Angeles : John Edwards Memorial Foundation, 1967. — I, 629.

Rosenfeld, Paul. An hour with American music / Paul Rosenfeld. — Philadelphia : Lippincott, 1929. — I, 277.

Rosenfeld, Paul. Discoveries of a music critic / Paul Rosenfeld. — New York : Harcourt, Brace, 1936. — I, 276.

Rosenfeld, Paul. Musical chronicle, 1917–1923 / Paul Rosenfeld. — New York : Harcourt, Brace, 1923. — I, 377.

Rosenfeld, Paul. Musical impressions / Paul Rosenfeld; ed. Herbert A. Leibowitz. — New York : Hill & Wang, 1969. — I, 278.

Rosenkrantz, Timme. Swing photo album 1939 / Timme Rosenkrantz. — Lowestoft, England : Scorpion, 1964. — I, A-219.

Rosenthal, David H. Hard bop : jazz and black music, 1955–1965 / David H. Rosenthal. — New York : Oxford, 1992. — III, 1123.

Rossi, Nick. Music of our time / Nick Rossi and Robert A. Choate. — Boston : Crescendo, 1969. — S 160.

Rossiter, Frank R. Charles Ives and his America / Frank R. Rossiter. — New York : Liveright, 1975. — I, 333.

Rothel, David. The singing cowboys / David Rothel. — South Brunswick, N.J. : Barnes, 1978. — II, 932.

Rourke, Constance. American humor : a study of the national character / Constance Rourke. — Rev. ed. — New York : Doubleday, 1953. — I, 1242.

Rourke, Constance. The roots of American culture, and other essays / Constance Rourke; ed., with preface by Van Wyck Brooks. — New York : Harcourt, 1942. — I, 41.

Rouse, Christopher. William Schuman documentary / Christopher Rouse. — Bryn Mawr, Pa. : Presser, 1980. — II, 198.

Roussel, Hubert. The Houston Symphony Orchestra, 1913–1971 / Hubert Roussel. — Austin : University of Texas Press, 1972. — I, 129.

Rowe, Mike. Chicago breakdown / Mike Rowe. — London : Eddison Press, 1973. — I, 826.

Rowell, Lois. American organ music on records / Lois Rowell. — Braintree, Mass. : Organ Literature Foundation, 1976. — II, 86.

Rowes, Barbara. Grace Slick : the biography / Barbara Rowes. — Garden City, N.Y. : Doubleday, 1980. — II, 1242.

Rowland, Mabel. Bert Williams, son of laughter / Mabel Rowland. — New York : The English Crafters, 1923. — I, 1235.

Rowland, Mark. Prince : his story in words and pictures : an unauthorized biography / Mark Rowland and Margy Rochlin. — New York : Lorevan, 1985. — III, 849.

Rowlands, John. Spotlight heroes / John Rowlands. — New York : McGraw-Hill, 1981. — II, A-753.

Rowley, Chris. Blood on the tracks : the story of Bob Dylan / Chris Rowley. — London : Proteus, 1984 — II, A-791.

Roxon, Lillian. Rock encyclopedia / Lillian Roxon. — New York : Grosset & Dunlap, 1969. — I, 1338.

Roy, Samuel. Elvis : prophet of power / Samuel Roy. — Brookline, Mass. : Branden, 1985. — III, 839.

Rozsa, Miklos. Double life : the autobiography of Miklos Rozsa / Miklos Rozsa. — Tunbridge Wells, England : Midas Books, 1982. — II, A-606.

Rubenstein, Raeanne. Honkytonk heroes : a photo album of country music / Raeanne Rubenstein. — New York : Harper & Row, 1975. — II, 365.

Rubin, D. The American South : portrait of a culture / D. Rubin. — Baton Rouge : Louisiana State University Press, 1980. — II, 370.

Rubin, Ruth. Voices of a people : Yiddish folk song / Ruth Rubin. — 2nd ed. — New York : McGraw-Hill, 1973. — II, 451.

Rubin, Stephen E. The new Met in profile / Stephen E. Rubin. — New York : Macmillan, 1974. — II, 75.

Rublowsky, John. Black music in America / John Rublowsky. — New York : Basic Books, 1971. — I, A-151.

Rublowsky, John. Music in America / John Rublowsky. — New York : Crowell-Collier, 1967. — I, 28.

Rublowsky, John. Popular music / John Rublowsky. — New York : Basic Books, 1967. — II, 842.

Ruff, Willie. A call to assembly : the autobiography of a musical storyteller / Willie Ruff. — New York : Viking, 1991. — III, 666.

Ruhlmann, William. The history of the Grateful Dead / William Ruhlmann. — New York : Smithmark, 1990. — III, 913.

Ruland, Hans. Duke Ellington : sein Leben, seine Musik, seine Schallplatten / Hans Ruland. — Gauting-Buchendorf, Germany : Oreos, 1983. — II, A-475.

Ruppli, Michel. Atlantic Records : a discography / Michel Ruppli. — Westport, Conn. : Greenwood, 1979. — II, 638.

Ruppli, Michel. Charles Mingus discography / Michel Ruppli. — Frankfurt, Germany : Ruecker, 1982. — II, A-380.

Ruppli, Michel. Prestige jazz records 1949–1960 / Michel Ruppli. — Copenhagen : Knudsen, 1972. — I, 935.

Ruppli, Michel. The Aladdin/Imperial labels : a discography / Michel Ruppli. — New York : Greenwood, 1991. — III, 197.

Ruppli, Michel. The Chess labels / Michel Ruppli. — Westport, Conn. : Greenwood, 1983. — II, A-312.

Ruppli, Michel. The Clef/Verve labels : a discography / Michel Ruppli and Bob Porter. — New York : Greenwood, 1986. — III, 201.

Ruppli, Michel. The Prestige label : a discography / Michel Ruppli. — Westport, Conn. : Greenwood, 1980. — III, 216.

Ruppli, Michel. The Savoy label : a discography / Michel Ruppli. — Westport, Conn. : Greenwood, 1980. — II, 639.

Rusch, Robert D. Jazztalk / Robert D. Rusch. — Secaucus, N.J. : Lyle Stuart, 1984. — II, A-451.

Rushmore, Robert. The life of George Gershwin / Robert Rushmore. — New York : Crowell-Collier, 1966. — I, A-263.

Rushton, William Faulkner. The Cajuns : from Acadia to Louisiana / William Faulkner Rushton. — New York : Farrar, Straus & Giroux, 1979. — II, 425.

Russell, Charles Edward. The American orchestra and Theodore Thomas / Charles Edward Russell. — Garden City, N.Y. : Doubleday, 1927. — I, 246.

Russell, Ethan A. Dear Mr. Fantasy : diary of a decade / Ethan A. Russell. — Boston : Houghton Mifflin, 1985. — II, A-702.

Russell, George. The Lydian concept of tonal organization for improvisation / George Russell. — New York : Concept, 1959. — I, 984.

Russell, Henry. Cheer! boys, cheer! / Henry Russell. — London : Macqueen, 1895. — I, 1221.

Russell, Henry. The passing show / Henry Russell. — Boston : Little, Brown, 1926. — I, A-58.

Russell, Ross. Bird lives : the high life and hard times of Charlie (Yardbird) Parker / Ross Russell. — New York : Charterhouse, 1973. — I, 1136.

Russell, Ross. Jazz style in Kansas City and the southwest / Ross Russell. — Berkeley : University of California Press, 1971. — I, 1074.

Russell, Tony. Blacks, whites and blues / Tony Russell. — London : Studio Vista, 1970. — I, 819.

Russell, William. Tumbleweed : best of the singing cowboys / William Russell. — Fairfax, Va. : Western Revue, 1977. — II, 1059.

Russo, William. Composing for the jazz orchestra / William Russo. — Chicago : University of Chicago Press, 1961. — I, 985.

Russo, William. Jazz composition and orchestration / William Russo. — Chicago : University of Chicago Press, 1968. — I, 986.

Rust, Brian. American dance band discography, 1917–1942 / Brian Rust. — New Rochelle, N.Y. : Arlington House, 1975. — I, 936.

Rust, Brian. Brian Rust's guide to discography / Brian Rust. — Westport, Conn. : Greenwood, 1980. — II, 657.

Rust, Brian. Jazz records, 1897–1942 / Brian Rust. — 5th ed. — Chigwell, Essex, England : Storyville, [1982]. — III, 242.

Rust, Brian. Jazz records, 1897–1942 / Brian Rust. — Rev. ed. — London : Storyville, 1970. — I, 930.

Rust, Brian. The American record label book / Brian Rust. — New Rochelle, N.Y. : Arlington House, 1978. — II, 815.

Rust, Brian. The complete entertainment discography / Brian Rust; with Allen G. Debus. — New Rochelle, N.Y. : Arlington House, 1973. — I, 1159.

Rust, Brian. The complete entertainment discography from 1897 to 1942 / Brian Rust and Allen G. Debus. — 2nd ed. — New York : Da Capo, 1989. — III, 269.

Rust, Brian. The dance bands / Brian Rust. — London : Allan, 1972. — I, 1044.

Rust, Brian. The Victor master book / Brian Rust. — Hatch End, Middlesex, England : Author, 1969. — I, 1160.

Ruttencutter, Helen Drees. Previn / Helen Drees Ruttencutter. — New York : St. Martin's, 1985. — II, A-152.

Ruuth, Marianne. Triumph & tragedy : the true story of the Supremes : a biography / Marianne Ruuth. — Los Angeles : Holloway House, 1987. — III, 937.

Ryan, Betsy Alayne. Gertrude Stein's theatre of the absolute / Betsy Alayne Ryan. — Ann Arbor, Mich. : UMI Research Press, 1984. — II, A-140.

Ryan, Jack. Recollections : the Detroit years / Jack Ryan. — [n.p.] : Author, 1982. — II, A-352.

Ryan, John. The production of culture in the music industry : the ASCAP-BMI controversy / John Ryan. — Lanham, Md. : University Press of America, 1985. — II, A-524.

Ryan, Thomas. Recollections of an old musician / Thomas Ryan. — New York : Dalton, 1899. — II, 149.

Sablosky, Irving. American music / Irving Sablosky. — Chicago : University of Chicago Press, 1969. — I, 31.

Sablosky, Irving. What they heard : music in America, 1852–1881, from the pages of Dwight's Journal of Music / Irving Sablosky. — Baton Rouge : Louisiana State University Press, 1986. — III, 373.

Sachse, Julius Friedrich. The German Pietists of provincial Pennsylvania / Julius Friedrich Sachse. — Philadelphia : Author, 1895. — I, 85.

Sachse, Julius Friedrich. The German sectarians of Pennsylvania, 1708–1800 / Julius Friedrich Sachse. — Philadelphia : Author, 1899–1900. — I, 86.

Sachse, Julius Friedrich. The music of the Ephrata Cloister / Julius Friedrich Sachse. — Lancaster, Pa. : Author, 1903. — I, 87.

Sackheim, Eric. The blues line : a collection of blues lyrics / Eric Sackheim. — New York : Grossman, 1969. — I, 880.

Sacred repository of anthems and hymns for devotional worship and praise. — Canterbury, N.H., 1852. — I, 556.

Sakol, Jeannie. The wonderful world of country music / Jeannie Sakol. — New York : Grosset & Dunlap, 1979. — II, 362.

Salem, James M. A guide to critical reviews, part II : the musical, 1909–1989 / James M. Salem. — Metuchen, N.J. : Scarecrow, 1991. — III, 133.

Salem, James M. A guide to critical reviews : part 2 : the musical from Rodgers and Hart to Lerner and Lowe / James M. Salem. — Metuchen, N.J. : Scarecrow, 1967. — I, 1260.

Saler, Dennis. Rock art : fifty-two album covers / Dennis Saler. — Seaside, Calif. : Comma Books, 1977. — II, 1276.

Sales, Grover. Jazz : America's classical music / Grover Sales. — Englewood Cliffs, N.J. : Prentice-Hall, 1984. — II, A-413.

Saleski, Gdal. Famous musicians of Jewish origin / Gdal Saleski. — New York : Bloch, 1949. — I, 18.

Sallee, James. A history of evangelistic hymnody / James Sallee. — Grand Rapids, Mich. : Baker Book House, 1978. — II, 112.

Sallis, James. The guitar players / James Sallis. — New York : Morrow, 1982. — II, A-60.

Salzman, Eric. Making changes : a practical guide to vernacular harmony / Eric Salzman and Michael Sahl. — New York : McGraw-Hill, 1977. — II, 858.

Salzman, Eric. Twentieth-century music : an introduction / Eric Salzman. —
  2nd ed. — Englewood Cliffs, N.J. : Prentice-Hall, 1974. — I, 266.
Samaroff Stokowski, Olga. An American musician's story / Olga Samaroff
  Stokowski. — New York : Norton, 1939. — I, A-44.
Saminsky, Lazare. Living music of the Americas / Lazare Saminsky. — New
  York : Howell, Soskin, 1949. — I, A-14.
Sampson, Henry T. Blacks in blackface : a source book on early black musical
  shows / Henry T. Sampson. — Metuchen, N.J. : Scarecrow, 1977. — II, 885.
Samuels, William Everett. Union and the black musician / William Everett
  Samuels. — Lanham, Md. : University Press of America, 1984. — II, A-303.
Sandahl, Linda J. Rock films : a viewer's guide to three decades of musicals,
  concerts, documentaries, and soundtracks, 1955–1986 / Linda J. Sandahl. —
  New York : Facts on File, 1987. — III, 1285.
Sandberg, Larry. The folk music sourcebook / Larry Sandberg and Dick Weiss-
  man. — New, updated ed. — New York : Da Capo, 1989. — III, 26.
Sandberg, Larry. The folk music sourcebook / Larry Sandberg and Dick Weiss-
  man. — New York : Knopf, 1976. — II, 275.
Sandburg, Carl. American songbag / Carl Sandburg. — New York : Harcourt,
  Brace, 1927. — I, 462.
Sander, Ellen. Trips : rock life in the sixties / Ellen Sander. — New York :
  Scribner's, 1973. — II, 1145.
Sanders, Ronald. The days grow short : the life and music of Kurt Weill / Ronald
  Sanders. — New York : Holt, Rinehart & Winston, 1980. — II, 966.
Sandford, Herb. Tommy and Jimmy : the Dorsey years / Herb Sandford. —
  New Rochelle, N.Y. : Arlington House, 1972. — I, 1104.
Sandner, Wolfgang. Jazz : zur Geschichte und stillistlischen Entwicklung
  afroamerikanishcer Musik / Wolfgang Sandner. — Laabe, Germany : Läber,
  1982. — II, A-419.
Sanfilippo, Luigi. General catalog of Duke Ellington's recorded music / Luigi
  Sanfilippo. — 2nd ed. — Palermo : Centro Studi di Musica Contemporanea,
  1966. — I, 949.
Sanjek, Russell. American popular music and its business : the first four hundred
  years / Russell Sanjek. — New York : Oxford, 1988. — III, 370.
Sanjek, Russell. American popular music business in the 20th century / Russell
  Sanjek and David Sanjek. — New York : Oxford, 1991. — III, 371.
Sanjek, Russell. From print to plastic : publishing and promoting America's
  popular music / Russell Sanjek. — Brooklyn : Institute for Studies in Ameri-
  can Music, 1983. — II, A-525.
Sankey, Ira D. My life and sacred songs / Ira D. Sankey. — London : Hodder
  and Stoughton, 1906. — I, 74.
Sankey, Ira D. Sankey's story of the gospel hymns, and of sacred songs and so-
  los / Ira D. Sankey. — Philadelphia : Sunday School Times, 1906. — I, 74.
Santelli, Robert. Aquarius rising : the rock festival years / Robert Santelli. —
  New York : Dell, 1980. — II, 1146.
Santelli, Robert. Sixties rock : a listener's guide / Robert Santelli. — Chicago :
  Contemporary Books, 1985. — II, A-689.
Santos, Raye. X-Capees : a San Francisco punk photo documentary / Raye San-
  tos [et al]. — Berkeley, Calif. : Last Gasp of San Francisco, 1980. — II, 1263.

Saporita, Jay. Pourin' it all out / Jay Saporita. — Secaucus, N.J. : Citadel, 1980. — II, 1176.

Sargeant, Winthrop. Jazz hot and hybrid / Winthrop Sargeant — 3rd ed. — New York : Da Capo, 1975. — I, 1037.

Sarlin, Bob. Turn it up! I can't hear the words / Bob Sarlin. — New York : Simon & Schuster, 1974. — II, 1140.

Sauers, Wendy. Elvis Presley : a complete reference / Wendy Sauers. — Jefferson, N.C. : McFarland, 1984. — II, A-820.

Saunders, Richard Drake. Music and dance in California and the West / ed. Richard Drake Saunders. — Hollywood : Bureau of Musical Research, 1948. — I, 89.

Saunders, Richard Drake. Music and dance in the central states / ed. Richard Drake Saunders. — Hollywood : Bureau of Musical Research, 1952. — I, 89.

Savage, William W. Singing cowboys and all that jazz : a short history of popular music in Oklahoma / William W. Savage. — Norman : University of Oklahoma Press, 1983. — II, A-543.

Savoy, Ann Allen. Cajun music : a reflection of a people / Ann Allen Savoy. — Eunice, La. : Bluebird Press, 1984. — II, A-275.

Sawyer, Charles. B. B. King : the authorized biography / Charles Sawyer. — Poole, Dorset, England : Blandford Press, 1981. — II, 549.

Sawyer, Charles. The arrival of B. B. King / Charles Sawyer. — Garden City, N.Y. : Doubleday, 1980. — II, 549.

Sawyer-Laucanno, Christopher. An invisible spectator : a biography of Paul Bowles / Christopher Sawyer-Laucanno. — London : Bloomsbury, 1989. — III, 1300.

Saxon, Lyle. Gumbo ya-ya : a collection of Louisiana folk tales / ed. Lyle Saxon. — Boston : Houghton Mifflin, 1945. — II, 492.

Sayers, Scott P. Sinatra, the man and his music : the recording artistry of Francis Albert Sinatra / Scott P. Sayers and Ed O'Brien. — Austin : TSD Press, 1992. — III, 359.

Saylor, Bruce. The writings of Henry Cowell : a descriptive bibliography / Bruce Saylor. — Brooklyn : Institute for Studies in American Music, 1977. — II, 184.

Scaduto, Anthony. Bob Dylan / Anthony Scaduto. — New York : Grosset & Dunlap, 1972. — I, 1378.

Scaduto, Tony. Frank Sinatra / Tony Scaduto. — London : Michael Joesph, 1976. — II, 1011.

Scarborough, Dorothy. A song catcher in the southern mountains / Dorothy Scarborough. — New York : Columbia University Press, 1937. — I, 468.

Scarborough, Dorothy. On the trail of negro folk-songs / Dorothy Scarborough. — Cambridge, Mass. : Harvard University Press, 1925. — I, 767.

Schaap, Phil. Louis Armstrong festival discography / New York : WKCR, 1982. — II, A-371.

Schabas, Ezra. Theodore Thomas : America's conductor and builder of orchestras, 1835–1905 / Ezra Schabas; foreword by Valerie Solti. — Urbana : University of Illinois Press, 1989. — III, 963.

Schafer, William J. Brass bands and New Orleans jazz / William J. Schafer. — Baton Rouge : Louisiana State University Press, 1977. — II, 727.

Schafer, William J. Rock music : where it's been, what it means, where it's going / William J. Schafer. — Minneapolis : Augsburg, 1972. — I, 1359.

Schafer, William J. The art of ragtime / William J. Schafer and Johannes Riedel. — Baton Rouge : Louisiana State University Press, 1973. — I, 803.

Schaffner, Nicholas. The British invasion : from the first wave to the new wave / Nicholas Schaffner. — New York : McGraw-Hill, 1982. — III, 1192.

Schauffler, Robert Haven. Music as a social force in America and the science of practice / Robert Haven Schauffler and Sigmund Spaeth. — New York : Caxton Institute, 1927. — I, 95.

Schebera, Jürgen. Kurt Weill : Leben und Werk / Jürgen Schebera. — Königstein, Germany : Athenäum, 1984. — II, A-609.

Schechter, Harold. Patterns in popular culture : a sourcebook for writers / Harold Schechter and Jonna Gormely Semeiks. — New York : Harper & Row, 1980. — II, 859.

Schenkel, Steven. The tools of jazz / Steven Schenkel. — Englewood Cliffs, N.J. : Prentice-Hall, 1983. — II, A-414.

Scheurer, Timothy E. Born in the U.S.A. : the myth of America in popular music from colonial times to the present / Timothy E. Scheurer. — Jackson : University Press of Mississippi, 1991. — III, 1060.

Scheurer, Timothy E. The age of rock / ed. Timothy E. Scheurer. — Bowling Green, Ohio : Bowling Green State University Popular Press, 1989. — III, 1193.

Scheurer, Timothy E. The nineteenth century and Tin Pan Alley / Timothy E. Scheurer. — Bowling Green, Ohio : Bowling Green State University Popular Press, 1989. — III, 1061.

Schicke, C. A. Revolution in sound : a biography of the recording industry / C. A. Schicke. — Boston : Little, Brown, 1975. — II, 106.

Schickel, Richard. Carnegie Hall : the first one hundred years / Richard Schickel and Michael Walsh. — New York : Abrams, 1987. — III, 396.

Schiedt, Duncan. The jazz state of Indiana / Duncan Schiedt. — Pittsboro, Ind. : Author, 1977. — II, 728.

Schiesel, Jane. The Otis Redding story / Jane Schiesel. — Garden City, N.Y. : Doubleday, 1973. — I, 889.

Schiff, David. The music of Elliott Carter / David Schiff. — London : Eulenburg, 1983. — II, A-116.

Schiffman, Jack. Harlem heyday / Jack Schiffman. — Buffalo, N.Y. : Prometheus Books, 1984. — II, A-560.

Schiffman, Jack. Uptown : the story of Harlem's Apollo Theatre / Jack Schiffman. — New York : Cowles, 1971. — II, 886.

Schipper, Henry. Broken record : the story of the Grammy awards / Henry Schipper. — New York : Birch Lane, 1992. — III, 60.

Schlappi, Elizabeth. Roy Acuff : the Smoky Mountain boy / Elizabeth Schlappi. — Gretna, La. : Pelican, 1978. — II, 391.

Schlappi, Elizabeth. Roy Acuff and his Smoky Mountain Boys / Elizabeth Schlappi. — Cheswold, Dela. : Disc Collector Publications, 1966. — I, A-133.

Schleifer, Martha Furman. William Wallace Gilchrist (1846–1916) / Martha Furman Schleifer. — Metuchen, N.J. : Scarecrow, 1985. — II, A-79.

Schleman, Hilton. Rhythm on record : a who's who and register of recorded dance music / Hilton Schleman. — London : Melody Maker, 1936. — I, 923.

Schlenker, Alma H. Music in Bethlehem / Alma H. Schlenker. — Bethlehem, Pa. : Oaks Printing, 1984. — II, A-41.

Schlesinger, Janet. Challenge to the urban orchestra : the case of the Pittsburgh Symphony / Janet Schlesinger. — Pittsburgh : Author, 1971. — II, 124.

Schlouch, Claude. In memory of Wardell Gray : a discography / Claude Schlouch. — Marseilles, France : Author, 1983. — II, A-375.

Schlundt, Christena L. Dance in the musical theatre : Jerome Robbins and his peers / Christena L. Schlundt. — New York : Garland, 1989. — III, 10.

Schmidt, John C. The life and works of John Knowles Paine / John C. Schmidt. — Ann Arbor, Mich. : UMI Research Press, 1980. — II, 145.

Schmidt, Mathias R. Bob Dylan und die sechziger Jahre / Mathias R. Schmidt. — Frankfurt : Fischer, 1983. — II, A-792.

Schmidt, Mathias R. Bob Dylan's message songs / Mathias R. Schmidt. — Bern, Switzerland : Lang, 1982. — II, A-792.

Schmidt, Paul William. Acquired of the angels : the lives and works of master guitar makers John D'Angelico and James L. D'Aquisto / Paul William Schmidt. — Metuchen, N.J. : Scarecrow, 1991. — III, 972.

Schmidt-Joos, Siegfried. — Das Musical / Siegried Schmidt-Joos. — Munich : DTV, 1965. — II, 1050.

Schmidt-Joos, Siegfried. Idole / Siegfried Schmidt-Joos. — Frankfurt : Ullstein, 1984. — II, A-759.

Schmidt-Joos, Siegfried. Rock Lexikon / Siegfried Schmidt-Joos and Barry Graves. — Rev. ed. — Reinbek bei Hamburg : Rowohlt, 1975. — II, 1104.

Schneider, David. The San Francisco Symphony Orchestra : music, maestros, and musicians / David Schneider; discography by Victor Ledin. — Novato, Calif. : Presidio, 1987. — III, 1001.

Schoen-Rene, Anna Eugenie. America's musical inheritance / Anna Eugenie Schoen-Rene. — New York : Putnam, 1941. — II, 107.

Schoener, Allon. Harlem on my mind / Allon Schoener. — New York : Random House, 1968. — I, 670.

Scholes, Percy A. The Puritans and music in England and New England / Percy A. Scholes. — Oxford : Clarendon Press, 1934. — I, 184.

Schonberg, Harold C. Horowitz : his life and his music / Harold C. Schonberg. — New York : Simon & Schuster, 1992. — III, 550.

Schoorl, Bob. George Gershwin : van Broadway tot Carnegie Hall / Bob Schoorl. — Amsterdam : Strengholt, 1952. — I, A-264.

Schouten, Martin. Billie en de president : verhalen uit de tijd van de jazz / Martin Schouten. — Amsterdam : De Arbeiderspers, 1977. — II, 706.

Schreiber, Flora Rheta. William Schuman / Flora Rheta Schreiber and Vincent Persichetti. — New York : Schirmer, 1954. — I, 345.

Schreiber, Norman. The ultimate guide to independent record labels and artists : an A-to-Z shop-by-mail source of great music, from rock, jazz, and blues to classical, avant-garde, and new age / Norman Schreiber. — New York : Pharos Books, 1992. — III, 41.

Schroeder, Fred. Twentieth-century popular culture in museums and libraries / Fred Schroeder. — Bowling Green, Ohio : Bowling Green State University Popular Press, 1981. — II, A-510.

Schrueers, Fred. Blondie / Fred Schruers. — New York : Grosset & Dunlap, 1980. — II, 1284.

Schuller, Gunther. Early jazz : its roots and musical development / Gunther Schuller. — New York : Oxford University Press, 1968. — I, 1038.

Schuller, Gunther. Musings : the musical worlds of Gunther Schuller / Gunther Schuller; foreword by Milton Babbitt. — New York : Oxford, 1986. — III, 515.

Schuller, Gunther. The swing era : the development of jazz, 1930–1945 / Gunther Schuller. — New York : Oxford, 1989. — III, 1090.

Schuyler, Phillipa Duke. Adventures in black and white / Philippa Duke Schuyler. — New York : Speller, 1960. — II, 592.

Schwartz, Charles. Cole Porter : a biography / Charles Schwartz. — New York : Dial, 1977. — II, 958.

Schwartz, Charles. George Gershwin : a selective bibliography and discography / Charles Schwartz. — Detroit : Information Coordinators, 1974. — I, 1286.

Schwartz, Charles. Gershwin : his life and music / Charles Schwartz. — New York : Bobbs-Merrill, 1973. — I, 1285.

Schwartz, Elliott. Contemporary composers on contemporary music / Elliott Schwartz and Barney Childs. — New York : Holt, Rinehart & Winston, 1967. — I, 263.

Schwartz, Elliott. Electronic music : a listener's guide / Elliott Schwartz. — New York : Praeger, 1973. — I, 283.

Schwartz, Harry Wayne. Bands of America / Harry Wayne Schwartz. — Garden City, N.Y. : Doubleday, 1957. — I, 1200.

Schwarzer Gesang. — Munich : Nymphenburg, 1961, 1962. — II, 527.

Schwerin, Jules. Got to tell it : Mahalia Jackson, queen of gospel / Jules Schwerin. — New York : Oxford, 1992. — III, 741.

Schwienher, William K. Lawrence Welk : an American institution / William K. Schwienher. — Chicago : Nelson-Hall, 1980. — II, 1095.

Scobey, Jan. He rambled! 'Til cancer cut him down : Bob Scobey, Dixieland jazz musician and bandleader, 1916–1963 / Jan Scobey. — Northridge, Calif. : Pal Publishing, 1976. — II, 767.

Scobey, Lola. Willie Nelson : country outlaw / Lola Scobey. — New York : Kensington, 1982. — II, A-260.

Scoppa, Bud. The Byrds / Bud Scoppa. — New York : Quick Fox, 1971. — II, 1285.

Scott, Frank. The Down Home guide to the blues / Frank Scott and the staff of Down Home Music. — Chicago : Chicago Review Press, 1991. — III, 223.

Scott, John. DeadBase IV : the complete guide to Grateful Dead song lists / John W. Scott, Mike Dogulshkin and Stu Nixon. — Hanover, N.H. : DeadBase, 1990. — III, 914.

Scott, John Anthony. The ballad of America : the history of the United States in song and story / John Anthony Scott. — New York : Bantam, 1966. — II, 862.

Scott, Michael. Maria Meneghini Callas / Michael Scott. — Boston : Northeastern University Press, 1992. — III, 694.

Scruggs, Earl. Earl Scruggs and the 5-string banjo / Earl Scruggs. — New York : Peer, 1968. — I, A-139.

Sculatti, Gene. San Francisco nights : the psychedelic music trip / Gene Sculatti and Davin Seay. — New York : St. Martin's, 1985. — II, A-707.

Sculatti, Gene. The catalog of cool / Gene Sculatti. — New York : Warner Books, 1983. — II, A-703.

Sears, Nelson. Jim and Jesse : Appalachia to the Grand Ole Opry / Nelson Sears. — [n.p.] : Author, 1976. — S. 409.

Sears, Richard S. V-Discs : a history and discography / Richard S. Sears. — Westport, Conn. : Greenwood, 1980. — II, 816.

Sedaka, Neil. Laughter in the rain : my own story / Neil Sedaka. — New York : Putnam, 1982. — II, A-839.

Seeger, Anthony. Early field recordings : a catalogue of cylinder collections at the Indiana University Archives of Traditional Music / Anthony Seeger and Louise S. Spear. — Bloomington : Indiana University Press, 1987. — III, 192.

Seeger, Pete. Carry it on : a history in song and pictures of the working men and women of America / Pete Seeger and Bob Reiser. — New York : Simon & Schuster, 1985. — II, A-209.

Seeger, Pete. Everybody says freedom / Pete Seeger and Bob Reiser. — New York : Norton, 1989. — III, 1213.

Seeger, Pete. How to play the 5-string banjo / Pete Seeger. — New York : People's Songs, 1948. — I, A-140.

Seeger, Pete. The incompleat folksinger / Pete Seeger. — New York : Simon & Schuster, 1972. — I, 590.

Segalini, Sergio. Callas : portrait of a diva / Sergio Segalini. — London : Hutchinson, 1980. — III, 695.

Seipt, Allen Anders. Schwenkfelder hymnology and the sources of the first Schwenkfelder hymn-book printed in America / Allen Anders Seipt. — Philadelphia : Americana Germanica Press, 1909. — I, A-23.

Seldes, Gilbert. The public arts / Gilbert Seldes. — New York : Simon & Schuster, 1956. — II, 1074.

Seldes, Gilbert. The seven lively arts / Gilbert Seldes. — 2nd ed. — New York : Sagamore, 1957. — I, 1166.

Seltsam, William H. Metropolitan Opera annals / William H. Seltsam. — New York : Wilson, 1947. Supplements 1957, 1968. — I, 155.

Seltzer, George. Music matters : the performer and the American Federation of Musicians / George Seltzer. — Metuchen, N.J. : Scarecrow, 1989. — III, 42.

Seltzer, George. The professional symphony orchestra in the United States / George Seltzer. — Metuchen, N.J. : Scarecrow, 1975. — II, 219.

Selvin, Joel. Rick Nelson : idol for a generation / Joel Selvin. — Chicago : Contemporary Books, 1990. — III, 801.

Semler, Isabel Parker. Horatio Parker : a memoir for his grandchildren / Isabel Parker Semler. — New York : Putnam, 1942. — I, 243.

Sendrey, Alfred. Bibliography of Jewish music / Alfred Sendrey. — New York : Columbia University Press, 1951. — I, 8.

Sennett, Ted. Hollywood musicals / Ted Sennett. — New York : Abrams, 1981. — II, A-590.

Sessions, Roger. Reflections on the music life in the United States / Roger Sessions. — New York : Merlin, 1956. — I, 370.

Sessions, Roger. The musical experience of a composer, performer and listener / Roger Sessions. — Princeton, N.J. : Princeton University Press, 1950. — I, 346.

Seton, Marie. Paul Robeson / Marie Seton. — London : Dobson, 1958. — I, 710.

Sewall, Samuel. Diary / Samuel Sewall. — New York : Macy-Masius 1927. — I, A-45.

Seward, Theodore F. Jubilee songs, as sung by the Jubilee Singers / Theodore F. Seward. — New York : Biglow & Main, 1872. — I, 784.

Seward, Theodore F. The educational work of Dr. Lowell Mason / Theodore F. Seward. — [no publisher or place] 1878[?]. — I, 173.

Shacter, James D. Piano man : the story of Ralph Sutton / James D. Shacter. — Chicago : Jaynar Press, 1975. — II, 768.

Shaffer, Karen A. Maud Powell : pioneer American violinist / Karen A. Shaffer and Neva Garner Greenwood; foreword by Yehudi Menuhin. — Arlington, Va. : Maud Powell Foundation; distributed by Iowa State University Press, 1988. — III, 590.

Shanet, Howard. Philharmonic : a history of New York's orchestra / Howard Shanet. — New York : Doubleday, 1975. — I, 115.

Shannon, Bob. Behind the hits / Bob Shannon. — New York : Warner Books, 1986. — III, 1062.

Shapiro, Bill. Thirty years of rock and roll on compact disc / Bill Shapiro. — New York : Andres & McMeel, 1988. — III, 270.

Shapiro, Doris. We danced all night : my life behind the scenes with Alan Jay Lerner / Doris Shapiro. — New York : Morrow, 1990. — III, 968.

Shapiro, Harry. Jimi Hendrix : electric gypsy / Harry Shapiro and Caesar Glebbeek. — London : Heinemann, 1990. — III, 584.

Shapiro, Nat. Hear me talkin' to ya : the story of jazz by the men who made it / Nat Shapiro and Nat Hentoff. — New York : Rinehart, 1955. — I, 1006.

Shapiro, Nat. Popular music : an annotated index of American popular songs / Nat Shapiro. — New York : Adrian, 1964–1973. — I, 1161.

Shapiro, Nat. The jazz makers / Nat Shapiro and Nat Hentoff. — New York : Rinehart, 1957. — I, 1079.

Sharp, Cecil J. English folk songs from the Southern Appalachians / Cecil J. Sharp. — London : Oxford University Press, 1932. — I, 469.

Shaver, Sean. Elvis' portrait portfolio / Sean Shaver. — Memphis : Timur, 1983. — II, A-832.

Shaver, Sean. The life of Elvis Presley / Sean Shaver. — Memphis : Timur, 1979. — II, 1303.

Shaw, Arnold. Belafonte : an unauthorized biography / Arnold Shaw. — Philadelphia : Chilton, 1960. — II, 1070.

Shaw, Arnold. Black popular music in America : from the spirituals, minstrels, and ragtime to soul, disco, and hip-hop / Arnold Shaw. — New York : Schirmer, 1986. — III, 1225.

Shaw, Arnold. Dictionary of American pop/rock / Arnold Shaw. — New York : Schirmer, 1982. — II, A-666.

Shaw, Arnold. Honkers and shouters : the golden years of rhythm and blues / Arnold Shaw. — New York : Collier Books, 1978. — II, 561.

Shaw, Arnold. Rock revolution / Arnold Shaw. — New York : Crowell-Collier, 1969. — I, 1360.

Shaw, Arnold. Sinatra / Arnold Shaw. — London : Allen, 1968. — I, 1337.

Shaw, Arnold. Sinatra the entertainer / Arnold Shaw. — New York : Delilah, 1982. — II, A-638.

Shaw, Arnold. The jazz age : popular music in the 1920s / Arnold Shaw. — New York : Oxford, 1987. — III, 1063.

Shaw, Arnold. The rockin' 50s : the decade that transformed the pop music scene / Arnold Shaw. — New York : Hawthorn, 1974. — II, 1128.

Shaw, Arnold. The street that never slept / Arnold Shaw. — New York : Coward, McCann & Geoghegan, 1971. — I, 978.

Shaw, Arnold. World of soul / Arnold Shaw. — New York : Cowles, 1970. — I, 895.

Shaw, Artie. The trouble with Cinderella / Artie Shaw. — New York : Farrar, Straus & Young, 1952. — I, 1138.

Shay, Frank. American sea songs and chanteys from the days of iron men and wooden ships / Frank Shay. — New York : Norton, 1948. — I, 576.

Shay, Frank. Iron men and wooden ships / Frank Shay. — Garden City, N.Y. : Doubleday, Page, 1924. — I, 576.

Shearin, Hubert G. A syllabus of Kentucky folk-songs / Hubert G. Shearin and Josiah H. Combs. — Lexington, Ky. : Transylvania Printing, 1911. — II, 455.

Sheean, Vincent. Oscar Hammerstein I : the life and exploits of an impresario / Vincent Sheean. — New York : Simon & Schuster, 1956. — I, 157.

Sheldon, Ruth. Hubbin' it : the life of Bob Wills / Ruth Sheldon. — Kingsport, Tenn. : Kingsport Press, 1938. — I, A-134.

Shellans, Herbert. Folk songs of the Blue Ridge Mountains / Herbert Shellans. — New York : Oak, 1968. — I, 506.

Shelton, Robert. No direction home : the life and music of Bob Dylan / Robert Shelton. — New York : Morrow, 1986. — III, 715.

Shelton, Robert. The country music story / Robert Shelton. — New Rochelle, N.Y. : Arlington House, 1966. — I, 608.

Shemel, Sidney. This business of music / Sidney Shemel and M. William Krasilovsky. — 6th ed. — New York : Billboard Books, 1990. — III, 1248.

Shepard, Sam. Rolling Thunder logbook / Sam Shepard. — New York : Viking, 1977. — II, 1202.

Shepherd, Don. Bing Crosby : the hollow man / Don Shepherd and Robert F. Slatzer. — New York : St. Martin's, 1981. — II, A-625.

Shepherd, John. Tin Pan Alley / John Shepherd. — London : Routledge & Kegan Paul, 1982. — II, A-536.

Shepherd, John. Whose music? : a sociology of musical languages / John Shepherd [et al]. — London : Latimer, 1977. — II, 18.

Sheridan, Chris. Count Basie : a bio-discography / Chris Sheridan. — New York : Greenwood, 1986. — III, 288.

Sherman, John K. Music and maestros : the story of the Minneapolis Symphony Orchestra / John K. Sherman. — Minneapolis : University of Minnesota Press, 1952. — I, 138.

Sherman, John K. Music and theater in Minnesota history / John K. Sherman. — Minneapolis : University of Minnesota Press, 1958. — II, 123.

Sherman, Michael W. The collector's guide to Victor records / Michael W. Sherman; in collaboration with William R. Moran and Kurt R. Nauck, III. — Dallas : Monarch Record Enterprises, 1992. — III, 218.

Sherwin, Sterling. Railroad songs of yesterday / Sterling Sherwin and Harry K. McClintock. — New York : Shapiro, Bernstein, 1943. — I, 572.

Shestack, Melvin. Country music encyclopedia / Melvin Shestack. — New York : Crowell, 1974. — I, 609.

Shetler, Donald J. In memoriam Howard Hanson / ed. Donald J. Shetler. — Rochester, N.Y. : Eastman School of Music, 1984. — II, A-67.

Shevey, Sandra. Ladies of pop-rock / Sandra Shevey. — New York : Scholastic Book Service, 1972. — II, 1282.

Shipton, Alyn. Fats Waller : his life & times / Alyn Shipton. — New York : Universe, 1988. — III, 574.

Shirley, Kay. Book of the blues / Kay Shirley [et al]. — New York : Leeds Music, 1963. — I, 881.

Shirley, Wayne D. *Modern Music*, published by the League of Composers, 1924–1946 : an analytic index / Wayne D. Shirley. — New York : AMS Press, 1976. — II, 166.

Shoemaker, Henry W. Mountain minstrelsy of Pennsylvania / Henry W. Shoemaker. — Philadelphia : McGirr, 1931. — I, 484.

Shoemaker, Henry W. North Pennsylvania minstrelsy / Henry W. Shoemaker. — Altoona, Pa. : Altoona Tribune, 1919. — I, 484.

Shore, Michael. The history of American Bandstand / Michael Shore and Dick Clark. — New York : Ballantine, 1985. — II, A-743.

Shore, Michael. The *Rolling Stone* book of rock video / Michael Shore. — New York : Quill, 1984. — II, A-754.

Short, Bobby. Black and white baby / Bobby Short. — New York : Dodd, Mead, 1971. — II, 1087.

Sidran, Ben. Black talk / Ben Sidran. — New York : Holt, Rinehart & Winston, 1971. — I, 696.

Sieben, Pearl. The immortal Jolson / Pearl Sieben. — New York : Fell, 1962. — I, 1333.

Siegel, Alan H. Breakin' in the music business / Alan H. Siegel. — Port Chester, N.Y. : Cherry Lane Books, 1983. — II, A-744.

Silber, Irwin. Soldier songs and home-front ballads of the Civil War / ed. Irwin Silber. — New York : Oak, 1964. — II, 874.

Silber, Irwin. Songs America voted by / ed. Irwin Silber. — Harrisburg, Pa. : Stackpole, 1971. — II, 1030.

Silber, Irwin. Songs of independence / ed. Irwin Silber. — Harrisburg, Pa. : Stackpole Books, 1973. — II, 863.

Silber, Irwin. Songs of the Civil War / Irwin Silber. — New York : Columbia University Press, 1960. — I, 1191.

Silber, Irwin. Songs of the great American west / Irwin Silber. — New York : Macmillan, 1967. — I, 512.

Silet, Charles L. The writings of Paul Rosenfeld : an annotated bibliography / Charles L. Silet. — New York : Garland, 1981. — II, A-153.

Sills, Beverly. Beverly : an autobiography / Beverly Sills and Lawrence Linderman. — New York : Bantam, 1987. — III, 855.

Silverman, Jerry. Folk blues : 110 American folk blues / Jerry Silverman. — New York : Macmillan, 1958. — I, 882.

Silverman, Jerry. The art of the folk blues guitar / Jerry Silverman. — New York : Oak, 1964. — I, A-187.

Silverman, Jerry. The flat-picker's guitar guide / Jerry Silverman. — New York : Oak, 1966. — I, A-141.

Silverman, Kenneth. A cultural history of the American Revolution / Kenneth Silverman. — New York : Crowell, 1976. — II, 140.

Silvester, Peter J. A left hand like God : a history of boogie-woogie piano / Peter J. Silvester; with a special contribution from Denis Harbinson. — London : Quartet, 1988. — III, 992a.

Simas, Rick. The musicals no one came to see : a guidebook to four decades of musical comedy casualties on Broadway, off-Broadway, and in out-of-town try-outs, 1943–1983 / Rick Simas. — New York : Garland, 1987. — III, 134.

Simkins, F. B. Art and music in the South / F. B. Simkins. — Farmville, Va. : Longwood College, 1961. — II, 125.

Simon, George T. The best of the music makers / George T. Simon [et al]. — Garden City, N.Y. : Doubleday, 1979. — II, 823.

Simon, George T. The big bands / George Thomas Simon. — 4th ed. — New York : Schirmer; London : Collier Macmillan, 1981. — III, 1142.

Simon, George T. The big bands / George Simon. — Rev. ed. — New York : Macmillan, 1971. — I, 1045.

Simon, George T. The big bands trivia quiz book / George Thomas Simon. — New York : Barnes & Noble, 1985. — III, 1143.

Simon, George T. Glenn Miller and his orchestra / George Simon. — New York : Crowell, 1974. — I, 1126.

Simon, George T. Simon says : the sights and sounds of the swing era, 1935–1955 / George Simon. — New Rochelle, N.Y. : Arlington House, 1971. — I, 1046.

Simone, Nina. I put a spell on you : the autobiography of Nina Simone / Nina Simone; with Stephen Cleary. — New York : Pantheon, 1992. — III, 858.

Simosko, Vladimir. Eric Dolphy : a musical biography and discography / Vladimir Simosko and Barry Tepperman. — Washington : Smithsonian Institution Press, 1974. — I, 1103.

Simpkins, Cuthbert Ormond. Coltrane : a biography / Cuthbert Ormond Simpkins. — Perth Amboy, N.J. : Herndon House, 1975. — II, 743.

Simpkins, Cuthbert Ormond. Coltrane : a biography / Cuthbert Ormond Simpkins. — New York : Herndon House, 1975. — I, A-220.

Simpson, Anne Key. Hard trials : the life and music of Harry T. Burleigh / Anne Key Simpson. — Metuchen, N.J. : Scarecrow, 1990. — III, 457.

Simpson, Eugene E. America's position in music / Eugene E. Simpson. — Boston : Four Seas, 1920. — I, A-15.

Sims, Jane L. Marian Anderson : an annotated bibliography and discography / Janet L. Sims. — Westport, Conn. : Greenwood, 1981. — II, A-307.

Sinatra, Frank. Sinatra in his own words / Frank Sinatra; comp. Guy Yarwood. — New York : Delilah, 1983. — II, A-640.

Sinatra, Frank. Sinatra on Sinatra / Frank Sinatra; comp. Guy Yarwood. — London : W. H. Allen, 1982. — II, A-640.

Sinatra, Nancy. Frank Sinatra, my father / Nancy Sinatra. — Garden City, N.Y. : Doubleday, 1985. — III, 861.

Sinclair, John. Guitar army : street writings, prison writings / John Sinclair. — New York : Douglas, 1972. — II, 1152.

Sinclair, John. Music and politics / John Sinclair and Robert Levin. — New York : World, 1971. — II, 722.

Singer, Barry. Black and blue : the life and lyrics of Andy Razaf / Barry
    Singer. — New York : Schirmer, 1992. — III, 510.
Singer, Kurt. The Danny Kaye saga / Kurt Singer. — London : Robert Hale,
    1957. — II, 1080.
Sive, Helen R. Music's Connecticut yankee : an introduction to the life and mu-
    sic of Charles Ives / Helen R. Sive. — New York : Atheneum, 1977. — II,
    192.
Sizer, Sandra S. Gospel hymns and social religion / Sandra S. Sizer. — Philadel-
    phia : Temple University Press, 1978. — II, 42.
Sjogren, Thorbjorn. The discography of Duke Jordan / Thorbjorn Sjogren. —
    Copenhagen : Author, 1982. — II, A-377.
Sjogren, Thorbjorn. The Duke Jordan discography / Thorbjorn Sjogren. — Rev.
    ed. — Copenhagen : Author, 1984. — III, 331.
Sjogren, Thorbjorn. The Sonny Rollins discography / Thorbjorn Sjogren. —
    Copenhagen : Author, 1982. — II, A-384.
Skiles, Martin. Music scoring for TV and motion pictures / Martin Skiles. —
    Blue Ridge Summit, Pa. : Tab Books, 1976. — II, 1060.
Sklar, Rick. Rocking America : how the all-hit radio stations took over : an in-
    sider's view / Rick Sklar. — New York : St. Martin's, 1984. — II, A-745.
Skowronski, JoAnn. Aaron Copland : a bio-bibliography / JoAnn Skowronski. —
    Westport, Conn. : Greenwood, 1985. — II, A-119.
Skowronski, JoAnn. Black music in America : a bibliography / JoAnn Skowron-
    ski. — Metuchen, N.J. : Scarecrow, 1981. — II, A-291.
Skowronski, JoAnn. Women in American music : a bibliography / JoAnn
    Skowronski. — Metuchen, N.J. : Scarecrow, 1978. — II, 24.
Slaughter, Todd. Elvis Presley / Todd Slaughter. — London : Mandabrook,
    1977. — II, 1304.
Slide, Anthony. The vaudevillians : a dictionary of vaudeville performers / An-
    thony Slide. — Westport, Conn. : Arlington House, 1981. — II, A-566.
Slobin, Mark. Chosen voices : the story of the American cantorate / Mark
    Slobin. — Urbana : University of Illinois Press, 1989. — III, 1045.
Slobin, Mark. Tenement songs : the popular music of the Jewish immigrant /
    Mark Slobin. — Urbana : University of Illinois Press, 1982. — II, A-544.
Sloman, Larry. On the road with Bob Dylan : rolling with the thunder / Larry
    Sloman. — New York : Bantam, 1978. — II, 1203.
Slonimsky, Nicolas. Lexicon of musical invective / Nicolas Slonimsky. — 2nd
    ed. — New York : Coleman-Ross, 1965. — I, 257.
Slonimsky, Nicolas. Music since 1900 / Nicolas Slonimsky. — 4th ed. — New
    York : Scribner's, 1971. — I, A-84.
Slonimsky, Nicolas. Perfect pitch : a life story / Nicolas Slonimsky. — New
    York : Oxford, 1988. — III, 971.
Small, Christopher. Music of the common tongue : survival and celebration in
    Afro-American music / Christopher Small. — London : Calder, 1987. — III,
    1226.
Small, Christopher. Music, society, education / Christopher Small. — 2nd ed. —
    London : Calder, 1980. — II, 19.
Smart, James R. The Sousa band : a discography / James R. Smart. — Wash-
    ington : Library of Congress, 1970. — I, 1206.

Smith, Bill. The vaudevillians / Bill Smith. — New York : Macmillan, 1976. — II, 894.

Smith, Carolina Estes. The Philharmonic Orchestra of Los Angeles : the first decade, 1919–1929 / Carolina Estes Smith. — Los Angeles, United Printing Co., 1930. — I, 130.

Smith, Catherine Parsons. Mary Carr Moore, American composer / Catherine Parsons Smith and Cynthia S. Richardson. — Ann Arbor : University of Michigan Press, 1987. — III, 502.

Smith, Cecil. Musical comedy in America / Cecil Smith. — New York : Theatre Arts Books, 1950. — I, 1228.

Smith, Charles Edward. The jazz record book / Charles Edward Smith [et al]. — New York : Smith & Durrell, 1942. — I, 954.

Smith, David. Peter Allen : between the moon and New York City / David Smith and Neal Peters. — New York : Delilah, 1983. — II, A-767.

Smith, Dwight L. Afro-American history : a bibliography / Dwight L. Smith. — Santa Barbara, Calif. : ABC-Clio, 1974. — I, 654.

Smith, Eric Ledell. Bert Williams : a biography of the pioneer black comedian / Eric Ledell Smith. — Jefferson, N.C. : McFarland, 1992. — III, 1296.

Smith, Gibbs M. Joe Hill / Gibbs M. Smith. — Salt Lake City : University of Utah Press, 1969. — I, 594.

Smith, Harry B. First nights and first editions / Harry B. Smith. — Boston : Little, Brown, 1931. — I, 1301.

Smith, Jay D. Jack Teagarden : the story of a jazz maverick / Jay D. Smith and Len Guttridge. — London : Cassell, 1960. — I, 1141.

Smith, Joe. Off the record : an oral history of popular music / Joe Smith; ed. Mitchell Fink. — New York : Warner Books, 1988. — III, 1064.

Smith, John L. The Johnny Cash discography / John L. Smith. — Westport, Conn. : Greenwood, 1985. — II, A-2247.

Smith, Julia. Aaron Copland : his work and contribution to American music / Julia Smith. — New York : Dutton, 1955. — I, 318.

Smith, Julia. Directory of American women composers / Julia Smith. — Chicago : National Federation of Music Clubs, 1970. — I, 47.

Smith, Kate. Living in a great big way / Kate Smith. — New York : Blue Ribbon Books, 1938. — II, 1013.

Smith, Kile. Catalog of music by Pennsylvania composers / Kile Smith. — Wynnewood, Pa. : Pennsylvania Composers Forum, 1992. — III, 107.

Smith, L. Allen. A catalogue of pre-revival Appalachian dulcimers / L. Allen Smith. — Columbia : University of Missouri Press, 1983. — III, 986.

Smith, L. Mayne. An introduction to bluegrass / L. Mayne Smith. — Los Angeles : John Edwards Memorial Foundation, 1966. — II, 479.

Smith, Michael P. A joyful noise : a celebration of New Orleans music / Michael P. Smith. — Dallas : Taylor, 1990. — III, 1128.

Smith, Michael P. New Orleans jazz fest : a pictorial history / Michael P. Smith. — Gretna, La. : Pelican, 1991. — III, 1129.

Smith, Moses. Koussevitzky / Moses Smith. — New York : Allen, Towne & Heath, 1947. — S. 220.

Smith, Patrick J. A year at the Met / Patrick J. Smith. — New York : Knopf, 1983. — II, A-49.

Smith, Reed. South Carolina ballads / ed. Reed Smith. — Cambridge, Mass. : Harvard University Press, 1928. — II, 316.

Smith, Steven C. A heart at fire's center : the life and music of Bernard Herrmann / Steven C. Smith. — Berkeley : University of California Press, 1991. — III, 485.

Smith, Stuff. Pure at heart / Stuff Smith; ed. Anthony Barnett and Eva Logager. — Lewes, England : Allardyce, Barnett, 1991. — III, 591.

Smith, W. O. (William Oscar). Sideman : the long gig of W. O. Smith : a memoir / W. O. Smith. — Nashville : Rutledge Hill, 1991. — III, 592.

Smith, William Ander. The mystery of Leopold Stokowski / William Ander Smith. — Rutherford, N.J. : Fairleigh Dickinson University Press, 1990. — III, 962.

Smith, Willie. Music on my mind : the memoirs of an American pianist / Willie Smith; with George Hoefer. — Garden City, N.Y. : Doubleday, 1964. — I, 1140.

Smitherman, Geneva. Talkin and testifyin : the language of black America / Geneva Smitherman. — Boston : Houghton Mifflin, 1977. — II, 493.

Smolian, Steven. A handbook of film, theater, and television music on record, 1948–1969 / Steven Smolian. — New York : Record Undertaker, 1970. — I, 1314.

Smyth, Willie. Country music recorded prior to 1943 : a discography of LP reissues / Willie Smyth. — Los Angeles : John Edwards Memorial Foundation, 1984. — II, A-219.

Smythe, Augustine T. The Carolina low country / Augustine T. Smythe. — New York : Macmillan, 1932. — I, 796.

Snow, George. Glenn Miller & the age of swing / George Snow and Jonathan Green. — London : Dempsey & Squires, 1976. — II, 762.

Soares, Janet Mansfield. Louis Horst : musician in a dancer's world / Janet Mansfield Soares. — Durham, N.C. : Duke University Press, 1992. — III, 488.

Sobel, Bernard. A pictorial history of burlesque / Bernard Sobel. — New York : Bonanza Books, 1956. — II, 895.

Sobel, Bernard. A pictorial history of vaudeville / Bernard Sobel. — New York : Citadel, 1961. — II, 896.

Sokol, Martin L. The New York City Opera : an American adventure / Martin L. Sokol. — London : Collier Macmillan, 1981. — II, A-50.

Sollinger, Charles. String class publications in the United States, 1851–1951 / Charles Sollinger. — Detroit : Information Coordinators, 1974. — I, 174.

Solomon, Clive. Record hits : the British top 50 charts / Clive Solomon [et al]. — London : Omnibus, 1979. — II, 1114.

Solow, Linda. Boston composers project : a bibliography of contemporary music / Linda Solow. — Cambridge, Mass. : MIT Press, 1983. — II, A-98.

Somma, Robert. No one waved good-bye : a casualty report on rock and roll / Robert Somma. — New York : Outerbridge & Dienstfrey, 1971. — I, 1372.

Sonneck, Oscar G. Bibliography of early secular American music / Oscar George Theodore Sonneck; revised and enlarged by William Treat Upton. — Washington : Library of Congress, 1945. — I, 2.

Sonneck, Oscar G. Catalogue of first editions of Edward MacDowell

(1861–1980) / Oscar G. Sonneck. — Washington : Library of Congress, 1917. — I, 240.

Sonneck, Oscar G. Early concert-life in America (1731–1800) / Oscar G. Sonneck. — Leipzig : Breitkopf & Härtel, 1949. — I, 210.

Sonneck, Oscar G. Early opera in America / Oscar G. Sonneck. — New York : Schirmer, 1915. — I, 144.

Sonneck, Oscar G. Francis Hopkinson, the first American poet composer (1737–1791) and James Lyon, patriot, preacher, psalmodist (1735–1794) / Oscar G. Sonneck. — Washington : H. L. McQueen, 1905. — I, 204.

Sonneck, Oscar G. Miscellaneous studies in the history of music / Oscar G. Sonneck. — New York : Macmillan, 1921. — I, A-16.

Sonneck, Oscar G. Report on The Star Spangled Banner, Hail Columbia, America, Yankee Doodle / Oscar G. Sonneck. — Washington : Government Printing Office, 1909. — I, 1187.

Sonneck, Oscar G. Suum cuique : essay in music / Oscar G. Sonneck. — New York : Schirmer, 1916. — I, 42.

Sonneck, Oscar G. The Star Spangled Banner / Oscar G. Sonneck. — Washington : Government Printing Office, 1914. — I, 1188.

Sonnier, Austin M. Willie Greary "Bunk" Johnson : the New Iberia years / Austin M. Sonnier. — New York : Crescendo, 1977. — II, 754.

Sousa, John Philip. Marching along : recollections of men, women and music / John Philip Sousa. — Boston : Hale, Cushman and Flint, 1928. — I, 1201.

Sousa, John Philip. Through the year with Sousa / John Philip Sousa. — New York : Crowell, 1910. — I, 1202.

Southall, Geneva H. Blind Tom / Geneva H. Southall. — Minneapolis : Challenge Productions, 1979. — II, 511.

Southern, Eileen. African-American traditions in song, sermon, tale, and dance, 1600s-1920 : an annotated bibliography of literature, collections, and artworks / Eileen Southern and Josephine Wright. — Westport, Conn. : Greenwood, 1990. — III, 1275.

Southern, Eileen. Biographical dictionary of Afro-American and African musicians / Eileen Southern. — Westport, Conn. : Greenwood, 1981. — II, A-298.

Southern, Eileen. Music of black Americans : a history / Eileen Southern. — New York : Norton, 1971. — I, 697.

Southern, Eileen. Readings in black American music / ed. Eileen Southern. — New York : Norton, 1971. — I, 698.

Southern, Eileen. Readings in black American music / Eileen Southern. — 2nd ed. — New York : Norton, 1983. — III, 1222.

Southern, Eileen. The music of black Americans : a history / Eileen Southern. — 2nd ed. — New York : Norton, 1983. — III, 1227.

Spackman, Stephen. Wallingford Rieger : two essay in musical biography / Stephen Spackman. — Brooklyn : Institute for Studies in American Music, 1982. — II, A-135.

Spada, James. Barbra : the first decade : the films and career of Barbra Streisand. — James Spada. — Secaucus, N.J. : Citadel, 1974. — II, 1092.

Spada, James. Judy and Liza / James Spada and Karen Swenson. — Garden City, N.Y. : Doubleday, 1983. — II, A-628.

Spada, James. Streisand : the woman and the legend / James Spada. — Garden City, N.Y. : Doubleday, 1982. — II, A-643.

Spada, James. The divine Bette Midler / James Spada. — New York : Collier 1984. — II, A-814.

Spaeth, Sigmund. A history of popular music in America / Sigmund Spaeth. — New York : Random House, 1948. — I, 1171.

Spaeth, Sigmund. Music and dance in New York State / ed. Sigmund Spaeth. — New York : Bureau of Musical Research, 1952. — I, 89.

Spaeth, Sigmund. Music and dance in Pennsylvania, New Jersey and Delaware / ed. Sigmund Spaeth. — New York : Bureau of Musical Research, 1954. — I, 89.

Spaeth, Sigmund. Music and dance in the New England states / ed. Sigmund Spaeth. — New York : Bureau of Musical Research, 1953. — I, 89.

Spaeth, Sigmund. Music and dance in the southeastern states / ed. Sigmund Spaeth. — New York : Bureau of Musical Research, 1952. — I, 89.

Spaeth, Sigmund. Read 'em and weep / Sigmund Spaeth. — Rev. ed. — New York : Arco, 1945. — I, 1181.

Spaeth, Sigmund. The facts of life in popular song / Sigmund Spaeth. — New York : Whittlesey House, 1934. — I, 1174.

Spaeth, Sigmund. Weep some more, my lady / Sigmund Spaeth. — Garden City, N.Y. : Doubleday, Page, 1927. — I, 1182.

Spagnardi, Ron. The great jazz drummers / Ron Spagnardi; ed. William F. Miller. — Cedar Grove, N.J. : Modern Drummer Publications, 1992. — III, 434.

Spalding, Walter Raymond. Music at Harvard : a historical review of men and events / Walter Raymond Spalding. — New York : Coward-McCann, 1935. — I, A-46.

Specht, Paul L. How they became name bands / Paul L. Specht. — New York : Fine Arts, 1941. — I, 1047.

Specht, R. John. Early American vocal music in modern editions / R. John Specht. — Albany, N.Y. : New York State American Revolution Bicentennial Commission, 1974. — II, 138.

Spector, Ronnie. Be my baby : how I survived mascara, miniskirts, and madness : or my life as a fabulous Ronette / Ronnie Spector. — New York : Harmony Books, 1990. — III, 862.

Spedale, Rhodes. A guide to jazz in New Orleans / Rhodes Spedale. — New Orleans : Hope Publications, 1984. — II, A-444.

Spell, Lota M. Music in Texas / Lota M. Spell. — Austin, Tex. : Author, 1936. — I, 131.

Spellman, A. B. Four lives in the bebop business / A. B. Spellman. — New York : Pantheon, 1967. — I, 1058.

Spencer, Jon Michael. As the black school sings : black music collections at black universities and colleges, with a union list of book holdings / Jon Michael Spencer. — New York : Greenwood, 1987. — III, 117.

Spencer, Jon Michael. Protest and praise : sacred music of black religion / Jon Michael Spencer. — Minneapolis : Fortress, 1990. — III, 1223.

Spencer, Jon Michael. Sacred music of the secular city : from blues to rap / Jon Michael Spencer. — Durham, N.C. : Duke University Press, 1992. — III, 1224.

Spencer, Ray. Piano player's jazz handbook / Ray Spencer. — Metuchen, N.J. : Scarecrow, 1985. — II, A-404.

Spillane, Daniel. History of the American pianoforte : its technical development and the trade / Daniel Spillane. — New York : Author, 1890. — I, 163.

Spiller, Robert E. Literary history of the United States / ed. Robert E. Spiller [et al]. — Vol. 3, Bibliography. — New York : Macmillan, 1948. — Supplements, 1959, 1972. — I, 9.

Spinden, Herbert Joseph. Songs of the Tewa / Herbert Joseph Spinden. — New York : Exposition of Indian Tribal Arts, 1933. — II, 256.

Spitz, Bob. Dylan : a biography / Bob Spitz. — New York : McGraw-Hill, 1988. — III, 716.

Spitz, Robert Stephen. Barefoot in Babylon : the creation of the Woodstock music festival, 1969 / Robert Stephen Spitz. — New York : Viking, 1978. — II, 1147.

Spitz, Robert Stephen. The making of superstars / Robert Stephen Spitz. — Garden City, N.Y. : Doubleday, 1978. — II, 1177.

Spitzer, David. Jazzshots : a photographic essay / David Spitzer. — Miami : Zerkim Press, 1979. — II, 785.

Spottswood, Richard K. Ethnic music on records : a discography of ethnic recordings produced in the United States, 1893 to 1942 / Richard K. Spottswood. — Urbana : University of Illinois Press, 1990. — III, 227.

Spradling, Mary Mace. In black and white : a guide to magazine articles, newspaper articles, and books concerning more than 15,000 black individuals and groups / Mary Mace Spradling. — 3rd ed. — Detroit : Gale, 1980. — II, 486.

Stagg, Jerry. The brothers Shubert / Jerry Stagg. — New York : Random House, 1968. — I, 1261.

Stagg, Tom. New Orleans, the revival / Tom Stagg and Charlie Crump. — Dublin : Bashall Eaves, 1973. — I, 937.

Stallings, Penny. Rock & roll confidential / Penny Stallings. — Boston : Little, Brown, 1984. — II, A-726.

Stambler, Irwin. Encyclopedia of folk, country and western music / Irwin Stambler and Grelun Landon. — Rev. ed. — New York : St. Martin's, 1983. — III, 68.

Stambler, Irwin. Encyclopedia of folk, country and western music / Irwin Stambler and Grelun Landon. — New York : St. Martin's, 1969. — I, 610.

Stambler, Irwin. Encyclopedia of pop, rock & soul / Irwin Stambler. — Rev. ed. — New York : St. Martin's, 1989. — III, 77.

Stambler, Irwin. Encyclopedia of pop, rock & soul / Irwin Stambler, — New York : St. Martin's, 1975. — I, 1339.

Stambler, Irwin. Guitar years : pop music from country and western to hard rock / Irwin Stambler. — Garden City, N.Y. : Doubleday, 1970. — I, A-245.

Stampp, Kenneth M. Negro slavery in the American South / Kenneth M. Stampp. — London : Eyre & Spottiswoode, 1964. — I, 671.

Stampp, Kenneth M. The peculiar institution : slavery in the American South / Kenneth M. Stampp. — New York : Knopf, 1956. — I, 671.

Stancioff, Nadia. Maria : Callas remembered / Nadia Stancioff. — New York : Dutton, 1987. — III, 696.

Standifer, James A. Source book of African and Afro-American materials for music educators / James A. Standifer and Barbara Reeder. — Washington : Contemporary Music Project, 1972. — I, 699.

Standish, L. W. The Old Stoughton Musical Society / L. W. Standish. — Stoughton, Mass. [no publisher], 1929. — I, A-47.

Stanislaw, Richard J. A checklist of four-shape shape-note tunebooks / Richard J. Stanislaw. — Brooklyn : Institute for Studies in American Music, 1978. — II, 335.

Stanley, Billy. Elvis, my brother / Billy Stanley; with George Erikson. — New York : St. Martin's, 1989. — III, 840.

Stanley, Lawrence A. Rap : the lyrics / Lawrence A. Stanley; introduction by Jefferson Morley. — New York : Penguin, 1992. — III, 51.

Stanley, Rick. Caught in a trap / Rick Stanley; with Paul Harold. — Dallas : Word, 1992. — III, 841.

Stanton, Kenneth. Jazz theory : a creative approach / Kenneth Stanton. — New York : Taplinger, 1982. — II, A-405.

Staples, Samuel E. The ancient psalmody and hymnology of New England / Samuel E. Staples. — Worcester, Mass. : Jillson, 1880. — I, A-69.

Starer, Robert. Continuio : a life in music / Robert Starer — New York : Random House, 1987. — III, 522.

Stark, Richard B. Music of the bailes in New Mexico / ed. Richard B. Stark. — Santa Fe, N.M. : International Folk Art Foundation, 1978. — II, 436.

Stark, Richard B. Music of the Spanish folk plays of New Mexico / ed. Richard B. Stark. — Santa Fe, N.M. : Museum of New Mexico Press, 1969. — II, 437.

Starr, Larry. A union of diversities : style in the music of Charles Ives / Larry Starr. — New York : Schirmer, 1992. — III, 491.

Starr, S. Frederick. Red and hot : the fate of jazz in the Soviet Union, 1917–1980 / S. Frederick Starr. — New York : Oxford University Press, 1983. — II, A-420.

Staten, Vince. The real Elvis : good old boy / Vince Staten. — Dayton, Ohio : Media Ventures, 1978. — II, 1305.

Stearn, Jess. The truth about Elvis / Jess Stearn and Larry Geller. — New York : Jove Books, 1980. — II, 1306.

Stearns, Harold E. Civilization in the United States : an enquiry by thirty Americans / Harold E. Stearns. — New York : Harcourt, Brace, 1922. — I, 297.

Stearns, Marshall. Jazz dance : the story of American vernacular dance / Marshall Stearns and Jean Stearns. — New York : Macmillan, 1968. — I, 1007.

Stearns, Marshall. The story of jazz / Marshall Stearns. — Rev. ed. — New York : New American Library, 1958. — I, 1008.

Stebbins, George C. Reminiscences and gospel hymn stories / George C. Stebbins. — New York : George H. Doran, 1924. — I, 75.

Stecheson, Anthony. The Stecheson classified song directory / Anthony Stecheson and Anne Stecheson. — Hollywood : Music Industry Press, 1961. — II, 807.

Steelman, Robert. Catalog of the Lititz congregation collection / Robert Steelman. — Chapel Hill : University of North Carolina Press, 1981. — II, A-29.

Steenson, Martin. Blues unlimited 1–50 : an index / Martin Steenson. — London : Author, 1971. — I, 810.

Stehman, Dan. Roy Harris : a bio bibliography / Dan Stehman. — New York : Greenwood, 1991. — III, 166.

Stehman, Dan. Roy Harris : an American musical pioneer / Dan Stehman. — Boston : Twayne, 1984. — II, A-125.

Stein, Charles W. American vaudeville as seen by its contemporaries / Charles W. Stein. — New York : Knopf, 1984. — II, A-567.

Steiner, Wendy. The sign in music and literature / ed. Wendy Steiner. — Austin : University of Texas Press, 1981. — II, A-472.

Steinzor, Curt Efram. American musicologists, c. 1890–1945 : a bio-bibliographical sourcebook to the formative period / Curt Efram Steinzor. — New York : Greenwood, 1989. — III, 136.

Stern, Jane. Elvis world / Jane Stern and Michael Stern. — New York : Knopf, 1987. — III, 842.

Stern, Lee Edward. Jeanette MacDonald / Lee Edward Stern. — New York : Jove Books, 1979. — II, 981.

Stern, Lee Edward. The movie musical / Lee Edward Stern. — New York : Pyramid, 1974. — II, 1061.

Sternfeld, F. W. Music in the modern age / F. W. Sternfeld. — New York : Praeger, 1973. — (History of western music, 5) — I, 267.

Stevens, Denis. History of song / Denis Stevens. — London : Hutchinson, 1960. — I, 49.

Stevenson, Arthur L. The story of southern hymnology / Arthur L. Stevenson. — Salem, Va. : Author, 1931. — I, 69.

Stevenson, Janet. Marian Anderson : singing to the world / Janet Stevenson. — Chicago : Encyclopaedia Britannica Press, 1963. — I, A-157.

Stevenson, Robert. Philosophies of American music history : a lecture / Robert Stevenson. — Washington : Library of Congress, 1970. — I, 43.

Stevenson, Robert. Protestant church music in America : a short survey of men and movements from 1564 to the present / Robert Stevenson. — New York : Norton, 1966. — I, 63.

Steward, Sue. Signed, sealed and delivered : true life stories of women in pop / Sue Steward and Cheryl Carratt. — London : Pluto, 1984. — II, A-765.

Stewart, Rex. Boy meets horn / Rex Stewart; ed. Claire P. Gordon. — Ann Arbor : University of Michigan Press, 1991. — III, 669.

Stewart, Rex. Jazz masters of the thirties / Rex Stewart. — New York : Macmillan, 1972. — I, 1039.

Stewart, Tony. Cool cats : 25 years of rock 'n' roll style / Tony Stewart. — London : Eel Pie, 1981. — II, A-755.

Stewart-Baxter, Derrick. Ma Rainey and the classic blues singers / Derrick Stewart-Baxter. — London : Studio Vista, 1970. — I, 833.

Still, Judith Anne. William Grant Still : a voice high-sounding / Judith Anne Still. — Flagstaff, Ariz. : Master-Player Library, 1990. — III, 523.

Stock, Dennis. Jazz street / Dennis Stock. — London : Deutsch, 1960. — I, A-221.

Stoddard, Hope. Symphony conductors of the U.S.A. / Hope Stoddard. — New York : Crowell, 1957. — I, 371.

Stoddard, Tom. Jazz on the Barbary Coast / Tom Stoddard. — Chigwell, Essex, England : Storyville, 1982. — II, A-446.

Stokes, Geoffrey. Star-making machinery : inside the business of rock and roll / Geoffrey Stokes. — Indianapolis : Bobbs-Merrill, 1976. — II, 1162.

Stokes, W. Royal. The jazz scene : an informal history from New Orleans to 1990 / W. Royal Stokes. — New York : Oxford, 1991. — III, 1091.

Stoller, Lee. One day at a time / Lee Stoller; with Pete Chaney. — New York : St. Martin's, 1986. — III, 759.

Stoneburner, Bryan C. Hawaiian music : an annotated bibliography / Bryan C. Stoneburner. — Westport, Conn. : Greenwood, 1986. — III, 105.

Story, Rosalyn M. And so I sing : African-American divas of opera and concert / Rosalyn M. Story. — New York : Warner Books, 1990. — III, 445.

Stoutamire, Albert. Music of the old South : colony to confederacy / Albert Stoutamire. — Rutherford, N.J. : Fairleigh Dickinson University Press, 1972. — I, 122.

Strachwitz, Chris. American folk music occasional, no. 2 / ed. Chris Strachwitz and Pete Welding. — New York : Oak, 1970. — I, 646.

Strait, Raymond. Lanza : his tragic life / Raymond Strait and Terry Robinson. — Englewood Cliffs, N.J. : Prentice-Hall, 1980. — II, 978.

Strang, Lewis C. Celebrated comedians of light opera and musical comedy in America / Lewis C. Strang. — Boston : L. C. Page, 1901. — II, 1051.

Strassburg, Robert. Roy Harris : a catalog of his works / Robert Strassburg. — Los Angeles : California State University Press, 1973. — II, 186.

Stratemann, Klaus. Buddy Rich and Gene Krupa : a filmo-discography / Klaus Stratemann. — Lübeck, Germany : Uhle & Kleimann, 1980. — II, 775.

Stratemann, Klaus. Duke Ellington day by day and film by film / Klaus Stratemann. — Copenhagen : JazzMedia, 1992. — III, 470.

Stratemann, Klaus. Negro bands on film / Klaus Stratemann. — Lübeck, Germany : Uhle & Kleimann, 1981. — II, A-366.

Stratman, Carl J. Bibliography of the American theater, excluding New York City / Carl J. Stratman. — Chicago : Loyola University Press, 1965. — I, A-64.

Street, John. "No satisfaction?" : politics and popular music / John Street. — Exeter, England : IASPM/UK, 1985. — II, A-736.

Strickland, Edward. American composers : dialogues on contemporary music / Edward Strickland. — Bloomington : Indiana University Press, 1991. — III, 414.

Stricklin, Al. My years with Bob Wills / Al Stricklin and Jon McConal. — San Antonio : Naylor, 1976. — II, 421.

Strobel, Jerry. Grand Ole Opry : WSM picture-history book / Jerry Strobel. — Nashville : WSM, 1979. — II, 480.

Stroff, Stephen M. Discovering great jazz : a new listener's guide to the sounds and styles of the top musicians and their recordings on CDs, LPs, and cassettes / Stephen M. Stroff. — New York : Newmarket, 1991. — III, 1092.

Strothoff, Wolfgang. Verzeichnis deutschsprächiger musikpädagogischer Schriften zur afro-americanischen Musik / Wolfgang Strothoff. — Bremen, Germany : Archiv für Populäre Musik, 1977. — II, 588.

Stuart, Jay Allison. Call him George / Jay Allison Stuart. — London : Peter Davies, 1961. — I, 1122.

Stuart, Philip. Igor Stravinsky : the composer in the recording studio : comprehensive discography / Philip Stuart. — New York : Greenwood, 1991. — III, 284.

Studies in jazz discography / ed. Walter C. Allen. — Newark, N.J. : Rutgers University, 1971. — I, 953.

Stuessy, Joe. Rock 'n' roll : its history and stylistic development / Joe Stuessy. — Englewood Cliffs, N.J. : Prentice-Hall, 1990. — III, 1194.

Sudhalter, Richard M. Bix : man and legend / Richard M. Sudhalter and Philip R. Evans. — New Rochelle, N.Y. : Arlington House, 1974. — I, 1091.

Sudhalter, Richard M. Henry "Red" Allen / Richard M. Sudhalter; notes on the music by John Chilton. — Alexandria, Va. : Time-Life Records, 1981. — III, 596.

Sugerman, Daniel. Appetite for destruction : the days of Guns 'n' Roses / Daniel Sugerman. — New York : St. Martin's, 1991. — III, 916.

Sugerman, Daniel. The Doors : the complete illustrated lyrics / Daniel Sugerman. — New York : Hyperion, 1991. — III, 52.

Sugerman, Daniel. The Doors : the illustrated history / Daniel Sugerman. — New York : Morrow, 1983. — II, A-779.

Summerfield, Maurice J. The jazz guitar : its evolution and its players / Maurice J. Summerfield. — Gateshead, England : Ashley Mark, 1978. — II, 634.

Sumner, Melody. The guests go in to supper / ed. Melody Sumner, Kathleen Burch, and Michael Sumner. — Oakland, Calif. : Burning Books, 1986. — III, 1260.

Suskin, Steven. Berlin, Kern, Rodgers, Hart, and Hammerstein : a complete song catalogue / Steven Suskin; foreword by Theodore S. Chapin. — Jefferson, N.C. : McFarland, 1990. — III, 143.

Suskin, Steven. Opening night on Broadway : a critical quotebook of the golden era of the musical theatre / Steven Suskin. — New York : Schirmer, 1990. — III, 1021.

Suskin, Steven. Show tunes, 1905–1985 : the songs, shows, and careers of Broadway's major composers / Steven Suskin. — Rev. ed. — New York : Limelight, 1992. — III, 415.

Sutton, Allan. A guide to pseudonyms on American records, 1892–1942 / Allan Sutton. — Westport, Conn. : Greenwood, 1993. — III, 365.

Svinin, Paul. Picturesque United States of America, 1811, 1812, 1813 / Paul Svinin. — New York : Rudge, 1930. — I, A-169.

Swain, Joseph P. The Broadway musical : a critical and musical survey / Joseph P. Swain. — New York : Oxford, 1990. — III, 1015.

Swan, Howard. Music in the southwest, 1825–1950 / Howard Swan. — San Marino, Calif. : Huntington Library, 1952. — I, 132.

Swan, Peter. Joan Baez : a bio-disco-bibliography / Peter Swan. — Brighton, England : John L. Noyce, 1977. — II, 355.

Swanekamp, Joan. Diamonds & rust : a bibliography and discography on Joan Baez / Joan Swanekamp. — Ann Arbor, Mich. : Pierian Press, 1980. — II, 356.

Swann, Brian. Smoothing the ground : essays on Native American oral literature. — Brian Swann. — Berkeley : University of California Press, 1983. — II, A-163.

Swartz, Jon D. Handbook of old-time radio : a comprehensive guide to golden age radio listening and collecting / Jon D. Swartz and Robert C. Reinehr. — Metuchen, N.J. : Scarecrow, 1992. — III, 59.

Sweet, Charles Filkins. A champion of the cross : being the life of John Henry Hopkins / Charles Filkins Sweet. — New York : Pott, 1894. — I, A-24.

Swenson, John. Bill Haley : the daddy of rock and roll, / John Swenson. — London : W. H. Allen, 1982. — II, A-799.

Swenson, John. Simon & Garfunkel / John Swenson. — London : W. H. Allen, 1984. — II, A-841.

Swenson, John. Stevie Wonder / John Swenson. — New York : Harper, 1986. — III, 892.

Swenson, John. The Eagles / John Swenson. — New York : Ace, 1981. — II, A-793.

Swenson, John. The *Rolling Stone* jazz record guide / John Swenson. — New York : Random House, 1985. — II, A-388.

Swenson, Karen. Barbra, the second decade / Karen Swenson. — Secaucus, N.J. : Citadel, 1986. — III, 870.

Swoboda, Henry. The American symphony orchestra / Henry Swoboda. — Washington : Voice of America, 1967. — I, 372.

Sylvester, Robert. No cover charge : a backward look at the night clubs / Robert Sylvester. — New York : Dial, 1956. — II, 831a.

Symmes, Thomas. The reasonableness of regular singing or singing by note / Thomas Symmes. — Boston : Samuel Gerrish, 1720. — I, 193.

Symmes, Thomas. Utile dulci, or a joc-serious dialogue concerning regular singing / Thomas Symmes. — Boston : Samuel Gerrish, 1723. — I, 199.

Szatmary, David P. Rockin' in time : a social history of rock and roll / David P. Szatmary. — 2nd ed. — Englewood Cliffs, N.J. : Prentice-Hall, 1987. — III, 1195.

Szwed, John F. Afro-American folk culture : an annotated bibliography / John F. Szwed and Roger D. Abrahams. — Philadelphia : Institute for the Study of Human Issues, 1978. — II, 487.

Szwed, John F. Black Americans / John F. Szwed. — New York : Basic Books, 1970. — I, 679.

Taft, Michael. Blues lyric poetry : a concordance / Michael Taft. — New York : Garland, 1984. — II, A-313.

Tagg, Philip. Kojak : 50 seconds of television music / Philip Tagg. — Gothenburg, Sweden : Gothenburg University, 1979. — II, 941.

Tallant, Robert. Mardi gras / Robert Tallant. — Garden City, N.Y. : Doubleday, 1948. — II, 494.

Tallant, Robert. Voodoo in New Orleans / Robert Tallant. — New York : Macmillan, 1946. — I, 1070.

Talley, John B. Secular music in colonial Annapolis : the Tuesday Club, 1745–56 / John B. Talley. — Urbana : University of Illinois Press, 1988. — III, 386.

Talley, Thomas W. Negro folk rhymes, wise and otherwise : with a study / Thomas W. Talley. — New York : Macmillan, 1922. — I, 752.

Tanner, Paul O. W. A study of jazz / Paul O. W. Tanner and Maurice Gerow. — 4th ed. — Dubuque, Iowa : Brown, 1981. — II, 666.

Tanner, Paul O. W. Jazz / Paul O. W. Tanner, David W. Megill, and Maurice Gerow. — 7th ed. — Dubuque, Iowa : W. C. Brown, 1992. — III, 1093.

Taraborrelli, J. Randy. Call her Miss Ross : the unauthorized biography of Diana Ross / J. Randy Taraborrelli. — New York : Birch Lane, 1989. — III, 853.

Taraborrelli, J. Randy. Cher! / Mark Bego. — New York : Pocket Books, 1986. — III, 701.

Taraborrelli, J. Randy. Michael Jackson : the magic and the madness / J. Randy Taraborrelli. — Secaucus, N.J. : Carol, 1991. — III, 747.

Taraborrelli, J. Randy. Motown : hot wax, city cool & solid gold / J. Randy Taraborrelli. — Garden City, N.Y. : Doubleday, 1986. — III, 1251.

Tassin, Myron. Fifty years at the Grand Ole Opry / Myron Tassin. — Gretna, La. : Pelican, 1975. — II, 380.

Tatar, Elizabeth. Nineteenth century Hawaiian chant / Elizabeth Tatar. — Honolulu : Department of Anthropology, Bishop Museum, 1982. — III, 382.

Tatar, Elizabeth. Strains of change : the impact of tourism on Hawaiian music / Elizabeth Tatar. — Honolulu : Bishop Museum Press, 1987. — III, 383.

Tate, Greg. Flyboy in the buttermilk : essays on contemporary America / Greg Tate. — New York : Simon & Schuster, 1992. — III, 1072.

Tatham, David. The lure of the striped pig : the illustration of popular music in America, 1820–1870 / David Tatham. — Barre, Mass. : Imprint Society, 1973. — I, A-246.

Taubman, Joseph. In tune with the music business / Joseph Taubman. — New York : Law Arts, 1980. — II, 221.

Taussig, Harry. Folk style autoharp / Harry Taussig. — New York : Oak, 1967. — I, A-142.

Taussig, Harry. Instrumental techniques of American folk guitar / Harry Taussig. — Laguna Beach, Calif. : Traditonal Stringed Instruments, 1965. — I, A-143.

Tawa, Nicholas E. A most wondrous babble : American art composers, their music, and the American scene, 1950–1985 / Nicholas E. Tawa. — Westport, Conn. : Greenwood, 1987. — III, 378.

Tawa, Nicholas E. A sound of strangers / Nicholas E. Tawa. — Metuchen, N.J. : Scarecrow, 1982. — II, A-180.

Tawa, Nicholas E. Art music in the American society : the condition of art music in the late twentieth century / Nicholas E. Tawa. — Metuchen, N.J. : Scarecrow, 1987. — III, 376.

Tawa, Nicholas E. Mainstream music of early twentieth-century America : the composers, their times, and their works / Nicholas E. Tawa. — New York : Greenwood, 1992. — III, 377.

Tawa, Nicholas E. Music for the millions : antebellum democratic attitudes and the birth of American popular music / Nicholas Tawa. — New York : Pendragon, 1984. — II, A-545.

Tawa, Nicholas E. Serenading the reluctant eagle : American musical life 1925–1945 / Nicholas E. Tawa. — New York : Schirmer, 1984. — II, A-154.

Tawa, Nicholas E. Sweet songs for gentle Americans : the parlor song in America, 1790–1860 / Nicholas E. Tawa. — Bowling Green, Ohio : Bowling Green State University Popular Press, 1980. — II, 878.

Tawa, Nicholas E. The coming of age of American art music : New England's classical romanticists / Nicholas E. Tawa. — New York : Greenwood, 1991. — III, 372.

Tawa, Nicholas E. The way to Tin Pan Alley : American popular song, 1866–1910 / Nicholas E. Tawa. — New York : Schirmer, 1990. — III, 1065.

Taylor, Arthur. Notes and tones : musician to musician interviews / Arthur Taylor. — Liege, Belgium : Author, 1977. — II, 723.

Taylor, Billy. Jazz piano : a jazz history / Billy Taylor. — Dubuque, Iowa : Brown, 1983. — II, A-421.

Taylor, Deems. Some enchanted evenings : the story of Rodgers and Hammerstein / Deems Taylor. — New York : Harper, 1953. — I, 1299.

Taylor, Frank C. Alberta Hunter : a celebration in blues / Frank C. Taylor; with Gerald Cook. — New York : McGraw-Hill, 1987. — III, 739.

Taylor, George H. The American high school band / George H. Taylor. — New York : Richard Rosen, 1977. — II, 1037.

Taylor, Jo Gray. Negro slavery in Louisiana / Jo Gray Taylor. — Baton Rouge : Louisiana Historical Association, 1963. — II, 595.

Taylor, John Russell. The Hollywood musical / John Russell Taylor and Arthur Jackson. — London : Secker & Warburg, 1971. — I, 1267.

Taylor, Marshall W. A collection of revival hymns and plantation melodies / ed. Marshall W. Taylor. — Cincinnati : M. W. Taylor & W. C. Echols, 1883. — II, 611.

Taylor, Paul. Popular music since 1955 : a critical guide to the literature / Paul Taylor. — Boston : G. K. Hall, 1985. — III, 140.

Taylor, Ronald. Kurt Weill : a composer in a divided world / Ronald Taylor. — Boston : Northeastern University Press, 1992. — III, 534.

Taylor, Theodore. Jule : the story of composer Jule Styne / Theodore Taylor. — New York : Random House, 1979. — II, 965.

Taylor, Togan. The death and resurrection show : from shaman to superstar / Rogan Taylor. — London : Blond & Briggs, 1984. — II, A-537.

Tee, Ralph. Soul music : who's who / Ralph Tee. — Rocklin, Calif. : Prima, 1992. — III, 82.

Tefft, Lulu Sanford. Little intimate stories of Charles Wakefield Cadman / Lulu Sanford Tefft. — Hollywood : David Graham Fischer, 1926. — I, A-85.

Teichmann, Howard. George II, Kaufman : an intimate portrait / Howard Teichmann. — New York : Atheneum, 1972. — II, 954.

Tellstrom, A. Music in American education past and present / A. Tellstrom . — New York : Holt, Rinehart & Winston, 1971. — II, 102.

Temperley, Nicholas. Fuging tunes in the eighteenth century / Nicholas Temperley and Charles G. Manns. — Detroit : Information Coordinators, 1983. — II, A-76.

Templeton, Steve. The best of Elvis collectibles / Steve Templeton and Rosalind Cranor; contributing editors John Diesso and Ted Young. — Johnson City, Tenn. : Overmountain, 1992. — III, 843.

Tenney, James. Meta (+) Hodos / James Tenney. — New Orleans : Inter-American Institute for Musical Research of Tulane University, 1964. — I, A-86.

Ténot, Frank. Le jazz / Frank Ténot and Philippe Carles. — Paris : Larousse, 1977. — II, 707.

Tercinet, Alain. Stan Getz / Alain Tercinet. — Montpellier, France : Limon, 1989. — III, 636.

Terenzio, Maurice. The Soundies Distributing Corporation of America : a his-

Thomas, Bob. The one and only Bing / Bob Thomas. — New York : Grosset & Dunlap, 1977. — II, 990.

Thomas, J. C. Chasin' the Trane : the music and mystique of John Coltrane / J. C. Thomas. — Garden City, N.Y. : Doubleday, 1975. — I, 1096.

Thomas, Jean. Ballad makin' in the mountains of Kentucky / Jean Thomas. — New York : Oak, 1964. — I, 493.

Thomas, Jean. Devil's ditties : being stories of the Kentucky mountain folk / Jean Thomas. — Chicago : Hatfield, 1931. — I, A-121.

Thomas, Jean. The singin' fiddler of Lost Hope Hollow / Jean Thomas. — New York : Dutton, 1938. — I, A-122.

Thomas, Jean. The singin' gatherin' : tunes from the southern Appalachians / Jean Thomas and Joseph A. Leeder. — New York : Silver Burdett, 1939. — I, 494.

Thomas, Jeffrey Ross. Forty years of steel : an annotated discography of steel band and pan recordings, 1951–1991 / Jeffrey Ross Thomas. — Westport, Conn. : Greenwood, 1992. — III, 283.

Thomas, Lawrence. The MGM years / Lawrence Thomas. — New York : Columbia House, 1972. — II, 933.

Thomas, Margaret F. Musical Alabama / Margaret F. Thomas. — Montgomery, Ala. : Paragon, 1925. — I, A-48.

Thomas, Rose Fay. Memoirs of Theodore Thomas / Rose Fay Thomas. — New York : Moffat, Yard, 1911. — I, 247.

Thomas, Theodore. A musical autobiography / Theodore Thomas; ed. George P. Upton. — Chicago : McClurg, 1905. — I, 248.

Thomas, Tony. Film score : the view from the podium / Tony Thomas. — South Brunswick, N.J. : Barnes, 1979. — II, 942.

Thomas, Tony. Harry Warren and the Hollywood musical / Tony Thomas. — Secaucus, N.J. : Citadel, 1975. — I, 1303.

Thomas, Tony. Music for the movies / Tony Thomas. — New York : Barnes, 1973. — I, 1315.

Thomas, Tony. That's dancing / Tony Thomas. — New York : Abrams, 1985. — II, A-578.

Thomas, Tony. The Busby Berkeley book / Tony Thomas and Jim Terry. — Greenwich, Conn. : New York Graphic Society, 1973. — II, 934.

Thomas, Tony. The films of Gene Kelly, song and dance man / Tony Thomas. — Secaucus, N.J. : Citadel, 1974. — II, 977.

Thomason, Jean. Shaker manuscript hymnals from South Union, Kentucky / Jean Thomason. — Bowling Green, Ky. : Kentucky Folklore Society, 1967. — II, 336.

Thompson, Charles. Bing : the authorized biography / Charles Thompson. — London : W. H. Allen, 1975. — II, 991.

Thompson, Charles C., II. The death of Elvis : what really happened / Charles C. Thompson, II. — New York : Delacorte, 1991. — III, 844.

Thompson, Donald. Music and dance in Puerto Rico from the age of Columbus to modern times : an annotated bibliography / Donald Thompson and Annie F. Thompson. — Metuchen, N.J. : Scarecrow, 1991. — III, 108.

Thompson, Douglas. Madonna revealed : the unauthorized biography / Douglas Thompson. — Secaucus, N.J. : Carol, 1991. — III, 776.

Thompson, Harold W. A pioneer songster / ed. Harold W. Thompson. — Ithaca, N.Y. : Cornell University Press, 1958. — II, 288.

Thompson, Kenneth. A dictionary of twentieth-century composers (1911–1971) / Kenneth Thompson. — London : Faber & Faber, 1973. — I, 258.

Thompson, Oscar. American singer : a hundred years of success in opera / Oscar Thompson. — New York : Dial, 1937. — I, 145.

Thompson, Toby. Positively main street : an unorthodox view of Bob Dylan / Toby Thompson. — New York : Coward-McCann, 1971. — I, A-302.

Thompson, Vance. The life of Ethelbert Nevin / Vance Thompson. — Boston : Boston Music Co., 1913. — I, A-73.

Thomson, David. Fats Waller / David Thomson. — Alexandria, Va. : Time-Life Records, 1980. — III, 575.

Thomson, Elizabeth M. Conclusions on the wall : new essays on Bob Dylan / ed. Elizabeth M. Thomson. — Manchester, England : Thin Man, 1980. — II, 1204.

Thomson, Elizabeth. The Dylan companion / ed. Elizabeth Thomson and David Gutman. — New York : Delta Books, 1991. — III, 711.

Thomson, Liz. New women in rock / Liz Thomson. — London : Omnibus, 1982. — II, A-766.

Thomson, Ryan J. The fiddler's almanac / Ryan J. Thomson. — Newmarket, N.H. : Captain Fiddle Publications, 1985. — III, 993.

Thomson, Virgil. A Virgil Thomson reader / Virgil Thomson. — Boston : Houghton Mifflin, 1981. — II, A-141.

Thomson, Virgil. American music since 1910 / Virgil Thomson. — New York : Holt, Rinehart & Winston, 1971. — I, 298.

Thomson, Virgil. Music reviewed, 1940–1954 / Virgil Thomson. — New York : Vintage, 1967. — I, 383.

Thomson, Virgil. Music, right and left / Virgil Thomson. — New York : Holt, 1951. — I, 382.

Thomson, Virgil. Music with words : a composer's view / Virgil Thomson. — New Haven, Conn. : Yale University Press, 1989. — III, 1007.

Thomson, Virgil. The art of judging music / Virgil Thomson. — New York : Knopf, 1948. — I, 381.

Thomson, Virgil. The musical scene / Virgil Thomson. — New York : Knopf, 1945. — I, 380.

Thomson, Virgil. The state of music / Virgil Thomson. — 2nd ed. — New York : Random House, 1962. — I, 379.

Thomson, Virgil. Virgil Thomson / Virgil Thomson. — New York : Knopf, 1966. — I, 349.

Thomson, William. Schoenberg's error / William Thomson. Philadelphia : University of Pennsylvania Press, 1991. — III, 514.

Thorgerson, Storm. Album cover album / Storm Thorgerson and Roger Dean. — Limpsfield, Surrey, England : Dragon's World, 1977. — II, 1168.

Thorp, N. Howard. Songs of the cowboys / N. Howard Thorp. — 2nd ed. — Boston : Houghton Mifflin, 1921. — I, 564.

Thorson, Scott. Behind the candelabra : my life with Liberace / Scott Thorson; with Alex Thorleifson. — New York : Dutton, 1988. — III, 561.

Thurman, Howard. Deep river / Howard Thurman. — 2nd ed. — New York : Harper, 1955. — I, 797.

Tick, Judith. American women composers before 1870 / Judith Tick. — Ann Arbor, Mich. : UMI Research Press, 1983. — II, A-19.

Tierney, Judith. A description of the George Korson Folklore Archive in the D. Leonard Corgan Library of Kings College, Wilkes Barre / Judith Tierney. — Wilkes Barre, Pa. : Kings College Press, 1973. — II, 462.

Tilch, K. D. Rock Musiker / K. D. Tilch. — Hamburg : Taurus Press, 1988. — III, 282a.

Tillis, Mel. Stutterin' boy : the autobiography of Mel Tillis / Mel Tillis. — New York : Rawson, 1984. — II, A-267.

Timner, W. E. Ellingtonia : the recorded music of Duke Ellington and his sidemen / W. E. Timner. — 2nd ed. — Metuchen, N.J. : Scarecrow, 1988. — III, 307.

Timner, W. E. The recorded music of Duke Ellington and his sidemen : a collector's manual / W. E. Timner. — Rev. ed. — Montreal : Author, 1979. — II, 648.

Tinker, Edward L. Corridos and calaveras / ed. Edward L. Tinker. — Austin : University of Texas Press, 1961. — II, 438.

Tinsley, Jim Bob. He was singin' this song / ed. Jim Bob Tinsley. — Gainseville : University Press of Florida, 1982. — II, A-211.

Tiomkin, Dimitri. Please don't hate me / Dimitri Tiomkin and Prosper Buranelli. — Garden City, N.Y. : Doubleday, 1961. — II, 1062.

Tirro, Frank. Jazz : a history / Frank Tirro. — New York : Norton, 1977. — II, 696.

Tischler, Alice. Fifteen black American composers : a bibliography of their works / Alice Tischler. — Detroit : Information Coordinators, 1981. — II, A-300.

Tischler, Barbara L. An American music : the search for an American musical identity / Barbara L. Tischler. — New York : Oxford, 1986. — III, 379.

Titon, Jeff Todd. Early downhome blues : a musical and cultural analysis / Jeff Todd Titon. — Urbana : University of Illinois Press, 1977. — II, 554.

Titon, Jeff Todd. From blues to pop / Jeff Titon. — Los Angeles : John Edwards Memorial Foundation, 1974. — I, 836.

Titon, Jeff Todd. Powerhouse for God : speech, chant, and song in an Appalachian Baptist church / Jeff Todd Titon. — Austin : University of Texas Press, 1988. — III, 3.

Titon, Jeff Todd. Worlds of music : an introduction to the music of the world's peoples / Jeff Todd Titon. — New York : Schirmer, 1984. — II, A-168.

Tobias, Henry. Music in my heart and borscht in my blood : an autobiography / Henry Tobias. — New York : Hippocrene, 1987. — III, 530.

Tobler, John. 25 years of rock / John Tobler and Pete Frame. — London : Hamlyn, 1980. — II, 1260.

Tobler, John. Elvis : the legend and the music / John Tobler and Richard Wootton. — London : Optimum Books, 1983. — II, A-833.

Tobler, John. Guitar greats / John Tobler and Stuart Grundy. — London : BBC, 1982. — II, A-61.

Tobler, John. Guitar heroes / John Tobler. — London : Marshall Cavendish, 1978. — II, 1178.

Tobler, John. The Beach Boys / John Tobler. — London : Phoebus, 1977. — II, 1188.

Tobler, John. The Buddy Holly story / John Tobler. — London : Plexus, 1979. — II, 1209.

Toll, Robert C. Blacking up : the minstrel show in nineteenth-century America / Robert C. Toll. — New York : Oxford University Press, 1974. — I, 1243.

Toll, Robert C. On with the show : the first century of show business in America / Robert C. Toll. — New York : Oxford University Press, 1976. — II, 883.

Toll, Robert C. The entertainment machine : American show business in the twentieth century / Robert C. Toll. — New York : Oxford University Press, 1982. — II, A-546.

Tolzmann, Don Heinrich. German-Americana : a bibliography / Don Heinrich Tolzmann. — Metuchen, N.J. : Scarecrow, 1975. — I, 10.

Tomkins, Calvin. The bride and the bachelors : five masters of the avant garde / Calvin Tomkins. — New York : Viking, 1968. — II, 181.

Tomkins, Calvin. The bride and the bachelors : the heretical courtship in modern art / Calvin Tomkins. — New York : Viking, 1965. — II, 181.

Tomlin, Pinky. The object of my affection : an autobiography / Pinky Tomlin; with Lynette Wert. — Norman : University of Oklahoma Press, 1981. — III, 873.

Tommasini, Anthony. Virgil Thomson's musical portraits / Anthony Tommasini. — New York : Pendragon, 1986. — III, 183.

Toop, David. The rap attack : African jive to New York hip hop / David Toop. — London : Pluto Press, 1984. — II, A-362.

Topping, Ray. New Orleans rhythm & blues record label listings / Ray Topping. — Bexhill-on-Sea, England : Flyright Records, 1978. — II, 562.

Torgoff, Martin. American fool : the roots and improbable rise of John Cougar Mellencamp / Martin Torgoff. — New York : St. Martin's, 1986. — III, 784.

Torgoff, Martin. The complete Elvis / Martin Torgoff. — New York : Delilah, 1982. — II, A-834.

Tormé, Mel. It wasn't all velvet : an autobiography / Mel Tormé. — New York : Viking, 1988. — III, 874.

Tormé, Mel. The other side of the rainbow : with Judy Garland on the dawn patrol / Mel Tormé. — New York : Morrow, 1970. — II, 1093.

Tormé, Mel. Traps, the drum wonder : the life of Buddy Rich / Mel Tormé. — New York : Oxford, 1991. — III, 663.

Tosches, Nick. Country : living legends and dying metaphors in America's biggest music / Nick Tosches. — New York : Scribner's, 1985. — II, 371.

Tosches, Nick. Country : the biggest music in America / Nick Tosches. — New York : Stein & Day, 1977. — II, 371.

Tosches, Nick. Daryl Hall/John Oates : dangerous dances / Nick Tosches. — New York : St. Martin's, 1984. — II, A-800.

Tosches, Nick. Dino : living high in the dirty business of dreams / Nick Tosches. — New York : Doubleday, 1992. — III, 780.

Tosches, Nick. Hellfire : the Jerry Lee Lewis story / Nick Tosches. — New York : Dell, 1982. — II, A-811.

Tosches, Nick. Unsung heroes of rock 'n' roll : the birth of rock in the wild years before Elvis / Nick Tosches. — Rev. ed. — New York : Harmony Books, 1991. — III, 425.

Tosches, Nick. Unsung heroes of rock & roll / Nick Tosches. — New York : Scribner's, 1984. — II, A-760.

Tourville, Tom W. Minnesota rocked! / Tom W. Tourville. — Spirit Lake, Iowa : Author, 1983. — II, A-708.

Townsend, Charles R. San Antonio rose : the life and music of Bob Wills / Charles R. Townsend. — Urbana : University of Illinois Press, 1976. — II, 422.

Tracey, Hugh. Chopi musicians : their music, poetry and instruments / Hugh Tracey. — New ed. — London : Oxford University Press, 1970. — I, A-162.

Traill, Sinclair. Concerning jazz / Sinclair Traill. — London : Faber & Faber, 1957. — II, 708.

Traill, Sinclair. Just jazz / Sinclair Traill and Gerald Lascelles. — London : Davies [varies] : 1957–1960. — I, 927.

Traill, Sinclair. Play that music : a guide to playing jazz / Sinclair Traill. — London : Faber, 1956. — I, A-224.

Traubel, Helen. St. Louis woman / Helen Traubel. — New York : Duell, Sloan & Pearce, 1959. — II, 73.

Traubner, Richard. Operetta : a theatrical history / Richard Traubner. — London : Gollancz, 1984. — II, A-558.

Traum, Happy. Finger-picking styles for guitar / Happy Traum. — New York : Oak, 1966. — I, A-144.

Travis, Dempsey. An autobiography of black jazz / Dempsey Travis. — Chicago : Urban Research Institute, 1983. — II, A-441.

Trent-Johns, Altona. Play songs of the deep South / Altona Trent-Johns. — Washington : Associated Publishers, 1944. — II, 613.

Trevena, Nigel. Lou Reed and the Velvets / Nigel Trevena. — Falmouth, Cornwall, England : Bantam, 1973. — II, 1313.

Tribe, Ivan M. Molly O'Day, Lynn Davis, and the Cumberland Mountain folks : a bio-discography / Ivan M. Tribe and John W. Morris. — Los Angeles : John Edwards Memorial Foundation, 1975. — II, 410.

Tribe, Ivan M. Mountaineer jamboree : country music in West Virginia / Ivan M. Tribe. — Lexington : University Press of Kentucky, 1984. — II, A-237.

Tricoire, Robert. Gian Carlo Menotti : l'homme et son oeuvre / Robert Tricoire. — Paris : Seghers, 1966. — I, 340.

Triggs, W. W. The great Harry Reser / W. W. Triggs. — London : Henry G. Waker, 1980. — II, 652.

Trolle, Frank H. James P. Johnson : father of the stride piano / Frank H. Trolle [et al]; ed. and annotated by Dick M. Bakker. — Alphen an de Rijn, Netherlands : Micrography, 1981. — III, 326.

Trotter, James M. Music and some highly musical people / James M. Trotter. — Boston : Lee & Shepard, 1878. — I, 700.

Trouser Press record guide / ed. Ira A. Robbins. — 4th ed. — New York : Collier Books, 1991. — III, 271.

Troxler, Niklaus. Jazzplakate / Niklaus Troxler. — Waakirchen, Germany : Oreos, 1991. — III, 64.

Troy, Sandy. One more Saturday night : reflections with the Grateful Dead family and Dead Heads / Sandy Troy. — New York : St. Martin's, 1991. — III, 915.

Tucker, Mark. Ellington : the early years / Mark Tucker. — Urbana : University of Illinois Press, 1991. — III, 471.

Tucker, Sophie. Some of these days / Sophie Tucker. — Garden City, N.Y. : Doubleday, 1948. — II, 1016.

Tudor, Dean. Black music / Dean Tudor and Nancy Tudor. — Littleton, Colo. : Libraries Unlimited, 1979. — II, 540.

Tudor, Dean. Contemporary popular music / Dean Tudor and Nancy Tudor. — Littleton, Colo. : Libraries Unlimited, 1979. — II, 817.

Tudor, Dean. Grass roots music / Dean Tudor and Nancy Tudor. — Littleton, Colo. : Libraries Unlimited, 1979. — II, 272.

Tudor, Dean. Jazz / Dean Tudor and Nancy Tudor. — Littleton, Colo. : Libraries Unlimited, 1979. — II, 661.

Tudor, Dean. Popular music : an annotated guide to recordings / Dean Tudor. — Littleton, Colo. : Libraries Unlimited, 1983. — II, A-517.

Tudor, Dean. Popular music periodicals index, 1973 / Dean Tudor and Nancy Tudor. — Metuchen, N.J. : Scarecrow, 1974. — I, 1162.

Tufts, John. An introduction to the singing of psalm-tunes, in a plain and easy method / John Tufts. — 5th ed. — Boston : S. Gerrish, 1726. — I, 196.

Tulane University. William Ransom Hogan Jazz Archive. Catalog of the William Ransom Hogan Jazz Archive : the collection of seventy-eight RPM phonograph recordings / Howard-Tilton Memorial Library, Tulane University. — Boston : G. K. Hall, 1984. — III, 193.

Tully, Marjorie. Annotated bibliography of Spanish folklore in New Mexico and southern Colorado / Marjorie Tully and Juan Rael. — Albuquerque : University of New Mexico Press, 1950. — II, 439.

Tumbusch, Tom. Guide to Broadway musical theatre / Tom Tumbusch. — New York : Richards Rosen, 1972. — I, 1262.

Turner, Frederick. Remembering song : encounters with the New Orleans jazz tradition / Frederick Turner. — New York : Viking, 1982. — II, A-445.

Turner, John Frayn. Frank Sinatra : a personal portrait / John Frayn Turner. — New York : Hippocrene, 1984. — II, A-639.

Turner, Martha Anne. The yellow rose of Texas : her saga and her song / Martha Anne Turner. — Austin, Tex. : Shoal Creek Publishers, 1976. — II, 866.

Turner, Patricia. Afro-American singers : an index and preliminary discography of long-playing recordings of opera, choral music, and song / Patricia Turner. — Minneapolis : Challenge Productions, 1977. — II, 509.

Turner, Patricia. Dictionary of Afro-American performers : 78 RPM and cylinder recordings of opera, choral music, and song, c.1900–1949 / Patricia Turner. — New York : Garland, 1990. — III, 87.

Turner, Tina. I, Tina : my life story / Tina Turner; with Kurt Loder. — New York : Morrow, 1986. — III, 878.

Turner, Tony. All that glittered : my life with the Supremes / Tony Turner; with Barbara Aria. — New York : Dutton, 1990. — III, 938.

Turner, Tony. Deliver us from temptation / Tony Turner; with Barbara Aria. — New York : Thunder's Mouth; Emeryville, Calif. : distributed by Publishers Group West, 1992. — III, 940.

Turpie, Mary C. American music for the study of American civilization / Mary

C. Turpie. — Minneapolis : University of Minnesota, Program in American Studies, 1954. — I, 19.

Tyler, Don. Hit parade : an encyclopedia of the top songs of the jazz, depression, swing, and sing eras / Don Tyler. — New York : Quill, 1985. — III, 78.

Tyler, Linda. Edward Burlingame Hill : a bio-bibliography / Linda Tyler. — New York : Greenwood, 1989. — III, 167.

Ulanov, Barry. A handbook of jazz / Barry Ulanov. — New York : Viking, 1957. — I, 970.

Ulanov, Barry. A history of jazz in America / Barry Ulanov. — New York : Viking, 1952. — I, 1009.

Ulanov, Barry. Duke Ellington / Barry Ulanov. — New York : Creative Age, 1946. — I, 1109.

Ulanov, Barry. The incredible Crosby / Barry Ulanov. — New York : McGraw-Hill, 1948. — I, A-282.

Ullman, Michael. Jazz lives : portrait in words and pictures / Michael Ullman. — Washington : New Republic Books, 1980. — II, 735.

Ulrich, Allan. The art of film music / Allan Ulrich. — Oakland, Calif. : Oakland Museum, 1976. — II, 943.

Ulrich, Homer. A centennial history of the Music Teachers National Association / Homer Ulrich. — Cincinnati : Music Teachers National Association, 1976. — II, 103.

Underhill, Ruth Murray. Singing for power : the song magic of the Papago Indians of southern Arizona / Ruth Murray Underhill. — Berkeley : University of California Press, 1938. — II, 257.

United States. Works Projects Administration. California. History of music in San Francisco. — San Francisco : W.P.A., 1939–1942. — I, 133.

University of Rochester. Institute of American Music. American composers' concerts, and festivals of American music, 1925–1971 : cumulative repertoire. — Rochester, N.Y. : The Institute, 1972. — II, 222.

University of Utah Library. Black bibliography. — Salt Lake City : The Library, 1974. — I, 655.

Unterbrink, Mary. Jazz women at the keyboard / Mary Unterbrink. — Jefferson, N.C. : McFarland, 1983. — II, A-454.

Upton, George P. Musical memories : my recollections of celebrities of the half century 1850–1900 / George P. Upton. — Chicago : McClurg, 1908. — I, 127.

Upton, William Treat. Anthony Philip Heinrich : a nineteenth-century composer in America / William Treat Upton. — New York : Columbia University Press, 1939. — I, 232.

Upton, William Treat. Art-song in America / William Treat Upton. — Boston : Ditson, 1930. — Supplement, 1969. — I, 50.

Upton, William Treat. William Henry Fry, American journalist and composer-critic / William Treat Upton. — New York : Crowell, 1954. — I, 224.

Urban, Peter. Rollende Worte : die Poesie des Rock / Peter Urban. — Frankfurt : Fischer, 1979. — II, 1141.

Uscher, Nancy. Your own way in music / Nancy Uscher. — New York : St. Martin's, 1992. — III, 1258.

Uslan, Michael. Dick Clark's the first 25 years of rock and roll / Michael Uslan and Bruce Solomon. — New York : Dell, 1981. — II, A-746.

Vehanen, Kosti. Marian Anderson : a portrait / Kosti Vehanen. — New York : McGraw-Hill, 1941. — I, 707.

Vellenga, Dirk. Elvis and the colonel / Dirk Vellenga; with Mick Farren. — New York : Delacorte, 1988. — III, 980.

Vennum, Thomas. The Ojibwa dance drum : its history and construction / Thomas Vennum, Jr. — Washington : Smithsonian Institution Press, 1982. — III, 998.

Venudor, Pete. The standard Kenton directory / Pete Venudor and Michael Sparke. — Amsterdam : Pete Venudor, 1968. — I, 950.

Vermorcken, Elizabeth Moorhead. These two were here : Louise Homer and Willa Cather / Elizabeth Moorhead Vermorcken. — Pittsburgh : University of Pittsburgh Press, 1950. — II, 233.

Vernon, Paul. The Sun legend / Paul Vernon. — London : Steve Lane, 1969. — I, 1346.

Vian, Boris. Autre écrits sur le jazz / Boris Vian. — Paris : Bourgeois, 1981–1982. — II, A-430.

Vian, Boris. Chroniques de jazz / Boris Vian. — Paris : Le Jeune Parque, 1967. — II, 786.

Vigeland, Carl A. In concert : onstage and offstage with the Boston Symphony Orchestra / Carl A. Vigeland. — New York : Morrow, 1989. — III, 389.

Villetard, Jean-François. Coleman Hawkins / Jean-François Villetard. — Amsterdam : Micrography, 1984- . — II, A-376.

Vinay, Gianfranco. L'America musicale di Charles Ives / Gianfranco Vinay. — Turin, Italy : Einaudi, 1974. — I, 334.

Vince, Alan. I remember Gene Vincent / Alan Vince. — Prescott, Lancs., England : Vintage Rock 'n' Roll Appreciation Society, 1977. — II, 1318.

Vinton, Bobby. The Polish prince / Bobby Vinton; with Robert E. Burger. — New York : M. Evans, 1978. — II, 1319.

Vinton, John. Dictionary of contemporary music / John Vinton. — New York : Dutton, 1974. — I, 259.

Vinton, John. Essays after a dictionary / John Vinton. — Lewisburg, Pa. : Bucknell University Press, 1977. — II, 161.

Virga, Patricia H. The American opera to 1790 / Patricia H. Virga. — Ann Arbor, Mich. : UMI Research Press, 1982. — II, A-23.

Vitz, Robert C. The queen and the arts : cultural life in nineteenth-century Cincinnati / Robert C. Vitz. — Kent, Ohio : Kent State University Press, 1989. — III, 1274.

Viva, Luigi. Pat Metheny / Luigi Viva. — Waakirchen, Germany : Oreos, 1990. — III, 587.

Vivier, Odile. Varèse / Odile Vivier. — Paris : Éditions du Seuil, 1973. — I, 355.

Vlach, John M. The Afro-American tradition in the decorative arts / John M. Vlach. — Cleveland : Cleveland Museum of Art, 1978. — II, 590.

Voce, Steve. Woody Herman / Steve Voce; discography by Tony Shoppee. — London : Apollo, 1986. — III, 645.

Voigt, John. Jazz music inprint / John Voigt and Randall Kane. — 2nd ed. — Boston : Hornpipe Music, 1978. Supplement, 1979. — II, 635.

Von Gunden, Heidi. The music of Ben Johnston / Heidi von Gunden. — Metuchen, N.J. : Scarecrow, 1986. — III, 492.

VonGunden, Heidi. The music of Pauline Oliveros / Heidi VonGunden. — Metuchen, N.J. : Scarecrow, 1983. — II, A-132.

VonSchmidt, Eric. Baby, let me follow you down : the illustrated story of the Cambridge folk years / Eric VonSchmidt and Jim Rooney. — Garden City, N.Y. : Anchor, 1979. — II, 352.

Vreede, Max E. Paramount 12000/13000 series / Max E. Vreede. — London : Storyville, 1971. — I, 811.

Vuijsje, Bert. De nieuwe jazz / Bert Vuijsje. — Baarn, Netherlands. — Bosch & Keuning, 1978. — II, 724.

Vulliamy, Graham. Jazz and blues / Graham Vulliamy. — London : Routledge & Kegan Paul, 1982. — II, A-415.

Wacholtz, Larry E. Inside country music / Larry E. Wacholtz. — New York : Billboard Publications, 1986. — III, 1253.

Waddington, C. H. Biology and the history of the future / ed. C. H. Waddington. — Edinburgh : Edinburgh University Press, 1972. — I, 311.

Wade, Dorothy. Music man : Ahmet Ertegun, Atlantic Records, and the triumph of rock 'n' roll / Dorothy Wade and Justine Picardie. — New York : Norton, 1990. — III, 977.

Wadhams, Wayne. Sound advice / Wayne Wadhams. — New York : Schirmer, 1990. — III, 1254.

Waldo, Terry. This is ragtime / Terry Waldo. — New York : Hawthorn, 1976. — II, 533.

Walker, Edward S. Don't jazz : it's music / Edward S. Walker. — Walsall, Staffs., England : Author, 1979. — II, 697.

Walker, Edward S. English ragtime : a discography / Edward S. Walker and Steven Walker. — Mastin Moor, England : Author, 1971. — I, 804.

Walker, Leo. The big band almanac / Leo Walker. — Pasadena, Calif. : Ward Ritchie Press, 1978. — II, 715.

Walker, Leo. The wonderful era of the great dance bands / Leo Walker. — Berkeley, Calif. : Howell-North, 1965. — I, A-225.

Walker, William. The Christian harmony / William Walker. — Philadelphia : Miller's Bible and Publishing House, 1866. — I, 535.

Walker, William. The southern harmony and musical companion / William Walker. — New ed. — Philadelphia : Miller, 1854. — I, 527.

Walker, Wyatt Tee. Somebody's calling my name : black sacred music and social change / Wyatt Tee Walker. — Valley Forge, Pa. : Judson Press, 1979. — II, 582.

Walker-Hill, Helen. Piano music by black women composers : a catalog of solo and ensemble works / Helen Walker-Hill. — New York : Greenwood, 1992. — III, 139.

Wall, Mick. Guns 'n' Roses : the most dangerous band in the world / Mick Wall. — London : Sidgwick & Jackson, 1991. — III, 917.

Wallace, Robert K. A century of music-making : the lives of Josef & Rosina Lhevinne / Robert K. Wallace. — Bloomington : Indiana University Press, 1976. — II, A-223.

Wallaschek, Richard. Primitive music / Richard Wallaschek. — New York : Longmans, Green, 1893. — I, A-188.

Waller, Don. The Motown story / Don Waller. — New York : Scribner's, 1985. — II, A-353.

Waller, Maurice. Fats Waller / Maurice Waller and Anthony Calabrese. — New York : Schirmer, 1977. — II, 770.

Walley, David. No commercial potential : the saga of Frank Zappa and the Mothers of Invention / David Walley. — New York : Dutton, 1972. — I, 1388.

Wallis, Roger. Big sounds from small peoples : the music industry in small countries / Roger Wallis and Krister Malm. — London : Constable, 1984. — II, A-526.

Wallraf, Rainer. Presley : eine Biographie / Rainer Wallraf. — Munich : Nüchtern, 1977. — II, 1307.

Walsh, Stephen. The music of Stravinsky / Stephen Walsh. — London : Routledge, 1987. — III, 529.

Walter, Thomas. The grounds and rules of musick explained / Thomas Walter. — Boston : S. Gerrish, 1721. — I, 197.

Walters, Raymond. Stephen Foster / Raymond Walters. — Princeton, N.J. : Princeton University Press, 1936. — I, 1213.

Walters, Raymond. The Bethlehem Bach Choir : an historical and interpretative sketch / Raymond Walters. — Boston : Houghton Mifflin, 1918. — I, 123.

Walthall, Daddy Bob. The history of country music / Daddy Bob Walthall. — Houston : Walthall, 1978. — II, 482.

Walton, Ortiz. Music : black, white and blue / Ortiz Walton. — New York : Morrow, 1972. — I, 701.

Ward, Ed. Michael Bloomfield : the rise and fall of an American guitar hero / Ed Ward. — Port Chester, N.Y. : Cherry Lane Books, 1983. — II, A-771.

Ward, Ed. Rock of ages : the *Rolling Stone* history of rock and roll / Ed Ward, Geoffrey Stokes, and Ken Tucker. — New York : Rolling Stone/Summit, 1986. — III, 1196.

Ware, W. Porter. P. T. Barnum presents Jenny Lind / W. Porter Ware. — Baton Rouge : Louisiana State University Press, 1980. — II, 153.

Wareing, Charles. Bugles for Beiderbecke / Charles Wareing and George Garlick. — London : Sidgwick & Jackson, 1958. — I, 1092.

Warfield, William. My music and my life / William Warfield; with Alton Miller. — Champaign, Ill. : Sagamore, 1991. — III, 883.

Warner, Alan. Who sang what (on the screen) / Alan Warner. — London : Angus & Robertson, 1984. — II, A-591.

Warner, Anne. Traditional American folk songs from the Anne & Frank Warner collection / ed. Anne Warner. — Syracuse, N.Y. : Syracuse University Press, 1984. — II, A-178.

Warner, Frank M. Folk songs and ballads of the Eastern seaboard / Frank M. Warner. — Macon, Ga. : Southern Press, 1963. — II, 289.

Warner, James A. Songs that made America / James A. Warner. — New York : Grossman, 1972. — II, 1031.

Warner, Jay. The *Billboard* book of American singing groups : a history, 1940–1990 / Jay Warner. — New York : Billboard Books, 1992. — III, 88.

Warner, Thomas E. Periodical literature on American music, 1620–1920 : a classified bibliography with annotations / Thomas E. Warner. — Warren, Mich. : Harmonie Park, 1988. — III, 103.

Warren, Fred. Music of Africa / Fred Warren and Lee Warren. — Englewood Cliffs, N.J. : Prentice-Hall, 1970. — I, 728.

Warren, Richard. Charles E. Ives : discography / Richard Warren. — New Haven, Conn. : Yale University Library, 1972. — I, 335.

Warrick, Mancel. The progress of gospel music / Mancel Warrick. — New York : Vantage, 1977. — II, 583.

Warrington, James. Short titles of books relating to or illustrating the history and practice of psalmody in the United States, 1620–1820 / James Warrington. — Philadelphia : Author, 1898. — I, 185.

Wasserman, Paul. Festivals sourcebook / Paul Wasserman. — 2nd ed. — Detroit : Gale, 1984. — II, A-172.

Waters, Edward N. Victor Herbert : a life in music / Edward N. Waters. — New York : Macmillan, 1955. — I, 1289.

Waters, Ethel. His eye is on the sparrow : an autobiography / Ethel Waters; with Charles Samuels. — Garden City, N.Y. : Doubleday, 1951. — I, 854.

Waters, Ethel. To me it's wonderful / Ethel Waters. — New York : Harper & Row, 1972. — I, 855.

Watson, Deek. The story of the Ink Spots / Deek Watson; with Lee Stephenson. — New York : Vantage, 1967. — II, 563.

Watson, John F. Methodist error / John F. Watson. — Trenton, N.J. : D. & E. Fenton, 1819. — I, 741.

Wattiau, Georges. Book's book : a discography of Booker Ervin / Georges Wattiau. — Amsterdam : Micrography, 1987. — III, 308.

Way, Chris. In the Miller mood : a history and discography of the Glenn Miller service band, 1942–1945 / Chris Way; preface by Herb Miller. — [n.p.] : Author, 1987. — III, 343.

Way, Chris. The big bands go to war / Chris Way. — Edinburgh, Scotland : Mainstream, 1991. — III, 1144.

Webber, Malcolm. Medicine show / Malcolm Webber. — Caldwell, Idaho : Caxton Printers, 1941. — I, A-266.

Weber, Bruce. Let's get lost : starring Chet Baker : a film journal / Bruce Weber. — New York : MCA, 1988. — III, 601.

Weber, Horst. Charles Mingus : sein Leben, seine Musik, seine Schallplatten / Horst Weber. — Gauting-Buchendorf, Germany : Oreos, 1984. — II, A-488.

Weber, J. F. Carter and Schuman / J. F. Weber. — Utica, N.Y. : Author, 1978. — II, 183.

Weber, J. F. Edgard Varèse / J. F. Weber. — Utica, N.Y. : Author, 1975. — II, 202.

Weber, J. F. Leonard Bernstein / J. F. Weber. — Utica, N.Y. : Author, 1975. — II, 176.

Wehmeyer, Grete. Edgard Varèse / Grete Wehmeyer. — Regensburg, Germany : Bosse, 1977. — II, 203.

Weichlein, William J. A checklist of American periodicals, 1850–1900 / William J. Weichlein. — Detroit : Information Coordinators, 1970. — I, 249.

Weil, Susanne. Steppin' out : a guide to live music in Manhattan / Susanne Weil and Barry Singer. — Charlotte, N.C. : East Woods Press, 1980. — II, 831b.

Weill, Gus. You are my sunshine : the Jimmie Davis story / Gus Weill. — Waco, Tex. : Word Books, 1977. — II, 398.

Weill, Kurt. Ausgewählte Schriften / Kurt Weill. — Frankfurt, Germany : Suhrkamp, 1975. — I, 1304.

Weinberg, Barbara. Jazz space Detroit / Barbara Weinberg. — Detroit : Jazz Research Institute, 1980. — II, 729.

Weinberg, Max. The big beat : conversations with rock's great drummers / Max Weinberg and Robert Santelli. — Chicago : Contemporary Books, 1984. — II, A-761.

Weinman, Paul L. A bibliography of the Iroquoian literature, paritally annotated / Paul L. Weinman. — Albany : State University of New York, 1969. — I, 418.

Weinstein, Deena. Heavy metal : a cultural sociology / Deena Weinstein. — New York : Lexington Books, 1991. — III, 1197.

Weinstein, Norman C. A night in Tunisia : imaginings of Africa in jazz / Norman C. Weinstein. — Metuchen, N.J. : Scarecrow, 1992. — III, 1094.

Weir, Bob. Buck Clayton discography / Bob Weir. — Chigwell, Essex, England : Storyville, 1989. — III, 294.

Weir, William J. The songwriting racket and how to beat it / William J. Weir and Uno Goddard. — Palm Springs, Calif. : Cherokee Publishing, 1977. — II, 1271.

Weisberger, Bernard A. They gathered at the river : the story of the great revivalists and their impact upon religion in America / Bernard A. Weisberger. — Boston : Little, Brown, 1958. — I, 76.

Weiss, Piero. Music in the western world : a history in documents / ed. Piero Weiss and Richard Taruskin. — New York : Schirmer, 1984. — II, A-91.

Weissman, Dick. Music making in America / Dick Weissman. — New York : Ungar, 1982. — II, A-521.

Welch, Chris. Hendrix : a biography / Chris Welch. — London : Ocean Books, 1972. — I, 1381.

Welch, Chris. Take you higher : the Tina Turner experience / Chris Welch. — London : W. H. Allen, 1986. — III, 879.

Welding, Pete. Bluesland : portraits of twelve major American blues masters / ed. Pete Welding and Toby Byron. — New York : Dutton, 1991. — III, 437.

Welk, Lawrence. Lawrence Welk's musical family album / Lawrence Welk; with Bernice McGeehan. — Englewood Cliffs, N.J. : Prentice-Hall, 1977. — II, 1021.

Wells, Amos R. A treasure of hymns / Amos R. Wells. — Boston : Wilde, 1945. — II, 37.

Wells, Dicky. The night people : reminiscences of a jazzman / Dicky Wells; as told to Stanley Dance. — Boston : Crescendo, 1971. — I, 1144.

Wells, Dicky. The night people : the jazz life of Dicky Wells / Dicky Wells and Stanley Dance. — Washington : Smithsonian Institution Press, 1991. — III, 671.

Wells, Evelyn Kendrick. The ballad tree / Evelyn Kendrick Wells. — London : Methuen, 1950. — I, 471.

Wells, Katherine Gladney. Symphony and song : the Saint Louis Symphony Orchestra / Katherine Gladney Wells. — Woodstock, Vt. : Countryman, 1980. — II, 63.

Wenberg, Thomas James. The violin makers of the United States / Thomas James Wenberg. — Mt. Hood, Ore. : Mt. Hood Publishing Co., 1986. — III, 446.

Wendrich, Kenneth A. Essays on music in American education and society / Kenneth A. Wendrich. — Washington : University Press of America, 1982. — II, A-68.

Wenk, Arthur. Analyses of twentieth-century music : supplement / Arthur Wenk. — 2nd ed. — Boston : Music Library Association, 1984. — II, 167.

Wenk, Arthur. Analyses of twentieth-century music : supplement, 1970–1975 / Arthur Wenk. — Ann Arbor, Mich. : Music Library Association, 1976. — II, 167.

Wenk, Arthur. Analyses of twentieth-century music, 1940–1970 / Arthur Wenk. — Ann Arbor, Mich. : Music Library Association, 1975. — II, 167.

Wenner, Jann S. Twenty years of *Rolling Stone* : what a long, strange trip it's been / ed. Jann S. Wenner. — New York : Friendly Press, 1987. — III, 1050.

Wenzel, Lynn. I hear America singing : a nostalgic tour of popular sheet music / Lynn Wenzel and Carol J. Binkowski. — New York : Crown, 1989. — III, 1066.

Werner, Otto. The origin and development of jazz / Otto Werner; foreword by Dick Gibson. — 2nd ed. — Dubuque, Iowa : Kendall/Hunt, 1989. — III, 1124.

Werner, Otto. The origin and development of jazz / Otto Werner. — Dubuque, Iowa : Kendall/Hunt, 1984. — II, A-422.

Wernick, Peter. Bluegrass songbook / ed. Peter Wernick. — New York : Oal, 1976. — II, 483.

Wertheimer, Alfred. Elvis '56 : in the beginning / Alfred Wertheimer. — New York : Collier, 1979. — II, 1234.

Weschler-Vered, Artur. Jascha Heifetz / Artur Weschler-Vered and Julian Futter. — New York : Schirmer; London : Hale, 1986. — III, 579.

Wescott, Steven D. A comprehensive bibliography of music for film and television / Steven D. Wescott. — Detroit : Information Coordinators, 1985. — II, A-597.

West, John Foster. The ballad of Tom Dula / John Foster West. — Durham, N.C. : Moore Publishing, 1970. — II, 314.

West, Red. Elvis : what happened? / Red West [et al]. — New York : Ballantine, 1977. — II, 1235.

Westerberg, Hans. Boy from New Orleans : Louis "Satchmo" Armstrong on records, films, radio and television / Hans Westerberg. — Copenhagen : Jazzmedia, 1981. — II, A-372.

Western folklore, XXX. 3, July 1971. — Los Angeles : California Folklore Society, 1971. — I, 618.

Westin, Helen. Introducing the song sheet : a collector's guide with current price list / Helen Westin. — Nashville : Nelson, 1976. — II, 856.

Westlake, Neda M. Marian Anderson : a catalog of the collection at the University of Pennsylvania Library / Neda M. Westlake and Otto E. Albrecht. — Philadelphia : University of Pennsylvania Press, 1981. — II, A-308.

Westmoreland, Kathy. Elvis and Kathy / Kathy Westmoreland. — Glendale, Calif. : Glendale House, 1987. — III, 845.

Wetmore, Susannah. Mountain songs of North Carolina / ed. Susannah Wetmore and Marshall Bartholomew. — New York : Schirmer, 1926. — II, 315.

Wetzel, Richard D. Frontier musicians on the Connoquenessing, Wabash, and

Ohio / Richard D. Wetzel. — Athens, Ohio : Ohio University Press, 1976. — II, 60.

Whannel, Paddy. Jazz on film / Paddy Whannel. — London : British Film Institute, 1962. — I, 922.

Wheeler, Mary. Kentucky mountain songs / Mary Wheeler. — Boston : Boston Music Co., 1937, — I, A-123.

Wheeler, Mary. Roustabout songs : a collection of Ohio River valley songs / Mary Wheeler. — New York : Remick, 1939. — I, A-189.

Wheeler, Mary. Steamboatin' days : folk songs of the river packet era / Mary Wheeler. — Baton Rouge : Louisiana State University Press, 1944. — I, A-190.

Wheeler, Tom. American guitars : an illustrated history / Tom Wheeler. — Rev. ed. — New York : HarperCollins, 1992. — III, 996.

Wheeler, Tom. American guitars : an illustrated history / Tom Wheeler. — New York : Harper & Row, 1982. — II, A-62.

Whelan, Keith. Directory of record and CD retailers / Keith Whelan. — Wharton, N.J. : Power Communication Group, 1990. — III, 31.

Whisler, John A. Elvis Presley : reference guide and discography / John A. Whisler. — Metuchen, N.J. : Scarecrow, 1981. — II, A-821.

Whisnant, David E. All that is native and fine : the politics of culture in an American region / David E. Whisnant. — Chapel Hill : University of North Carolina Press, 1983. — II, A-187.

Whisnant, David E. Folk festival issues : report from a seminar, March 2–3, 1978 / David E. Whisnant. — Los Angeles : John Edwards Memorial Foundation, 1979. — II, 353.

Whitburn, Joel. *Billboard* 1990 music and video yearbook / Joel Whitburn. — Menomonee Falls, Wisc. : Record Research, 1992. — III, 277.

Whitburn, Joel. *Billboard* top 1000 singles, 1955–1990 / Joel Whitburn. — Milwaukee, Wisc. : Hal Leonard, 1991. — III, 274.

Whitburn, Joel. *Billboard's* top 3000, 1955–1987 / Joel Whitburn. — Menomonee Falls, Wisc. : Record Research, 1988. — III, 275.

Whitburn, Joel. Bubbling under the hot 100, 1959–1981 / Joel Whitburn. — Menomonee Falls, Wisc. : Record Research, 1982. — II, A-681.

Whitburn, Joel. Joel Whitburn presents the *Billboard* hot 100 charts : the eighties / Joel Whitburn. — Menomonee Falls, Wisc. : Record Research, 1991. — III, 276.

Whitburn, Joel. Pop annual 1955–1977 / Joel Whitburn. — Menomonee Falls, Wisc. : Record Research, 1978. — II, 1115.

Whitburn, Joel. Record research / Joel Whitburn. — Menomonee Falls, Wisc. : Record Research, 1970. — I, 1340.

Whitburn, Joel. The *Billboard* book of top 40 albums / Joel Whitburn. — Rev. ed. — New York : Billboard Books, 1991. — III, 272.

Whitburn, Joel. The *Billboard* book of top 40 hits / Joel Whitburn. — 5th ed. — New York : Billboard Books, 1989. — III, 273.

Whitburn, Joel. Top country and western records, 1949–1971 / Joel Whitburn. — Menomonee Falls, Wisc. : Record Research, 1972. — I, 632.

Whitburn, Joel. Top easy listening records 1961–1974 / Joel Whitburn. — Menomonee Falls, Wisc. : Record Research, 1975. — II, 818.

White, Mark. You must remember this : popular songwriters 1900–1980 / Mark White. — London : Warne, 1983. — II, A-518.

White, Newman Ivey. American negro folk-songs / Newman Ivey White. — Cambridge, Mass. : Harvard University Press, 1928. — I, 753.

White, Roger. Walk right back : the story of the Everly Brothers / Roger White. — London : Plexus, 1984. — II, A-794.

White, Timothy. Rock stars / Timothy White. — New York : Stewart, Tabori & Chang, 1984. — II, A-762.

White, William Carter. A history of military music in America / William Carter White. — New York : Exposition, 1944. — I, 1207.

Whiteley, Sheila. The space between the notes : rock and the counter-culture / Sheila Whiteley. — London and New York : Routledge, 1992. — III, 1198.

Whiteman, Paul. How to be a bandleader / Paul Whiteman and Leslie Lieber. — New York : McBride, 1941. — I, A-226.

Whiteman, Paul. Jazz / Paul Whiteman and Margaret McBride. — New York : Sears, 1926. — II, 713.

Whitesitt, Linda. The life and music of George Antheil / Linda Whitesitt. — Ann Arbor, Mich. : UMI Research Press, 1983. — III, 449.

Whitfield, Irene Therese. Louisiana French folk songs / Irene Therese Whitfield. — 2nd ed. — New York : Dover, 1969. — I, 495.

Whiting, Margaret. It might as well be spring : a musical autobiography / Margaret Whiting and Will Holt. — New York : Morrow, 1987. — III, 885.

Whitlock, E. Clyde. Music and dance in Texas, Oklahoma and the Southwest / ed. E. Clyde Whitlock and Richard Drake Saunders. — Hollywood : Bureau of Musical Research. — I, 89.

Whittall, Arnold. Music since the First World War / Arnold Whittall. — London : Dent, 1977. — II, 162.

Whitten, Norman E. Afro-American anthropology : contemporary perspectives / Norman E. Whitten and John F. Szwed. — New York : Free Press, 1970. — I, 680.

Whittle, D. W. Memoirs of Philip P. Bliss / ed. D. W. Whittle. — New York : Barnes, 1877. — I, 77.

Whittlesey, Walter R. Catalogue of first editions of Stephen C. Foster / Walter R. Whittlesey and Oscar G. Sonneck. — Washington : Library of Congress, 1915. — I, 1214.

Whitton, Joseph. The naked truth : an inside story of the Black Crook / Joseph Whitton. — Philadelphia : H. W. Shaw, 1897. — II, 1052.

Whitwell, David. The Longy Club : a professional wind ensemble in Boston (1900–1917) / David Whitwell. — Northridge, Calif. : WINDS, 1988. — III, 922.

Who's who in American music : classical. — New York : Bowker, 1984. — II, A-99.

Whole booke of psalmes faithfully translated into English metre [Bay psalm book]. — Cambridge, Mass. : Stephen Daye, 1640. — I, 188.

Wicke, Peter. Handbuch der populären Musik / Pete Wicke and Wieland Ziegenrücker. — Berlin : Deutscher Verlag für Musik, 1985. — II, A-511.

Wicke, Peter. Rock music : culture, aesthetics, and sociology / Peter Wicke. — New York : Cambridge University Press, 1990. — III, 1199.

Widner, Ellis. The Oak Ridge Boys : our story / Ellis Widner and Walter Carter. — Chicago : Contemporary Books, 1987. — III, 931.

Wienandt, Elwyn A. The anthem in England and America / Elwyn A. Wienandt and Robert H. Young. — New York : Free Press, 1970. — I, 64.

Wiessmüller, Peter. Miles Davis : sein Leben, seine Musik, seine Schallplatten / Peter Wiessemüller, — Gauting-Buchendorf, Germany : Oreos, 1984. — II, A-473.

Wiessmüller, Peter. Miles Davis : sein Leben, sein Musik, seine Schallplatten / Peter Wiessmuller. — 2nd ed. — Schaftlach, Germany : Oreos, 1988. — III, 630.

Wiggins, Gene. Fiddlin' Georgia crazy : fiddlin' John Carson, his real world, and the world of his songs / Gene Wiggins and Norm Cohen. — Urbana : University of Illinois Press, 1987. — III, 698.

Wilber, Bob. Music was not enough / Bob Wilber. — Basingstoke, England : Macmillan, 1987; New York : Oxford, 1988. — III, 674.

Wilbraham, Roy. Charles Mingus : a biography and discography / Roy Wilbraham. — London : Author, 1967. — I, 951.

Wilbraham, Roy. Jackie McLean : a discography with biography / Roy Wilbraham. — London : Author, 1967. — I, 951.

Wilbraham, Roy. Milt Jackson : a discography and biography / Roy Wilbraham. — London : Author, 1968. — I, 951.

Wild, David. Ornette Coleman 1958–1979 : a discography / David Wild and Michael Cuscuna. — Ann Arbor, Mich. : Wildmusic, 1980. — II, 644.

Wild, David. The recordings of John Coltrane : a discography / David Wild. — Ann Arbor, Mich. : Wildmusic, 1977. — II, 646.

Wildbihler, Hubert. The musical : an international annotated bibliography / Hubert Wildbihler and Sonja Völklein; foreword by Thomas Siedhoff. — London : K. G. Saur, 1986. — III, 135.

Wilder, Alec. American popular songs : the great innovators, 1900–1950 / Alec Wilder. — New York : Oxford University Press, 1972. — I, 1175.

Wile, Raymond R. Edison disc artists and records, 1910–1929 / Raymond R. Wile; ed. Ronald Dethlefson. — 2nd ed. — Brooklyn : APM Press, 1990. — III, 207.

Wile, Raymond R. Edison disc recordings / Raymond R. Wile. — Philadelphia : Eastern National Park and Monument Association, 1978. — II, 820.

Wilgus, D. K. Anglo-American folksong scholarship since 1898 / D. K. Wilgus. — New Brunswick, N.J. : Rutgers University Press, 1959. — I, 472.

Wilgus, D. K. Country-western music and the urban hillbilly / D. K. Wilgus. — Los Angeles : John Edwards Memorial Foundation, 1970. — I, 619.

Wilk, Max. Memory lane / Max Wilk. — London : Studioart, 1973. — II, 857.

Wilk, Max. They're playing our song / Max Wilk. — New York : Atheneum, 1973. — I, 1176.

Wilkinson, Todd R. Kansas City jazz and blues nightlife survival kit / Todd R. Wilkinson. — Kansas City, Mo. : The Ambassadors; distributed by Westport Publishers, 1990. — III, 32.

Willadeene. In the shadow of a song : the story of the Parton family / Willadeene. — New York : Bantam, 1985. — II, A-262.

Willens, Doris. Lonesome traveler : the life of Lee Hays / Doris Willens. — New York : Norton, 1988. — III, 729.

Williams, Brett. John Henry : a bio-bibliography / Brett Williams. — Westport, Conn. : Greenwood, 1983. — II, A-309.

Williams, Ethel L. Afro-American religious studies : a comprehensive bibliography with locations in American libraries / Ethel L. Williams. — Metuchen, N.J. : Scarecrow, 1972. — II, 530.

Williams, George. The songwriter's demo manual and success guide / George Williams. — Riverside, Calif. : Music Business Books, 1984. — II, A-747.

Williams, Hank, Jr. Living proof : an autobiography / Hank Williams, Jr. ; with Michael Bane. — New York : Putnam, 1979. — II, 420.

Williams, Jett. Ain't nothing' as sweet as my baby : the story of Hank Williams' lost daughter / Jett Williams; with Pamela Thomas. — New York : Harcourt Brace Jovanovich, 1990. — III, 886.

Williams, John A. Amistad 2 / ed. John A. Williams and Charles F. Harris. — New York : Random House, 1971. — II, 564.

Williams, John R. This was "Your Hit Parade" / John R. Williams. — Camden, Maine : Courier-Gazette, 1973. — II, 1116.

Williams, Lycrecia. Still in love with you : the story of Hank and Audrey Williams / Lycrecia Williams and Dale Vinicur. — Nashville : Rutledge Hill, 1989. — III, 888.

Williams, Martin. Jazz changes / Martin Williams. — New York : Oxford, 1992. — III, 1102.

Williams, Martin. Jazz heritage / Martin Williams. — New York : Oxford, 1985. — III, 1103.

Williams, Martin. Jazz in its time / Martin Williams. — New York : Oxford, 1989. — III, 1104.

Williams, Martin. Jazz masters in transition, 1957–69 / Martin Williams. — New York : Macmillan, 1970. — I, 1059.

Williams, Martin. Jazz masters of New Orleans / Martin Williams. — New York : Macmillan, 1967. — I, 1071.

Williams, Martin. Jazz panorama : from the pages of *The Jazz Review* / Martin Williams. — New York : Crowell-Collier, 1962. — I, 1024.

Williams, Martin. Jazz tradition / Martin Williams. — New York : Oxford, 1993. — III, 1105.

Williams, Martin. Jelly Roll Morton / Martin Williams. — London : Cassell, 1962. — I, 1129.

Williams, Martin. King Oliver / Martin Williams. — London : Cassell, 1960. — I, 1131.

Williams, Martin. The art of jazz / Martin Williams. — New York : Oxford University Press, 1959. — I, 1023.

Williams, Martin. The jazz tradition / Martin Williams. — New York : Oxford University Press, 1970. — I, 1080.

Williams, Martin. Where's the melody? A listener's introduction to jazz / Martin Williams. — Rev. ed. — New York : Pantheon, 1969. — I, 971.

Williams, Michael D. Source : music of the avant garde / Michael D. Williams. — Ann Arbor, Mich. : Music Library Association, 1978. — II, 168.

Williams, Ora. American black women in the arts and social sciences : a bibliographic survey / Ora Williams. — Metuchen, N.J. : Scarecrow, 1973. — I, 48.

Wilson, Earl. Sinatra : an unauthorized biography / Earl Wilson. — New York : Macmillan, 1976. — II, 1012.

Wilson, James Grant. The memorial history of the city of New York : from its first settlement to the year 1892 / James Grant Wilson. — New York : New York History Co., 1893. — I, 111.

Wilson, John S. Jazz : the transition years, 1940–1960 / John S. Wilson. — New York : Appleton-Century-Crofts, 1966. — I, 1061.

Wilson, John S. The collector's jazz : modern / John S. Wilson. — Philadelphia : Lippincott, 1959. — I, A-229.

Wilson, John S. The collector's jazz : traditional and swing / John S. Wilson. — Philadelphia : Lippincott, 1958. — I, A-230.

Wilson, Mary. Dreamgirl : my life as a supreme / Mary Wilson; with Patricia Romanowski and Ahrgus Juilliard. — New York : St. Martin's, 1986. — III, 890.

Wilson, Peter Niklas. Charlie Parker : sein Leben, seine Musik, seine Schallplatten / Peter Niklas Wilson and Ulfert Goeman. — Schaftlach, Germany : Oreos, 1988. — III, 658.

Wilson, Peter Niklas. Ornette Coleman : sein Leben, seine Musik, seine Schallplatten / Peter Niklas Wilson. — Schaftlach, Germany : Oreos, 1989. — III, 621.

Wilson, Peter Niklas. Sonny Rollins : sein Leben, seine Musik, seine Schallplatten / Peter Niklas Wilson. — Schaftlach, Germany : Oreos, 1991. — III, 665.

Wilson, Ruth Mack. Connecticut's music in the revolutionary era / Ruth Mack Wilson. — Hartford, Conn. : American Revolution Bicentennial Commission of Connecticut, 1980. — II, 50.

Winsor, Justin. The memorial history of Boston, including Suffolk County, Massachusetts, 1630–1880 / Justin Winsor. — Boston : Osgood, 1881. — I, 100.

Wise, Herbert H. Professional rock and roll / Herbert H. Wise. — New York : Amsco, 1967 — I, 1361.

Wiseman, Rich. Jackson Browne : the story of a hold out / Rich Wiseman. — Garden City, N.Y. : Doubleday, 1982. — II, A-773.

Wiseman, Rich. Neil Diamond : solitary star / Rich Wiseman. — New York : Dodd, Mead, 1987. — III, 709.

Wister, Frances Anne. Twenty-five years of the Philadelphia Orchestra, 1900–1925 / Frances Anne Wister. — Philadelphia : Author, 1925. — I, 124.

Witmark, Isidore. From ragtime to swingtime : the story of the House of Witmark / Isidore Witmark and Isaac Goldberg. — New York : Furman, 1939. — I, 1173.

Wittke, Carl. Tambo and bones : a history of the American musical stage / Carl Wittke. — Durham, N.C. : Duke University Press, 1930. — I, 1244.

Wodehouse, P. G. Bring on the girls! / P. G. Wodehouse and Guy Bolton. — New York : Simon & Schuster, 1953. — II, 969.

Wolf, Edwin. American song sheets, slip ballads and political broadsides, 1850–1870 / Edwin Wolf. — Philadelphia : Library Company of Philadelphia, 1963. — II, 808.

Wolfe, Charles. Lefty Frizell : his life, his music / Charles Wolfe. — Bremen : Bear Family Records, 1984. — II, A-250.

Wolfe, Charles. The life and legend of Leadbelly / Charles Wolfe and Kip Lornell. — New York : HarperCollins, 1992. — III, 761.

Wolfe, Charles K. Kentucky country / Charles K. Wolfe. — Lexington : University Press of Kentucky, 1984. — II, A-232.

Wolfe, Charles K. Tennessee strings : the story of country music in Tennessee / Charles K. Wolfe. — Knoxville : University of Tennessee Press, 1977. — II, 381.

Wolfe, Charles K. The Grand Ole Opry : the early years, 1925–1935 / Charles K. Wolfe. — London : Old Time Music, 1975. — I, 622.

Wolfe, Richard J. Early American music engraving and printing / Richard J. Wolfe. — Urbana : University of Illinois Press, 1980. — II, 101.

Wolfe, Richard J. Secular music in America, 1801–1825 : a bibliography / Richard J. Wolfe; introduction by Carleton Sprague Smith. — New York : New York Public Library, 1964. — I, 4.

Wölfer, Jürgen. Die Rock- und Popmusik / Jürgen Wölfer. — Munich : Heyne, 1980. — II, 1264.

Wölfer, Jürgen. Dizzy Gillespie : sein Leben, seine Musik, seine Schallplatten / Jürgen Wölfer. — Waakirchen, Germany : Oreos, 1987. — III, 638.

Wölfer, Jürgen. Handbuch des Jazz / Jürgen Wölfer. — Munich : Heyne, 1979. — II, 636.

Woliver, Robbie. Bringing it all back home : 25 years of American music at Folk City / Robbie Woliver. — New York : Pantheon, 1986. — III, 1067.

Woll, Allen L. Black musical theatre : from *Coontown* to *Dreamgirls* / Allen Woll. — Baton Rouge : Louisiana State University Press, 1989. — III, 1016.

Woll, Allen L. Dictionary of black theatre / Allen Woll. — Westport, Conn. : Greenwood, 1983. — II, A-561.

Woll, Allen L. Songs from Hollywood musical comedies, 1927 to the present : a dictionary / Allen L. Woll. — New York : Garland, 1976. — II, 809.

Woll, Allen L. The Hollywood musical goes to war / Allen L. Woll. — Chicago : Nelson-Hall, 1982. — II, A-592.

Wood, Graham. An A-Z of rock and roll / Graham Wood. — London : Studio Vista, 1971. — I, 1341.

Woods, Brenda. Louisville's own : an illustrated encyclopedia of Louisville area recorded pop music from 1953 to 1983 / Brenda Woods and Bill Woods. — Louisville : De Forest, 1983. — II, A-709.

Woods, W. Raymond. Anthropology on the Great Plains / W. Raymond Woods and Margot Liberty. — Lincoln : University of Nebraska Press, 1980. — II, 258.

Wooldridge, David. Charles Ives : a portrait / David Wooldridge. — London : Faber, 1975. — I, 336.

Wooldridge, David. From the steeples and mountains : a study of Charles Ives / David Wooldridge. — New York : Knopf, 1974. — I, 336.

Woollcott, Alexander. The story of Irving Berlin / Alexander Woollcott. New York : Putnam, 1925. — I, 1271.

Woollcott, Alexander. While Rome burns / Alexander Woollcott. — New York : Viking, 1934. — I, 711.

Wootton, Richard. Honky tonkin' / Richard Wootton and Charlie McKissack. — 3rd ed. — London : Travelaid Publishing, 1980. — II, 832.

Work, John W. American negro songs and spirituals / John W. Work. — New York : Howell, Soskin, 1940. — I, 781.
Work, John Wesley. Folk song of the American negro / John Wesley Work. — Nashville : Press of Fisk University, 1915. — I, 798.
Work, Monroe N. Bibliography of the negro in Africa and America / Monroe N. Work. — New York : Wilson, 1928. — I, 656.
Works Progress Administration, New Mexico. The Spanish-American song and game book. — New York : Barnes, 1942. — II, 441.
Worth, Fred L. All about Elvis / Fred L. Worth and Steve D. Tamerius. — New York : Bantam, 1981. — II, A-835.
Worth, Fred L. Elvis : his life from A to Z / Fred L. Worth and Steve D. Tamerius. — Chicago : Contemporary Books, 1988. — III, 846.
Worth, Fred L. The country and western book / Fred L. Worth. — New York : Drake, 1977. — II, 484.
Worth, Paul W. John McCormack : a comprehensive discography / Paul W. Worth and Jim Cartwright. — Westport, Conn. : Greenwood, 1986. — III, 342.
Wren, Christopher S. Johnny Cash : winners got scars too / Christopher S. Wren. — London : Allen, 1973. — I, 637.
Wren, Christopher S. Winners got scars too : the life and legend of Johnny Cash / Christopher S. Wren. — New York : Dial, 1971. — I, 637.
Wright, John. Ralph Stanley and the Clinch Mountain Boys : a discography / John Wright. — Evanston, Ill. : Author, 1983. — II, A-266.
Wright, Josephine. New perspectives on music : essays in honor of Eileen Southern / ed. Joesphine Wright and Samuel A. Floyd, Jr. — Warren, Mich. : Harmonie Park, 1992. — III, 1228.
Wright, Laurie. Mr. Jelly lord / Laurie Wright [et al]. — Chigwell, Essex, England : Storyville, 1980. — II, 651.
Wright, Robert L. Swedish emigrant ballads / Robert L. Wright. — Lincoln : University of Nebraska Press, 1965. — II, 302.
Wyeth, John. Repository of sacred music / John Wyeth. — 2nd ed. — Harrisburg, Pa. : Author, 1820. — I, 524.
Wyler, Michael. A glimpse at the past : an illustrated history of some early record companies that made jazz history / Michael Wyler. — West Moors, Dorset, England : Jazz Publications, 1957. — II, 658.
Wyman, Leland C. Navaho classification of their song ceremonials / Leland C. Wyman and Clyde Kluckhohn. — Menasha, Wisc. : American Anthropological Association, 1938. — I, 419.
Wyman, Loraine. Twenty Kentucky mountain songs / Loraine Wyman and Howard Brockway. — Boston : Ditson, 1920. — I, A-125.
Wynette, Tammy. Stand by your man / Tammy Wynette. — New York : Simon & Schuster, 1979. — II, 423.
Wynn, Ron. Tina : the Tina Turner story / Ron Wynn. — London : Sidgwick & Jackson, 1985. — II, A-848.
Yancey, Becky. My life with Elvis / Becky Yancey and Cliff Linedecker. — New York : St. Martin's, 1978. — II, 1308.
Yates, Peter. Twentieth century music : its evolution from the end of the harmonic era into the present era of sound / Peter Yates. — New York : Pantheon, 1967. — I, 268.

Zaretsky, Irving I. Religious movements in contemporary America / Irving I. Zaretsky. — Princeton, N.J. : Princeton University Press, 1974. — II, 584.

Zec, Donald. Barbra : a biography of Barbra Streisand / Donald Zec and Anthony Fowles. — New York : St. Martin's, 1982. — II, A-644.

Zeidman, Irving. The American burlesque show / Irving Zeidman. — New York : Hawthorn, 1967. — II, 897.

Zelzer, Sarah Schectman. Impresario : the Zelzer era, 1930–1990 / Sarah Schectman Zelzer; with Phyllis Dreazen. — Chicago : Academy Chicago Publishers, 1990. — III, 985.

Zimmer, Dave. Crosby, Stills & Nash : the authorized biography / Dave Zimmer and Henry Diltz. — New York : St. Martin's, 1984. — II, A-775.

Zimmermann, Walter. Desert plants : conversations with 23 American musicians / Walter Zimmermann. — Vancouver : Author, 1976. — II, 234.

Zinsser, William. Willie and Dwike : an American profile / William Zinsser. — New York : Harper & Row, 1984. — III, 429.

Zmijewsky, Steven. The films and career of Elvis Presley / Steven Zmijewsky and Boris Zmijewsky. — Secaucus, N.J. : Citadel, 1976. — II, 1236.

Zollo, Paul. Songwriters on songwriting / Paul Zollo. — Cincinnati : Writer's Digest Books, 1991. — III, 1068.

Zuck, Barbara A. A history of musical Americanism / Barbara A. Zuck. — Ann Arbor, Mich. : UMI Research Press, 1980. — II, 12.

Zur Heide, Karl Gert. Deep south piano : the story of Little Brother Montgomery / Karl Gert Zur Heide. — London : Studio Vista, 1970. — I, 849.

Zwerin, Mike. Broken up and down / Mike Zwerin. — Paris : Handshake Editions, 1982. — II, A-434.

Zwerin, Mike. Close enough for jazz / Mike Zwerin. — London : Quartet, 1983. — II, A-433.

Zwisohn, Laurence J. Bing Crosby : a lifetime of music / Laurence J. Zwisohn. — Los Angeles : Palm Tree Library, 1978. — II, 992.

Zwisohn, Laurence J. Loretta Lynn's world of music / Laurence J. Zwisohn. — II, 408.

ABOUT THE AUTHOR

Guy A. Marco has been a Senior Fellow at the Graduate School of Library and Information Science, Rosary College (River Forest, Illinois) since 1989. He has a master's degree in library science and a Ph.D in musicology from the University of Chicago. His positions have included: Dean, School of Library Science, Kent State University; Chief, General Reference and Bibliography Division, Library of Congress; and Chief of Library Activities, U.S. Army, Fort Dix. Marco is the author of *The Art of Counterpoint* (1968), *Information on Music* (3 vols.; 1975–1984), *Opera: A Research and Information Guide* (1984), and *Encyclopedia of Recorded Sound in the United States* (1993). He edited the second edition of E. T. Bryant's *Music Librarianship* (1985) and is editor of the Composer Resource Manuals series for Garland Publishing.